DATE DUE

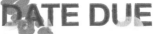

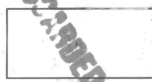

JUSTICE LEAGUE of AMERICA

DARK THINGS

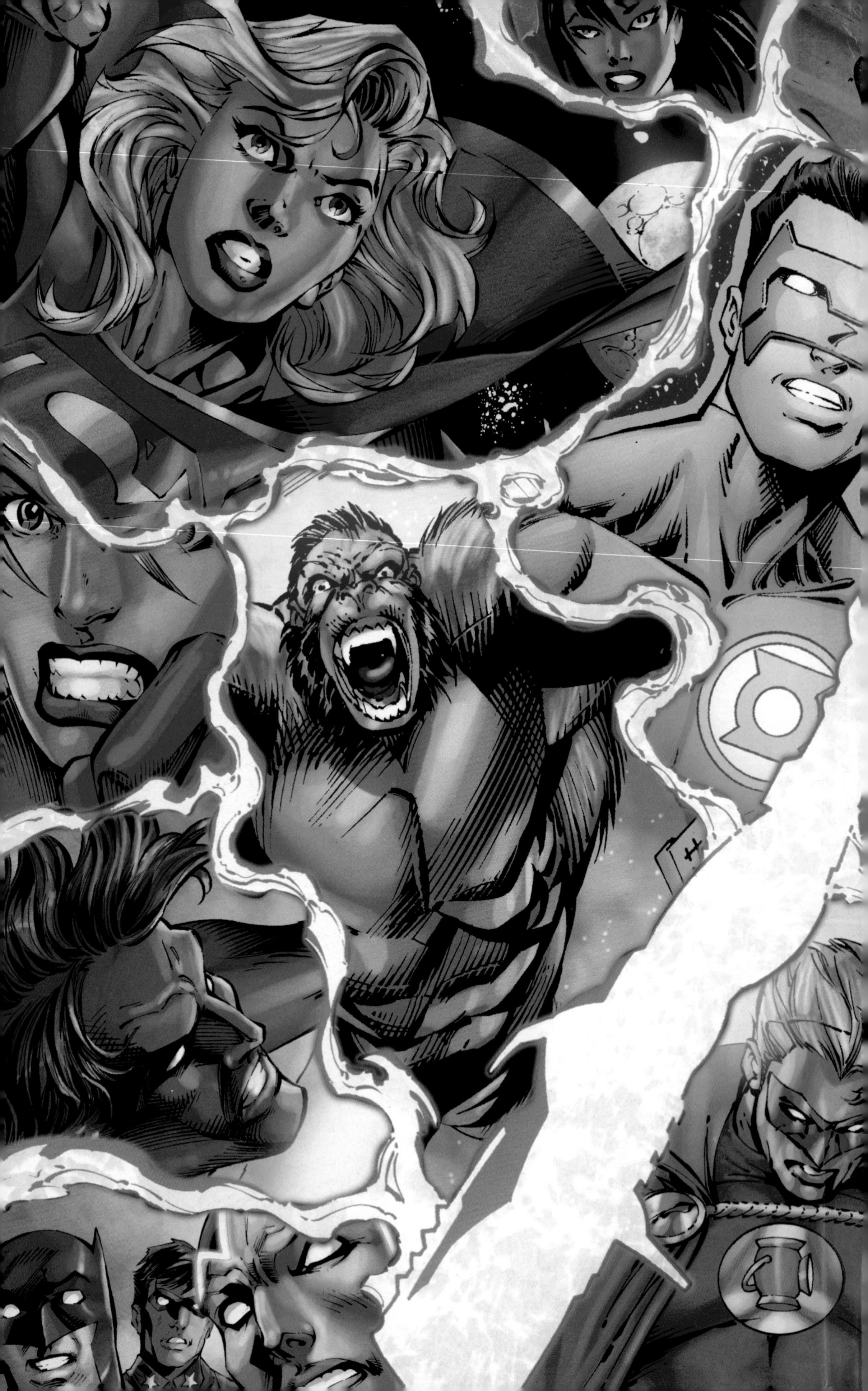

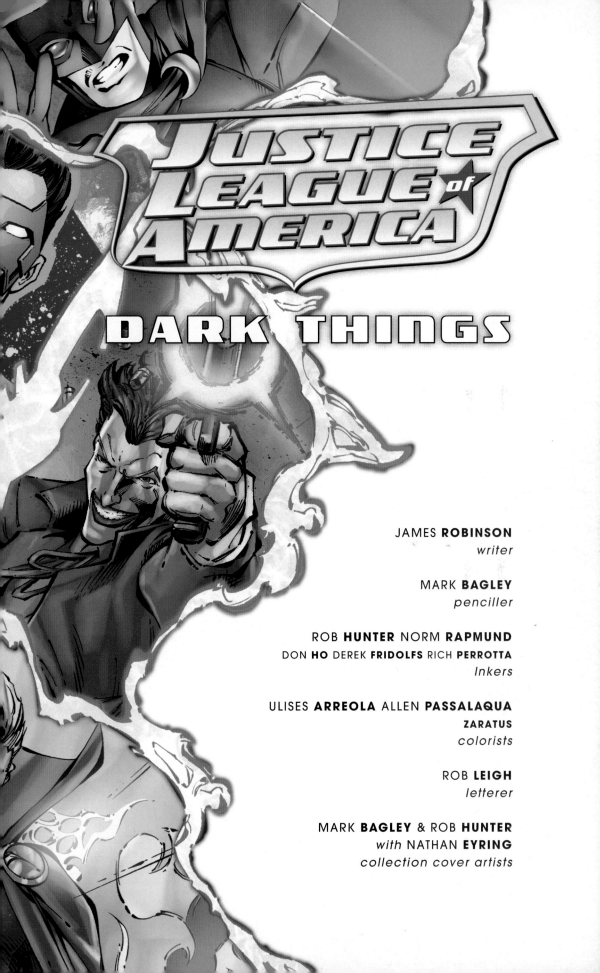

JUSTICE LEAGUE of AMERICA

DARK THINGS

JAMES **ROBINSON**
writer

MARK **BAGLEY**
penciller

ROB **HUNTER** NORM **RAPMUND**
DON **HO** DEREK **FRIDOLFS** RICH **PERROTTA**
Inkers

ULISES **ARREOLA** ALLEN **PASSALAQUA**
ZARATUS
colorists

ROB **LEIGH**
letterer

MARK **BAGLEY** & ROB **HUNTER**
with NATHAN **EYRING**
collection cover artists

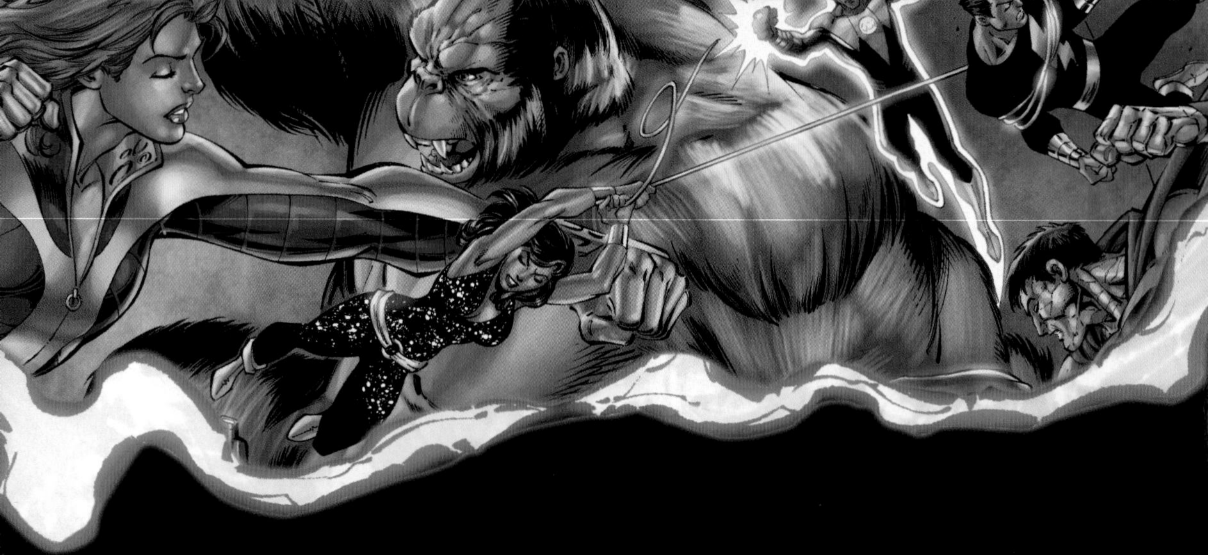

Eddie Berganza Mike Carlin Editors-original series
Adam Schlagman Rachel Gluckstern Associate Editors-original series
Rex Ogle Assistant Editor-original series
Bob Harras Group Editor-Collected Editions
Robbin Brosterman Design Director-Books

DC COMICS
Diane Nelson President
Dan DiDio and Jim Lee Co-Publishers
Geoff Johns Chief Creative Officer
Patrick Caldon EVP-Finance and Administration
John Rood EVP-Sales, Marketing and Business Development
Amy Genkins SVP-Business and Legal Affairs
Steve Rotterdam SVP-Sales and Marketing
John Cunningham VP-Marketing
Terri Cunningham VP-Managing Editor
Alison Gill VP-Manufacturing
David Hyde VP-Publicity
Sue Pohja VP-Book Trade Sales
Alysse Soll VP-Advertising and Custom Publishing
Bob Wayne VP-Sales
Mark Chiarello Art Director

Publication design by Robbie Biederman

JUSTICE LEAGUE OF AMERICA: DARK THINGS

DC Comics, 1700 Broadway, New York, NY 10019
A Warner Bros. Entertainment Company
Printed by Quad/Graphics, Versailles, KY, USA. 2/16/11. First printing.
HC ISBN: 978-1-4012-3011-1 SC ISBN: 978-1-4012-3193-4

Fiber used in this product line meets the sourcing requirements of the SFI program. www.sfiprogram.org PWC-SFICOC-260

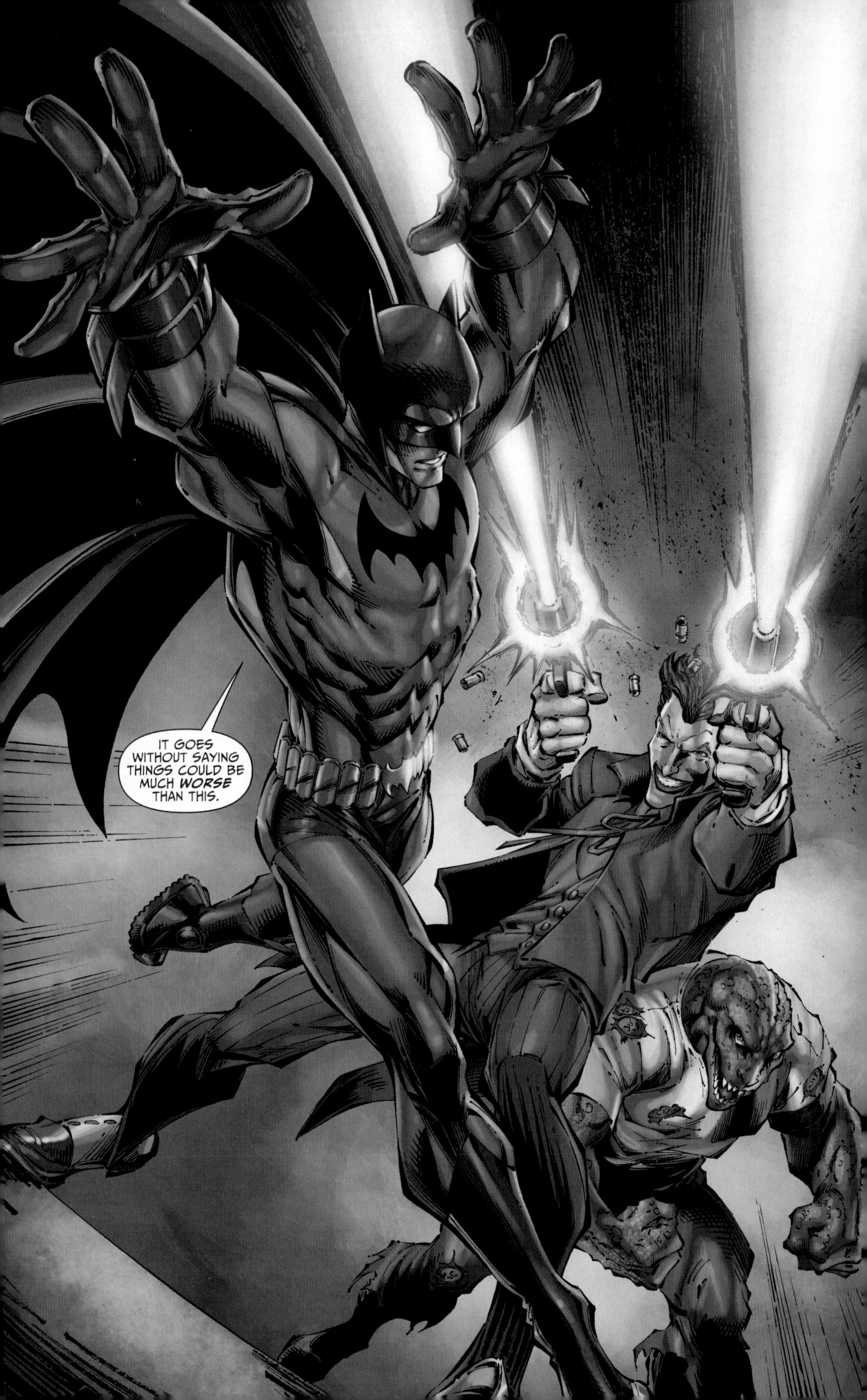
IT GOES WITHOUT SAYING THINGS COULD BE MUCH *WORSE* THAN THIS.

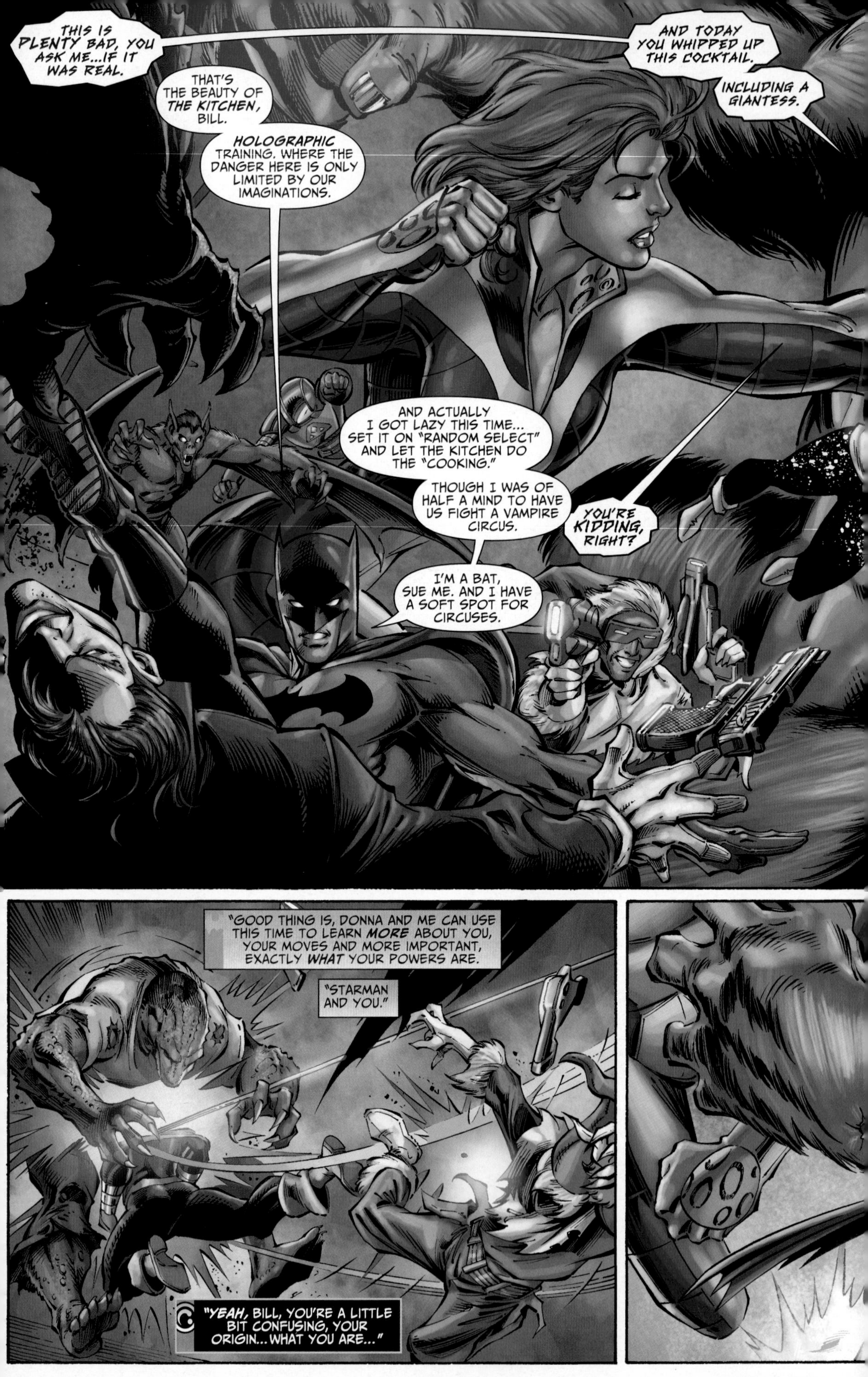
THIS IS PLENTY BAD, YOU ASK ME...IF IT WAS REAL.
AND TODAY YOU WHIPPED UP THIS COCKTAIL.
INCLUDING A GIANTESS.
THAT'S THE BEAUTY OF THE KITCHEN, BILL.
HOLOGRAPHIC TRAINING. WHERE THE DANGER HERE IS ONLY LIMITED BY OUR IMAGINATIONS.
AND ACTUALLY I GOT LAZY THIS TIME... SET IT ON "RANDOM SELECT" AND LET THE KITCHEN DO THE "COOKING."
THOUGH I WAS OF HALF A MIND TO HAVE US FIGHT A VAMPIRE CIRCUS.
YOU'RE KIDDING, RIGHT?
I'M A BAT, SUE ME. AND I HAVE A SOFT SPOT FOR CIRCUSES.
"GOOD THING IS, DONNA AND ME CAN USE THIS TIME TO LEARN MORE ABOUT YOU, YOUR MOVES AND MORE IMPORTANT, EXACTLY WHAT YOUR POWERS ARE.
"STARMAN AND YOU."
"YEAH, BILL, YOU'RE A LITTLE BIT CONFUSING, YOUR ORIGIN...WHAT YOU ARE..."

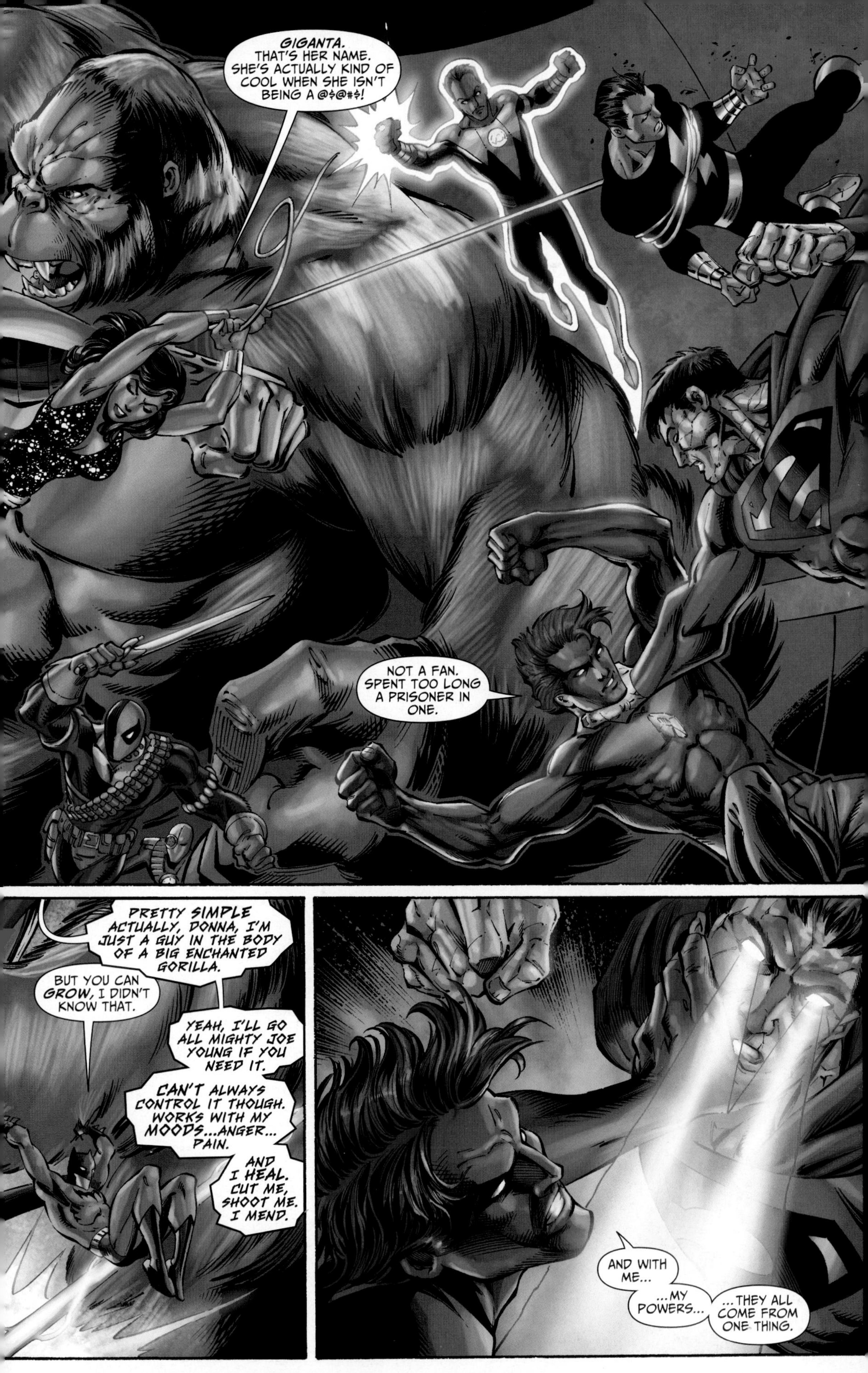
GIGANTA. THAT'S HER NAME. SHE'S ACTUALLY KIND OF COOL WHEN SHE ISN'T BEING A @$@#$!
NOT A FAN. SPENT TOO LONG A PRISONER IN ONE.
PRETTY SIMPLE ACTUALLY, DONNA, I'M JUST A GUY IN THE BODY OF A BIG ENCHANTED GORILLA.
BUT YOU CAN GROW, I DIDN'T KNOW THAT.
YEAH, I'LL GO ALL MIGHTY JOE YOUNG IF YOU NEED IT.
CAN'T ALWAYS CONTROL IT THOUGH. WORKS WITH MY MOODS...ANGER... PAIN.
AND I HEAL. CUT ME, SHOOT ME. I MEND.
AND WITH ME...
...MY POWERS...
...THEY ALL COME FROM ONE THING.

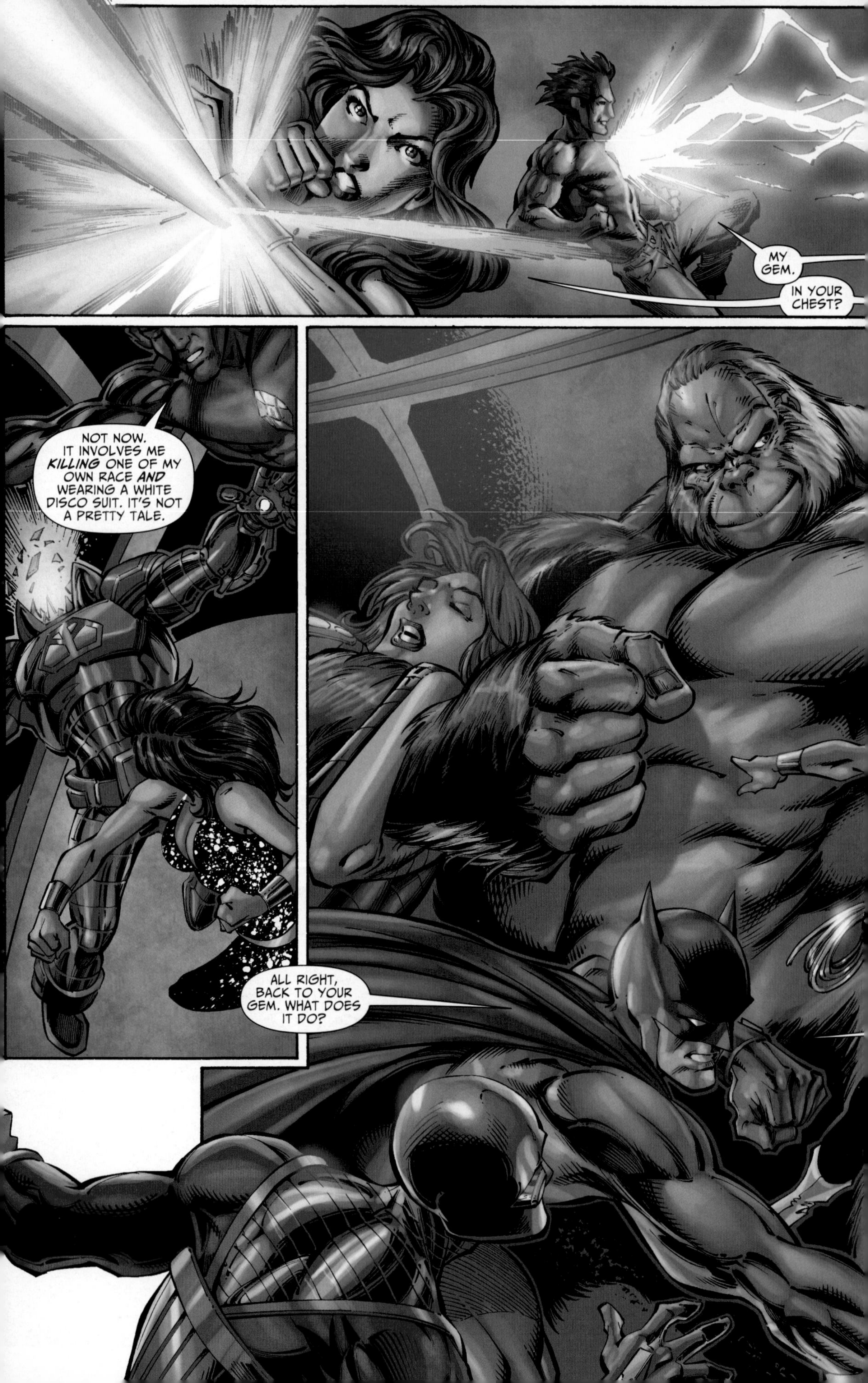
MY GEM.
IN YOUR CHEST?
NOT NOW. IT INVOLVES ME *KILLING* ONE OF MY OWN RACE *AND* WEARING A WHITE DISCO SUIT. IT'S NOT A PRETTY TALE.
ALL RIGHT, BACK TO YOUR GEM. WHAT DOES IT DO?

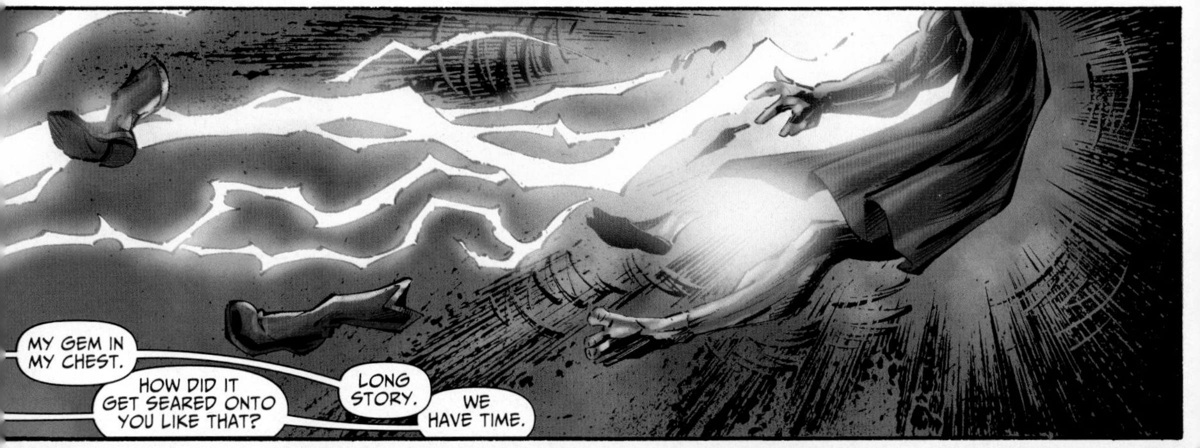
MY GEM IN MY CHEST.
HOW DID IT GET SEARED ONTO YOU LIKE THAT?
LONG STORY.
WE HAVE TIME.

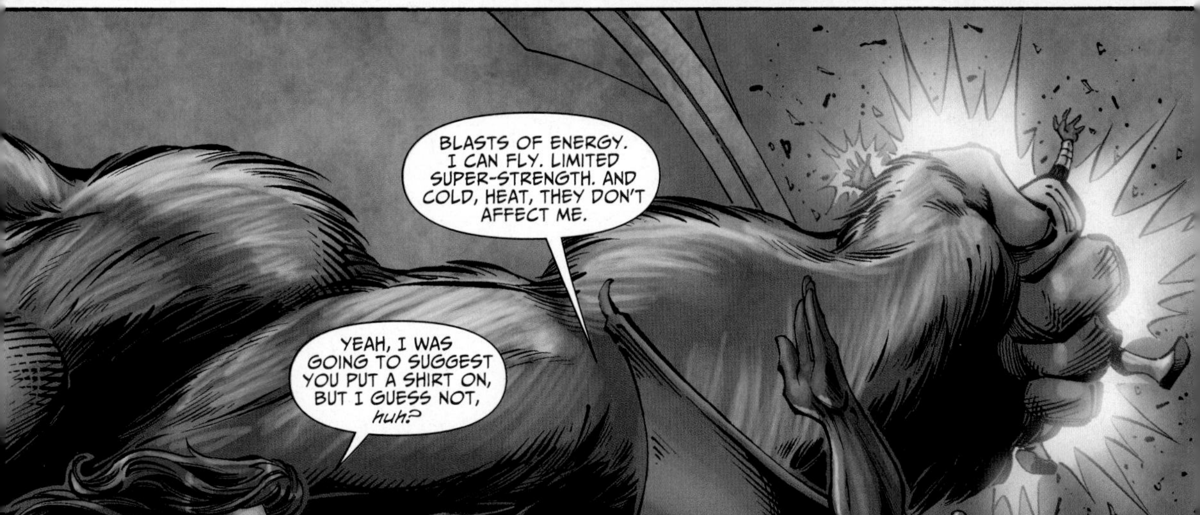
BLASTS OF ENERGY. I CAN FLY. LIMITED SUPER-STRENGTH. AND COLD, HEAT, THEY DON'T AFFECT ME.
YEAH, I WAS GOING TO SUGGEST YOU PUT A SHIRT ON, BUT I GUESS NOT, *huh?*
SERIOUSLY, YOU SURE YOU DON'T WANT SOME KIND OF COSTUME, "STARMAN"?
I'M A BLUE-SKINNED ALIEN AND I KICK ASS. THAT'S **PLENTY** COSTUME.

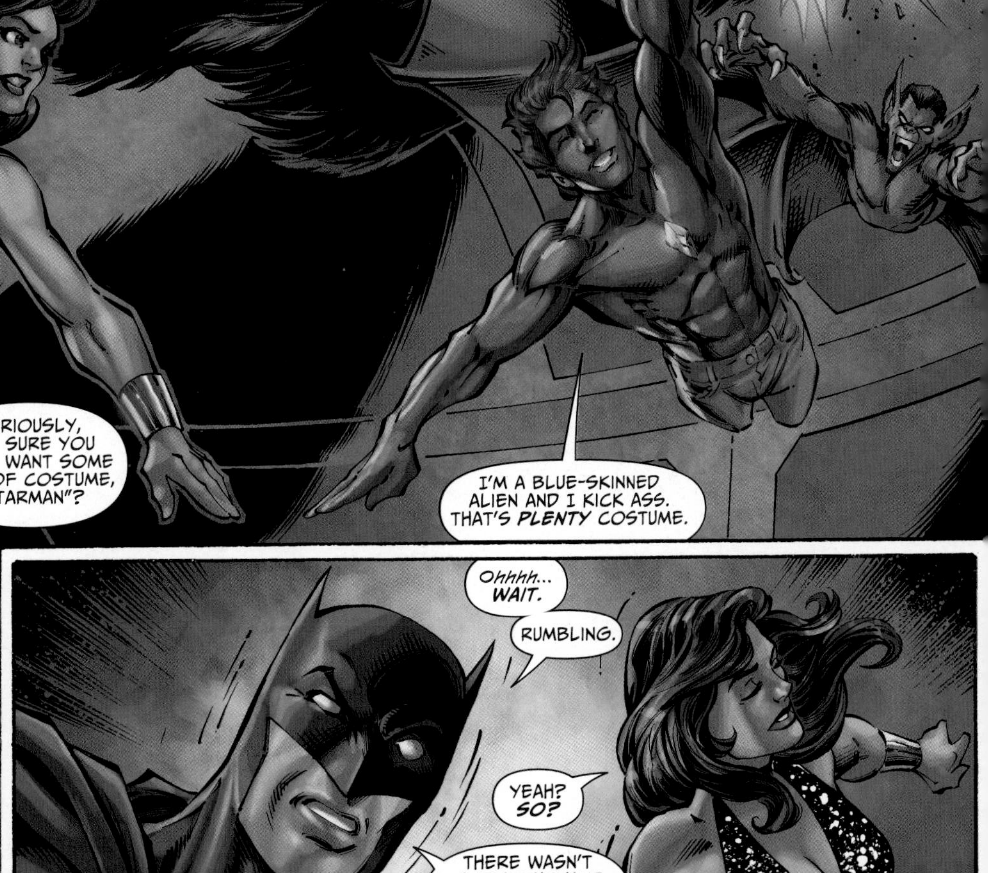
Ohhhh... **WAIT.**
RUMBLING.
YEAH? **SO?**
THERE WASN'T AN EARTHQUAKE PROGRAM. THIS IS--

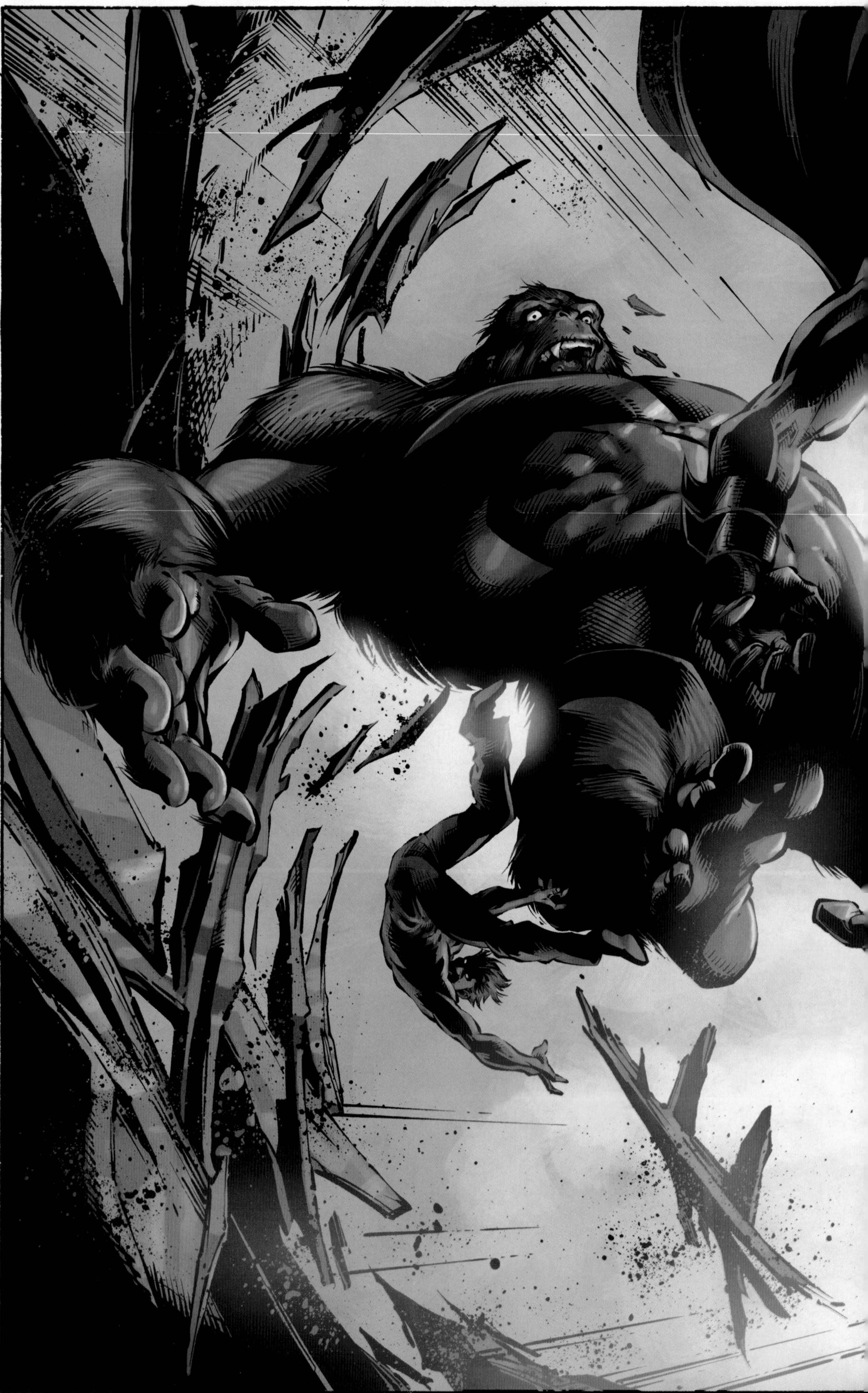

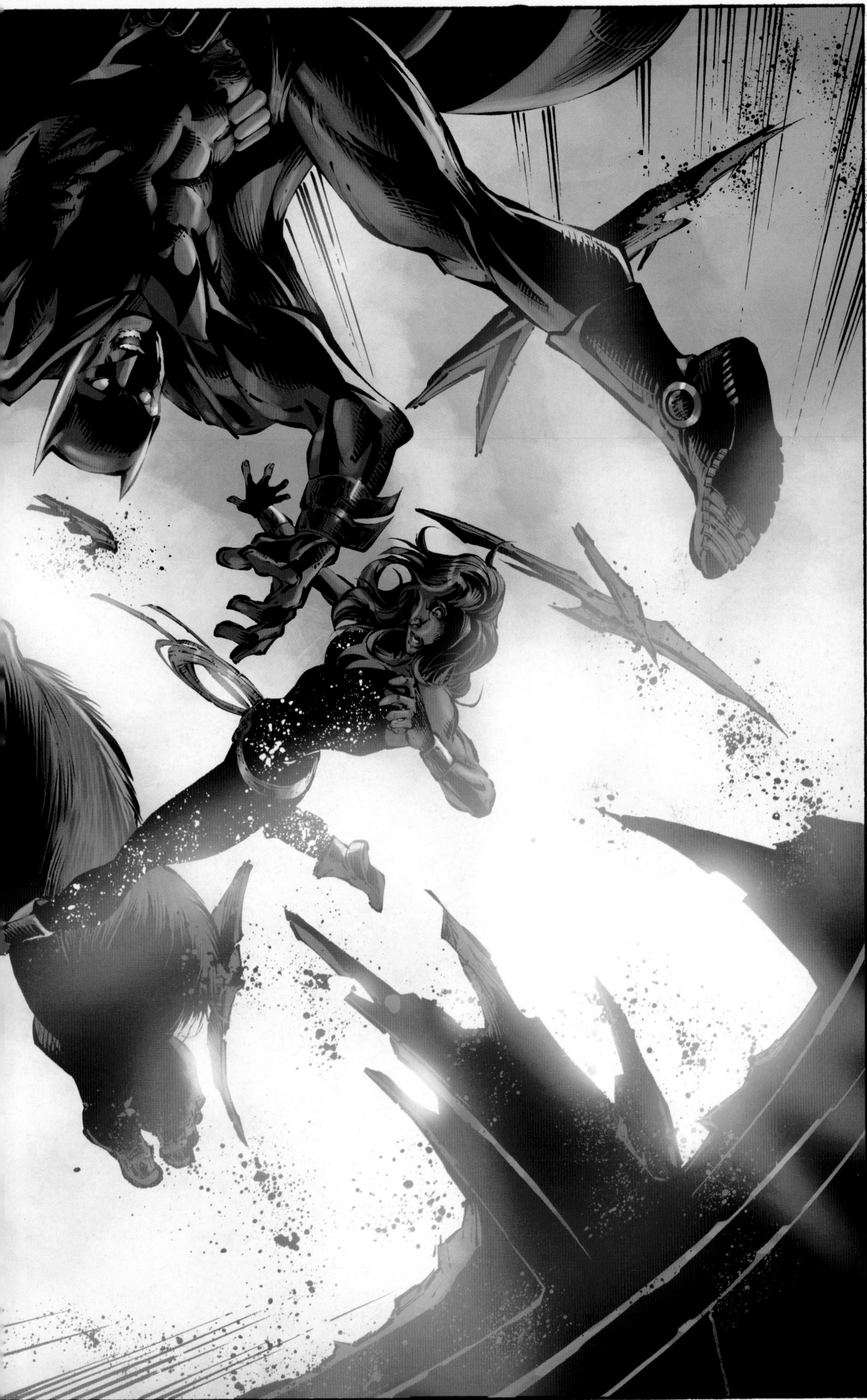

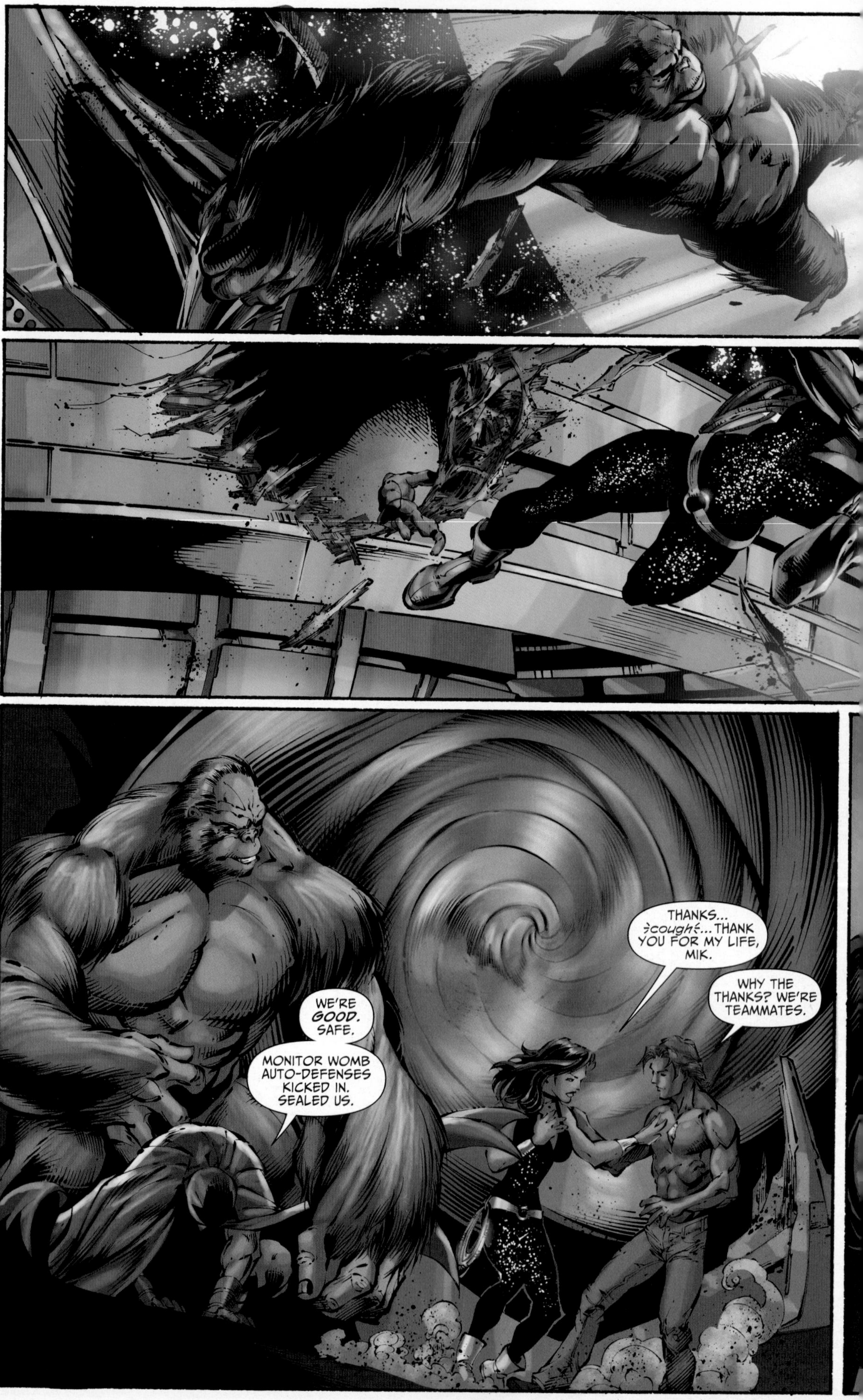
THANKS... ≈cough≈... THANK YOU FOR MY LIFE, MIK.
WHY THE THANKS? WE'RE TEAMMATES.
WE'RE GOOD. SAFE.
MONITOR WOMB AUTO-DEFENSES KICKED IN. SEALED US.

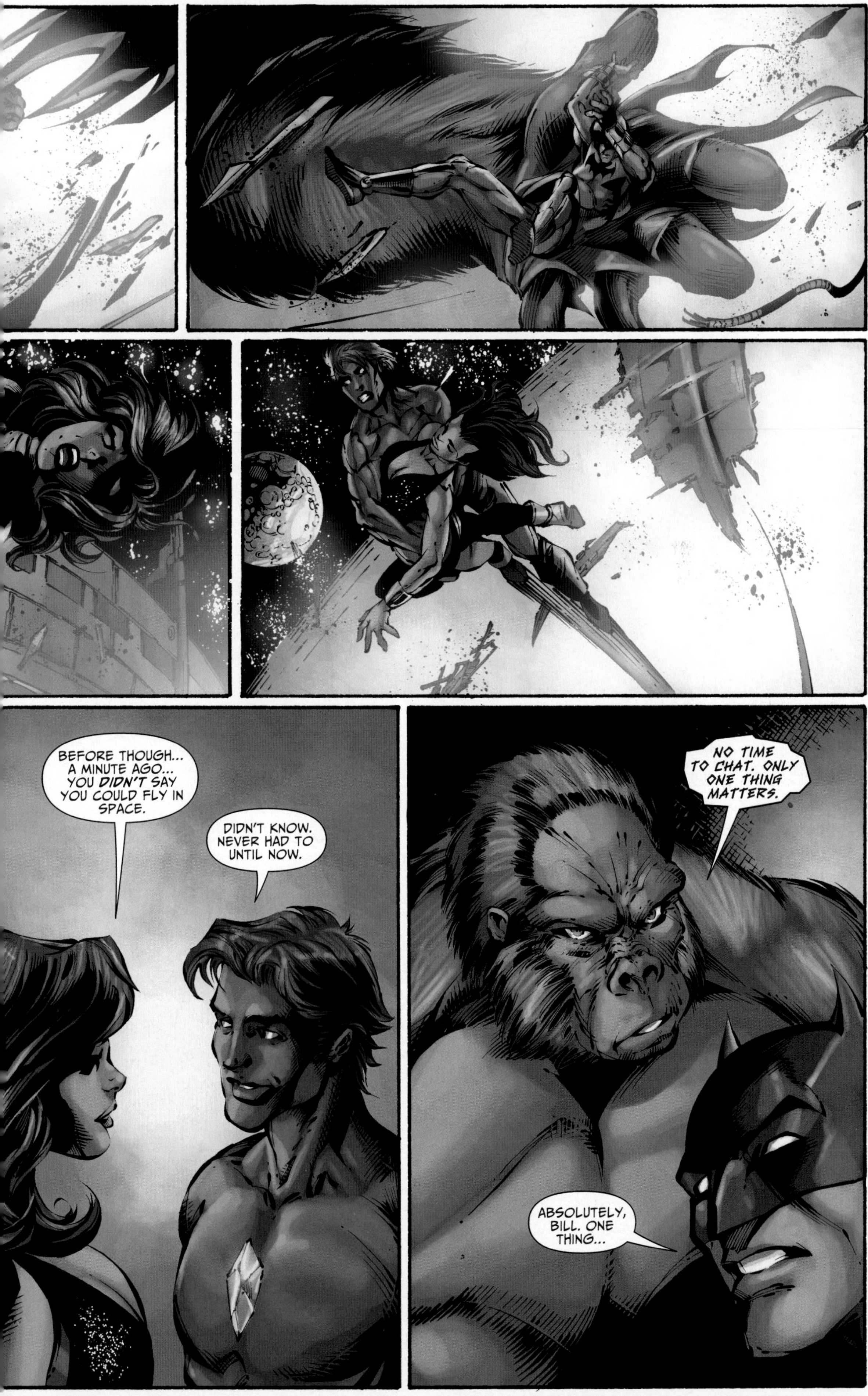
BEFORE THOUGH... A MINUTE AGO... YOU DIDN'T SAY YOU COULD FLY IN SPACE.
DIDN'T KNOW. NEVER HAD TO UNTIL NOW.
NO TIME TO CHAT. ONLY ONE THING MATTERS.
ABSOLUTELY, BILL. ONE THING...

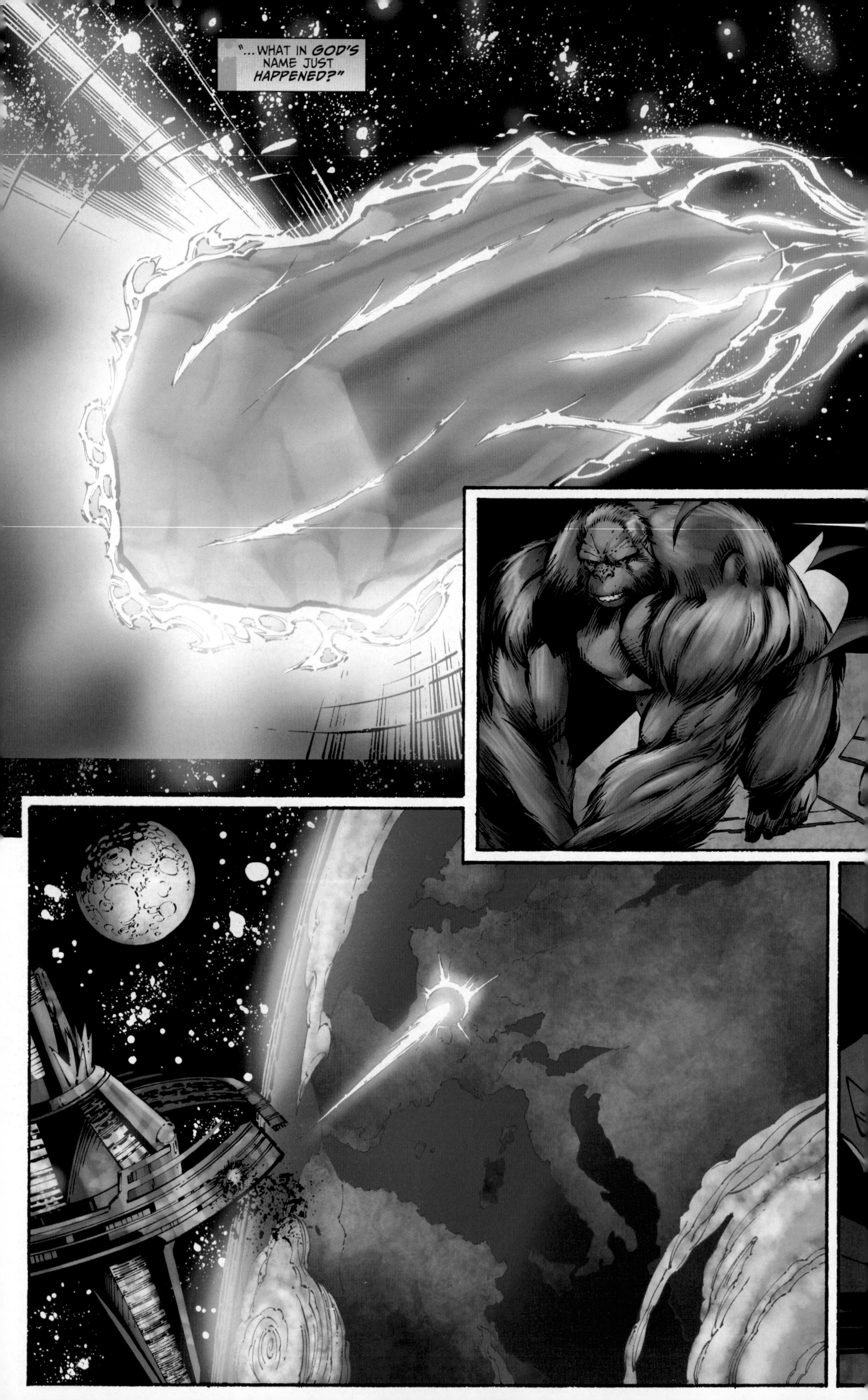
"...WHAT IN GOD'S NAME JUST HAPPENED?"

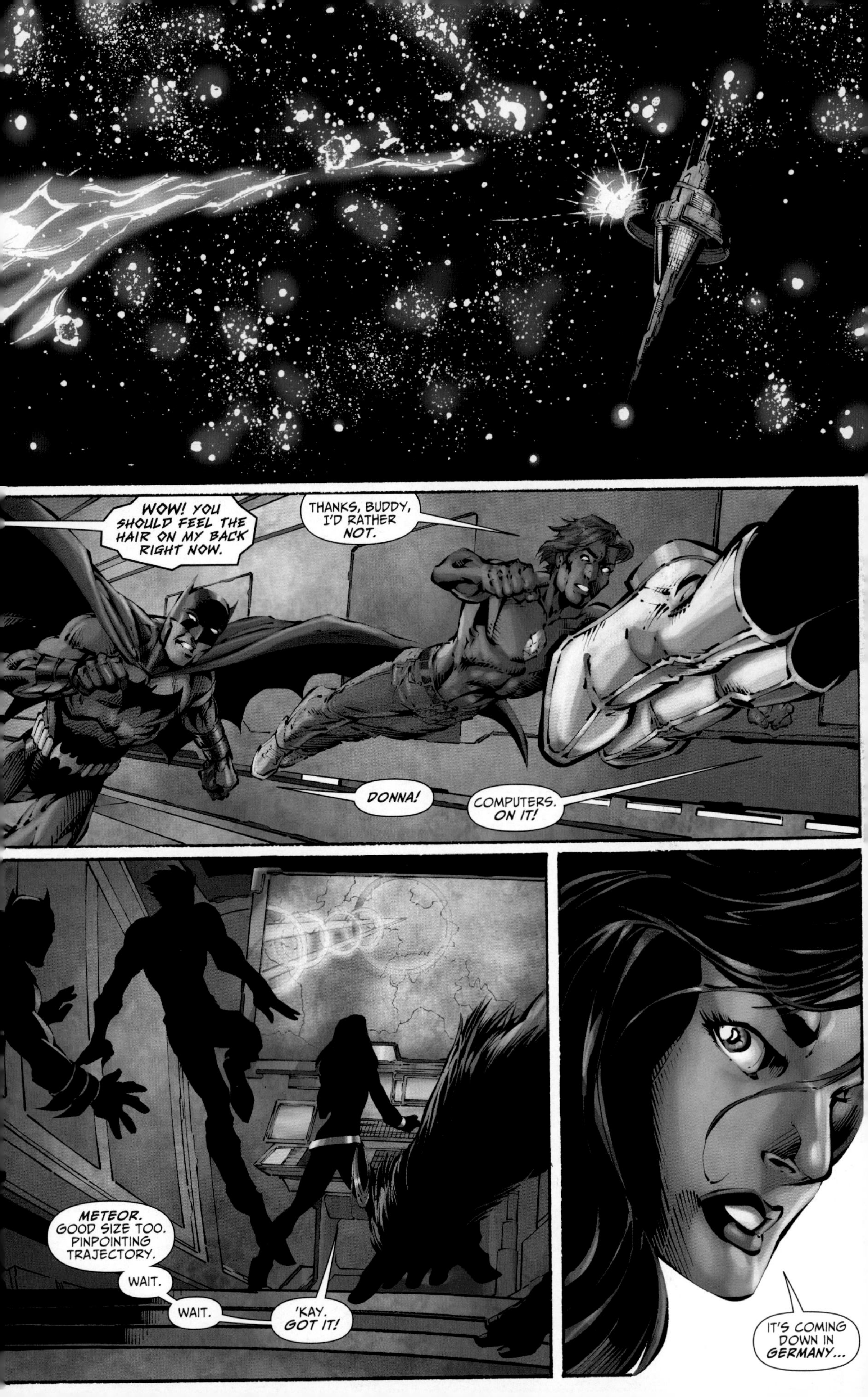
WOW! YOU SHOULD FEEL THE HAIR ON MY BACK RIGHT NOW.
THANKS, BUDDY, I'D RATHER NOT.
DONNA!
COMPUTERS. ON IT!
METEOR. GOOD SIZE TOO. PINPOINTING TRAJECTORY.
WAIT.
WAIT.
'KAY. GOT IT!
IT'S COMING DOWN IN GERMANY...

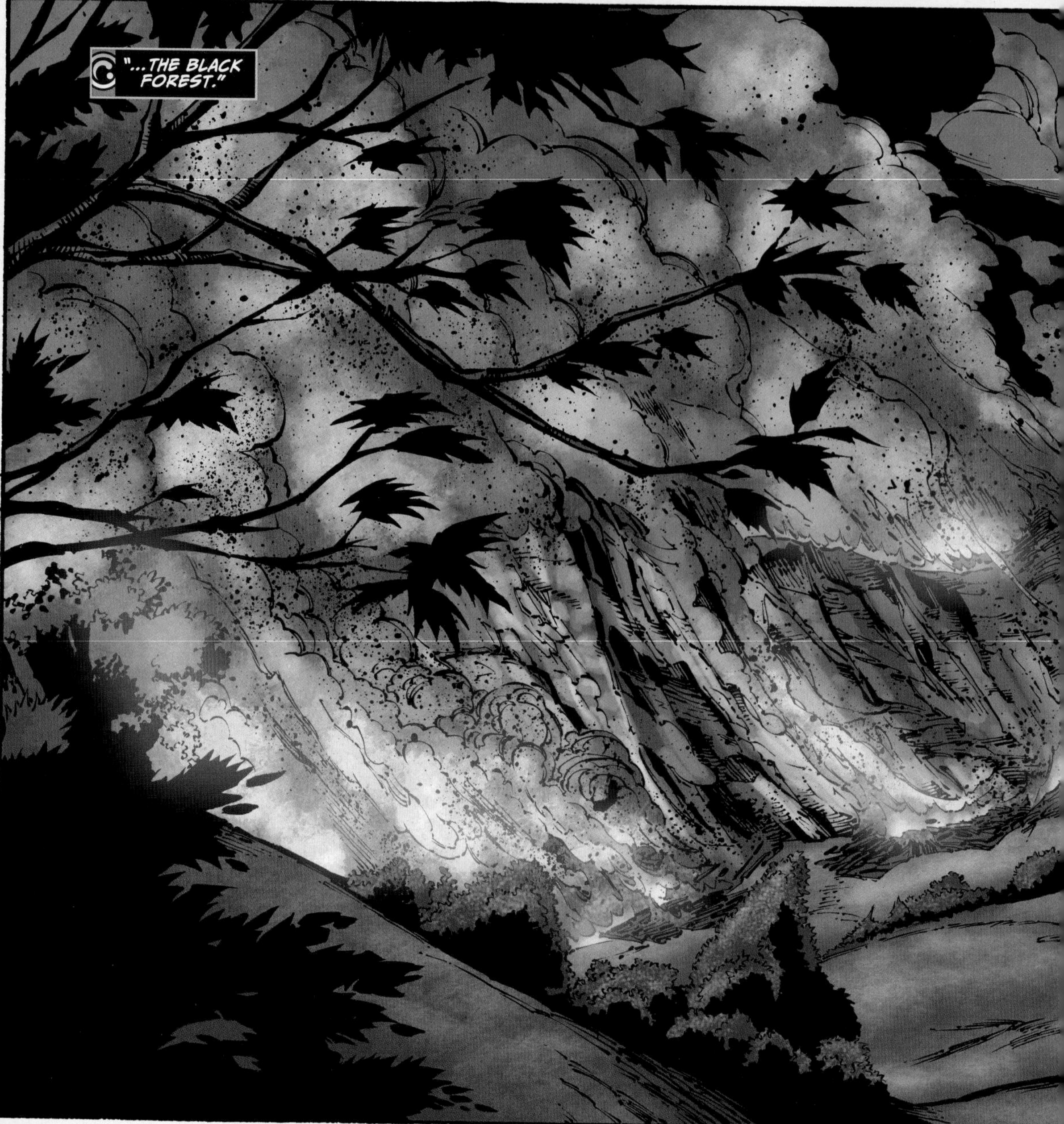
"...THE BLACK FOREST."

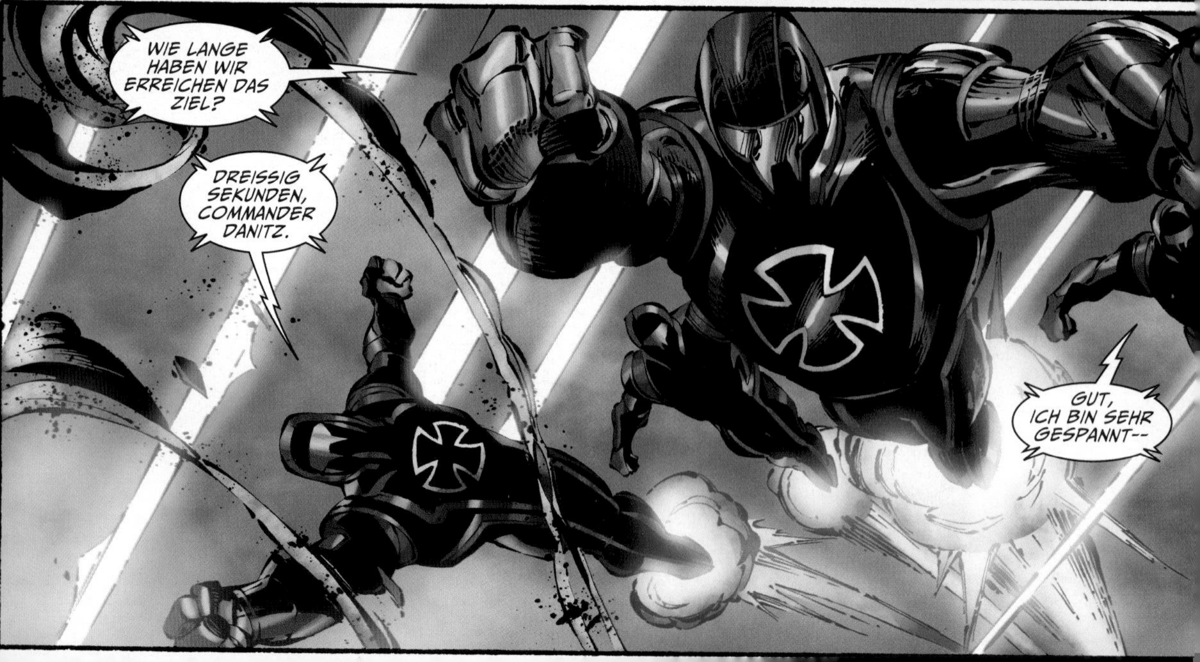
WIE LANGE HABEN WIR ERREICHEN DAS ZIEL?
DREISSIG SEKUNDEN, COMMANDER DANITZ.
GUT, ICH BIN SEHR GESPANNT--

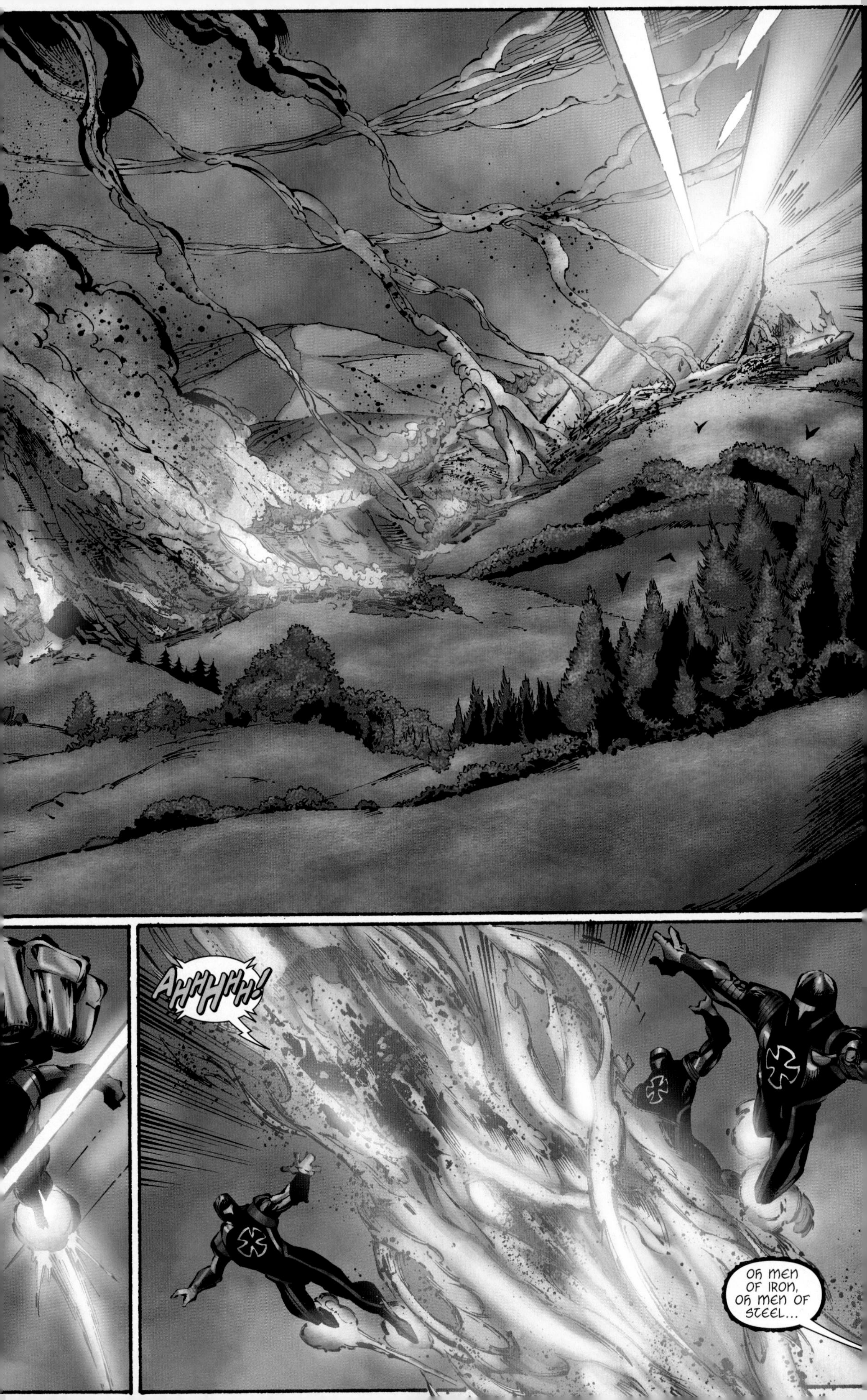
AHHHHH!
OH MEN OF IRON, OH MEN OF STEEL...

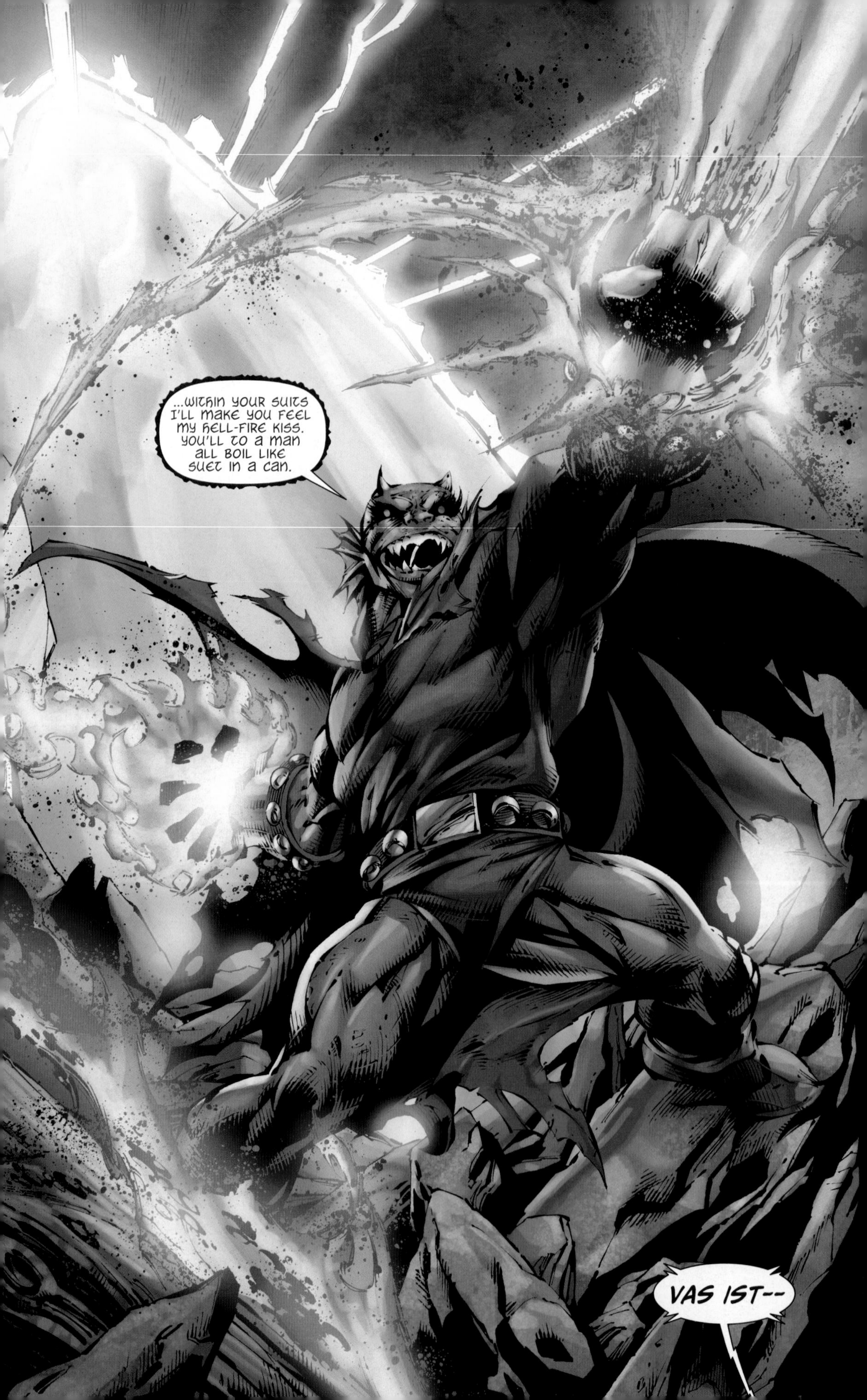
...WITHIN YOUR SUITS I'LL MAKE YOU FEEL MY HELL-FIRE KISS. YOU'LL TO A MAN ALL BOIL LIKE SUET IN A CAN.
VAS IST--

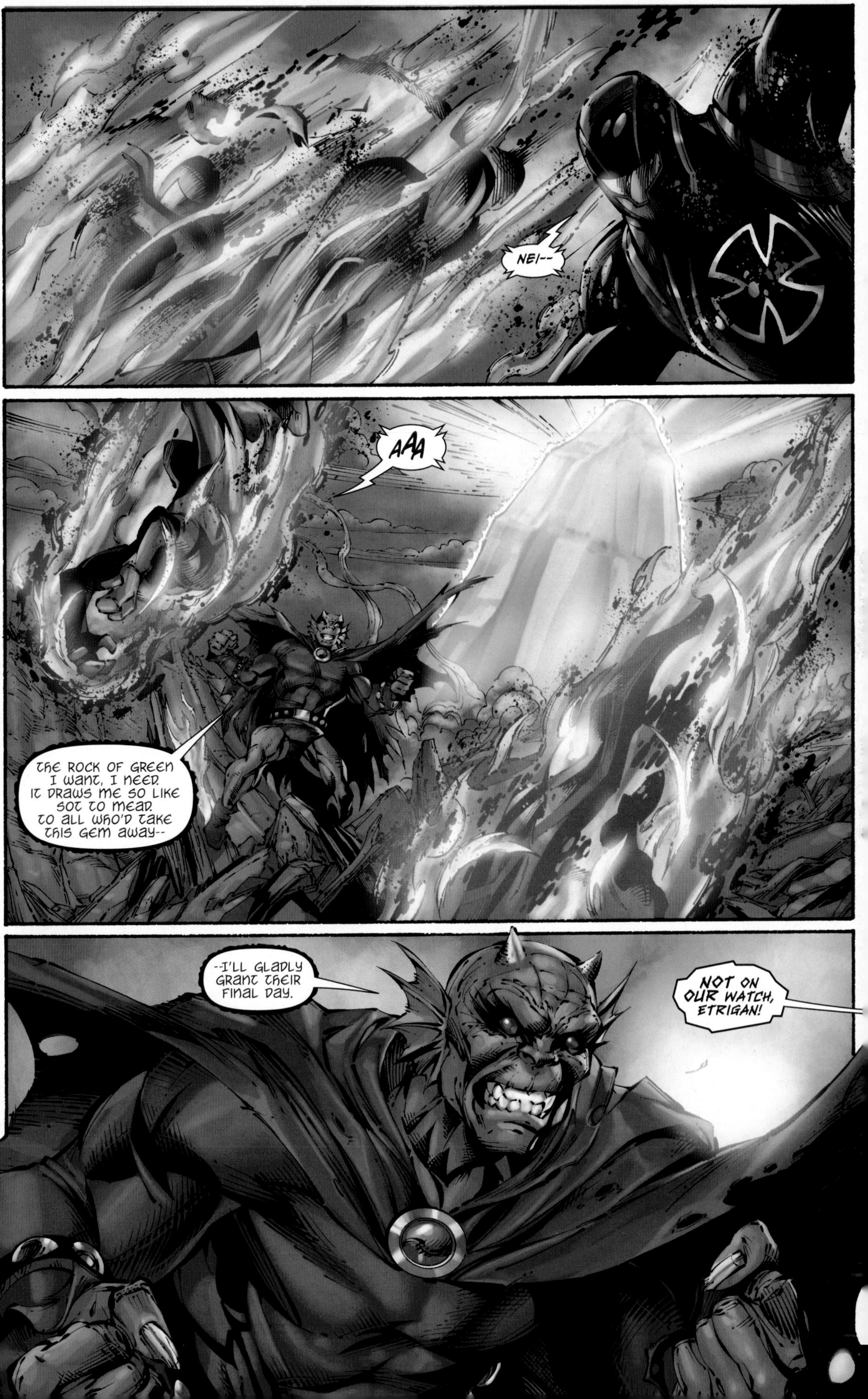
NEI--
AAA
THE ROCK OF GREEN I WANT, I NEED. IT DRAWS ME SO LIKE SOT TO MEAD. TO ALL WHO'D TAKE THIS GEM AWAY--
--I'LL GLADLY GRANT THEIR FINAL DAY.
NOT ON OUR WATCH, ETRIGAN!

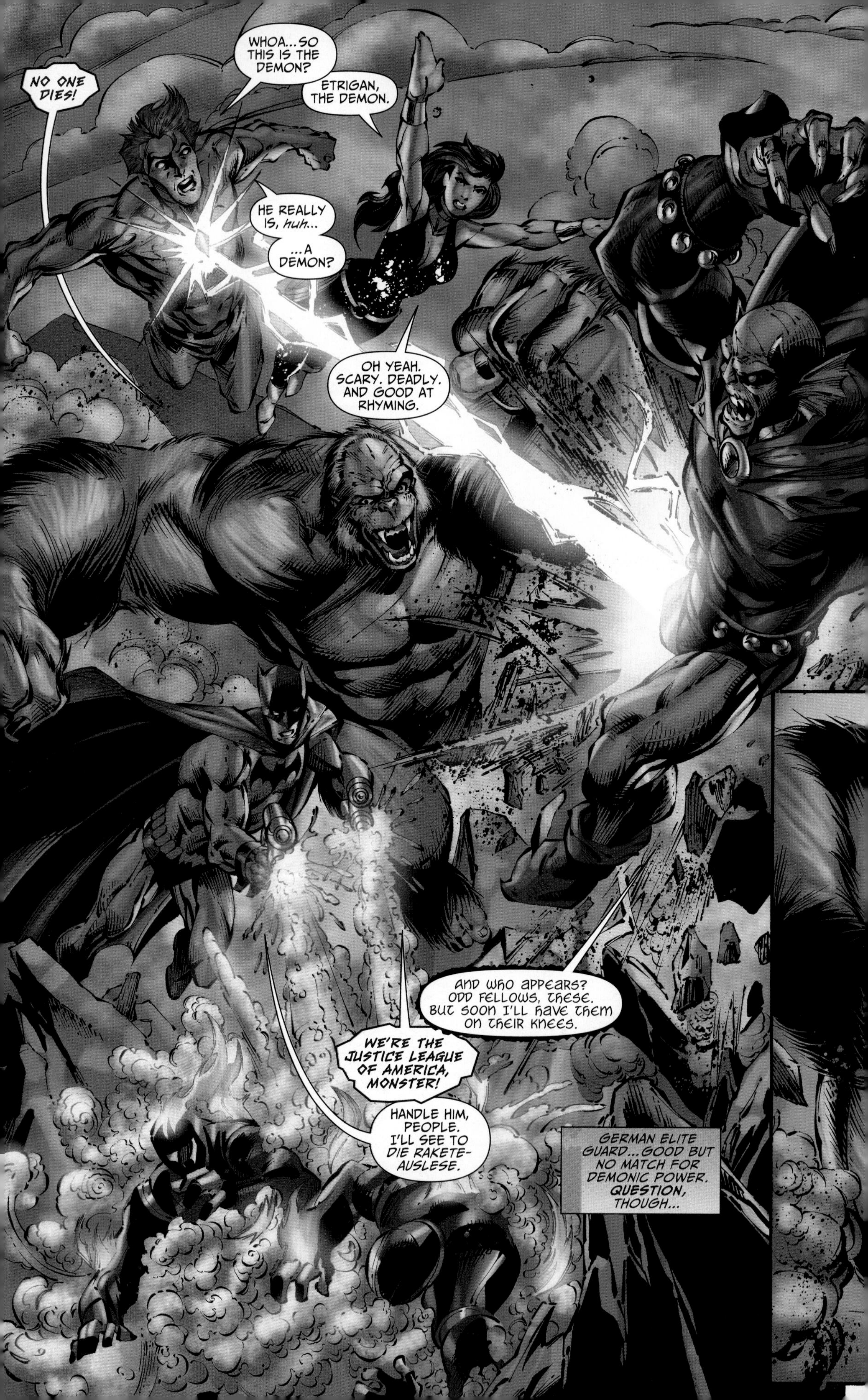
NO ONE DIES!
WHOA... SO THIS IS THE DEMON?
ETRIGAN, THE DEMON.
HE REALLY IS, *huh*...
...A DEMON?
OH YEAH. SCARY. DEADLY. AND GOOD AT RHYMING.
AND WHO APPEARS? ODD FELLOWS, THESE. BUT SOON I'LL HAVE THEM ON THEIR KNEES.
WE'RE THE JUSTICE LEAGUE OF AMERICA, MONSTER!
HANDLE HIM, PEOPLE. I'LL SEE TO DIE RAKETE-AUSLESE.
GERMAN ELITE GUARD...GOOD BUT NO MATCH FOR DEMONIC POWER. ***QUESTION,*** *THOUGH...*

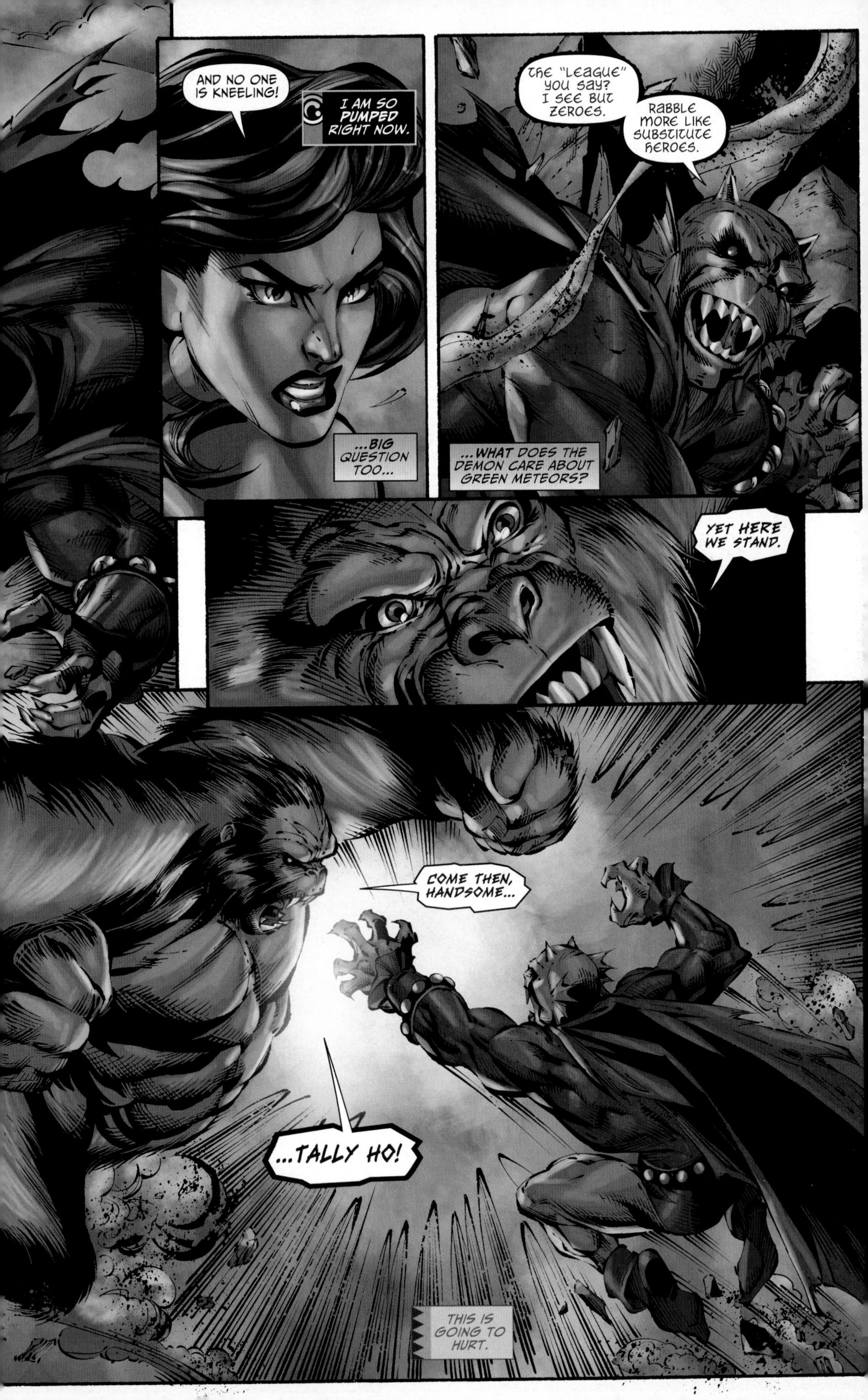
AND NO ONE IS KNEELING!
I AM SO PUMPED RIGHT NOW.
...BIG QUESTION TOO...
THE "LEAGUE" YOU SAY? I SEE BUT ZEROES.
RABBLE MORE LIKE SUBSTITUTE HEROES.
...WHAT DOES THE DEMON CARE ABOUT GREEN METEORS?
YET HERE WE STAND.
COME THEN, HANDSOME...
...TALLY HO!
THIS IS GOING TO HURT.

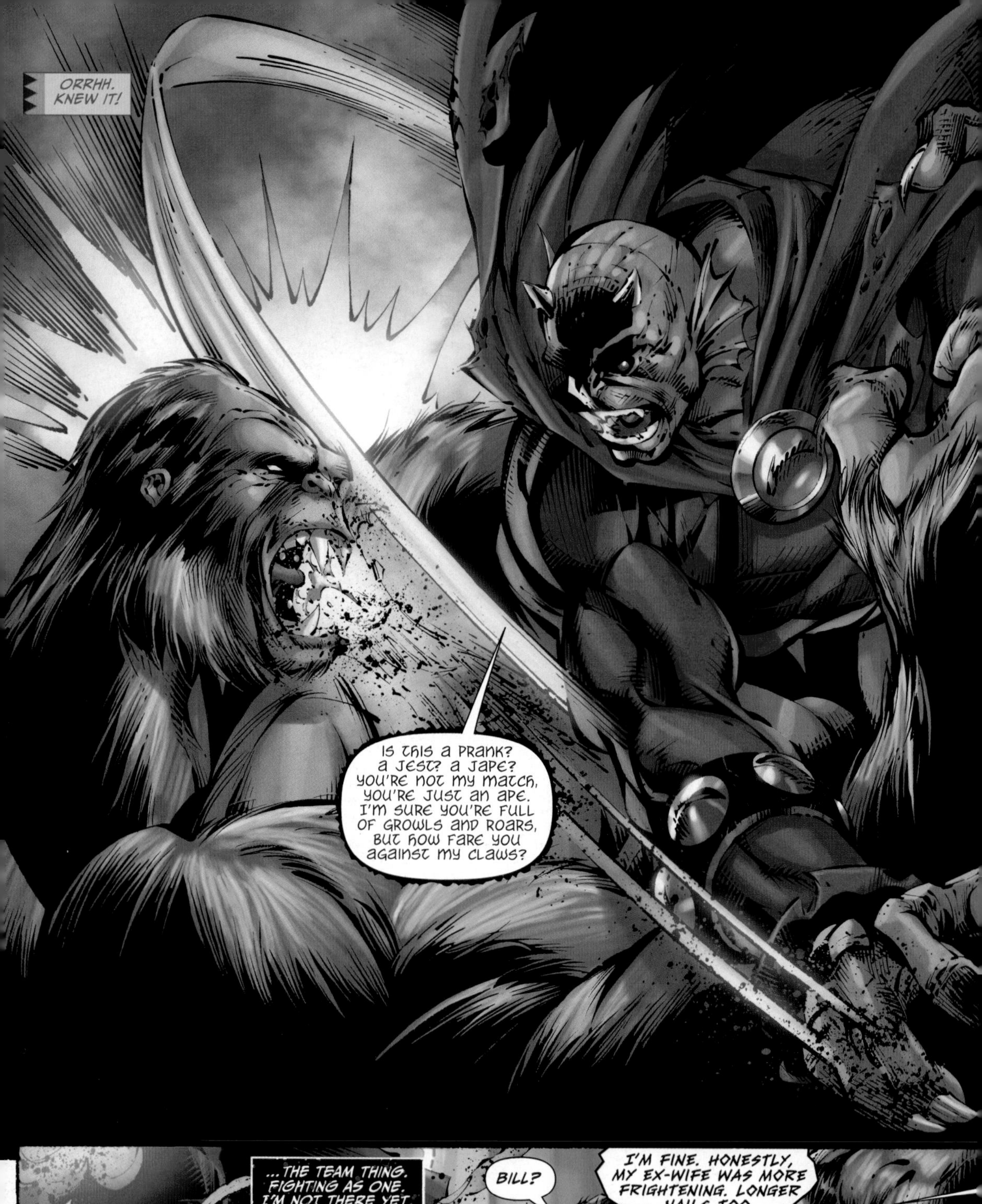
ORRHH. KNEW IT!
IS THIS A PRANK? A JEST? A JAPE? YOU'RE NOT MY MATCH, YOU'RE JUST AN APE. I'M SURE YOU'RE FULL OF GROWLS AND ROARS, BUT HOW FARE YOU AGAINST MY CLAWS?

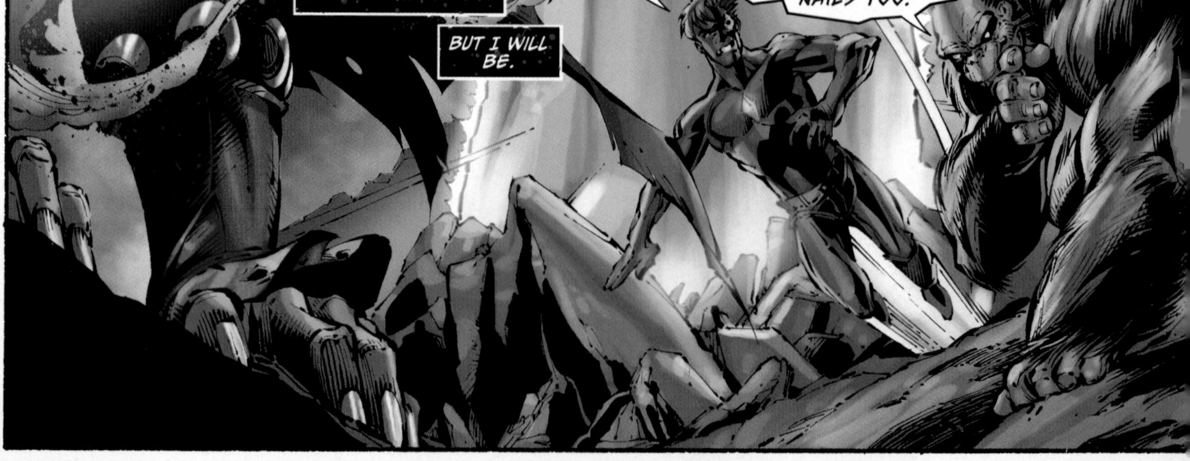
...THE TEAM THING. FIGHTING AS ONE. I'M NOT THERE YET.
BUT I WILL BE.
BILL?
I'M FINE. HONESTLY, MY EX-WIFE WAS MORE FRIGHTENING. LONGER NAILS TOO.

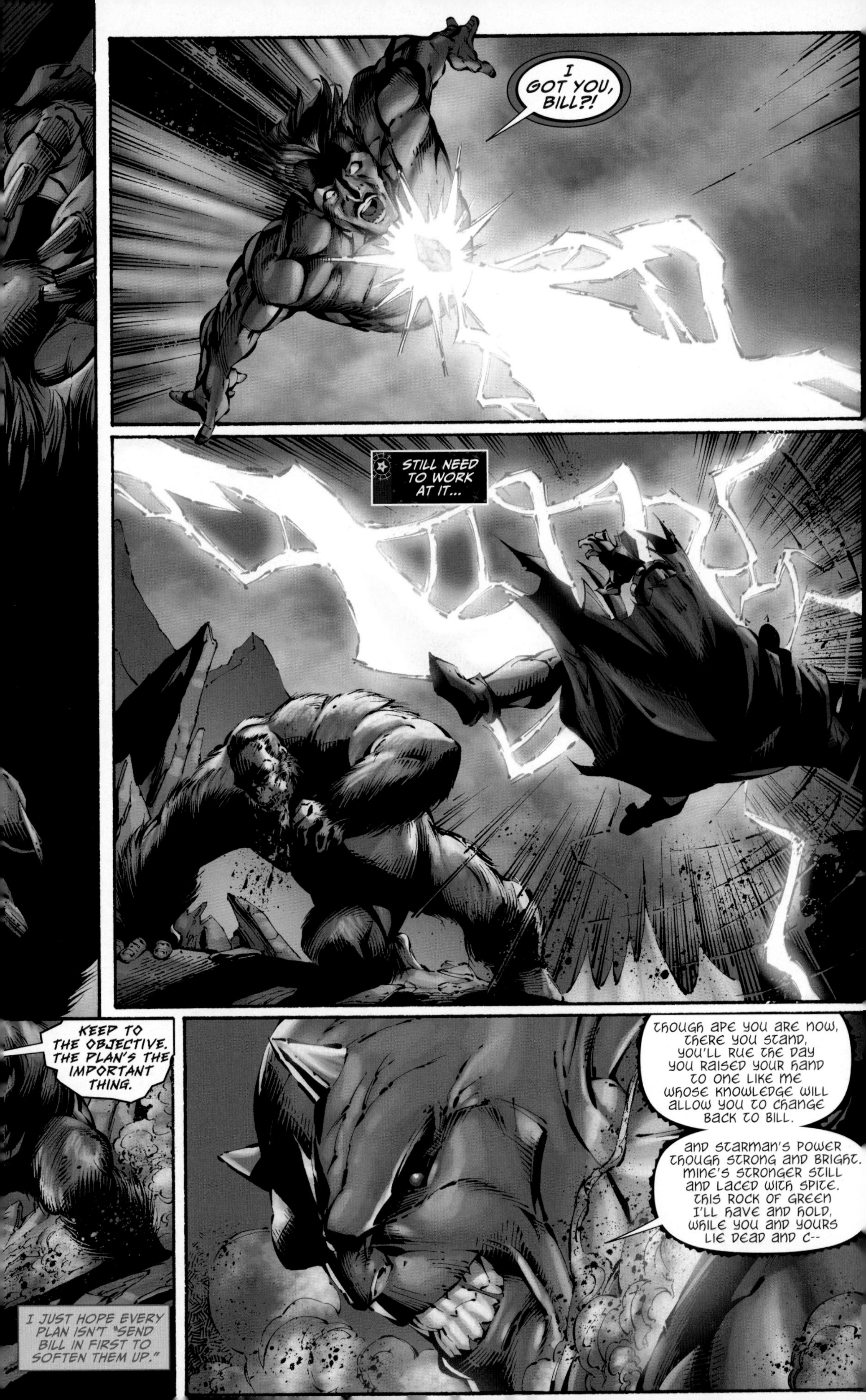
I GOT YOU, BILL?!
STILL NEED TO WORK AT IT...
KEEP TO THE OBJECTIVE. THE PLAN'S THE IMPORTANT THING.
I JUST HOPE EVERY PLAN ISN'T "SEND BILL IN FIRST TO SOFTEN THEM UP."
THOUGH APE YOU ARE NOW, THERE YOU STAND, YOU'LL RUE THE DAY YOU RAISED YOUR HAND TO ONE LIKE ME WHOSE KNOWLEDGE WILL ALLOW YOU TO CHANGE BACK TO BILL.
AND STARMAN'S POWER THOUGH STRONG AND BRIGHT, MINE'S STRONGER STILL AND LACED WITH SPITE. THIS ROCK OF GREEN I'LL HAVE AND HOLD, WHILE YOU AND YOURS LIE DEAD AND C--

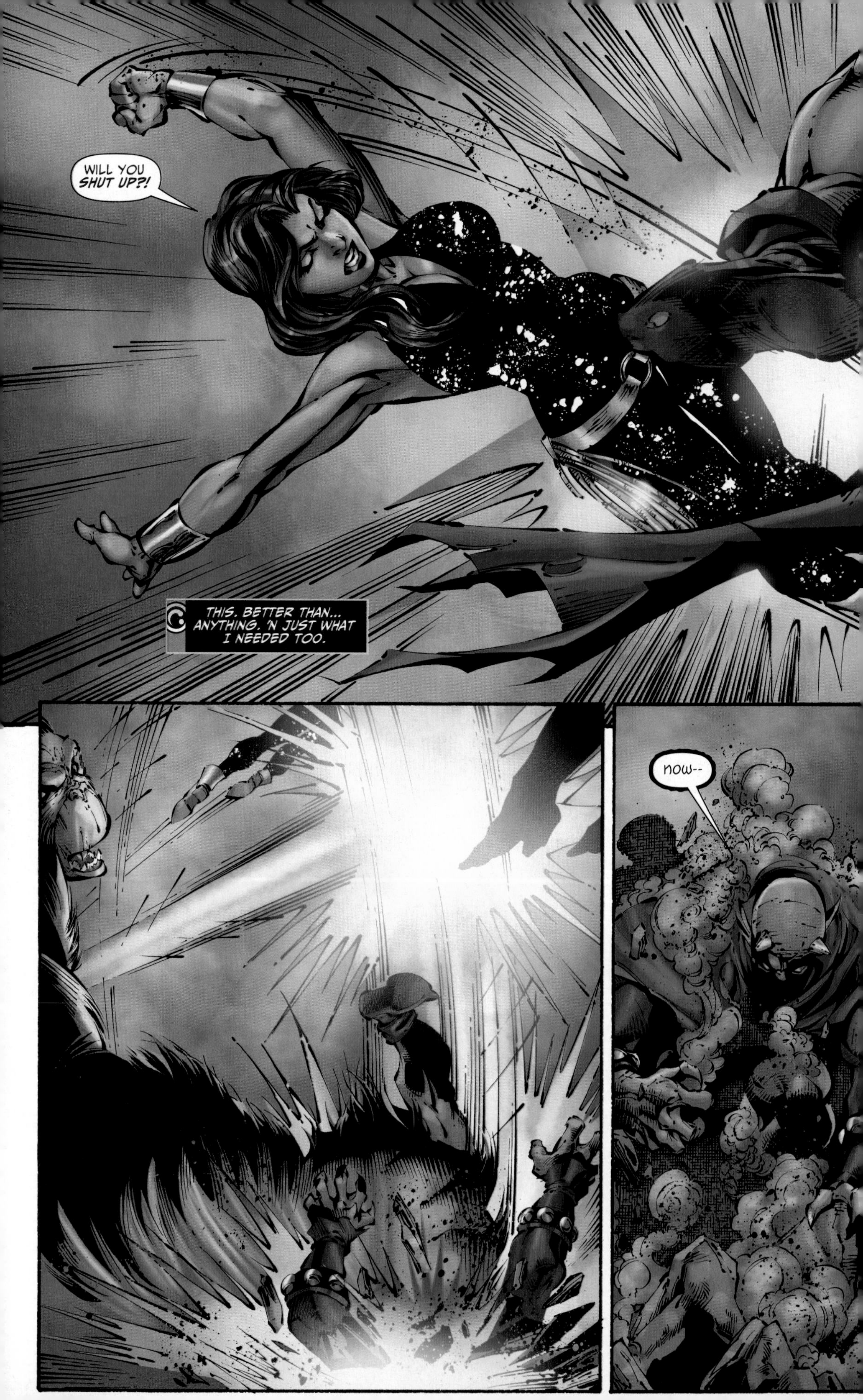
WILL YOU SHUT UP?!
THIS. BETTER THAN... ANYTHING. 'N JUST WHAT I NEEDED TOO.
now--

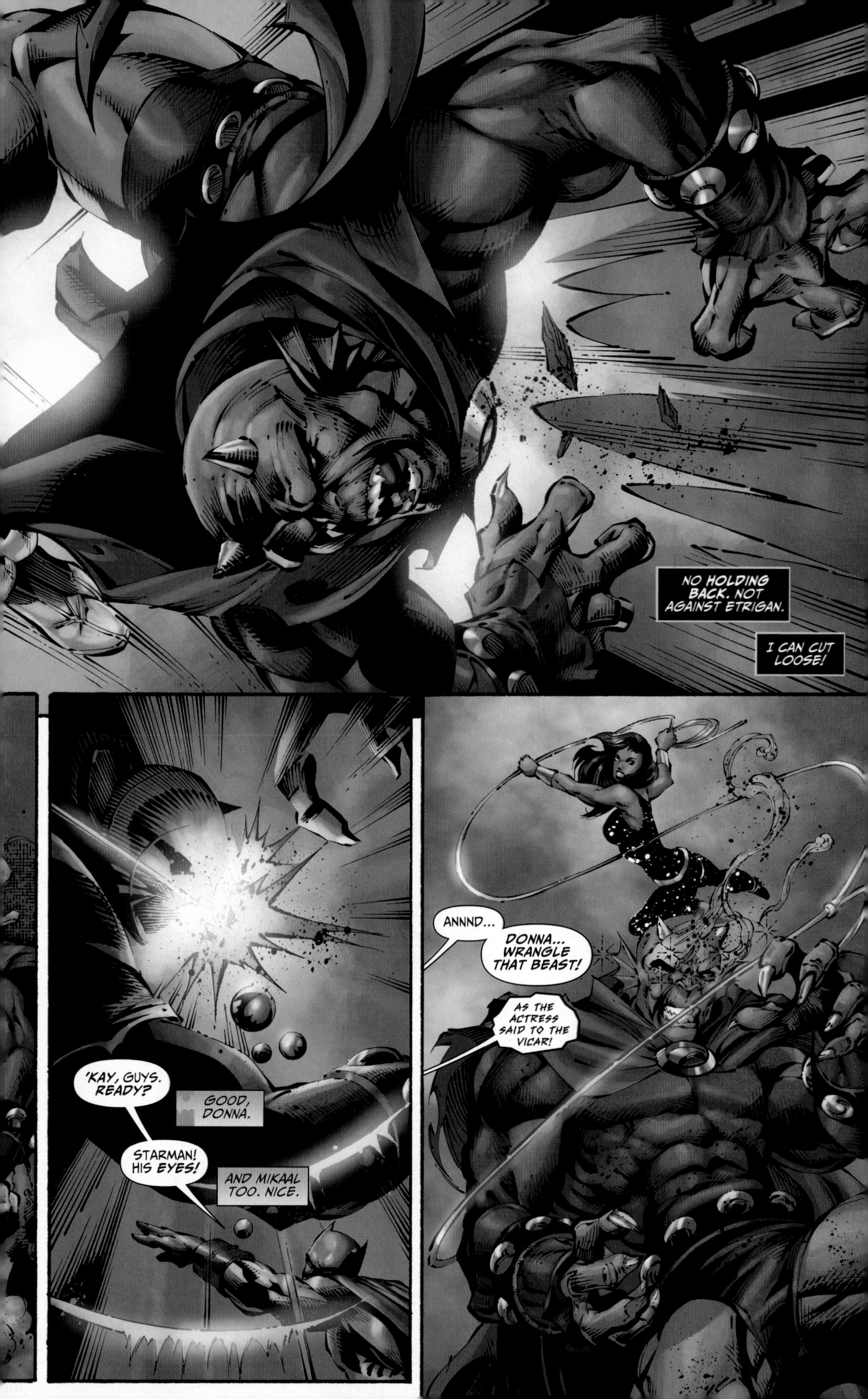
NO HOLDING BACK. NOT AGAINST ETRIGAN.
I CAN CUT LOOSE!
'KAY, GUYS. READY?
GOOD, DONNA.
STARMAN! HIS EYES!
AND MIKAAL TOO. NICE.
ANNND...
DONNA... WRANGLE THAT BEAST!
AS THE ACTRESS SAID TO THE VICAR!

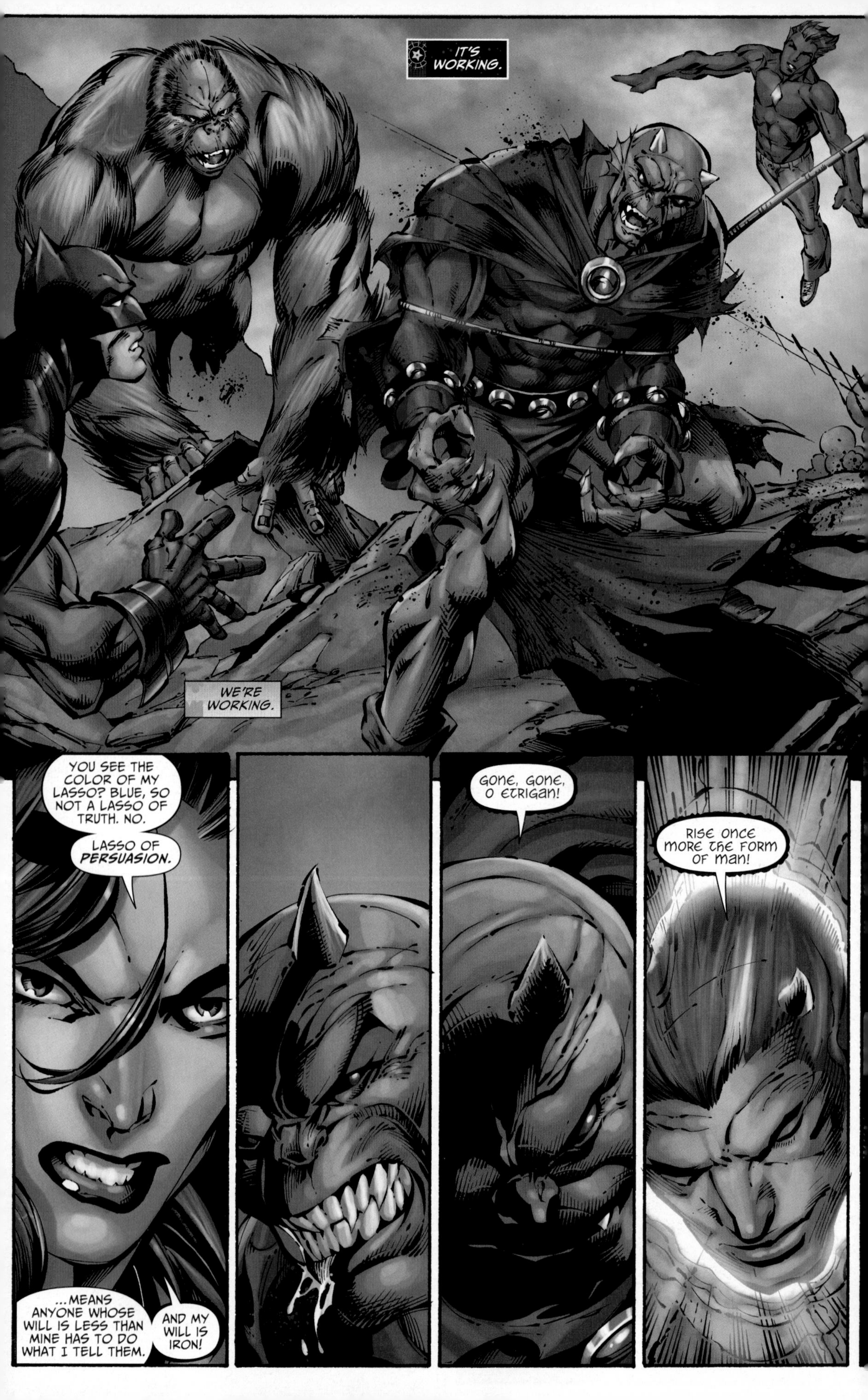
IT'S WORKING.
WE'RE WORKING.
YOU SEE THE COLOR OF MY LASSO? BLUE, SO NOT A LASSO OF TRUTH. NO.
LASSO OF PERSUASION.
...MEANS ANYONE WHOSE WILL IS LESS THAN MINE HAS TO DO WHAT I TELL THEM.
AND MY WILL IS IRON!
GONE, GONE, O ETRIGAN!
RISE ONCE MORE THE FORM OF MAN!

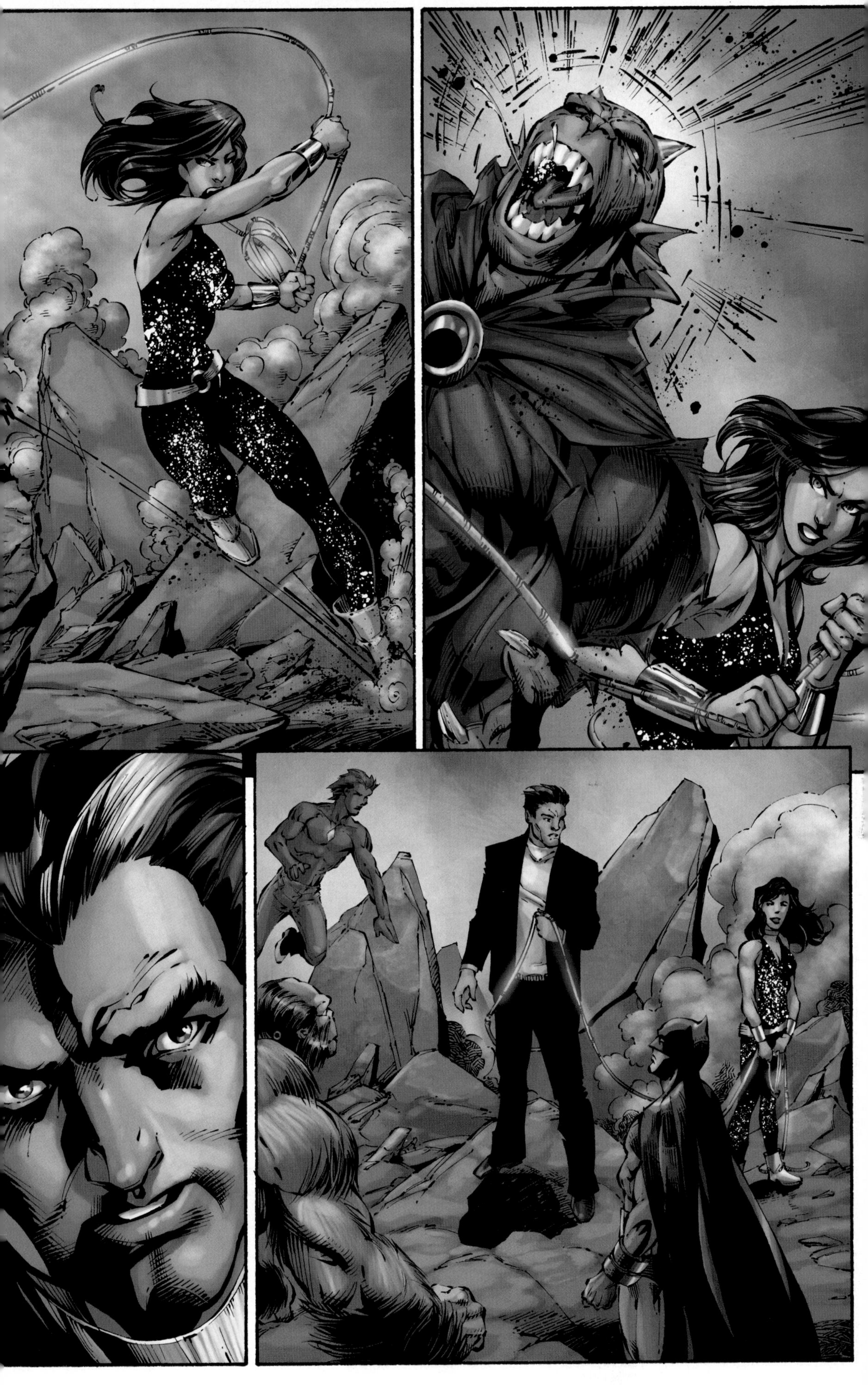

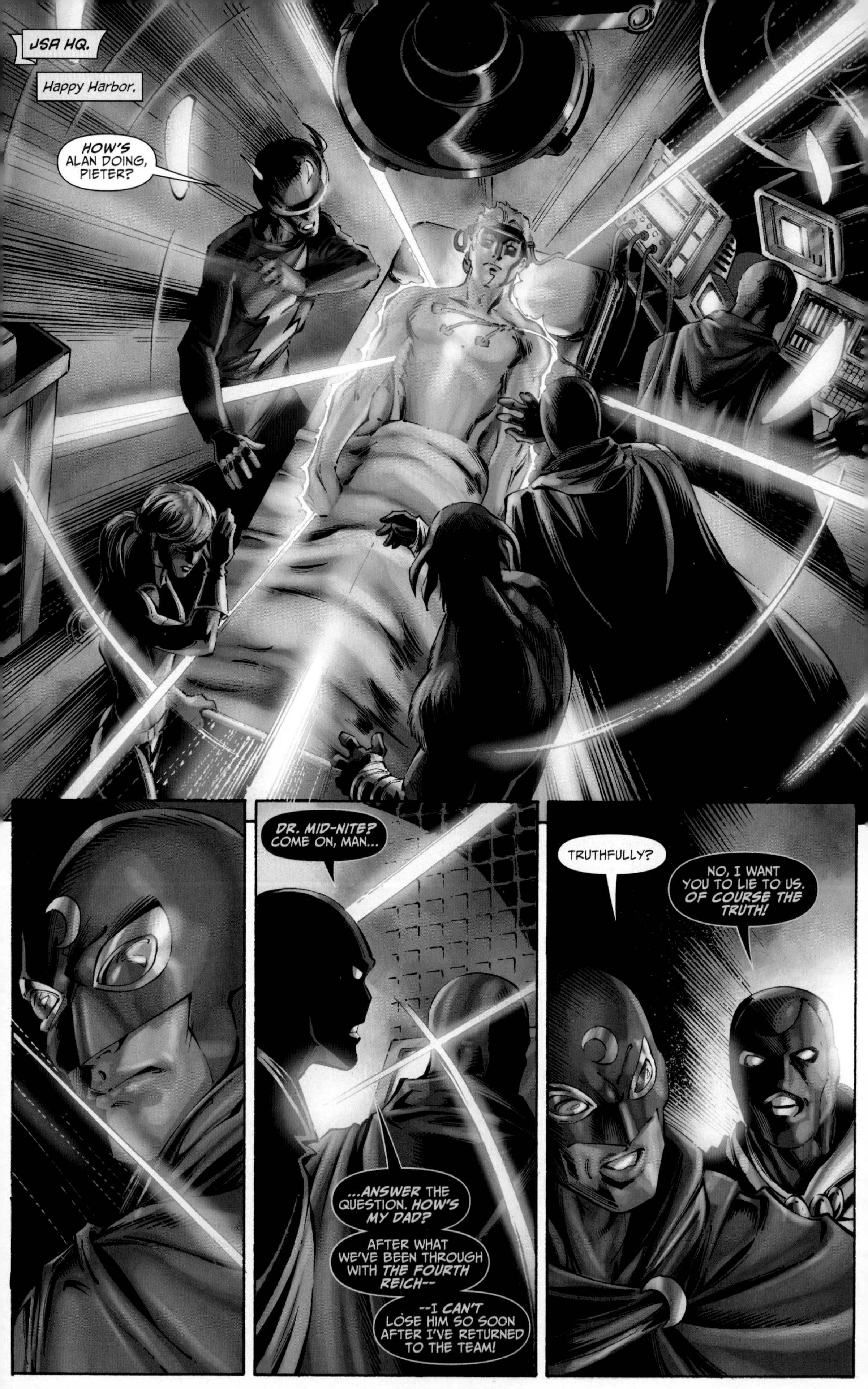
JSA HQ.
Happy Harbor.
HOW'S ALAN DOING, PIETER?
DR. MID-NITE? COME ON, MAN...
...ANSWER THE QUESTION. HOW'S MY DAD?
AFTER WHAT WE'VE BEEN THROUGH WITH THE FOURTH REICH--
--I CAN'T LOSE HIM SO SOON AFTER I'VE RETURNED TO THE TEAM!
TRUTHFULLY?
NO, I WANT YOU TO LIE TO US. OF COURSE THE TRUTH!

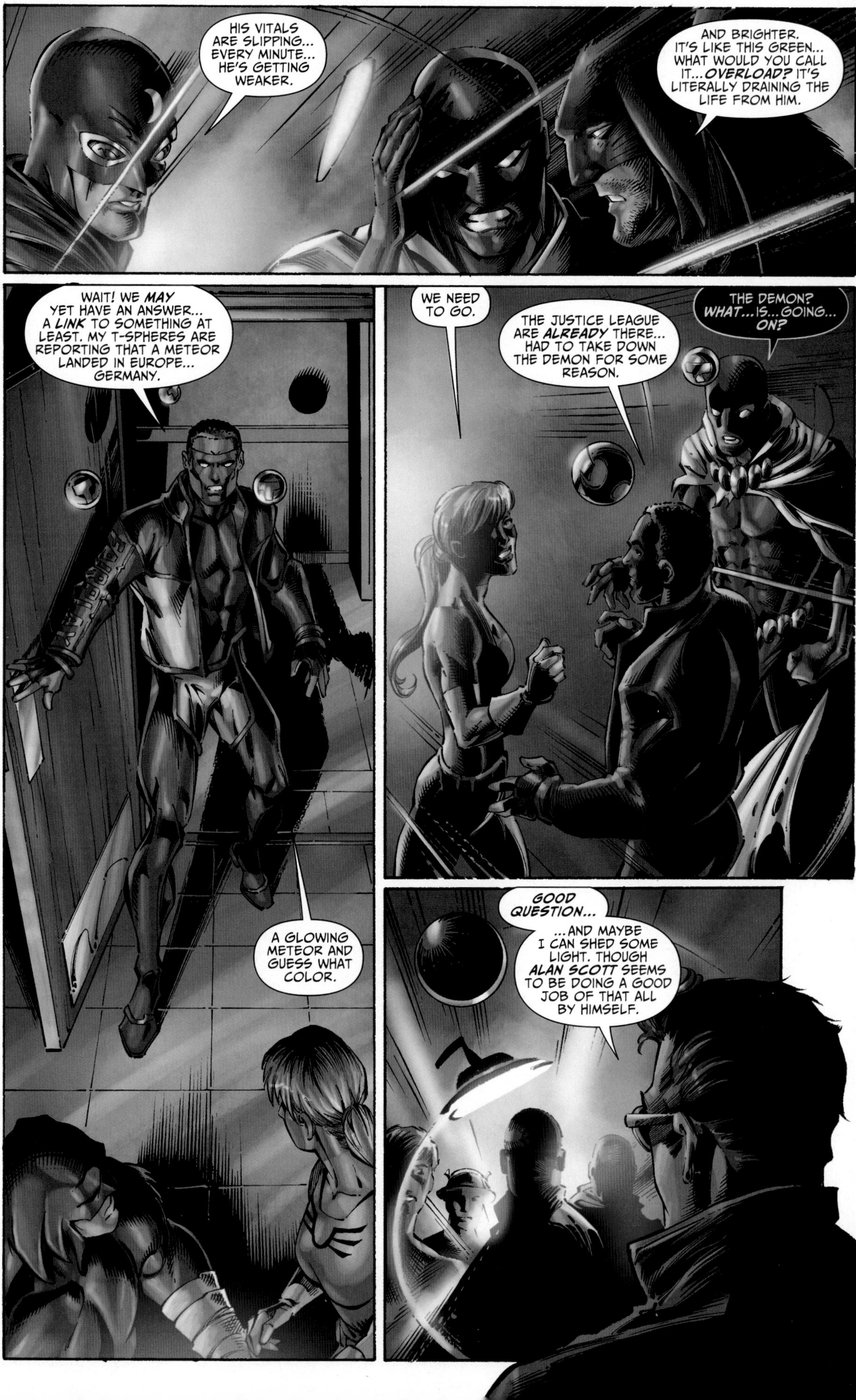
HIS VITALS ARE SLIPPING... EVERY MINUTE... HE'S GETTING WEAKER.
AND BRIGHTER. IT'S LIKE THIS GREEN... WHAT WOULD YOU CALL IT...*OVERLOAD?* IT'S LITERALLY DRAINING THE LIFE FROM HIM.
WAIT! WE *MAY* YET HAVE AN ANSWER... A *LINK* TO SOMETHING AT LEAST. MY T-SPHERES ARE REPORTING THAT A METEOR LANDED IN EUROPE... GERMANY.
A GLOWING METEOR AND GUESS WHAT COLOR.
WE NEED TO GO.
THE JUSTICE LEAGUE ARE *ALREADY* THERE... HAD TO TAKE DOWN THE DEMON FOR SOME REASON.
THE DEMON? *WHAT...*IS...GOING... *ON?*
GOOD QUESTION...
...AND MAYBE I CAN SHED SOME LIGHT. THOUGH *ALAN SCOTT* SEEMS TO BE DOING A GOOD JOB OF THAT ALL BY HIMSELF.

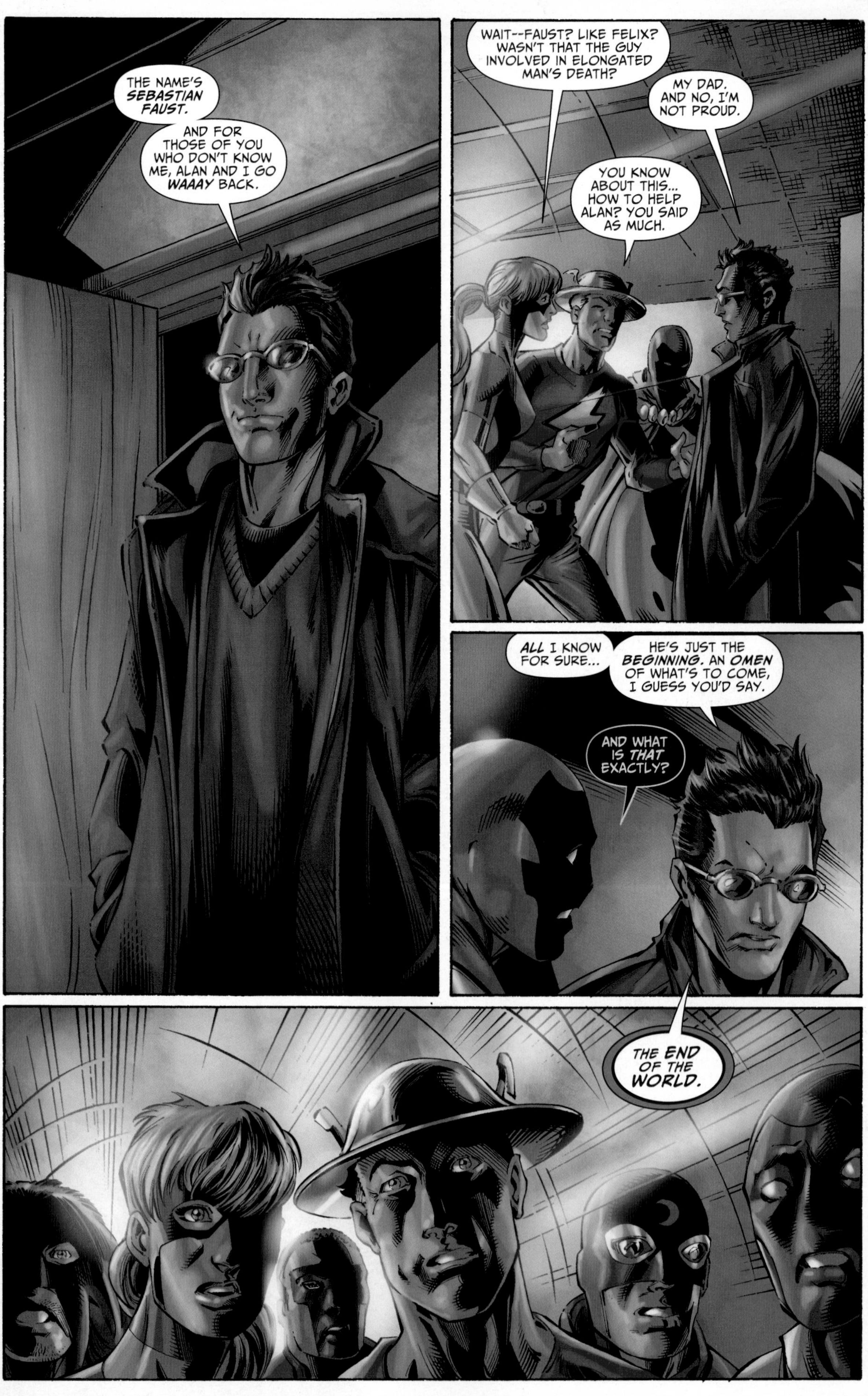
THE NAME'S *SEBASTIAN FAUST.*
AND FOR THOSE OF YOU WHO DON'T KNOW ME, ALAN AND I GO *WAAAY* BACK.
WAIT--FAUST? LIKE FELIX? WASN'T THAT THE GUY INVOLVED IN ELONGATED MAN'S DEATH?
MY DAD. AND NO, I'M NOT PROUD.
YOU KNOW ABOUT THIS... HOW TO HELP ALAN? YOU SAID AS MUCH.
ALL I KNOW FOR SURE...
HE'S JUST THE *BEGINNING.* AN *OMEN* OF WHAT'S TO COME, I GUESS YOU'D SAY.
AND WHAT IS *THAT* EXACTLY?
THE END OF THE WORLD.

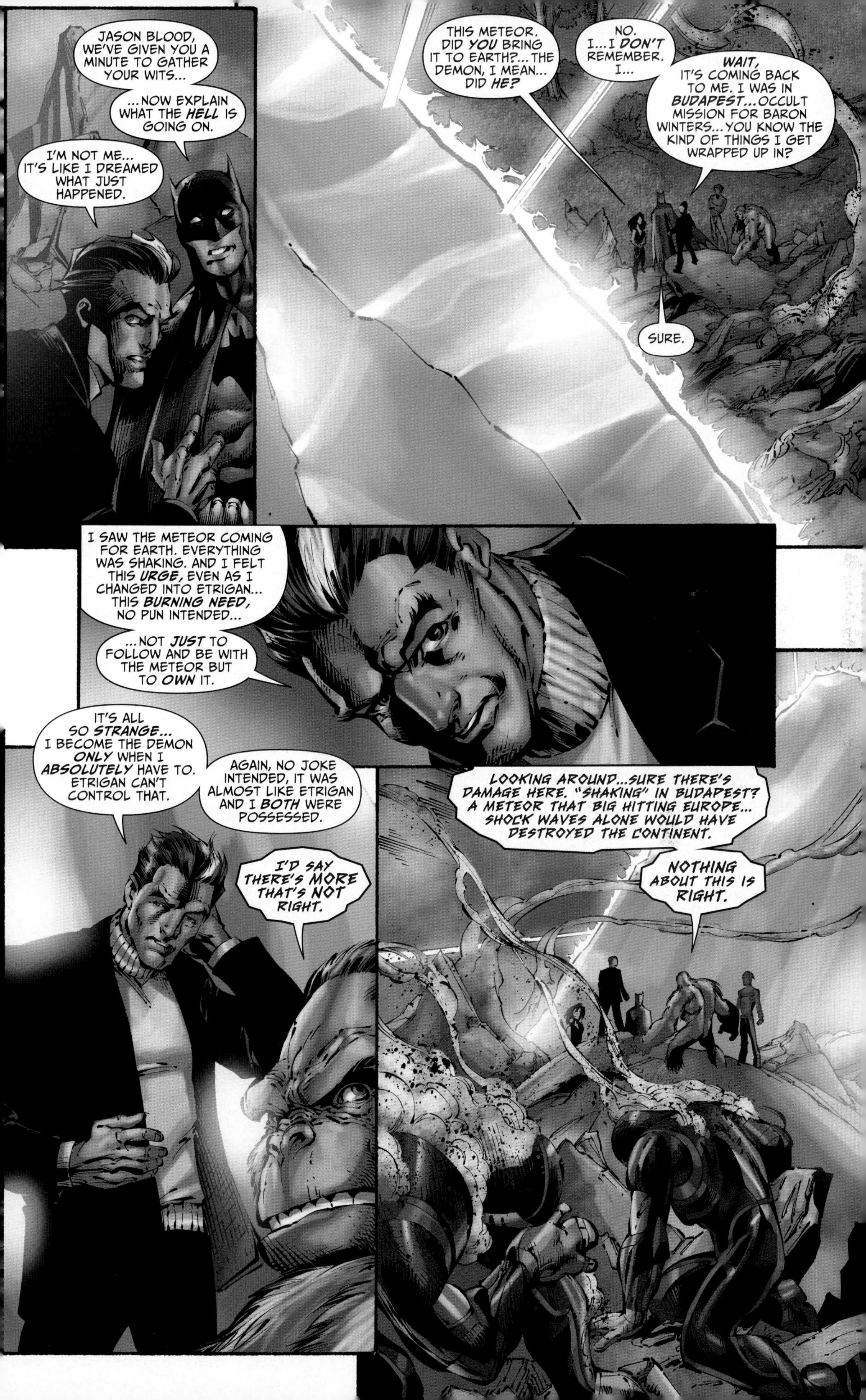

JASON BLOOD, WE'VE GIVEN YOU A MINUTE TO GATHER YOUR WITS...
...NOW EXPLAIN WHAT THE HELL IS GOING ON.
I'M NOT ME... IT'S LIKE I DREAMED WHAT JUST HAPPENED.
THIS METEOR. DID YOU BRING IT TO EARTH?... THE DEMON, I MEAN... DID HE?
NO. I...I DON'T REMEMBER. I...
WAIT, IT'S COMING BACK TO ME. I WAS IN BUDAPEST...OCCULT MISSION FOR BARON WINTERS...YOU KNOW THE KIND OF THINGS I GET WRAPPED UP IN?
SURE.
I SAW THE METEOR COMING FOR EARTH. EVERYTHING WAS SHAKING. AND I FELT THIS URGE, EVEN AS I CHANGED INTO ETRIGAN... THIS BURNING NEED, NO PUN INTENDED...
...NOT JUST TO FOLLOW AND BE WITH THE METEOR BUT TO OWN IT.
IT'S ALL SO STRANGE... I BECOME THE DEMON ONLY WHEN I ABSOLUTELY HAVE TO. ETRIGAN CAN'T CONTROL THAT.
AGAIN, NO JOKE INTENDED, IT WAS ALMOST LIKE ETRIGAN AND I BOTH WERE POSSESSED.
I'D SAY THERE'S MORE THAT'S NOT RIGHT.
LOOKING AROUND...SURE THERE'S DAMAGE HERE. "SHAKING" IN BUDAPEST? A METEOR THAT BIG HITTING EUROPE... SHOCK WAVES ALONE WOULD HAVE DESTROYED THE CONTINENT.
NOTHING ABOUT THIS IS RIGHT.

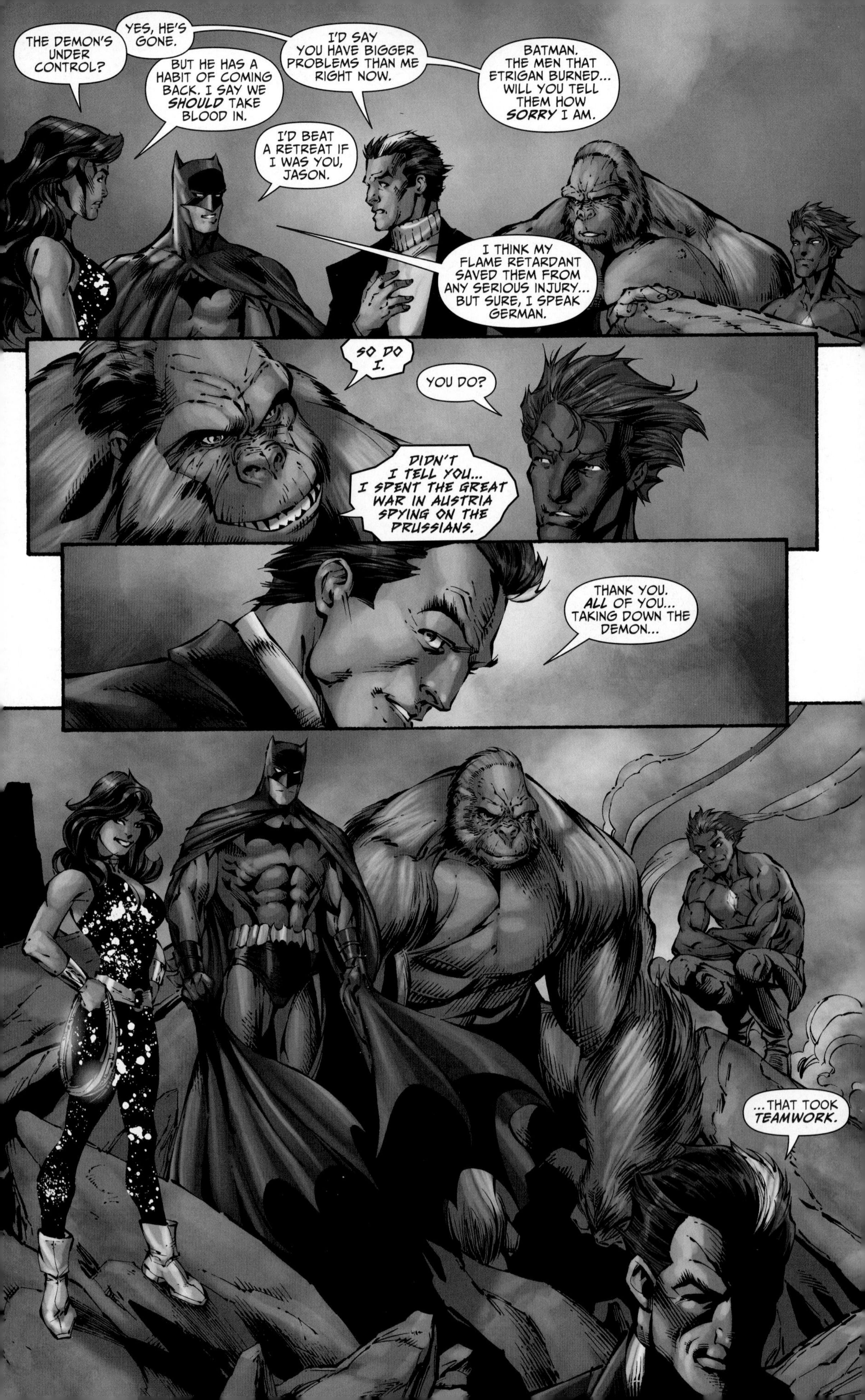
THE DEMON'S UNDER CONTROL?
YES, HE'S GONE.
BUT HE HAS A HABIT OF COMING BACK. I SAY WE SHOULD TAKE BLOOD IN.
I'D SAY YOU HAVE BIGGER PROBLEMS THAN ME RIGHT NOW.
BATMAN. THE MEN THAT ETRIGAN BURNED... WILL YOU TELL THEM HOW SORRY I AM.
I'D BEAT A RETREAT IF I WAS YOU, JASON.
I THINK MY FLAME RETARDANT SAVED THEM FROM ANY SERIOUS INJURY... BUT SURE, I SPEAK GERMAN.
SO DO I.
YOU DO?
DIDN'T I TELL YOU... I SPENT THE GREAT WAR IN AUSTRIA SPYING ON THE PRUSSIANS.
THANK YOU. ALL OF YOU... TAKING DOWN THE DEMON...
...THAT TOOK TEAMWORK.

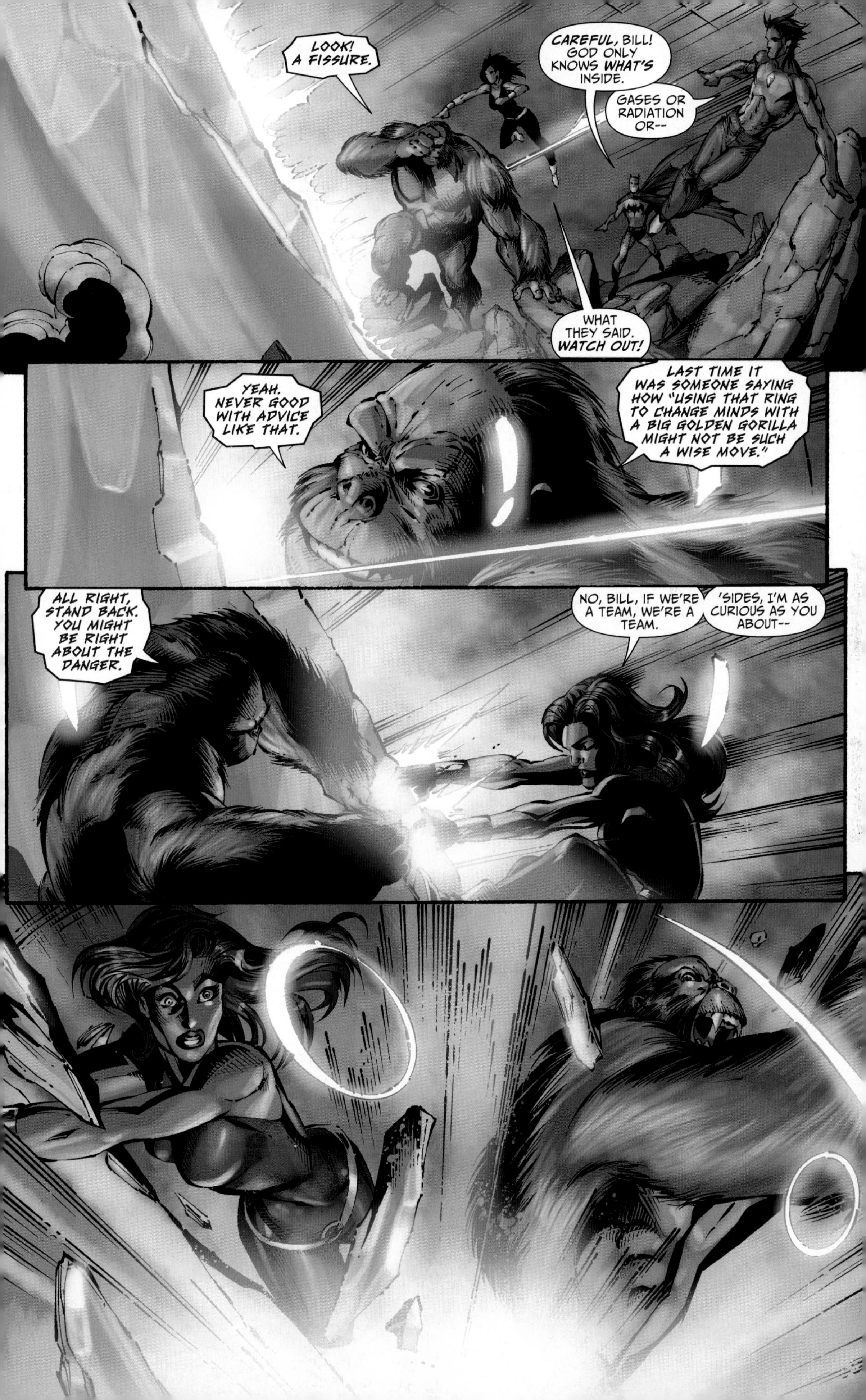
LOOK! A FISSURE.
CAREFUL, BILL! GOD ONLY KNOWS WHAT'S INSIDE.
GASES OR RADIATION OR--
WHAT THEY SAID. WATCH OUT!
YEAH. NEVER GOOD WITH ADVICE LIKE THAT.
LAST TIME IT WAS SOMEONE SAYING HOW "USING THAT RING TO CHANGE MINDS WITH A BIG GOLDEN GORILLA MIGHT NOT BE SUCH A WISE MOVE."
ALL RIGHT, STAND BACK. YOU MIGHT BE RIGHT ABOUT THE DANGER.
NO, BILL, IF WE'RE A TEAM, WE'RE A TEAM.
'SIDES, I'M AS CURIOUS AS YOU ABOUT--

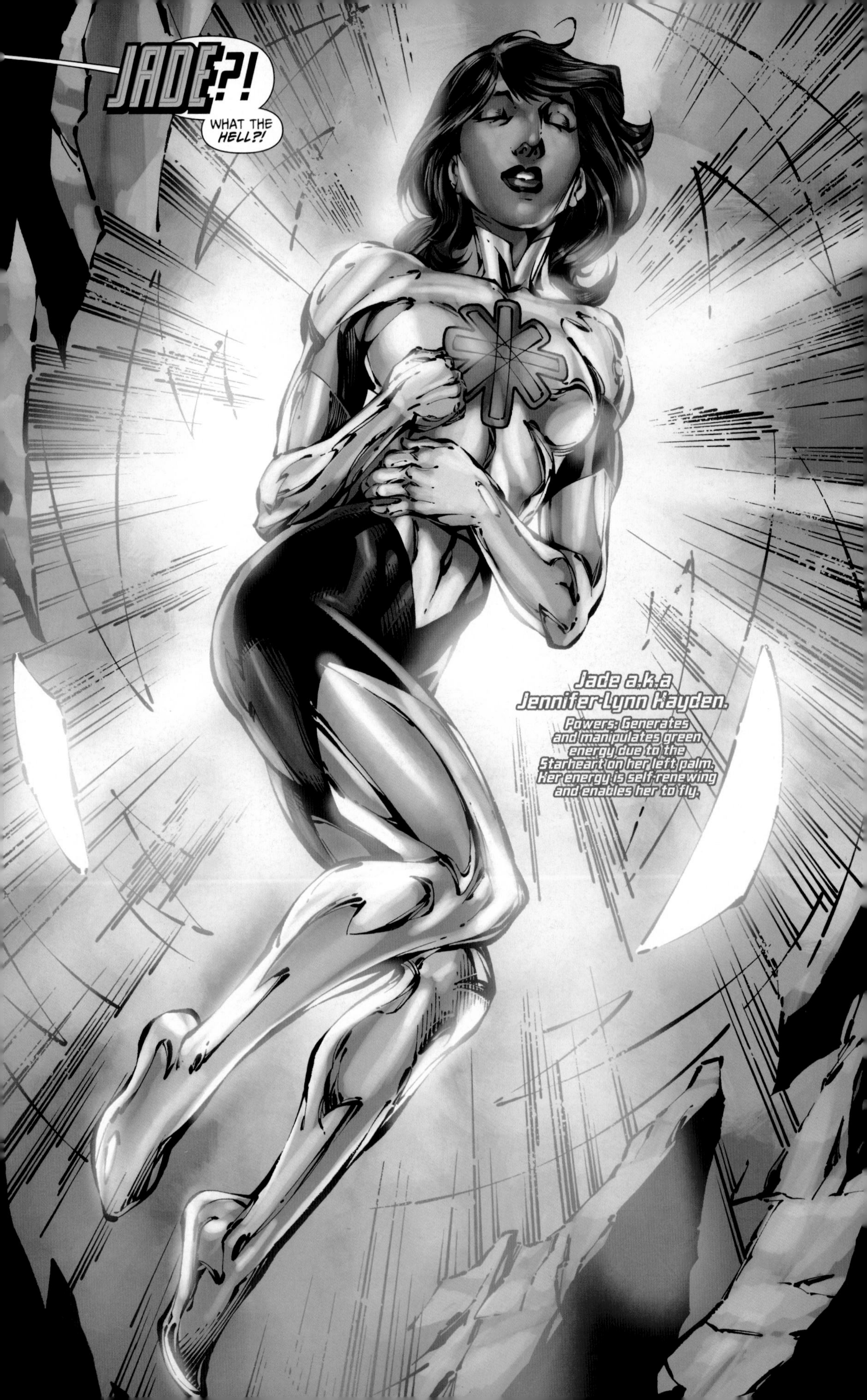
JADE?!
WHAT THE HELL?!
Jade a.k.a
Jennifer-Lynn Hayden.
Powers: Generates and manipulates green energy due to the Starheart on her left palm. Her energy is self-renewing and enables her to fly.

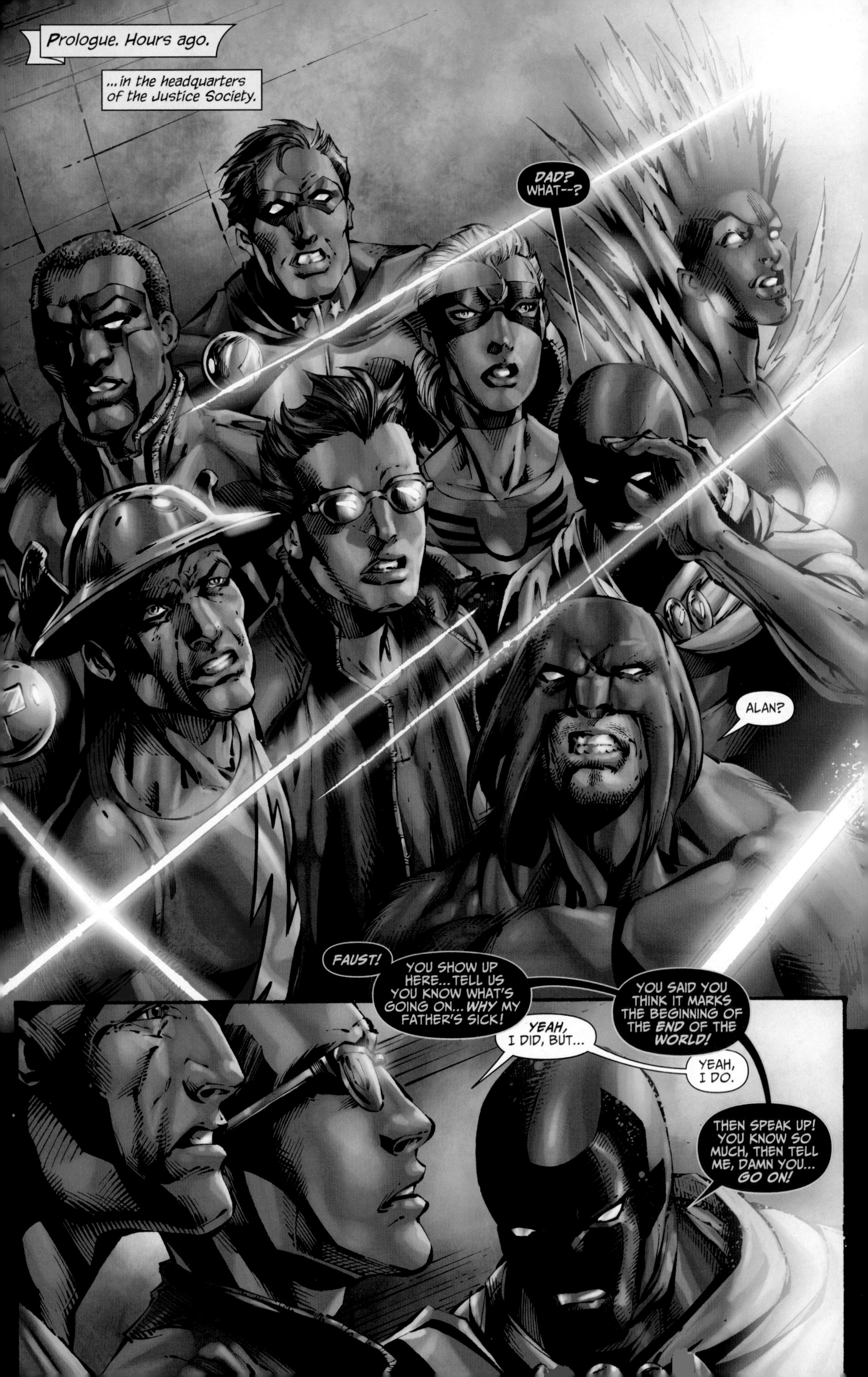
Prologue. Hours ago.
...in the headquarters of the Justice Society.
DAD? WHAT--?
ALAN?
FAUST!
YOU SHOW UP HERE...TELL US YOU KNOW WHAT'S GOING ON...WHY MY FATHER'S SICK!
YOU SAID YOU THINK IT MARKS THE BEGINNING OF THE END OF THE WORLD!
YEAH, I DID, BUT...
YEAH, I DO.
THEN SPEAK UP! YOU KNOW SO MUCH, THEN TELL ME, DAMN YOU... GO ON!

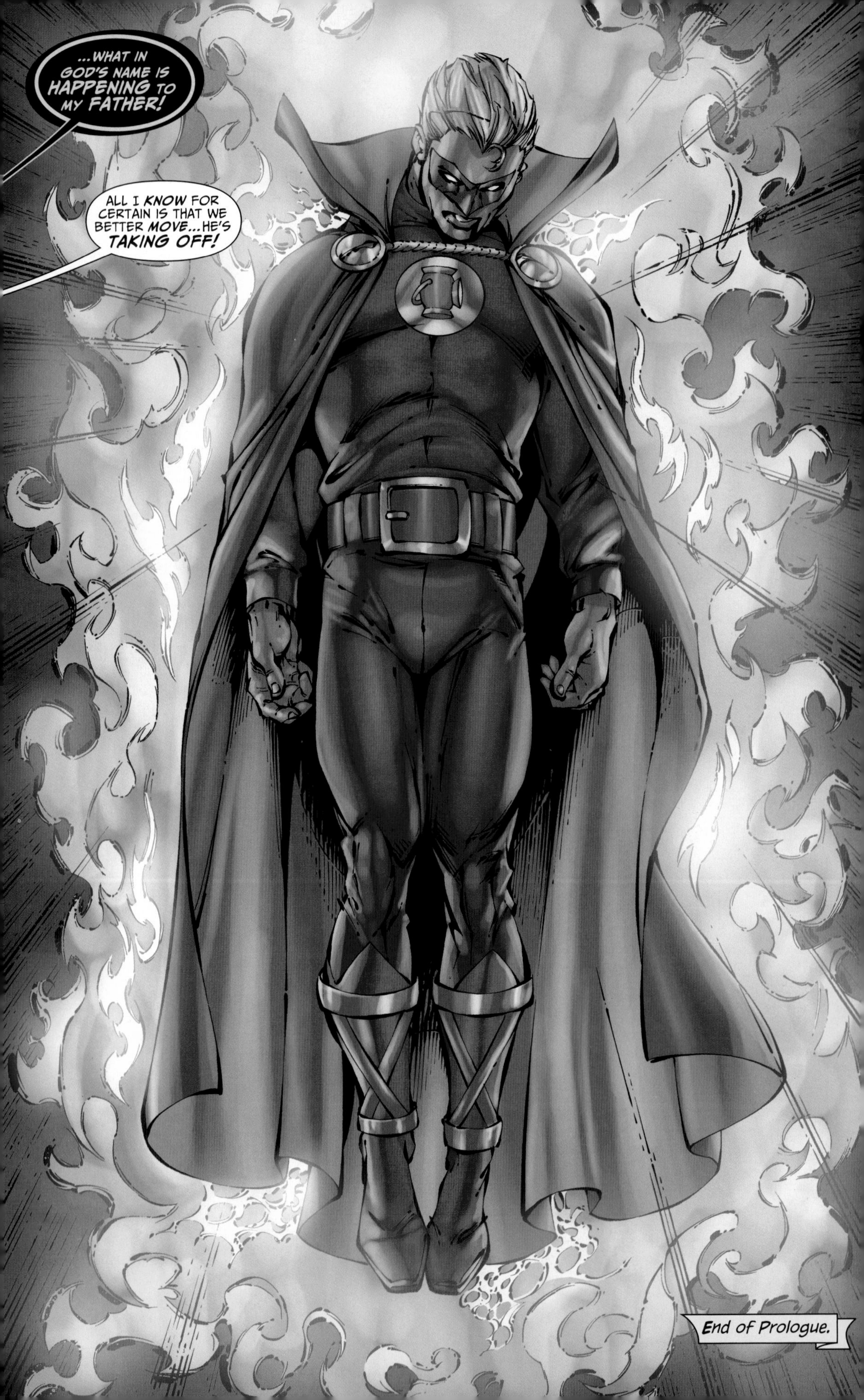
...WHAT IN GOD'S NAME IS HAPPENING TO MY FATHER!
ALL I KNOW FOR CERTAIN IS THAT WE BETTER MOVE...HE'S TAKING OFF!
End of Prologue.

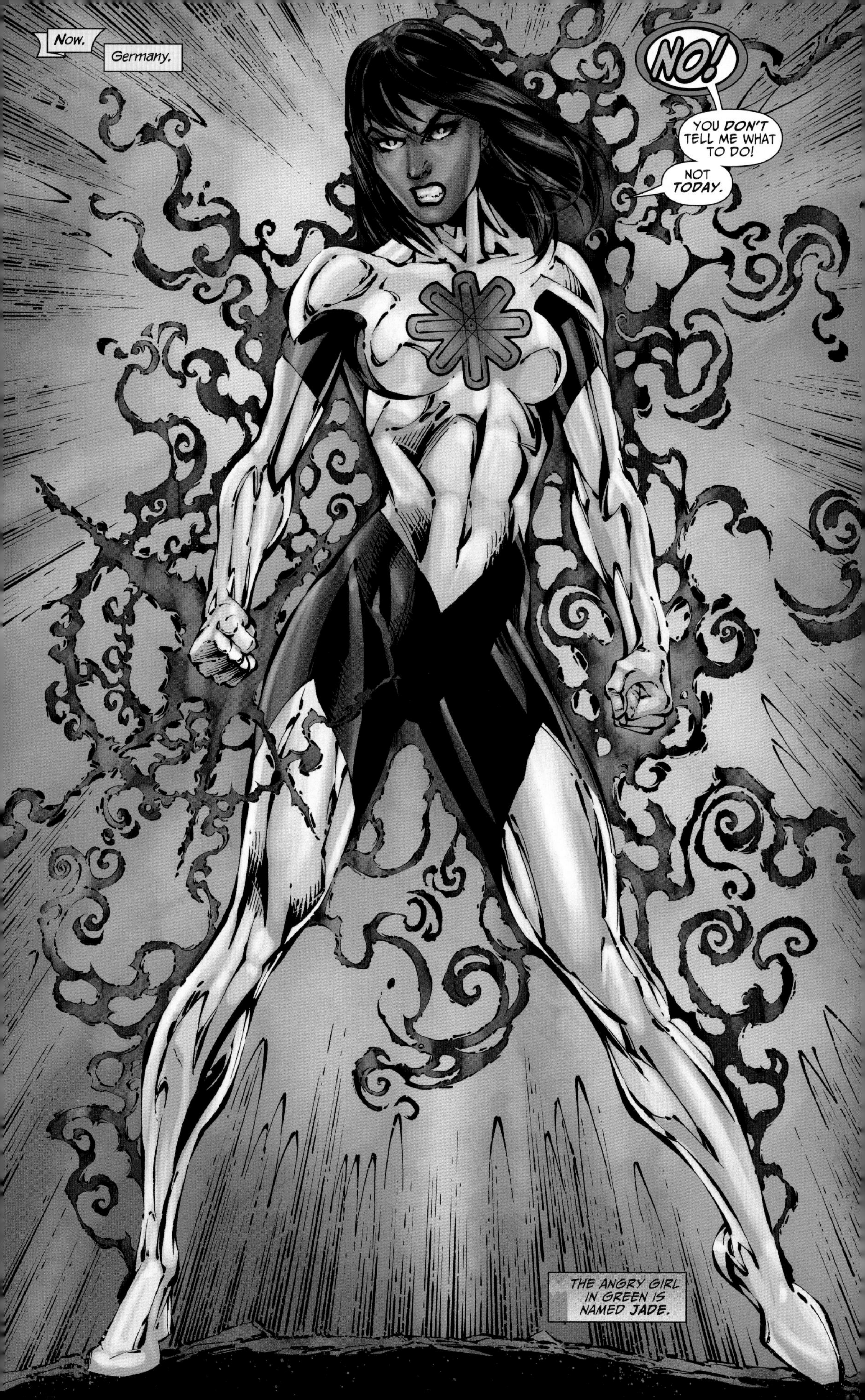
Now.
Germany.
NO!
YOU DON'T TELL ME WHAT TO DO!
NOT TODAY.
THE ANGRY GIRL IN GREEN IS NAMED JADE.

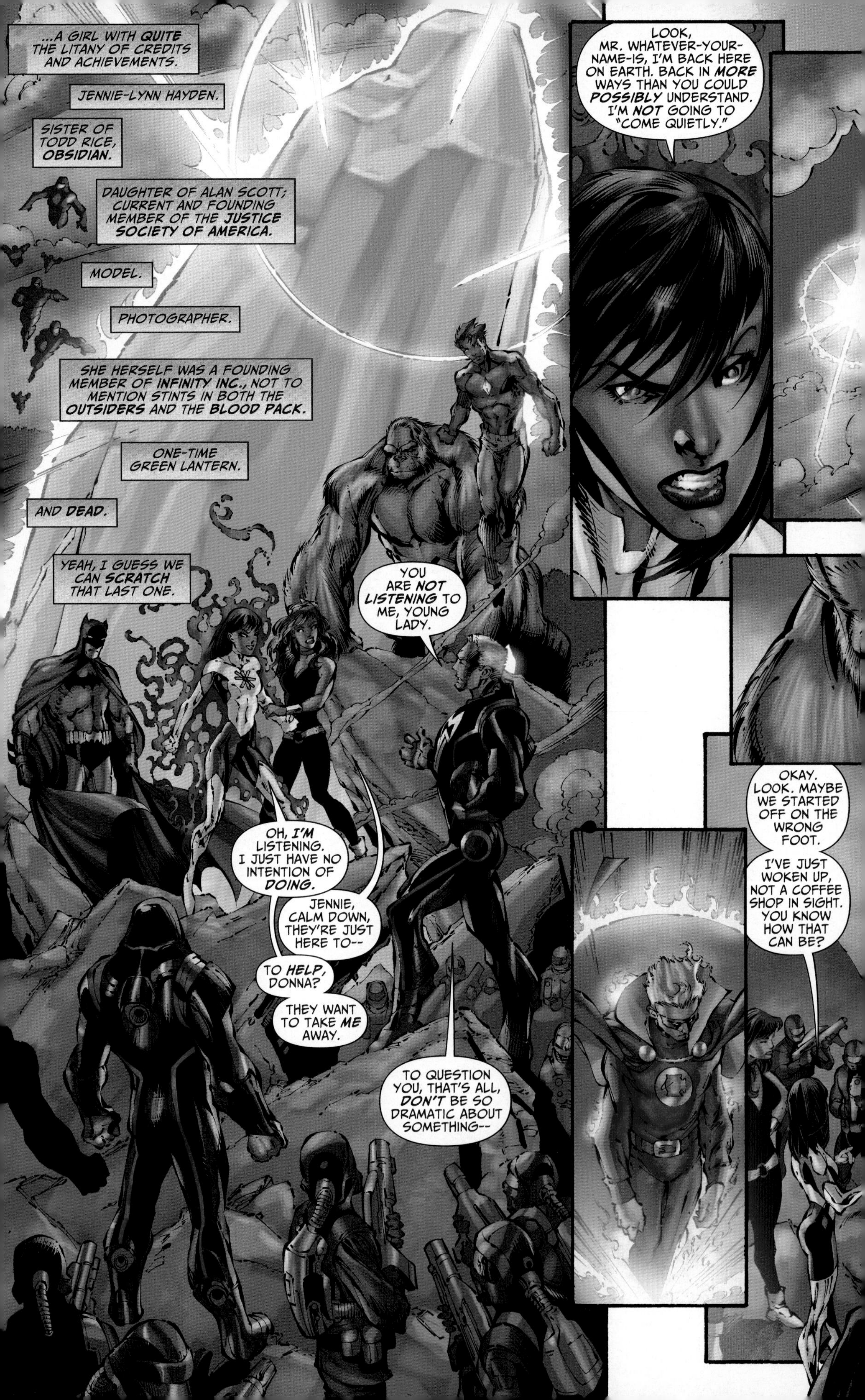

...A GIRL WITH QUITE THE LITANY OF CREDITS AND ACHIEVEMENTS.
JENNIE-LYNN HAYDEN.
SISTER OF TODD RICE, OBSIDIAN.
DAUGHTER OF ALAN SCOTT; CURRENT AND FOUNDING MEMBER OF THE JUSTICE SOCIETY OF AMERICA.
MODEL.
PHOTOGRAPHER.
SHE HERSELF WAS A FOUNDING MEMBER OF INFINITY INC., NOT TO MENTION STINTS IN BOTH THE OUTSIDERS AND THE BLOOD PACK.
ONE-TIME GREEN LANTERN.
AND DEAD.
YEAH, I GUESS WE CAN SCRATCH THAT LAST ONE.
YOU ARE NOT LISTENING TO ME, YOUNG LADY.
OH, I'M LISTENING. I JUST HAVE NO INTENTION OF DOING.
JENNIE, CALM DOWN, THEY'RE JUST HERE TO--
TO HELP, DONNA?
THEY WANT TO TAKE ME AWAY.
TO QUESTION YOU, THAT'S ALL, DON'T BE SO DRAMATIC ABOUT SOMETHING--
LOOK, MR. WHATEVER-YOUR-NAME-IS, I'M BACK HERE ON EARTH. BACK IN MORE WAYS THAN YOU COULD POSSIBLY UNDERSTAND. I'M NOT GOING TO "COME QUIETLY."
OKAY. LOOK. MAYBE WE STARTED OFF ON THE WRONG FOOT.
I'VE JUST WOKEN UP, NOT A COFFEE SHOP IN SIGHT. YOU KNOW HOW THAT CAN BE?

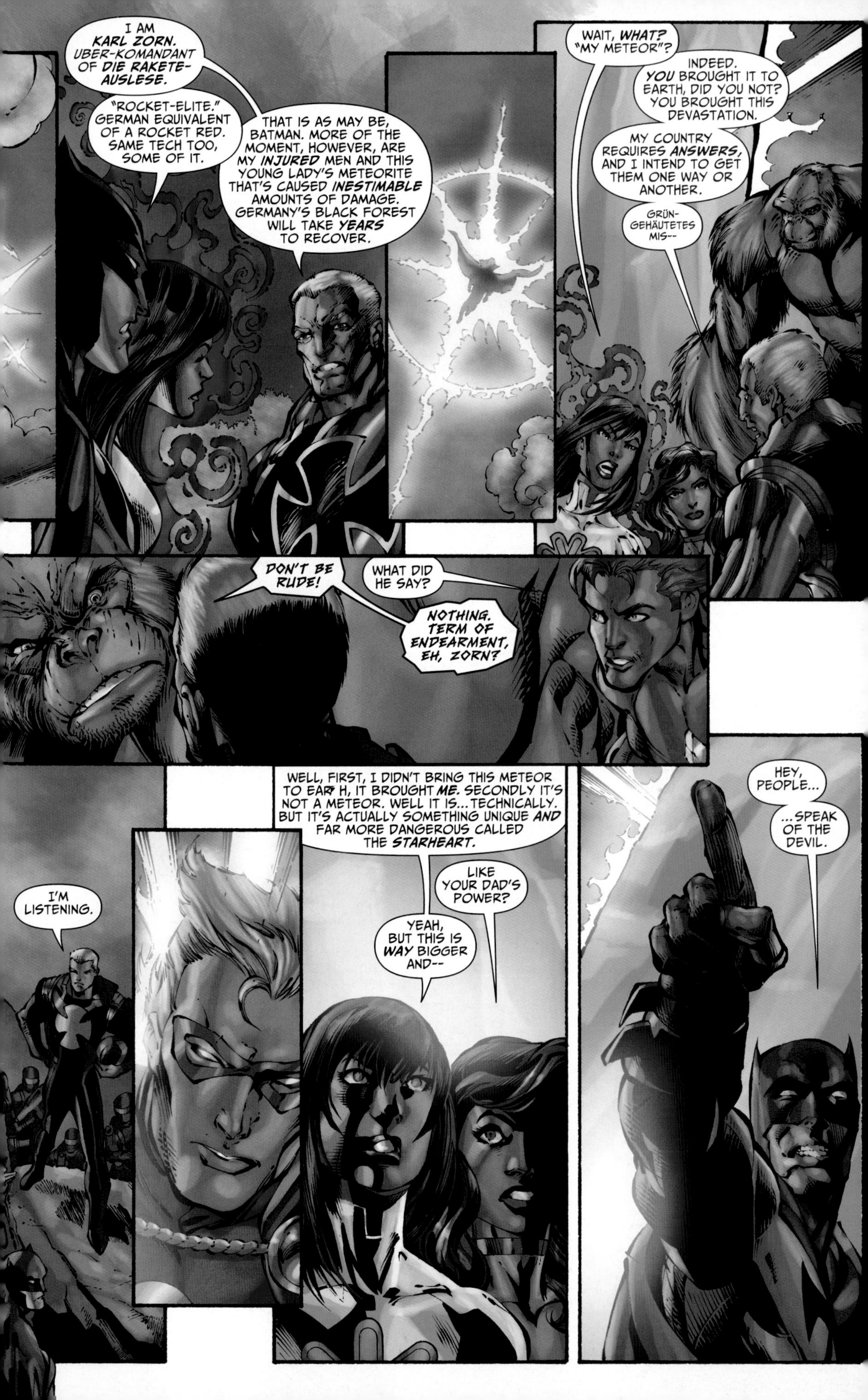
I AM KARL ZORN. UBER-KOMANDANT OF DIE RAKETE-AUSLESE.
"ROCKET-ELITE." GERMAN EQUIVALENT OF A ROCKET RED. SAME TECH TOO, SOME OF IT.
THAT IS AS MAY BE, BATMAN. MORE OF THE MOMENT, HOWEVER, ARE MY INJURED MEN AND THIS YOUNG LADY'S METEORITE THAT'S CAUSED INESTIMABLE AMOUNTS OF DAMAGE. GERMANY'S BLACK FOREST WILL TAKE YEARS TO RECOVER.
WAIT, WHAT? "MY METEOR"?
INDEED. YOU BROUGHT IT TO EARTH, DID YOU NOT? YOU BROUGHT THIS DEVASTATION.
MY COUNTRY REQUIRES ANSWERS, AND I INTEND TO GET THEM ONE WAY OR ANOTHER.
GRÜN-GEHÄUTETES MIS--
DON'T BE RUDE!
WHAT DID HE SAY?
NOTHING. TERM OF ENDEARMENT, EH, ZORN?
I'M LISTENING.
WELL, FIRST, I DIDN'T BRING THIS METEOR TO EARTH, IT BROUGHT ME. SECONDLY IT'S NOT A METEOR. WELL IT IS... TECHNICALLY. BUT IT'S ACTUALLY SOMETHING UNIQUE AND FAR MORE DANGEROUS CALLED THE STARHEART.
LIKE YOUR DAD'S POWER?
YEAH, BUT THIS IS WAY BIGGER AND--
HEY, PEOPLE...
...SPEAK OF THE DEVIL.

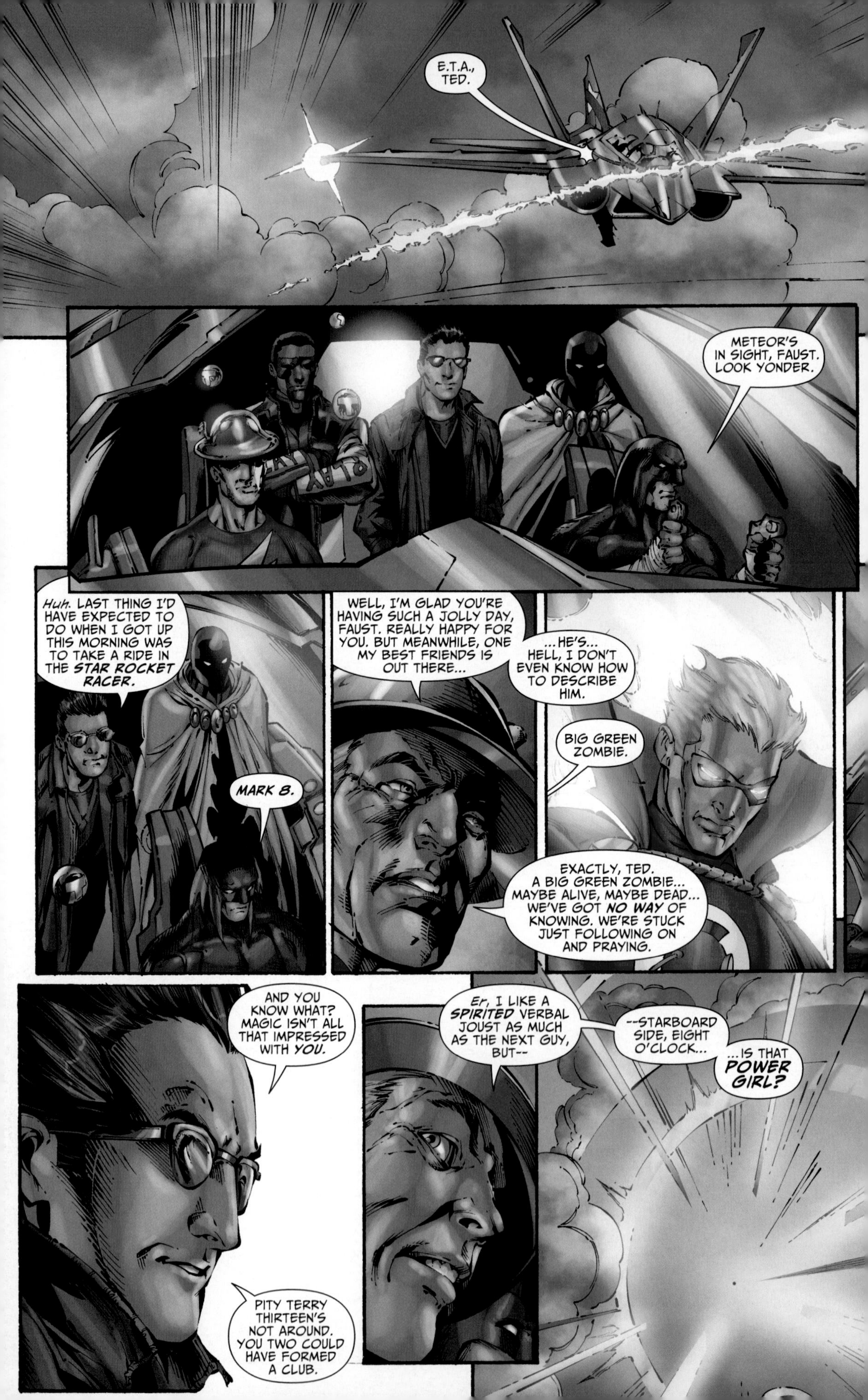
E.T.A., TED.
METEOR'S IN SIGHT, FAUST. LOOK YONDER.
Huh. LAST THING I'D HAVE EXPECTED TO DO WHEN I GOT UP THIS MORNING WAS TO TAKE A RIDE IN THE ***STAR ROCKET RACER.***
MARK 8.
WELL, I'M GLAD YOU'RE HAVING SUCH A JOLLY DAY, FAUST. REALLY HAPPY FOR YOU. BUT MEANWHILE, ONE MY BEST FRIENDS IS OUT THERE...
...HE'S... HELL, I DON'T EVEN KNOW HOW TO DESCRIBE HIM.
BIG GREEN ZOMBIE.
EXACTLY, TED. A BIG GREEN ZOMBIE... MAYBE ALIVE, MAYBE DEAD... WE'VE GOT ***NO WAY*** OF KNOWING. WE'RE STUCK JUST FOLLOWING ON AND PRAYING.
AND YOU KNOW WHAT? MAGIC ISN'T ALL THAT IMPRESSED WITH ***YOU.***
PITY TERRY THIRTEEN'S NOT AROUND. YOU TWO COULD HAVE FORMED A CLUB.
Er, I LIKE A ***SPIRITED*** VERBAL JOUST AS MUCH AS THE NEXT GUY, BUT--
--STARBOARD SIDE, EIGHT O'CLOCK...
...IS THAT ***POWER GIRL?***

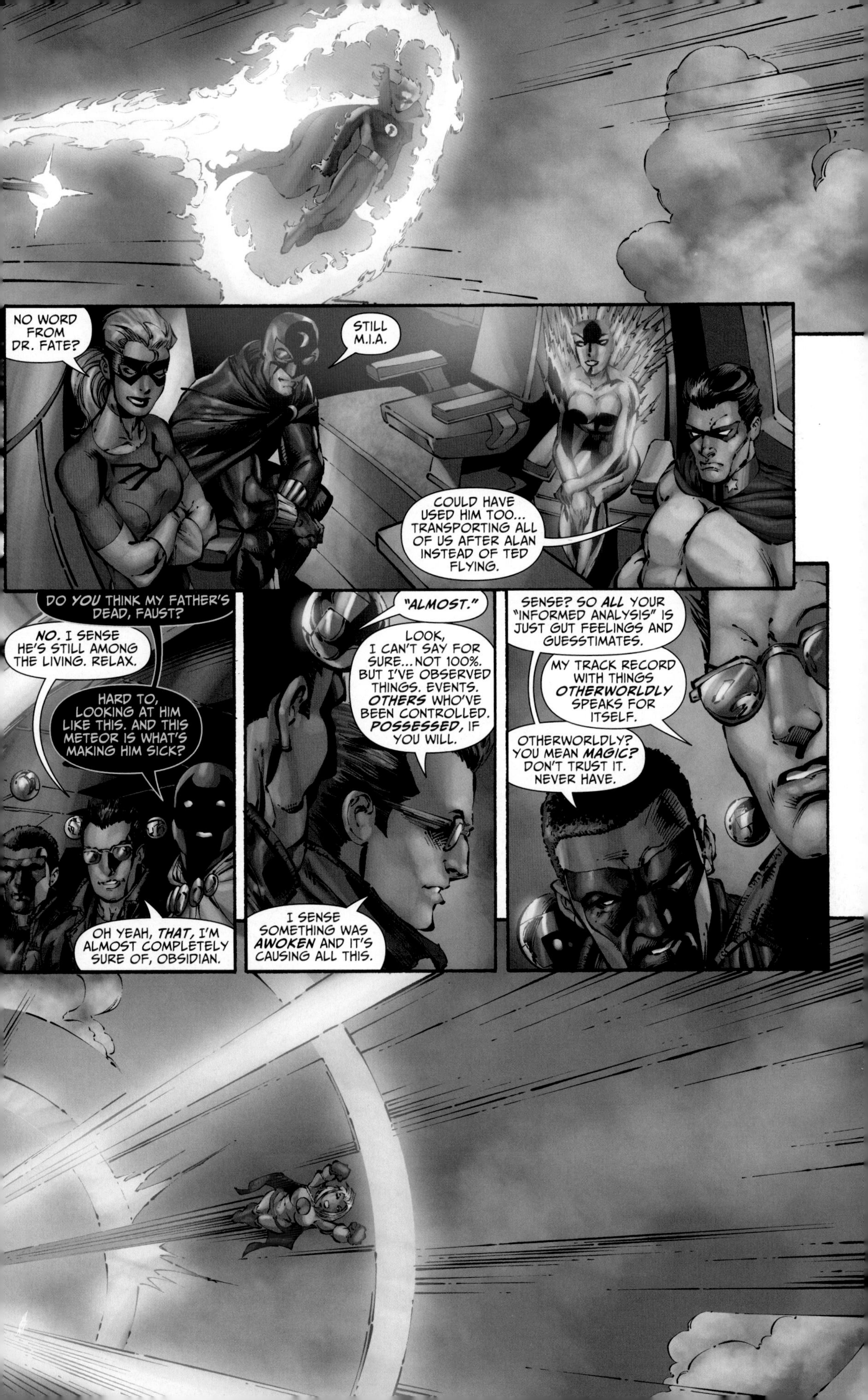
NO WORD FROM DR. FATE?
STILL M.I.A.
COULD HAVE USED HIM TOO... TRANSPORTING ALL OF US AFTER ALAN INSTEAD OF TED FLYING.
DO YOU THINK MY FATHER'S DEAD, FAUST?
NO. I SENSE HE'S STILL AMONG THE LIVING. RELAX.
HARD TO, LOOKING AT HIM LIKE THIS. AND THIS METEOR IS WHAT'S MAKING HIM SICK?
OH YEAH, THAT, I'M ALMOST COMPLETELY SURE OF, OBSIDIAN.
"ALMOST."
LOOK, I CAN'T SAY FOR SURE... NOT 100%. BUT I'VE OBSERVED THINGS. EVENTS. OTHERS WHO'VE BEEN CONTROLLED. POSSESSED, IF YOU WILL.
I SENSE SOMETHING WAS AWOKEN AND IT'S CAUSING ALL THIS.
SENSE? SO ALL YOUR "INFORMED ANALYSIS" IS JUST GUT FEELINGS AND GUESSTIMATES.
MY TRACK RECORD WITH THINGS OTHERWORLDLY SPEAKS FOR ITSELF.
OTHERWORLDLY? YOU MEAN MAGIC? DON'T TRUST IT. NEVER HAVE.

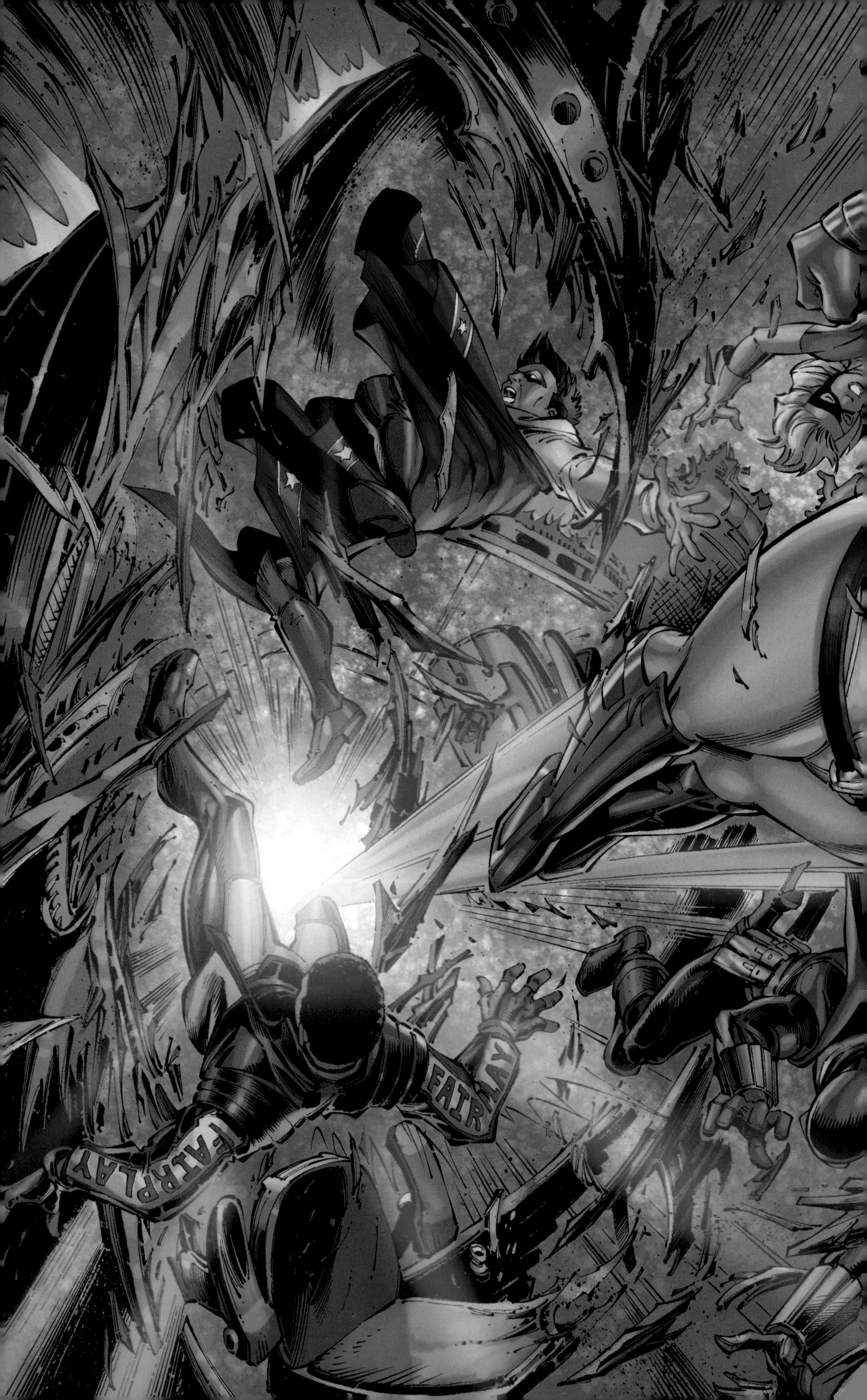
FAIRPLAY

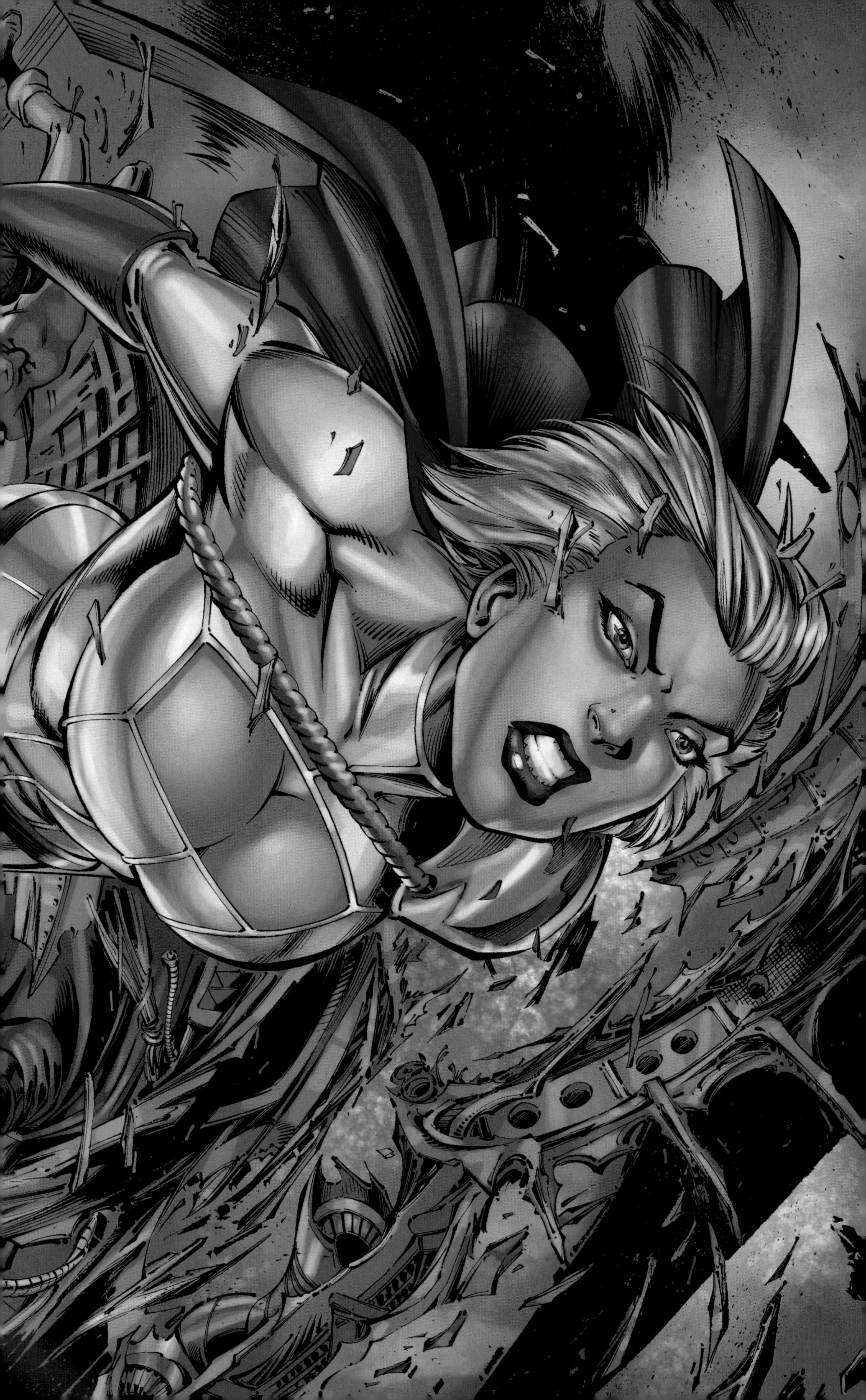

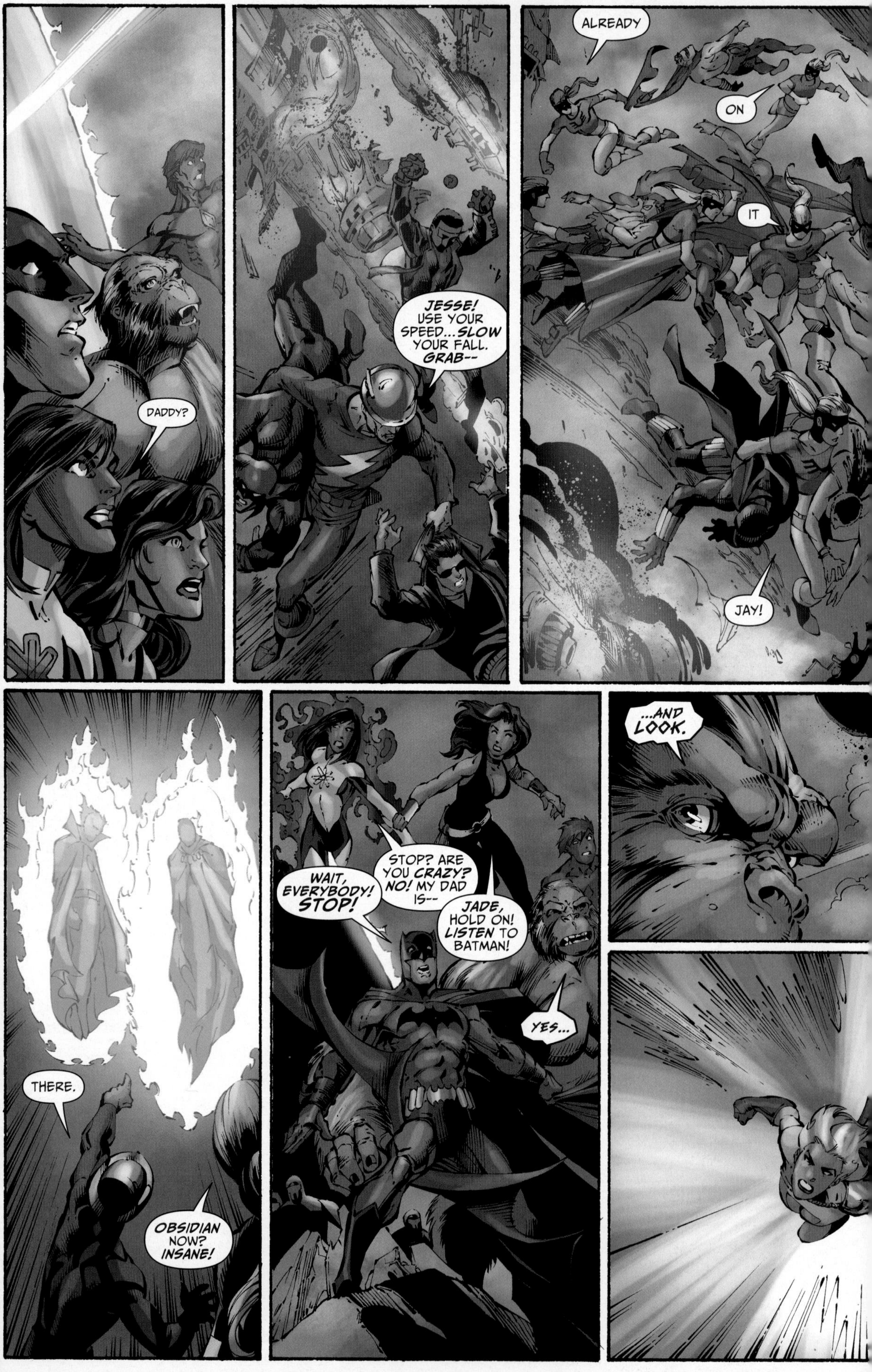
DADDY?
JESSE! USE YOUR SPEED...SLOW YOUR FALL. GRAB--
ALREADY
ON
IT
JAY!
THERE.
OBSIDIAN NOW? INSANE!
WAIT, EVERYBODY! STOP!
STOP? ARE YOU CRAZY? NO! MY DAD IS--
JADE, HOLD ON! LISTEN TO BATMAN!
YES...
...AND LOOK.

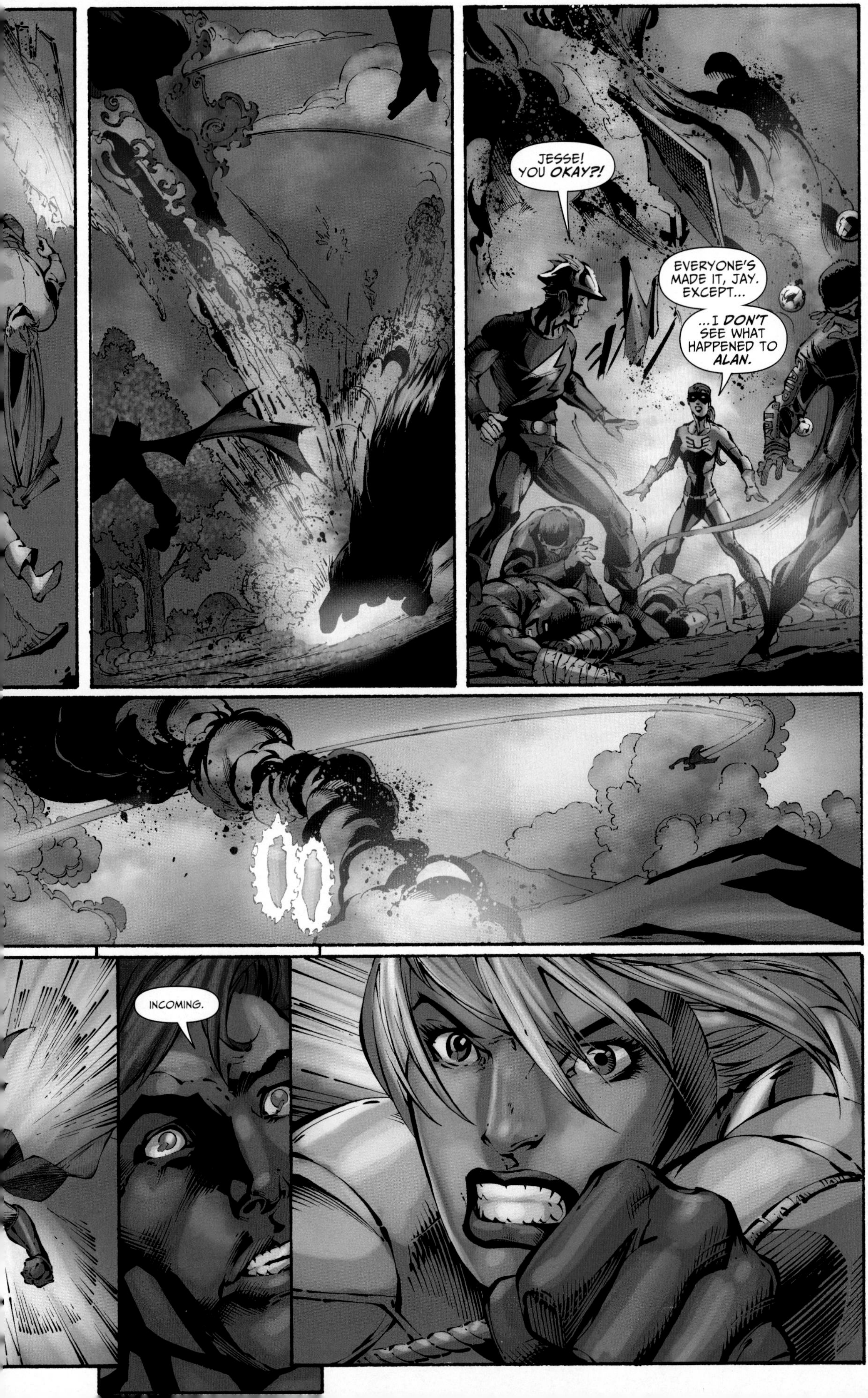
JESSE! YOU OKAY?!
EVERYONE'S MADE IT, JAY. EXCEPT...
...I DON'T SEE WHAT HAPPENED TO ALAN.
INCOMING.

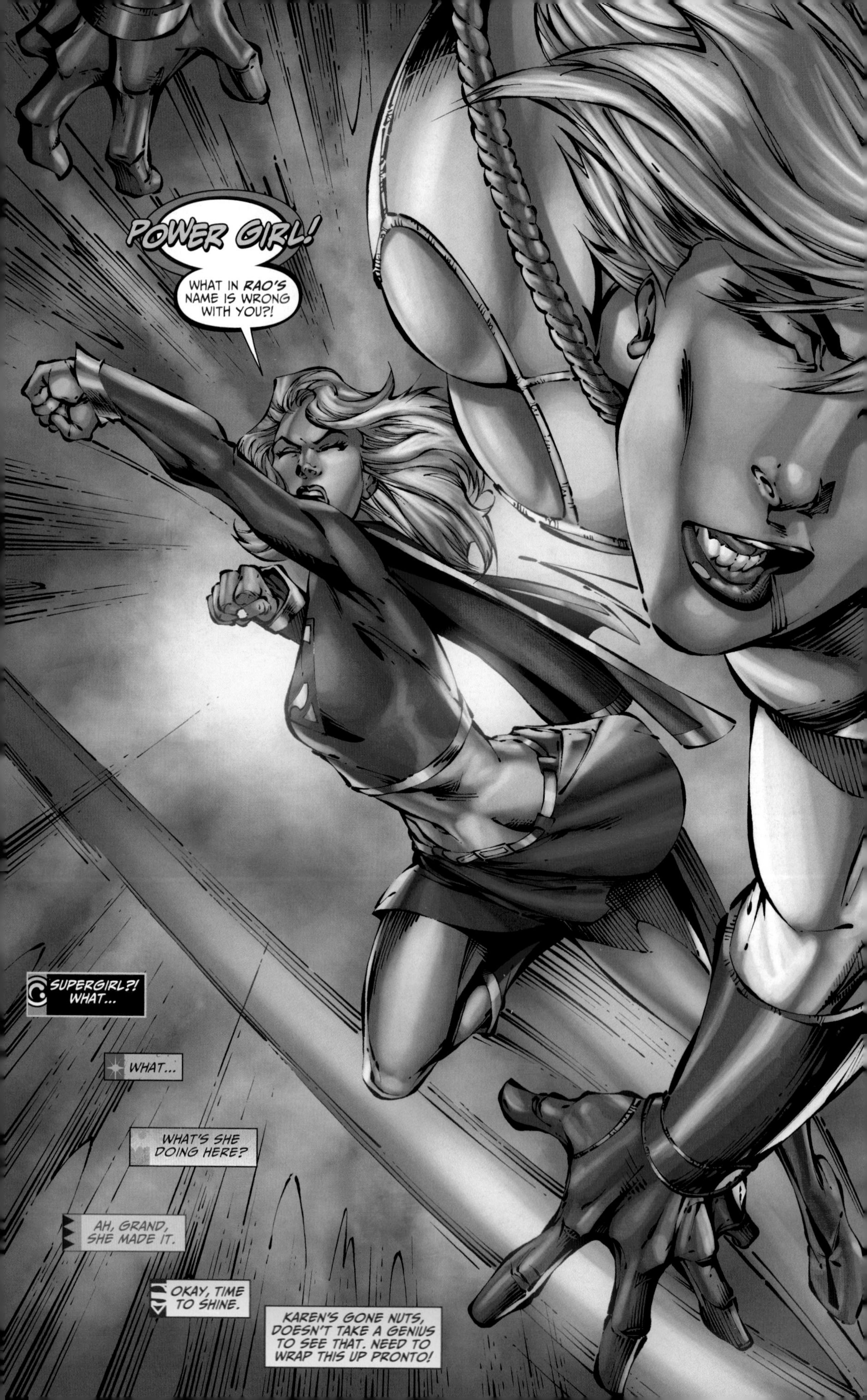
POWER GIRL!
WHAT IN RAO'S NAME IS WRONG WITH YOU?!
SUPERGIRL?! WHAT...
WHAT...
WHAT'S SHE DOING HERE?
AH, GRAND, SHE MADE IT.
OKAY, TIME TO SHINE.
KAREN'S GONE NUTS, DOESN'T TAKE A GENIUS TO SEE THAT. NEED TO WRAP THIS UP PRONTO!

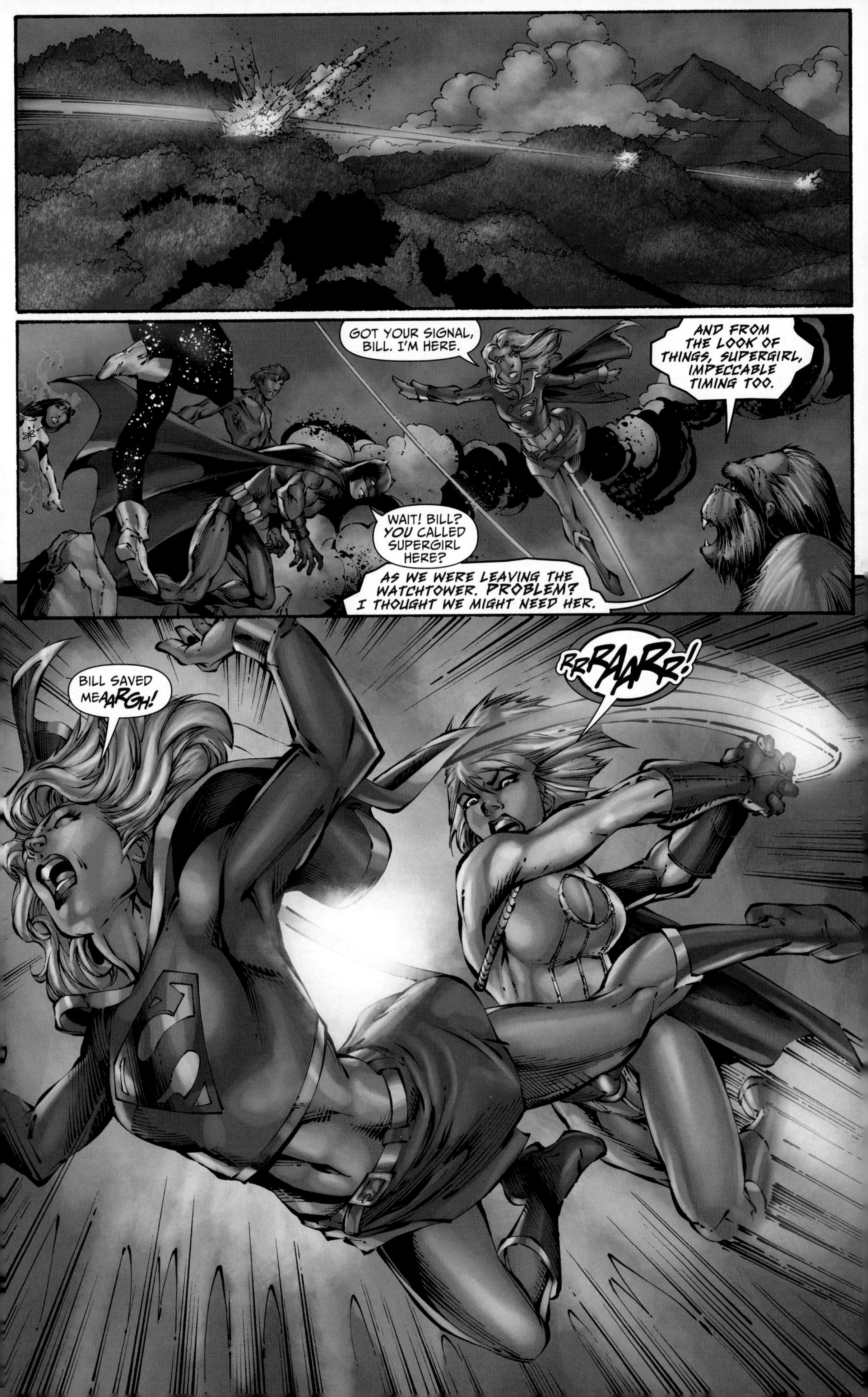
GOT YOUR SIGNAL, BILL. I'M HERE.
AND FROM THE LOOK OF THINGS, SUPERGIRL, IMPECCABLE TIMING TOO.
WAIT! BILL? YOU CALLED SUPERGIRL HERE?
AS WE WERE LEAVING THE WATCHTOWER. PROBLEM? I THOUGHT WE MIGHT NEED HER.
BILL SAVED MEAARGH!
RRRAARR!

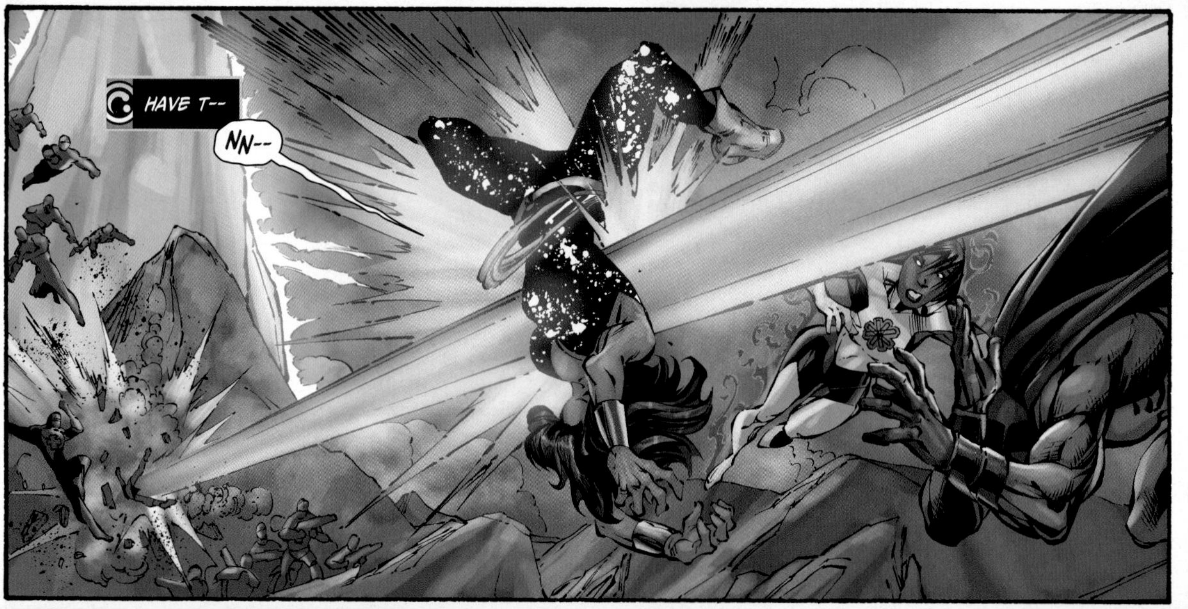
HAVE T--
NN--

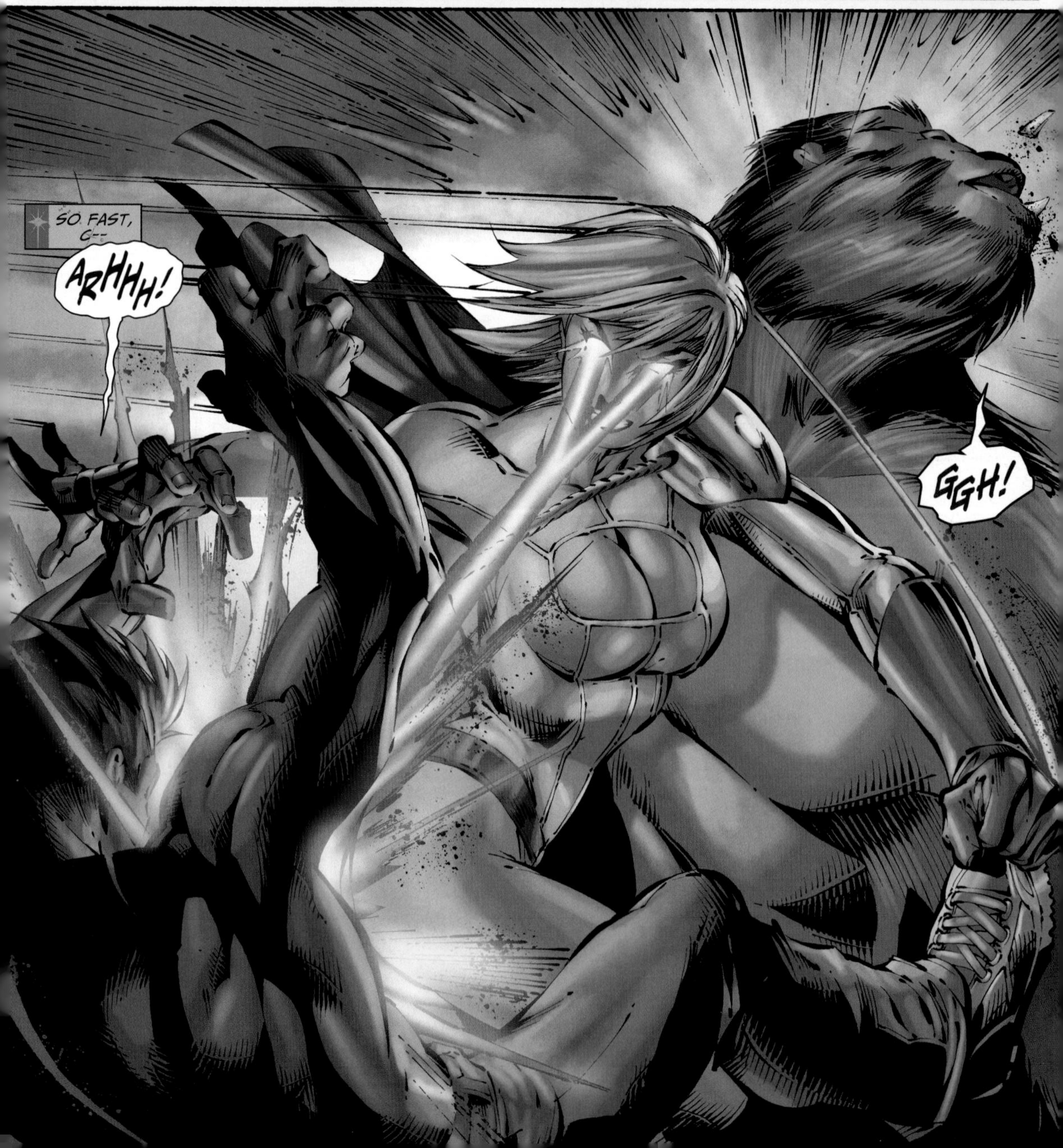
SO. FAST, C--
ARHHH!
GGH!

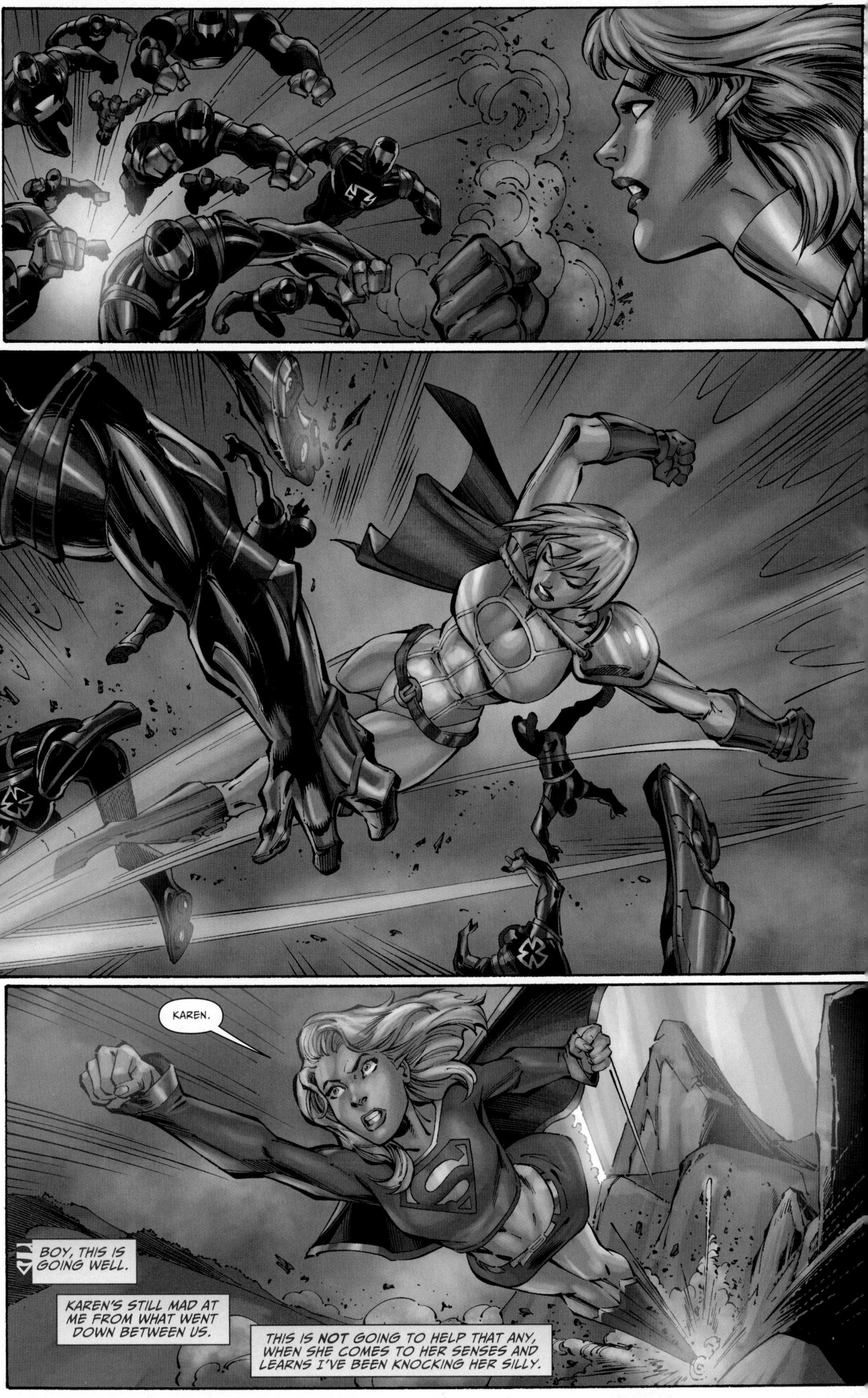

KAREN.
BOY, THIS IS GOING WELL.
KAREN'S STILL MAD AT ME FROM WHAT WENT DOWN BETWEEN US.
THIS IS **NOT** GOING TO HELP THAT ANY, WHEN SHE COMES TO HER SENSES AND LEARNS I'VE BEEN KNOCKING HER SILLY.

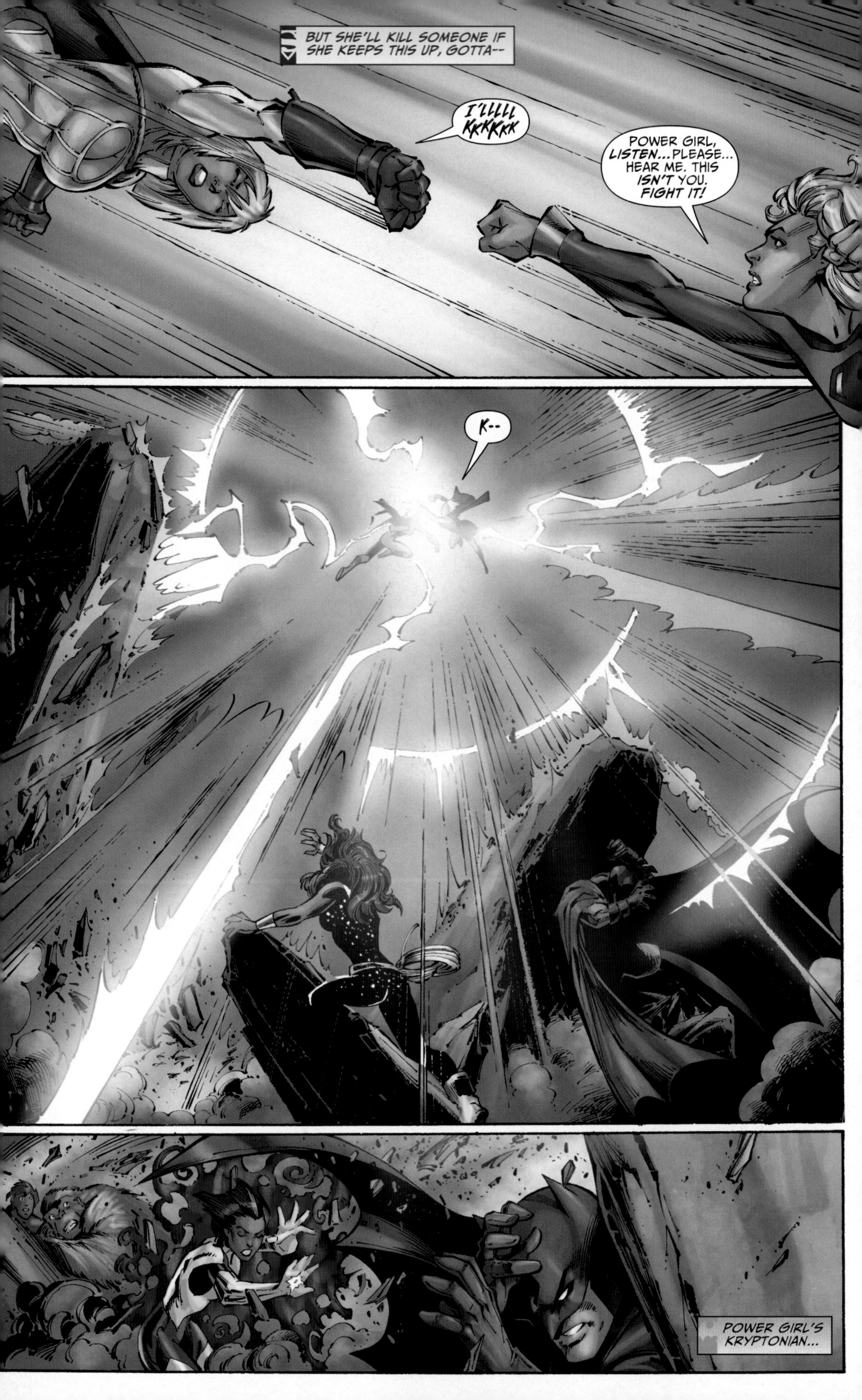

BUT SHE'LL KILL SOMEONE IF SHE KEEPS THIS UP, GOTTA--
I'LLLLL KKKKKK
POWER GIRL, LISTEN...PLEASE... HEAR ME. THIS ISN'T YOU. FIGHT IT!
K--
POWER GIRL'S KRYPTONIAN...

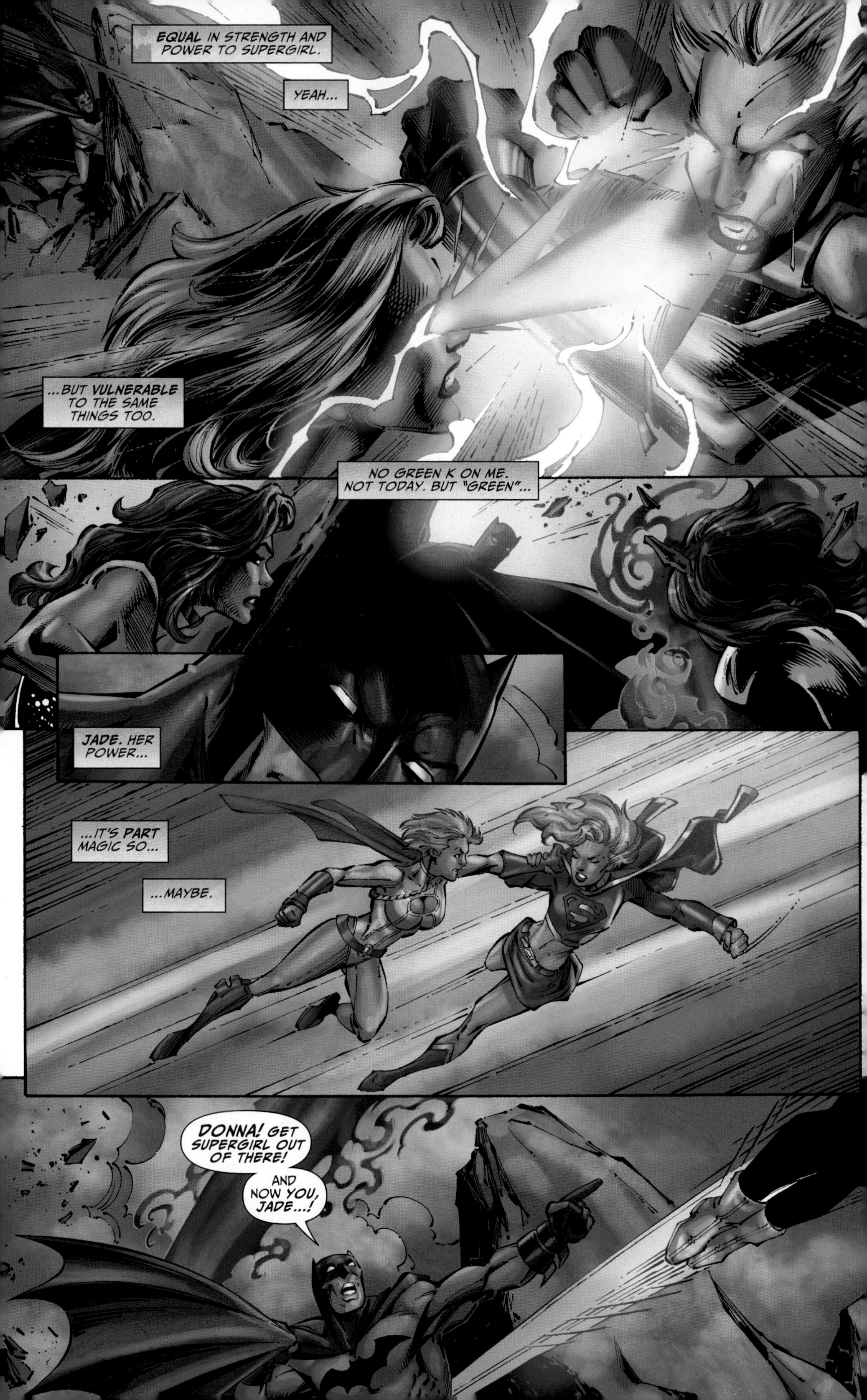
EQUAL IN STRENGTH AND POWER TO SUPERGIRL.
YEAH...
...BUT VULNERABLE TO THE SAME THINGS TOO.
NO GREEN K ON ME. NOT TODAY. BUT "GREEN"...
JADE. HER POWER...
...IT'S PART MAGIC SO...
...MAYBE.
DONNA! GET SUPERGIRL OUT OF THERE!
AND NOW YOU, JADE...!

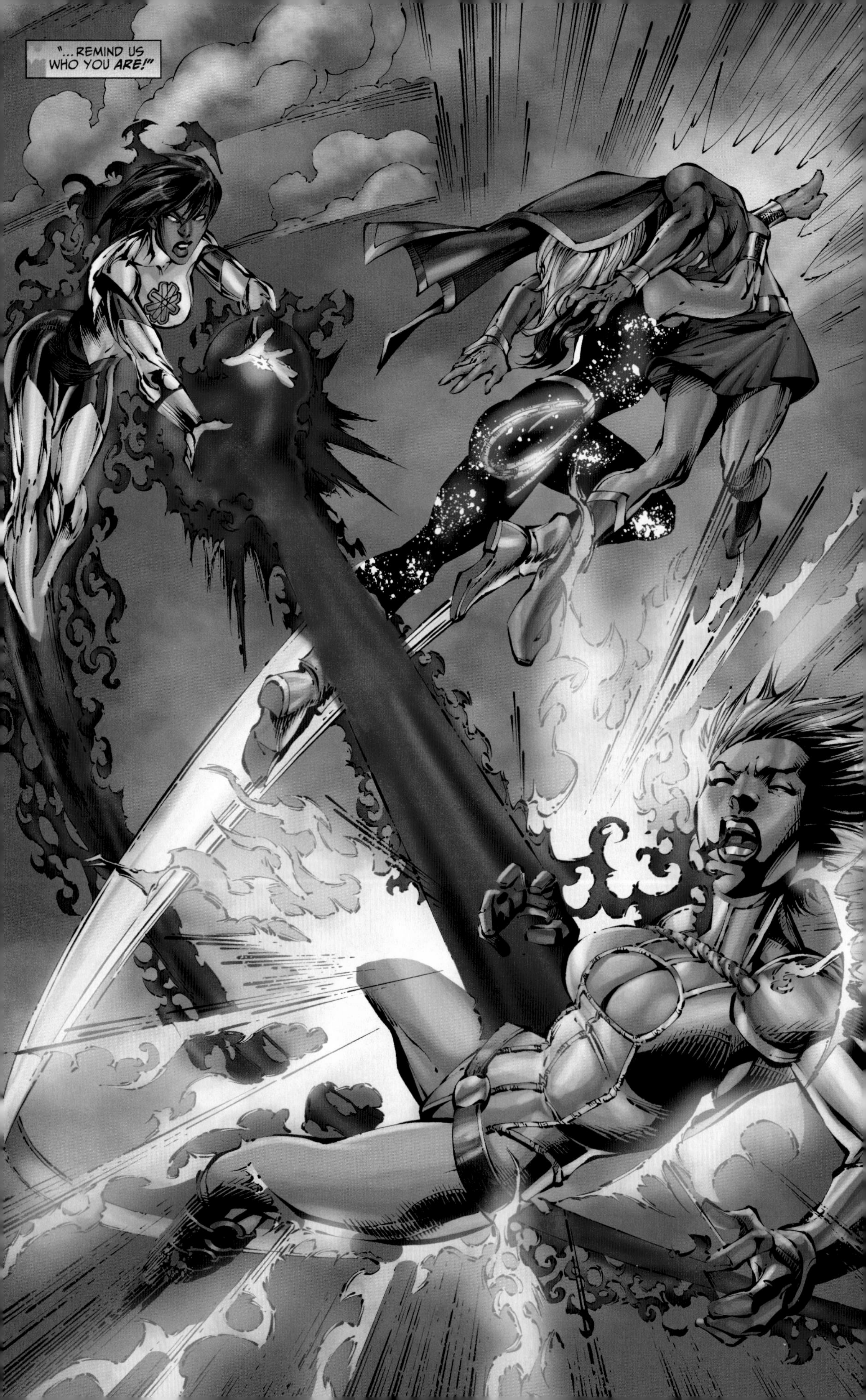
"...REMIND US WHO YOU ARE!"

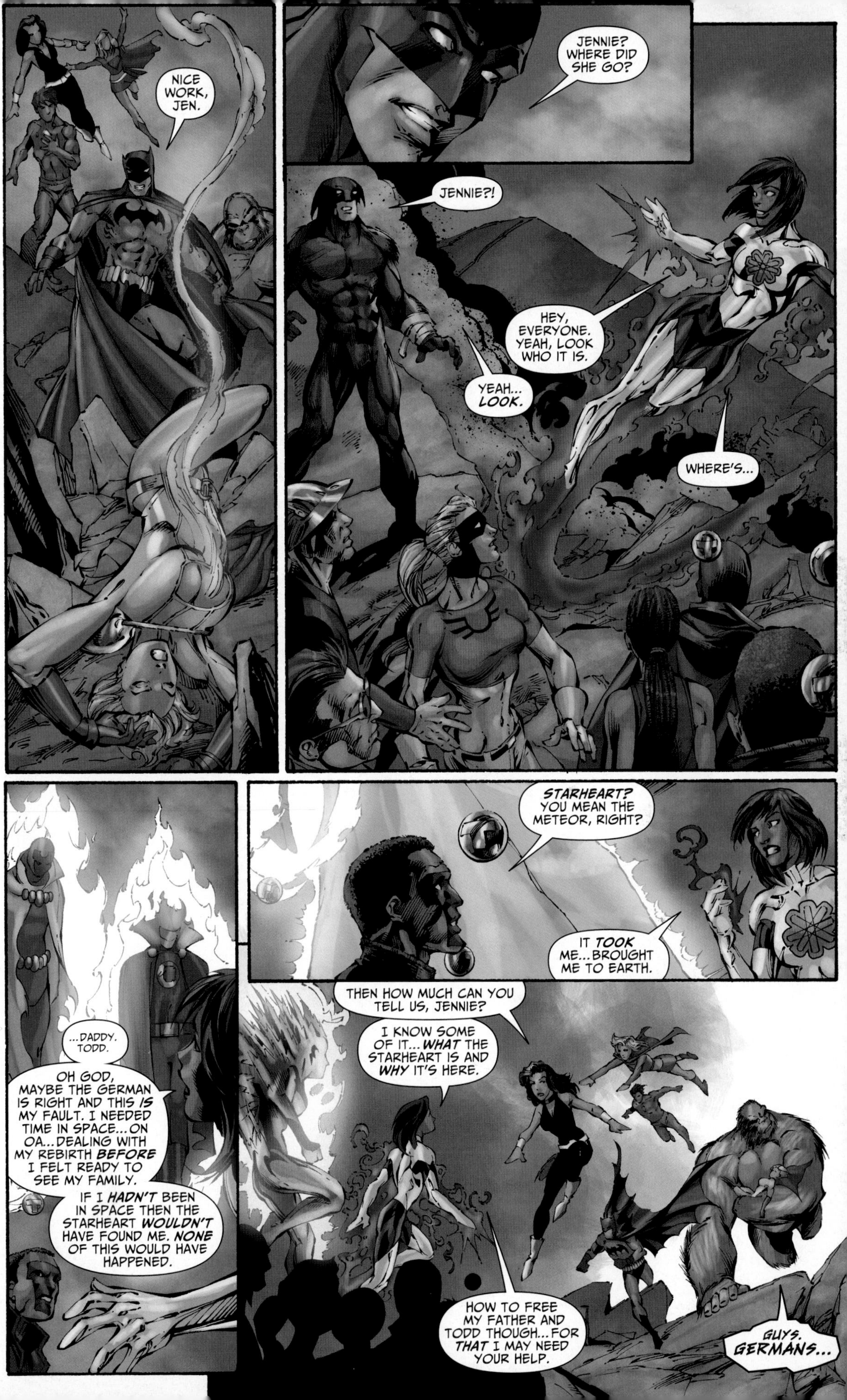

NICE WORK, JEN.
JENNIE? WHERE DID SHE GO?
JENNIE?!
HEY, EVERYONE. YEAH, LOOK WHO IT IS.
YEAH... *LOOK.*
WHERE'S...
...DADDY. TODD.
OH GOD, MAYBE THE GERMAN IS RIGHT AND THIS *IS* MY FAULT. I NEEDED TIME IN SPACE...ON OA...DEALING WITH MY REBIRTH *BEFORE* I FELT READY TO SEE MY FAMILY.
IF I *HADN'T* BEEN IN SPACE THEN THE STARHEART *WOULDN'T* HAVE FOUND ME. *NONE* OF THIS WOULD HAVE HAPPENED.
STARHEART? YOU MEAN THE METEOR, RIGHT?
IT *TOOK* ME...BROUGHT ME TO EARTH.
THEN HOW MUCH CAN YOU TELL US, JENNIE?
I KNOW SOME OF IT... *WHAT* THE STARHEART IS AND *WHY* IT'S HERE.
HOW TO FREE MY FATHER AND TODD THOUGH...FOR *THAT* I MAY NEED YOUR HELP.
GUYS. **GERMANS...**

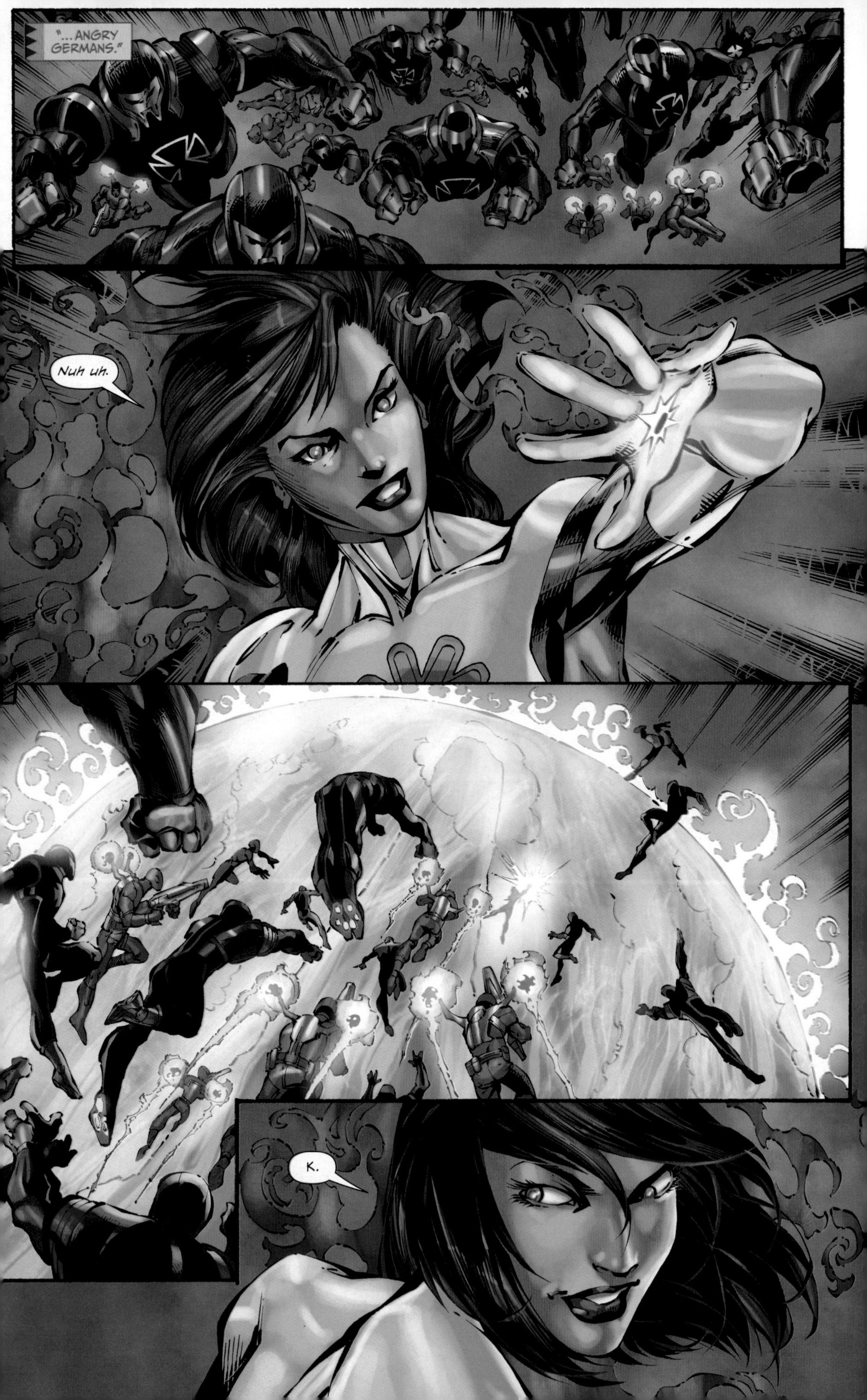
"...ANGRY GERMANS."
Nuh uh.
K.

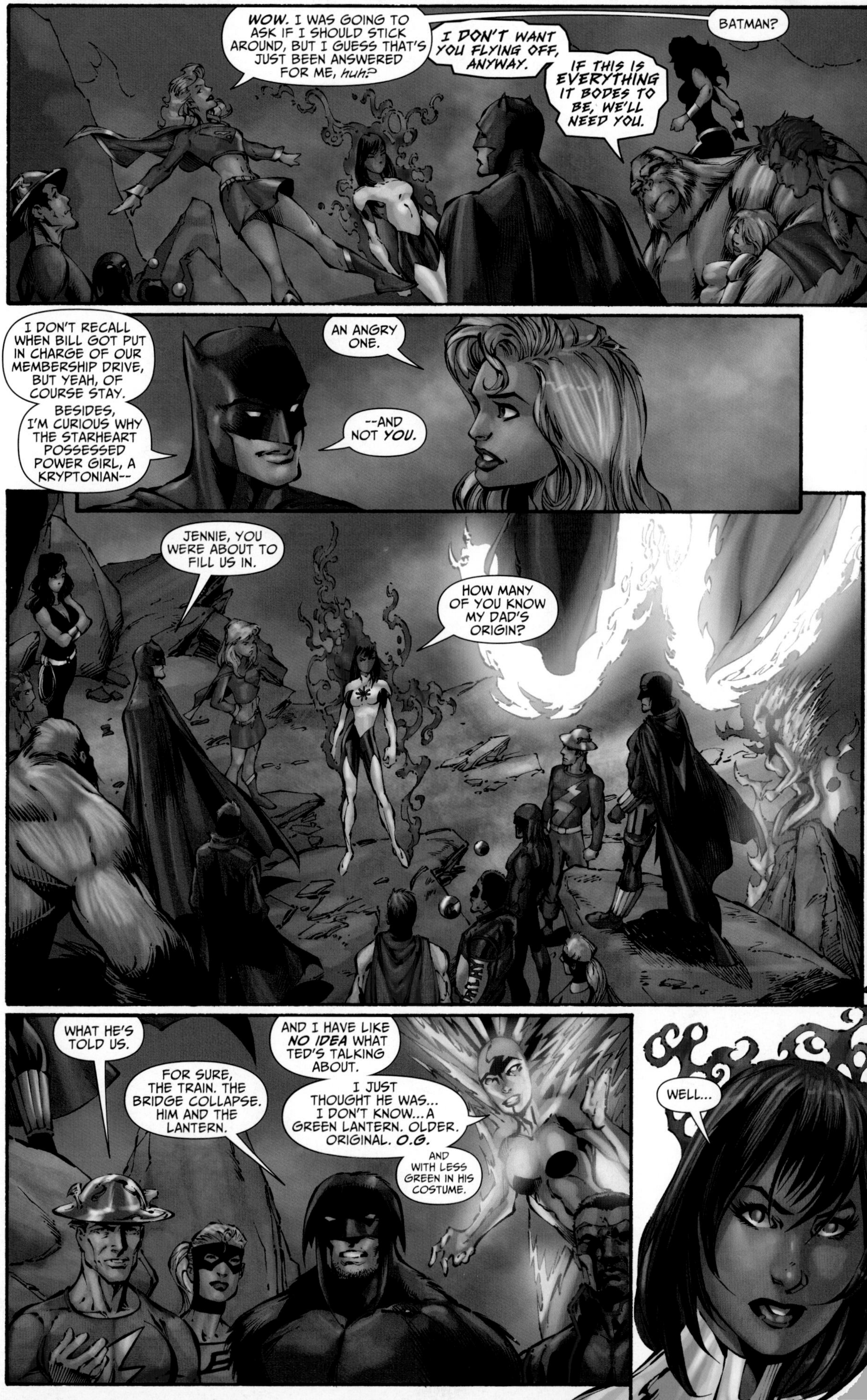
WOW. I WAS GOING TO ASK IF I SHOULD STICK AROUND, BUT I GUESS THAT'S JUST BEEN ANSWERED FOR ME, huh?
I DON'T WANT YOU FLYING OFF, ANYWAY.
BATMAN?
IF THIS IS EVERYTHING IT BODES TO BE, WE'LL NEED YOU.
I DON'T RECALL WHEN BILL GOT PUT IN CHARGE OF OUR MEMBERSHIP DRIVE, BUT YEAH, OF COURSE STAY.
BESIDES, I'M CURIOUS WHY THE STARHEART POSSESSED POWER GIRL, A KRYPTONIAN--
AN ANGRY ONE.
--AND NOT YOU.
JENNIE, YOU WERE ABOUT TO FILL US IN.
HOW MANY OF YOU KNOW MY DAD'S ORIGIN?
WHAT HE'S TOLD US.
FOR SURE, THE TRAIN. THE BRIDGE COLLAPSE. HIM AND THE LANTERN.
AND I HAVE LIKE NO IDEA WHAT TED'S TALKING ABOUT.
I JUST THOUGHT HE WAS... I DON'T KNOW... A GREEN LANTERN. OLDER. ORIGINAL. O.G.
AND WITH LESS GREEN IN HIS COSTUME.
WELL...

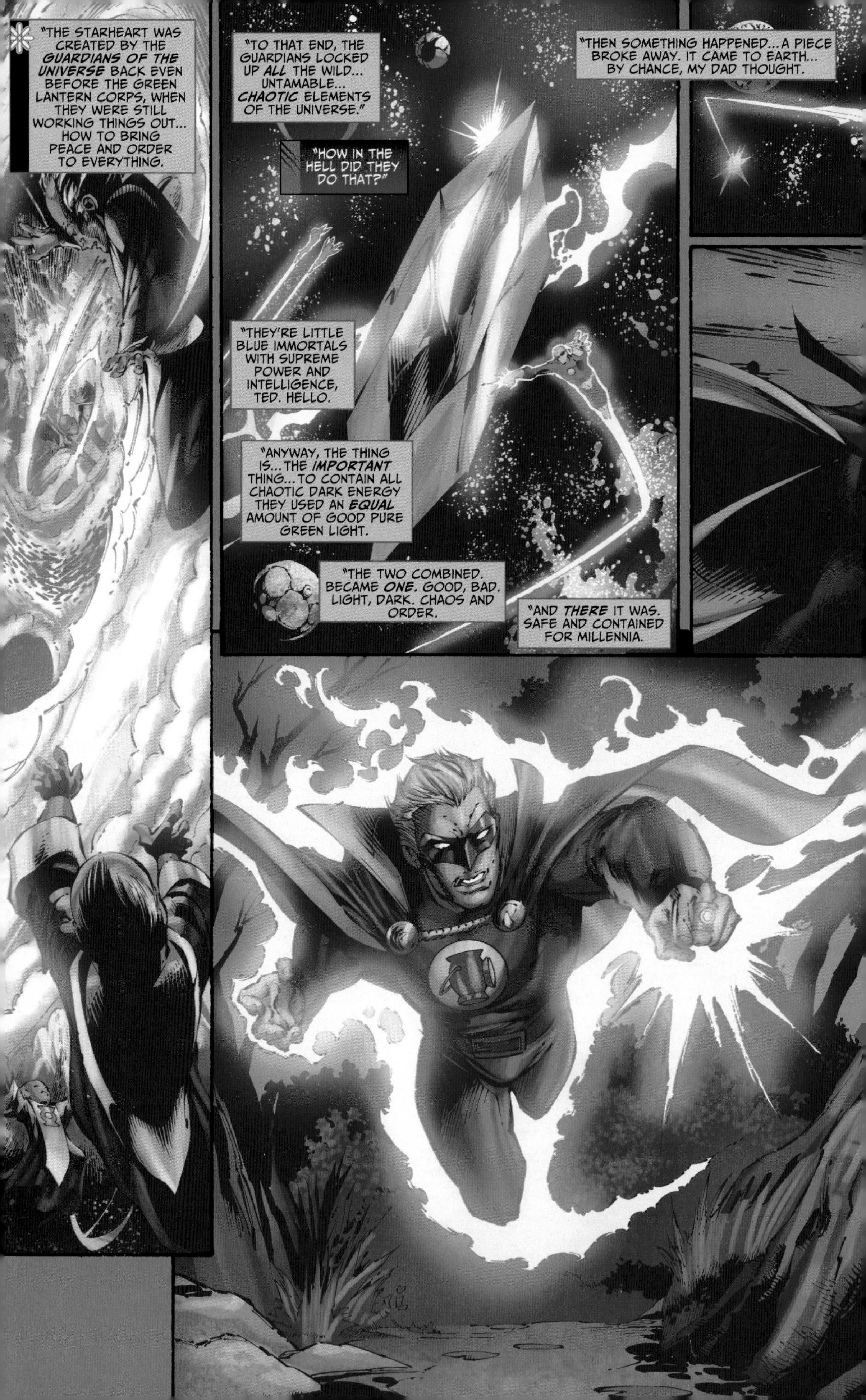
"THE STARHEART WAS CREATED BY THE GUARDIANS OF THE UNIVERSE BACK EVEN BEFORE THE GREEN LANTERN CORPS, WHEN THEY WERE STILL WORKING THINGS OUT... HOW TO BRING PEACE AND ORDER TO EVERYTHING.
"TO THAT END, THE GUARDIANS LOCKED UP ALL THE WILD... UNTAMABLE... CHAOTIC ELEMENTS OF THE UNIVERSE."
"HOW IN THE HELL DID THEY DO THAT?"
"THEY'RE LITTLE BLUE IMMORTALS WITH SUPREME POWER AND INTELLIGENCE, TED. HELLO.
"ANYWAY, THE THING IS...THE IMPORTANT THING...TO CONTAIN ALL CHAOTIC DARK ENERGY THEY USED AN EQUAL AMOUNT OF GOOD PURE GREEN LIGHT.
"THE TWO COMBINED. BECAME ONE. GOOD, BAD. LIGHT, DARK. CHAOS AND ORDER.
"AND THERE IT WAS. SAFE AND CONTAINED FOR MILLENNIA.
"THEN SOMETHING HAPPENED...A PIECE BROKE AWAY. IT CAME TO EARTH... BY CHANCE, MY DAD THOUGHT.

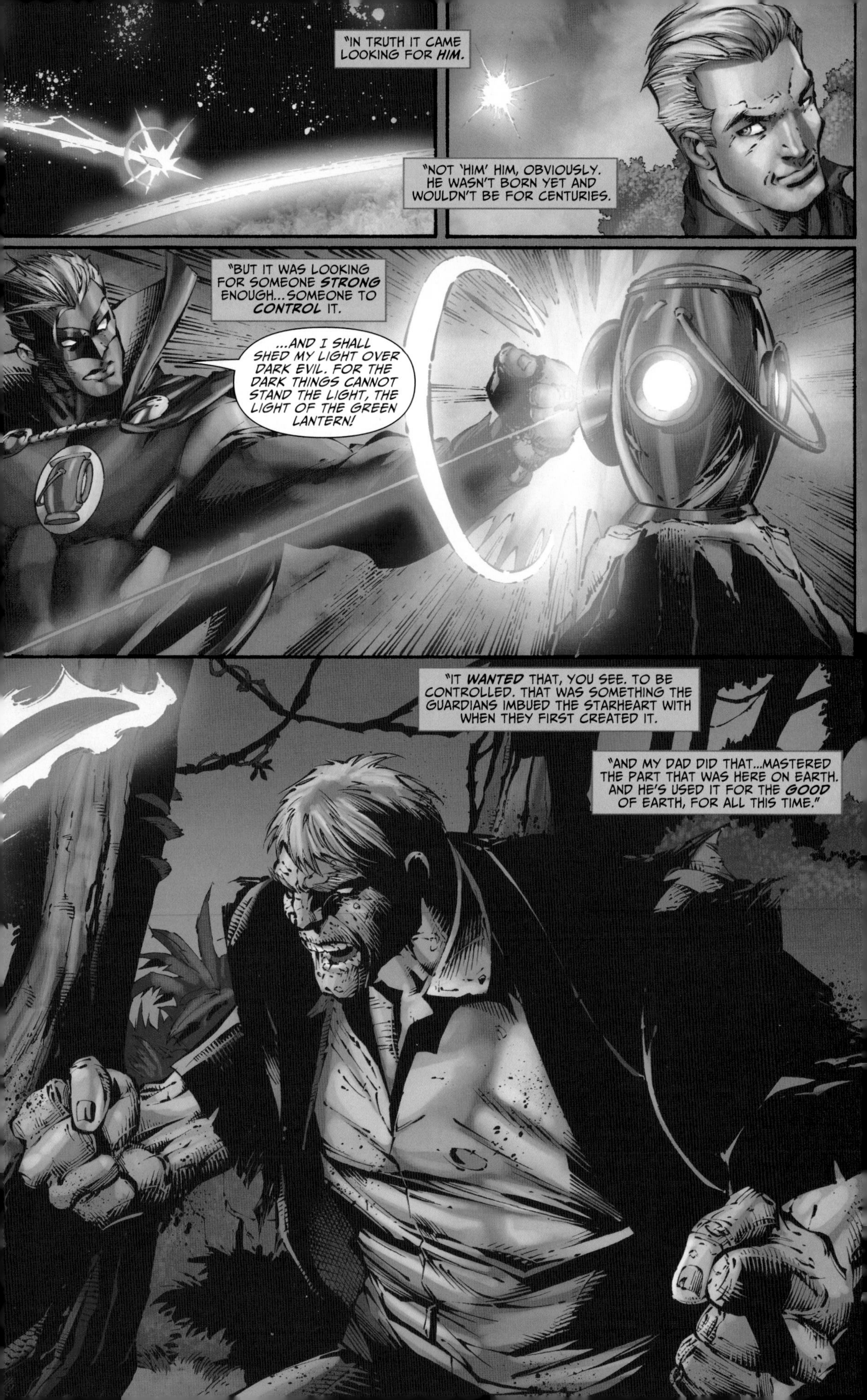
"IN TRUTH IT CAME LOOKING FOR HIM.
"NOT 'HIM' HIM, OBVIOUSLY. HE WASN'T BORN YET AND WOULDN'T BE FOR CENTURIES.
"BUT IT WAS LOOKING FOR SOMEONE STRONG ENOUGH...SOMEONE TO CONTROL IT.
...AND I SHALL SHED MY LIGHT OVER DARK EVIL. FOR THE DARK THINGS CANNOT STAND THE LIGHT, THE LIGHT OF THE GREEN LANTERN!
"IT WANTED THAT, YOU SEE. TO BE CONTROLLED. THAT WAS SOMETHING THE GUARDIANS IMBUED THE STARHEART WITH WHEN THEY FIRST CREATED IT.
"AND MY DAD DID THAT...MASTERED THE PART THAT WAS HERE ON EARTH. AND HE'S USED IT FOR THE GOOD OF EARTH, FOR ALL THIS TIME."

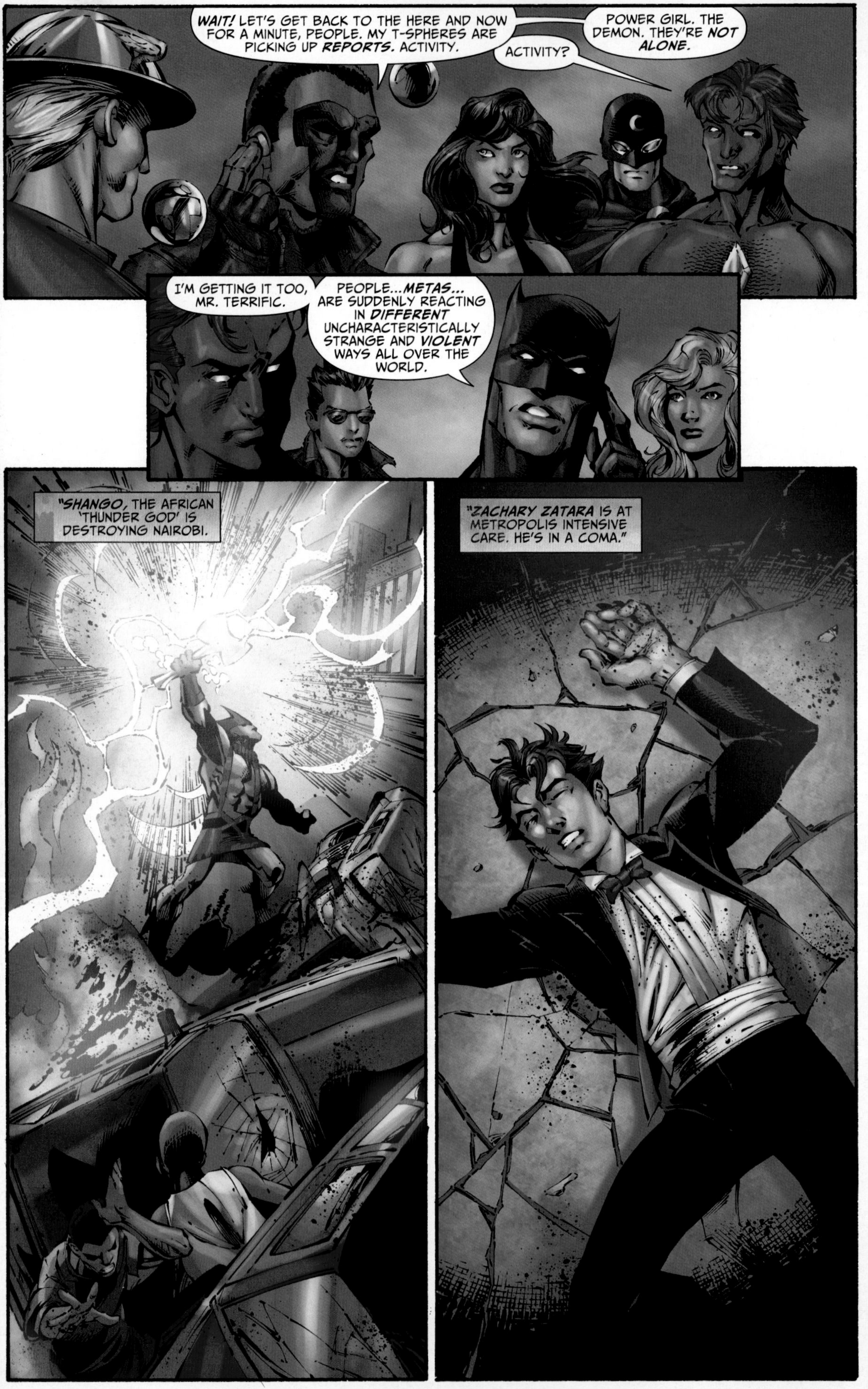
WAIT! LET'S GET BACK TO THE HERE AND NOW FOR A MINUTE, PEOPLE. MY T-SPHERES ARE PICKING UP REPORTS. ACTIVITY.
ACTIVITY?
POWER GIRL. THE DEMON. THEY'RE NOT ALONE.
I'M GETTING IT TOO, MR. TERRIFIC.
PEOPLE...METAS... ARE SUDDENLY REACTING IN DIFFERENT UNCHARACTERISTICALLY STRANGE AND VIOLENT WAYS ALL OVER THE WORLD.
"SHANGO, THE AFRICAN 'THUNDER GOD' IS DESTROYING NAIROBI.
"ZACHARY ZATARA IS AT METROPOLIS INTENSIVE CARE. HE'S IN A COMA."

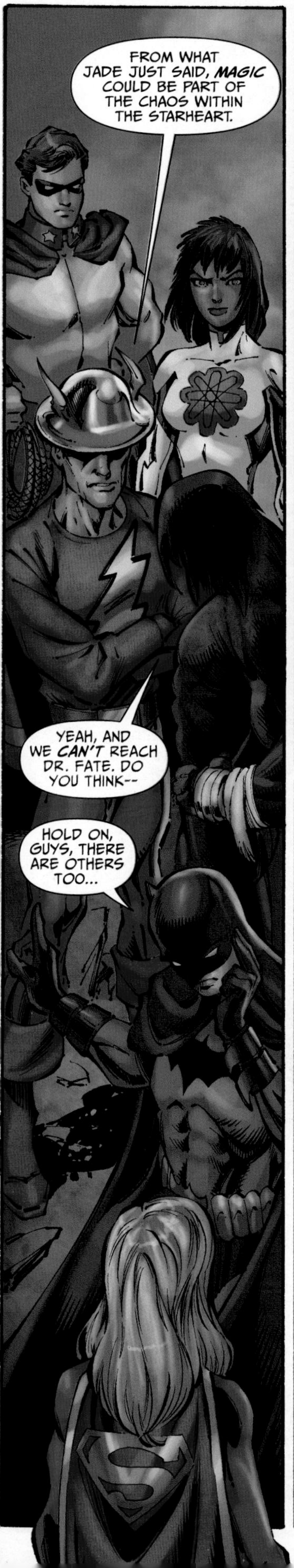
FROM WHAT JADE JUST SAID, MAGIC COULD BE PART OF THE CHAOS WITHIN THE STARHEART.
YEAH, AND WE CAN'T REACH DR. FATE. DO YOU THINK--
HOLD ON, GUYS, THERE ARE OTHERS TOO...

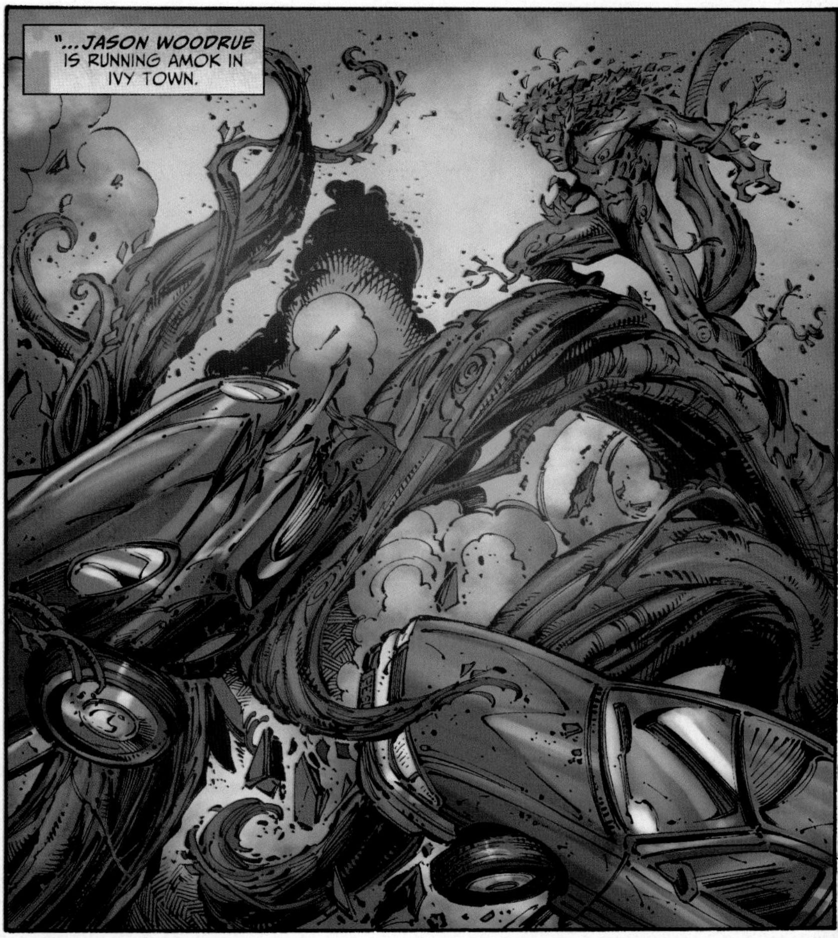
"...JASON WOODRUE IS RUNNING AMOK IN IVY TOWN.

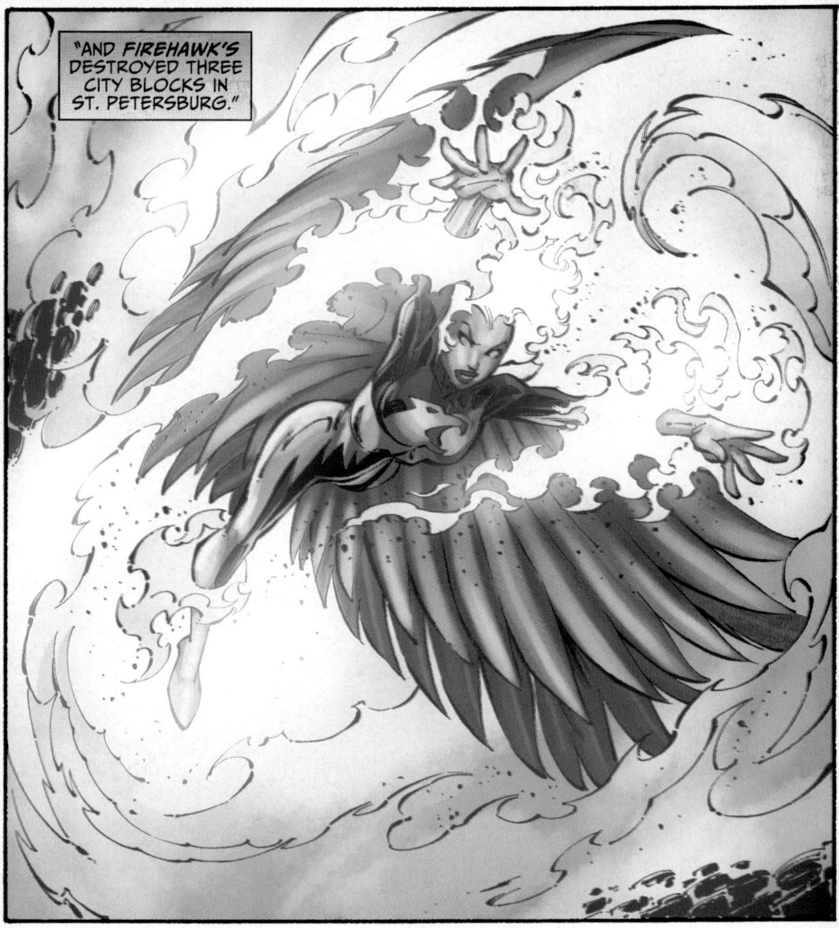
"AND FIREHAWK'S DESTROYED THREE CITY BLOCKS IN ST. PETERSBURG."

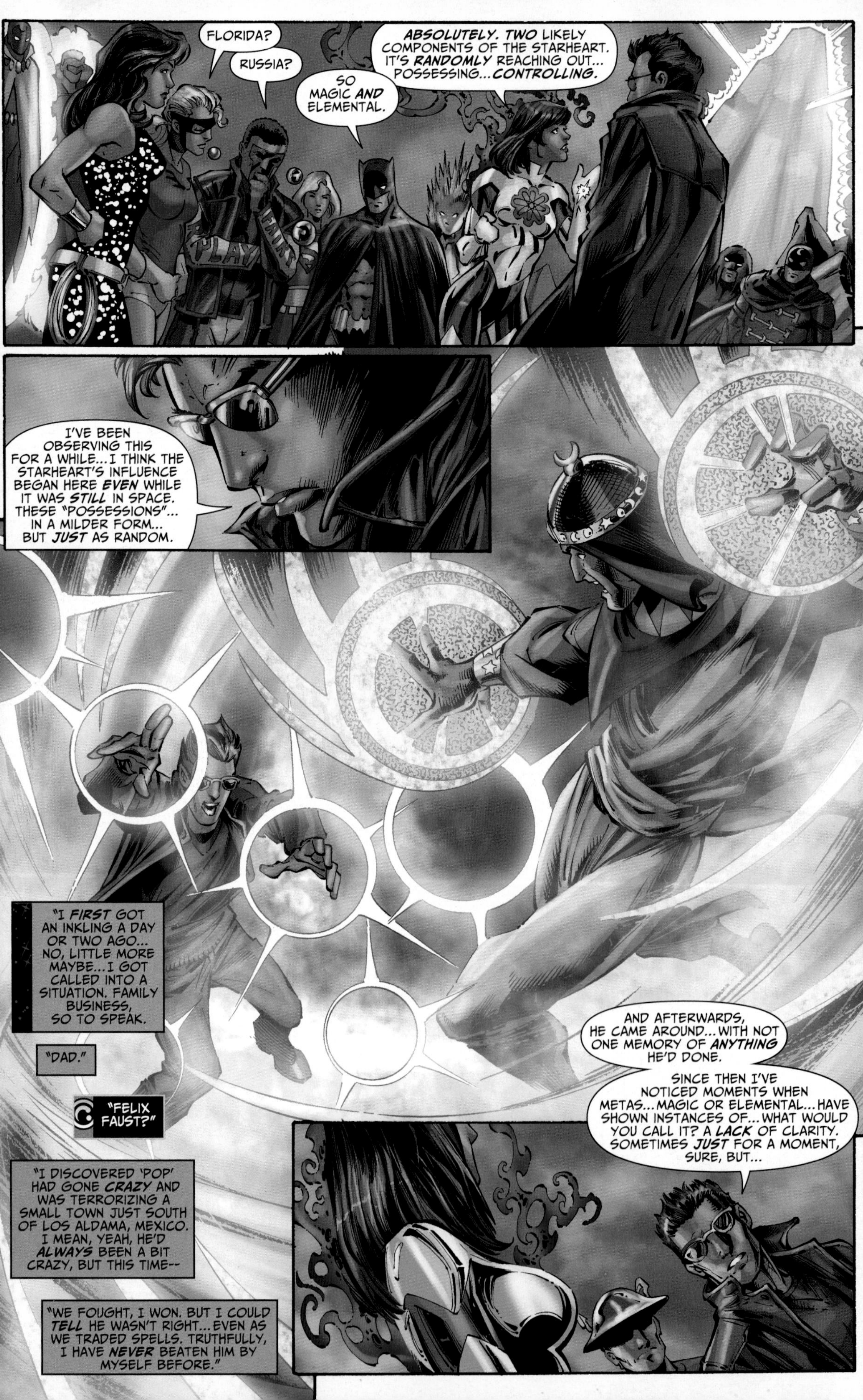
FLORIDA?
RUSSIA?
SO MAGIC AND ELEMENTAL.
ABSOLUTELY. TWO LIKELY COMPONENTS OF THE STARHEART. IT'S RANDOMLY REACHING OUT... POSSESSING...CONTROLLING.
I'VE BEEN OBSERVING THIS FOR A WHILE...I THINK THE STARHEART'S INFLUENCE BEGAN HERE EVEN WHILE IT WAS STILL IN SPACE. THESE "POSSESSIONS"... IN A MILDER FORM... BUT JUST AS RANDOM.
"I FIRST GOT AN INKLING A DAY OR TWO AGO... NO, LITTLE MORE MAYBE...I GOT CALLED INTO A SITUATION. FAMILY BUSINESS, SO TO SPEAK.
"DAD."
"FELIX FAUST?"
"I DISCOVERED 'POP' HAD GONE CRAZY AND WAS TERRORIZING A SMALL TOWN JUST SOUTH OF LOS ALDAMA, MEXICO. I MEAN, YEAH, HE'D ALWAYS BEEN A BIT CRAZY, BUT THIS TIME--
"WE FOUGHT, I WON. BUT I COULD TELL HE WASN'T RIGHT...EVEN AS WE TRADED SPELLS. TRUTHFULLY, I HAVE NEVER BEATEN HIM BY MYSELF BEFORE."
AND AFTERWARDS, HE CAME AROUND...WITH NOT ONE MEMORY OF ANYTHING HE'D DONE.
SINCE THEN I'VE NOTICED MOMENTS WHEN METAS...MAGIC OR ELEMENTAL...HAVE SHOWN INSTANCES OF...WHAT WOULD YOU CALL IT? A LACK OF CLARITY. SOMETIMES JUST FOR A MOMENT, SURE, BUT...

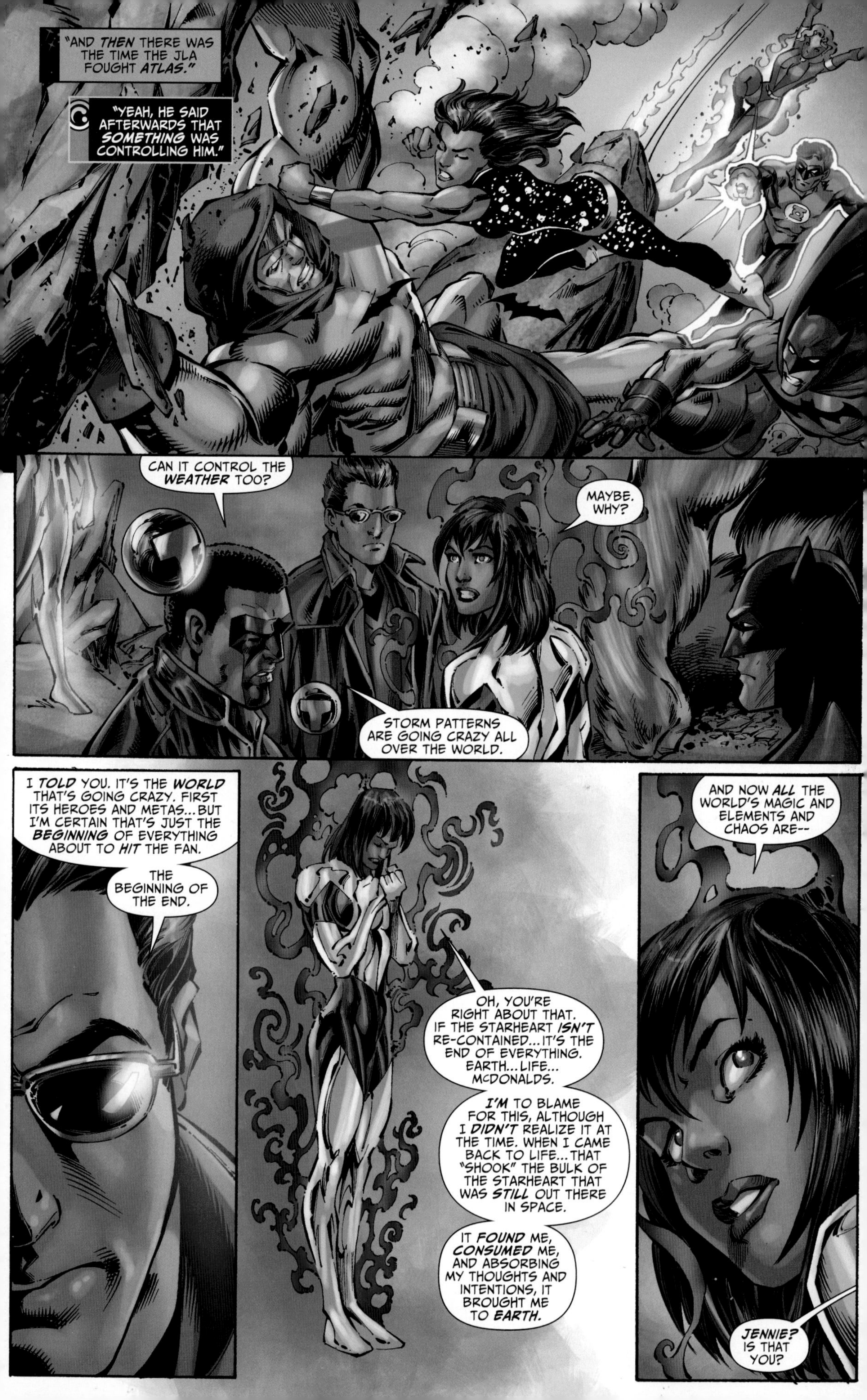
"AND THEN THERE WAS THE TIME THE JLA FOUGHT ATLAS."
"YEAH, HE SAID AFTERWARDS THAT SOMETHING WAS CONTROLLING HIM."
CAN IT CONTROL THE WEATHER TOO?
MAYBE. WHY?
STORM PATTERNS ARE GOING CRAZY ALL OVER THE WORLD.
I TOLD YOU. IT'S THE WORLD THAT'S GOING CRAZY. FIRST ITS HEROES AND METAS... BUT I'M CERTAIN THAT'S JUST THE BEGINNING OF EVERYTHING ABOUT TO HIT THE FAN.
THE BEGINNING OF THE END.
OH, YOU'RE RIGHT ABOUT THAT. IF THE STARHEART ISN'T RE-CONTAINED... IT'S THE END OF EVERYTHING. EARTH... LIFE... McDONALDS.
I'M TO BLAME FOR THIS, ALTHOUGH I DIDN'T REALIZE IT AT THE TIME. WHEN I CAME BACK TO LIFE... THAT "SHOOK" THE BULK OF THE STARHEART THAT WAS STILL OUT THERE IN SPACE.
IT FOUND ME, CONSUMED ME, AND ABSORBING MY THOUGHTS AND INTENTIONS, IT BROUGHT ME TO EARTH.
AND NOW ALL THE WORLD'S MAGIC AND ELEMENTS AND CHAOS ARE--
JENNIE? IS THAT YOU?

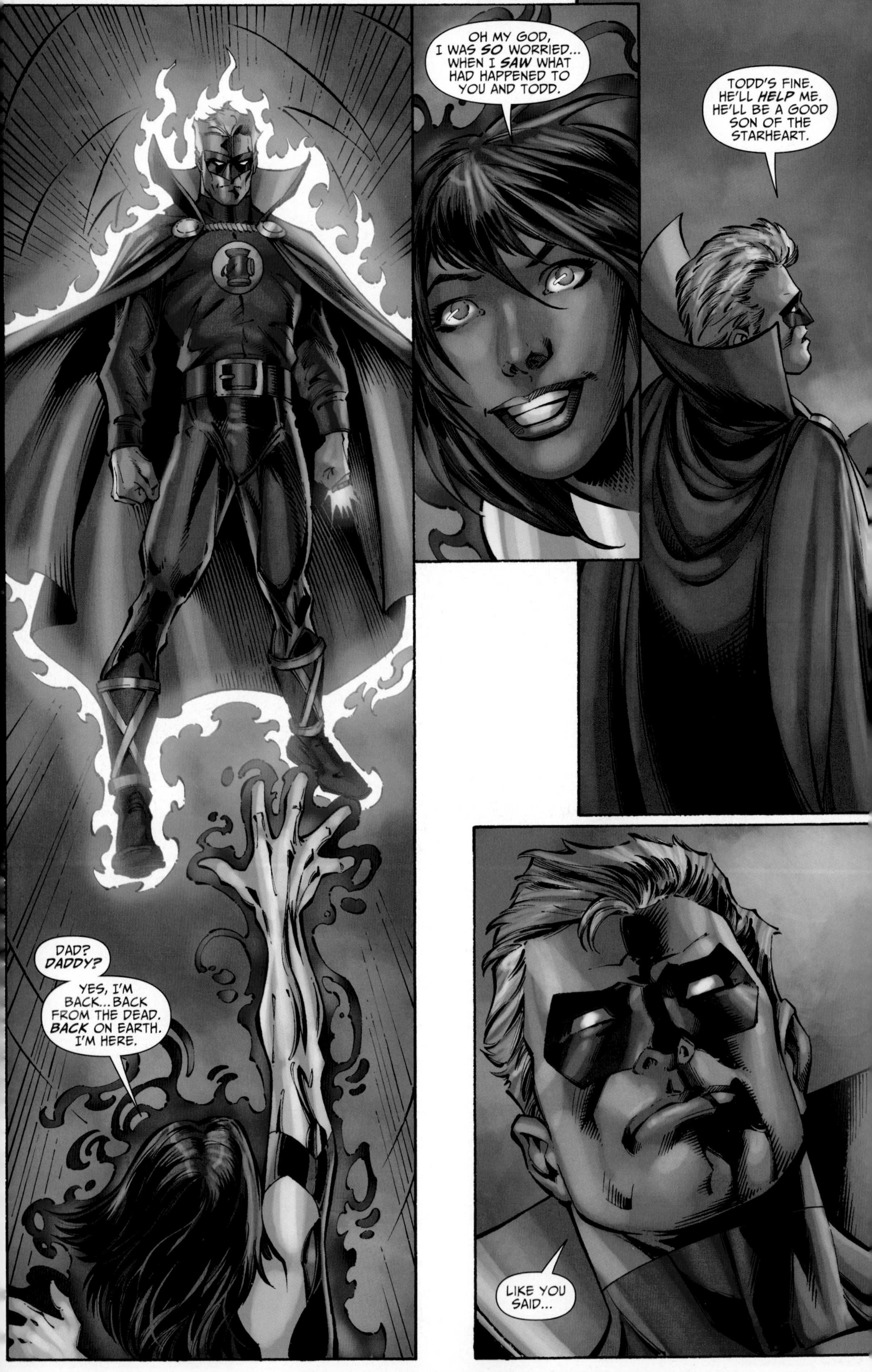
OH MY GOD, I WAS SO WORRIED... WHEN I SAW WHAT HAD HAPPENED TO YOU AND TODD.
TODD'S FINE. HE'LL HELP ME. HE'LL BE A GOOD SON OF THE STARHEART.
DAD? DADDY?
YES, I'M BACK...BACK FROM THE DEAD. BACK ON EARTH. I'M HERE.
LIKE YOU SAID...

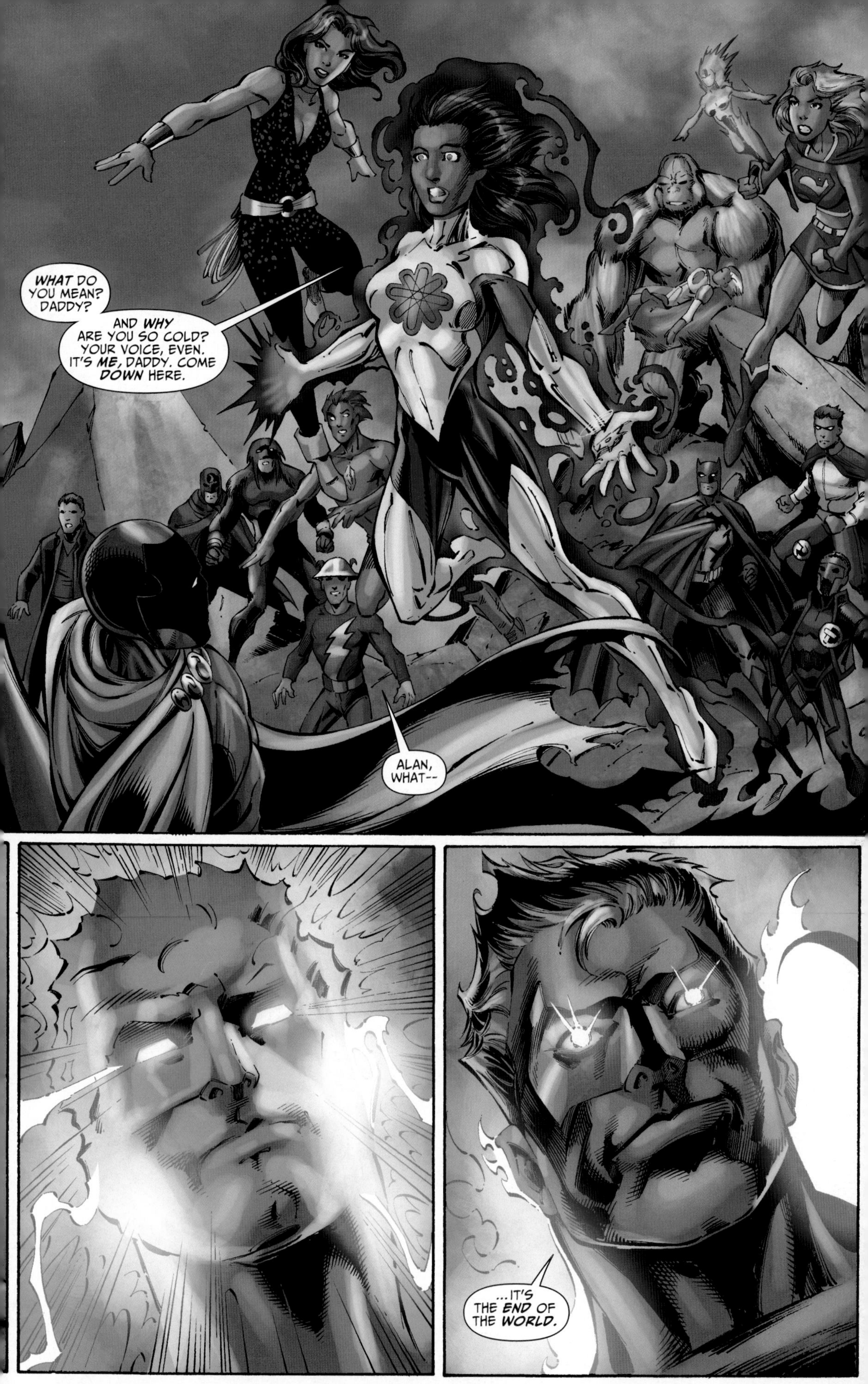
WHAT DO YOU MEAN? DADDY?
AND WHY ARE YOU SO COLD? YOUR VOICE, EVEN. IT'S ME, DADDY. COME DOWN HERE.
ALAN, WHAT--
...IT'S THE END OF THE WORLD.

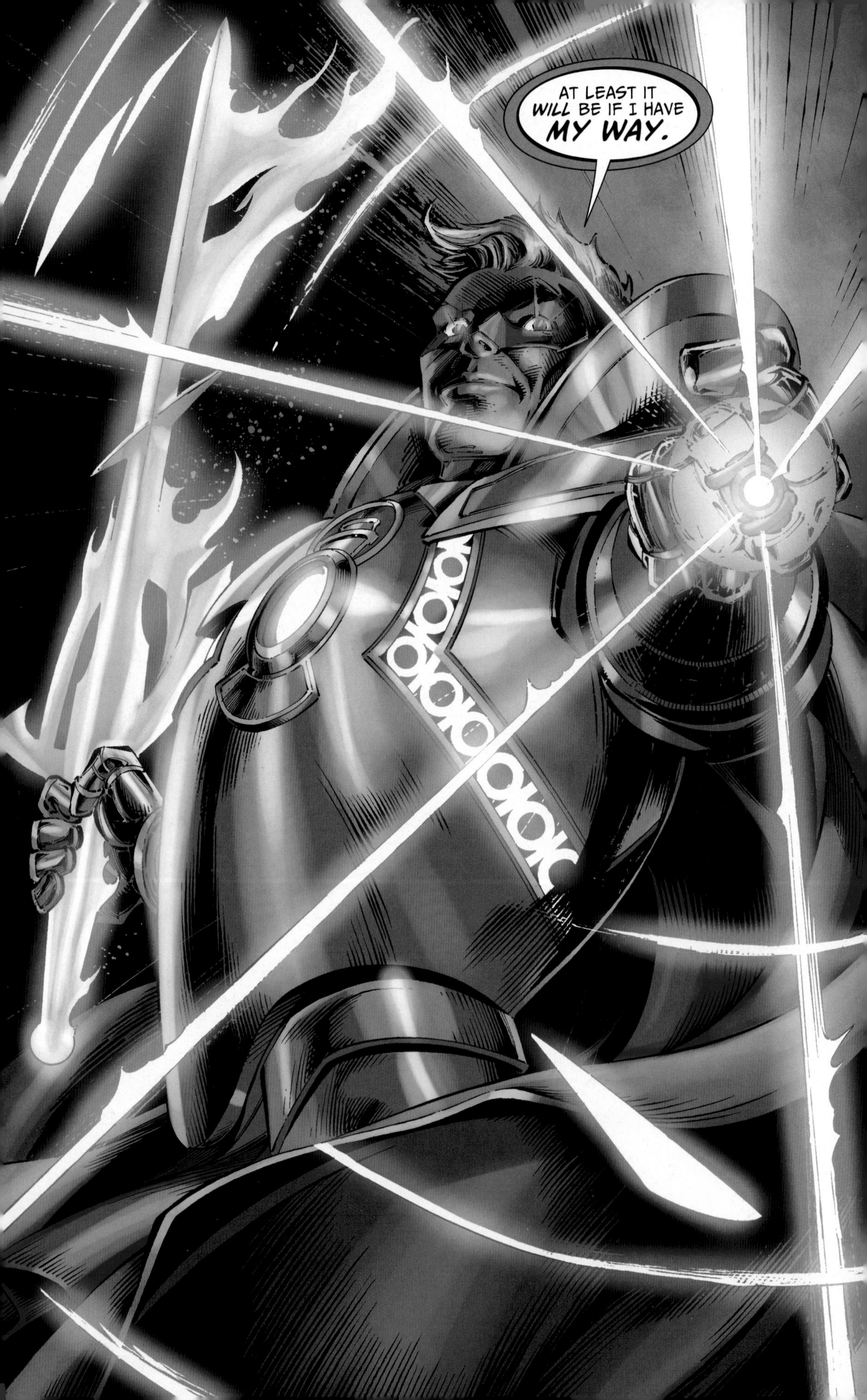
AT LEAST IT *WILL* BE IF I HAVE **MY WAY.**

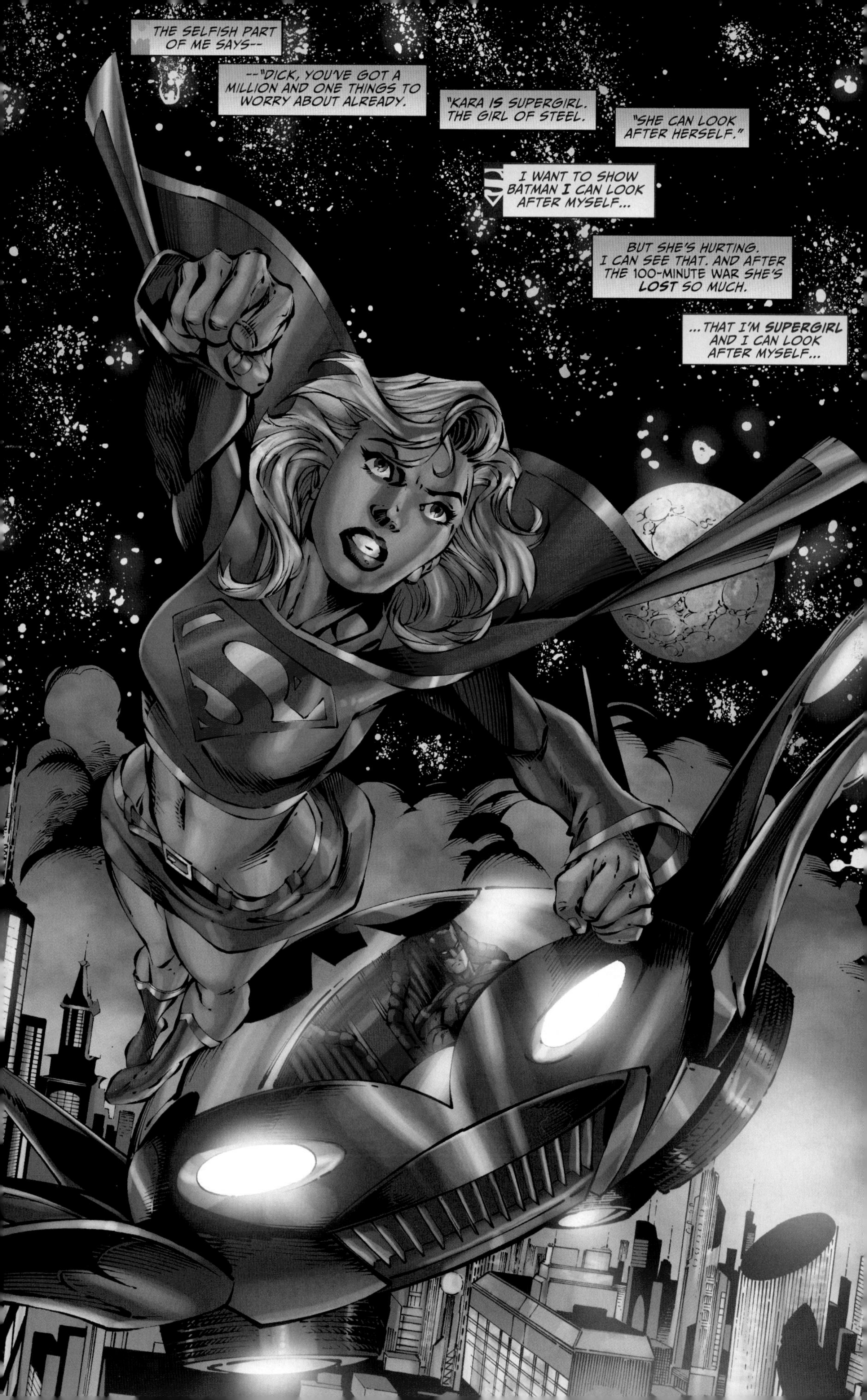
THE SELFISH PART OF ME SAYS--
--"DICK, YOU'VE GOT A MILLION AND ONE THINGS TO WORRY ABOUT ALREADY.
"KARA IS SUPERGIRL. THE GIRL OF STEEL.
"SHE CAN LOOK AFTER HERSELF."
I WANT TO SHOW BATMAN I CAN LOOK AFTER MYSELF...
BUT SHE'S HURTING. I CAN SEE THAT. AND AFTER THE 100-MINUTE WAR SHE'S LOST SO MUCH.
...THAT I'M SUPERGIRL AND I CAN LOOK AFTER MYSELF...

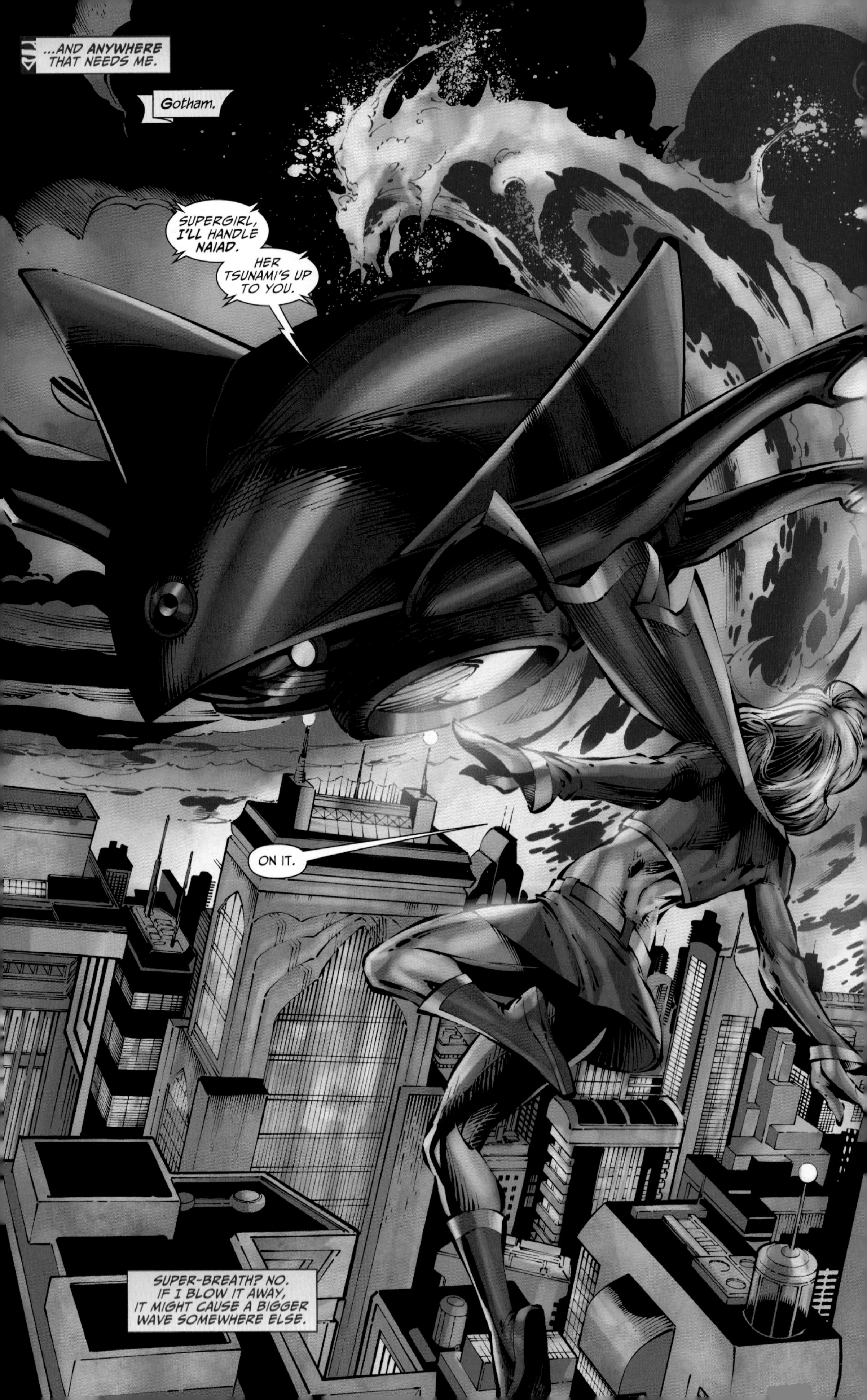
...AND ANYWHERE THAT NEEDS ME.
Gotham.
SUPERGIRL, I'LL HANDLE NAIAD.
HER TSUNAMI'S UP TO YOU.
ON IT.
SUPER-BREATH? NO. IF I BLOW IT AWAY, IT MIGHT CAUSE A BIGGER WAVE SOMEWHERE ELSE.

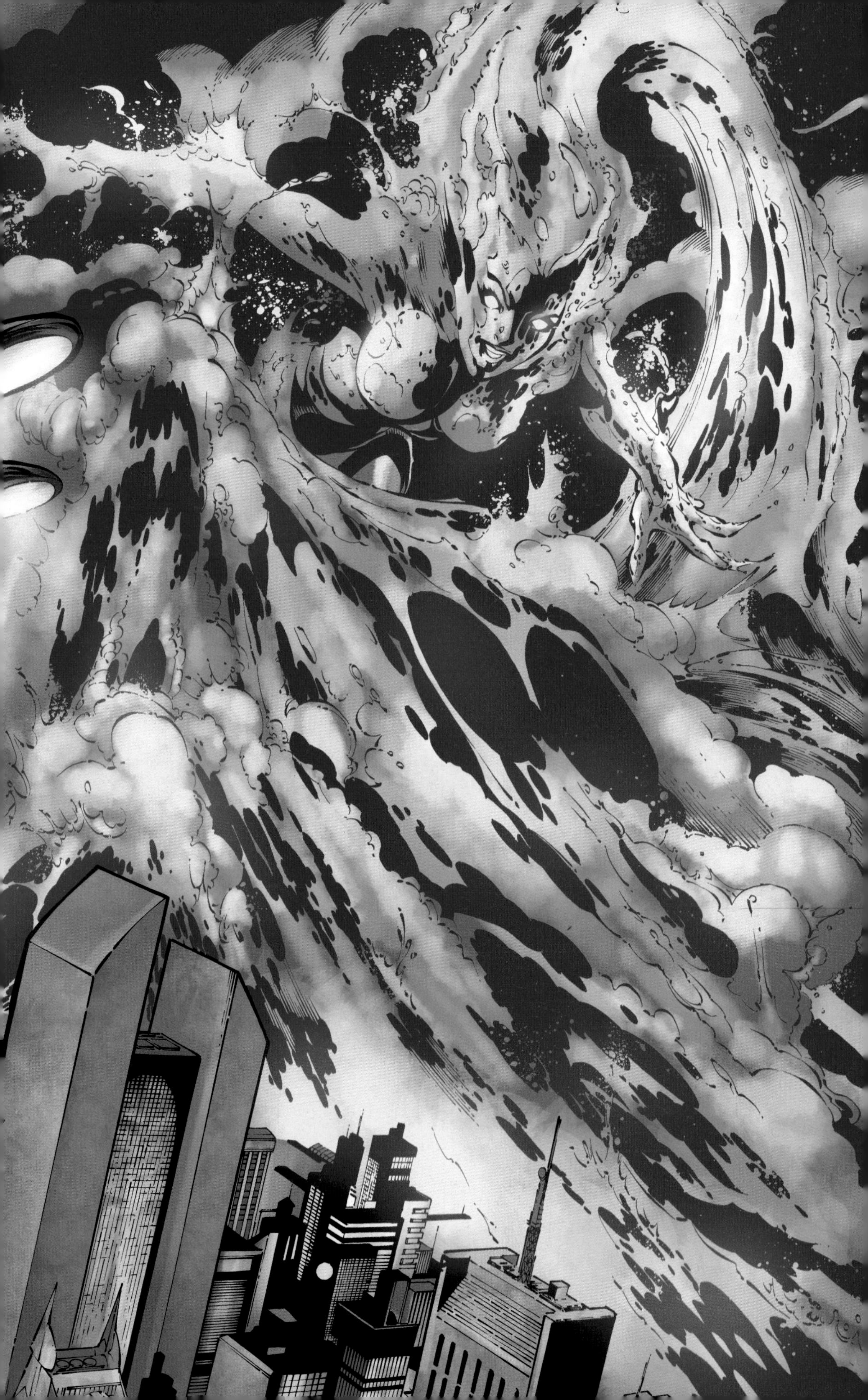

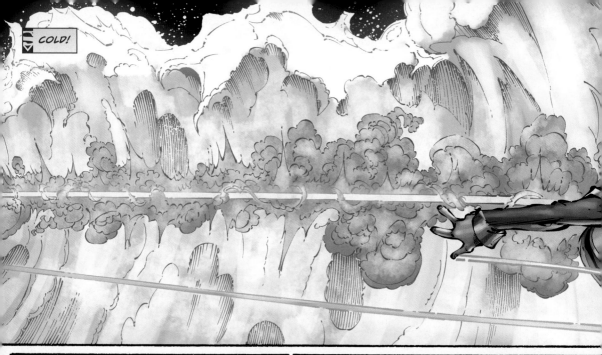

COLD!

LUCKY THE BATCAVE'S COMPUTERS HAD DATA ON NAIAD FROM HER TIME AS A MEMBER OF *PRIMAL FORCE.*

NO. BRUCE. NOTHING LUCKY ABOUT IT.

NAIAD'S AN *ELEMENTAL...WATER* ELEMENTAL, WHICH IS WHY SHE'S ON A RAMPAGE IN THE FIRST PLACE UNDER THE INFLUENCE OF THE *STARHEART--*

LIKE *NAIAD* HERE. HER ONE *WEAKNESS...*

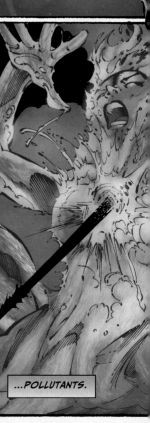

...*POLLUTANTS.*

--AND UNTIL WE'VE FOUND THE STARHEART... THE GIANT "SPACE ROCK" THAT CORRUPTED ALAN SCOTT AND OBSIDIAN WHO'VE BOTH VANISHED ALONG WITH IT...

...AND WHILE THE STARHEART'S POWER OF CHAOTIC ENERGY IS RANDOMLY POSSESSING AND MADDENING MAGIC AND ELEMENTAL METAHUMANS THE WORLD OVER...

...KEEPING CRAZY AT BAY THE WORLD OVER IS ALL THE J.L.A. CAN DO.

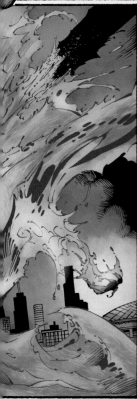

SUPERGIRL, YOU OKAY?

DUH. WHY WOULDN'T I BE?

I GUESS, YEAH. WHY WOULDN'T YOU? ANYWAY--

Y'KNOW, THAT COWL HIDES TOO MUCH OF YOUR FACE, GRAYSON.

RIIIGHT. ANYWAY... GOOD WORK.

AND I NEVER GOT THE CHANCE TO SAY IT EARLIER...

...WELCOME TO THE J.L.A.

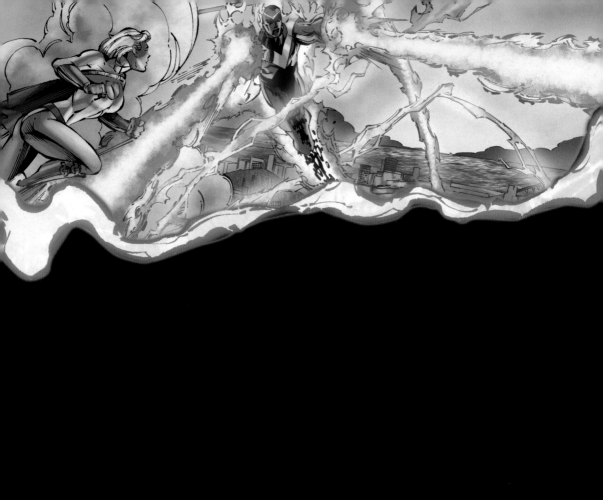

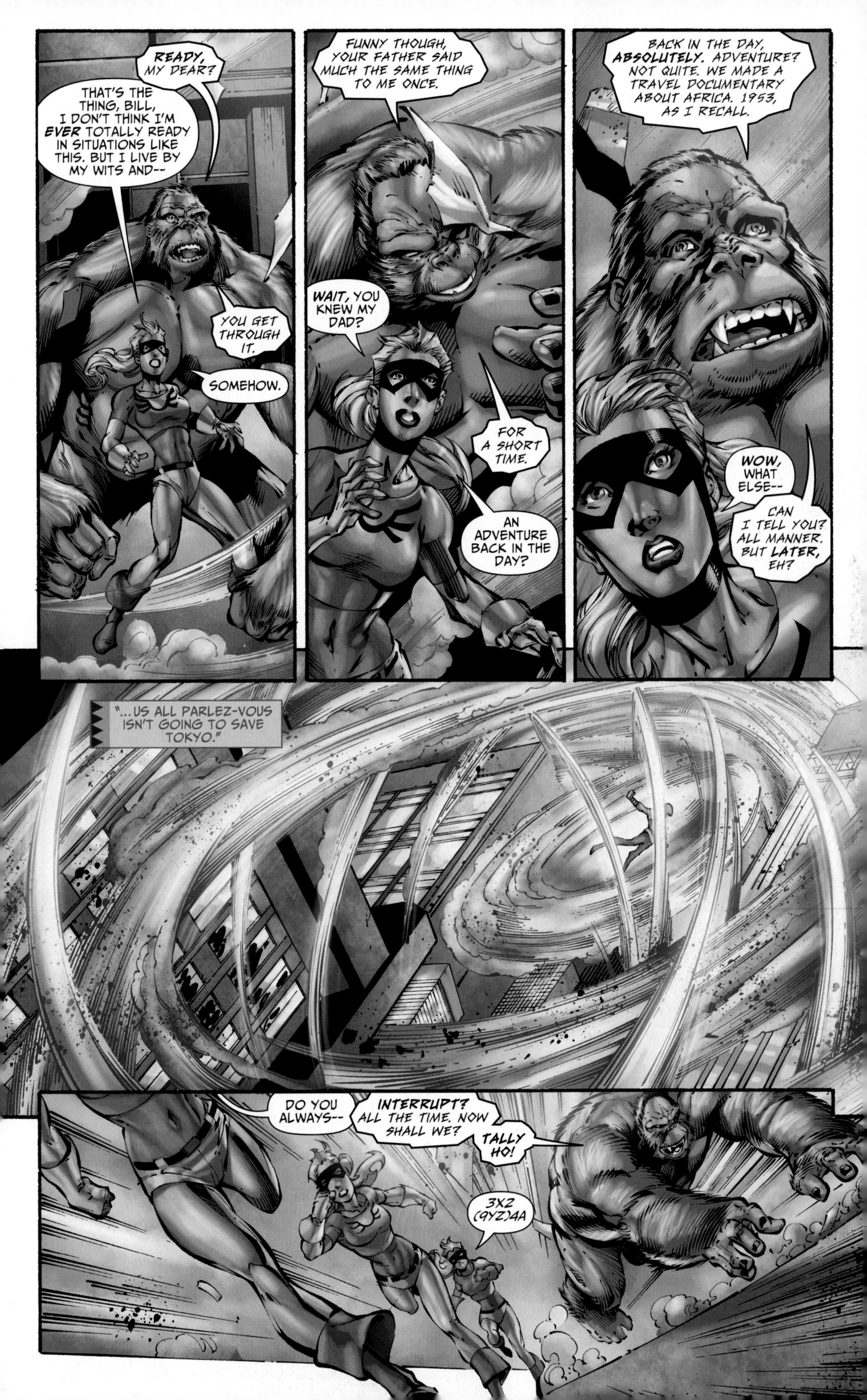
READY, MY DEAR?
THAT'S THE THING, BILL, I DON'T THINK I'M EVER TOTALLY READY IN SITUATIONS LIKE THIS. BUT I LIVE BY MY WITS AND--
YOU GET THROUGH IT.
SOMEHOW.
FUNNY THOUGH, YOUR FATHER SAID MUCH THE SAME THING TO ME ONCE.
WAIT, YOU KNEW MY DAD?
FOR A SHORT TIME.
AN ADVENTURE BACK IN THE DAY?
BACK IN THE DAY, ABSOLUTELY. ADVENTURE? NOT QUITE. WE MADE A TRAVEL DOCUMENTARY ABOUT AFRICA. 1953, AS I RECALL.
WOW, WHAT ELSE--
CAN I TELL YOU? ALL MANNER. BUT LATER, EH?
"...US ALL PARLEZ-VOUS ISN'T GOING TO SAVE TOKYO."
DO YOU ALWAYS--
INTERRUPT? ALL THE TIME. NOW SHALL WE?
TALLY HO!
3X2 (9YZ)4A

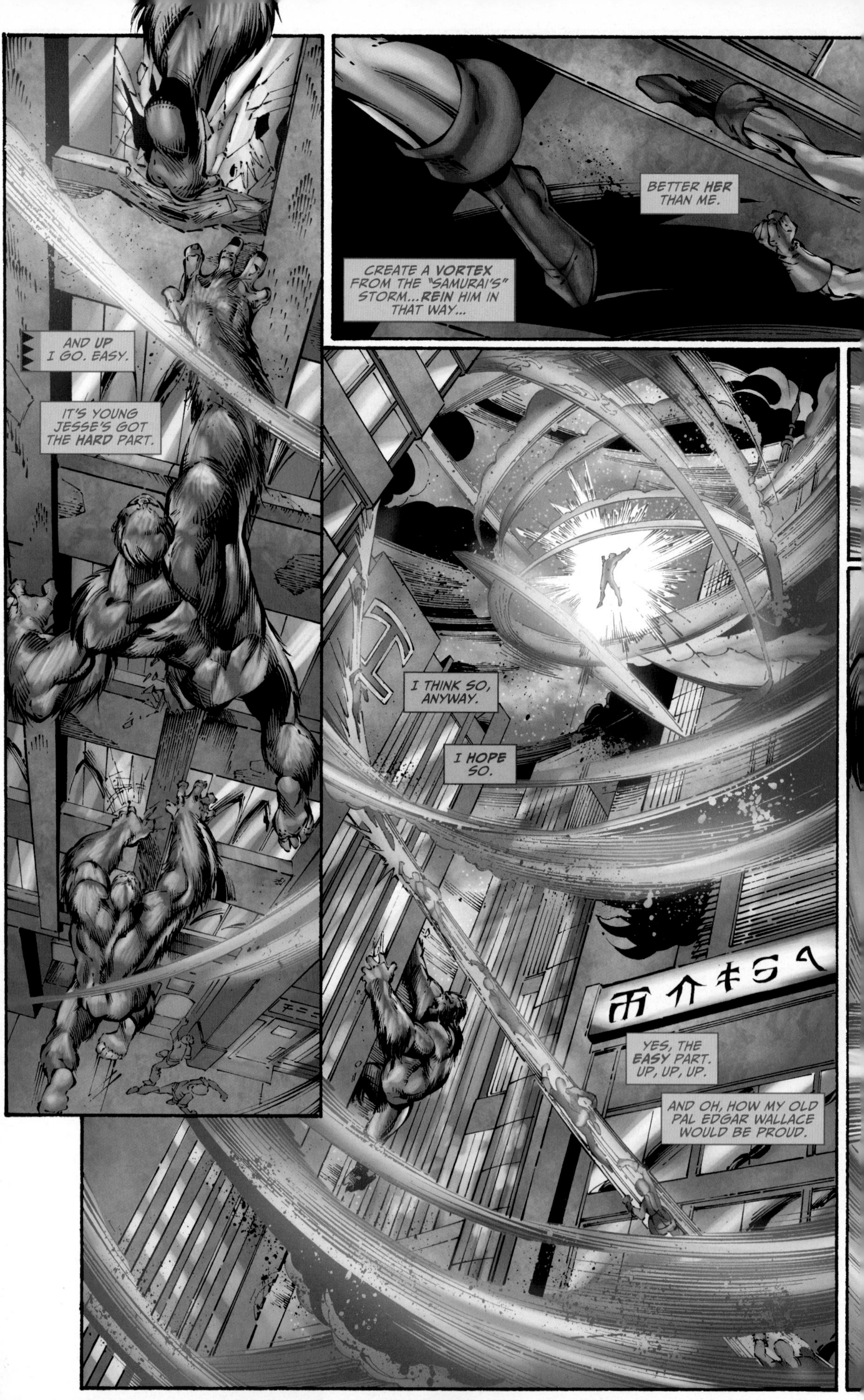
BETTER HER THAN ME.
CREATE A VORTEX FROM THE "SAMURAI'S" STORM...REIN HIM IN THAT WAY...
AND UP I GO. EASY.
IT'S YOUNG JESSE'S GOT THE HARD PART.
I THINK SO, ANYWAY.
I HOPE SO.
YES, THE EASY PART. UP, UP, UP.
AND OH, HOW MY OLD PAL EDGAR WALLACE WOULD BE PROUD.

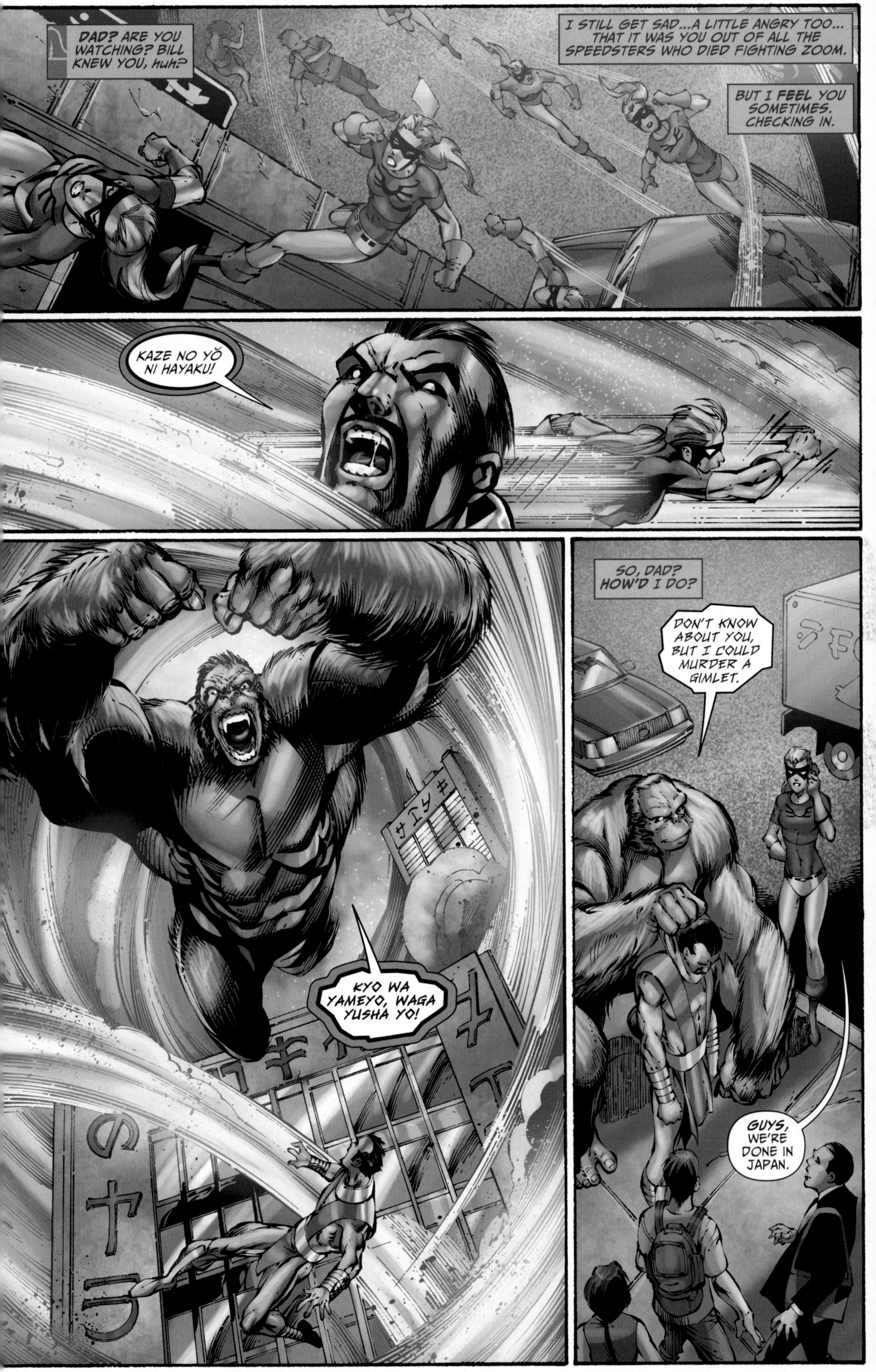
DAD? ARE YOU WATCHING? BILL KNEW YOU, huh?
I STILL GET SAD...A LITTLE ANGRY TOO... THAT IT WAS YOU OUT OF ALL THE SPEEDSTERS WHO DIED FIGHTING ZOOM.
BUT I FEEL YOU SOMETIMES. CHECKING IN.
KAZE NO YŎ NI HAYAKU!
KYO WA YAMEYO, WAGA YUSHA YO!
SO, DAD? HOW'D I DO?
DON'T KNOW ABOUT YOU, BUT I COULD MURDER A GIMLET.
GUYS, WE'RE DONE IN JAPAN.

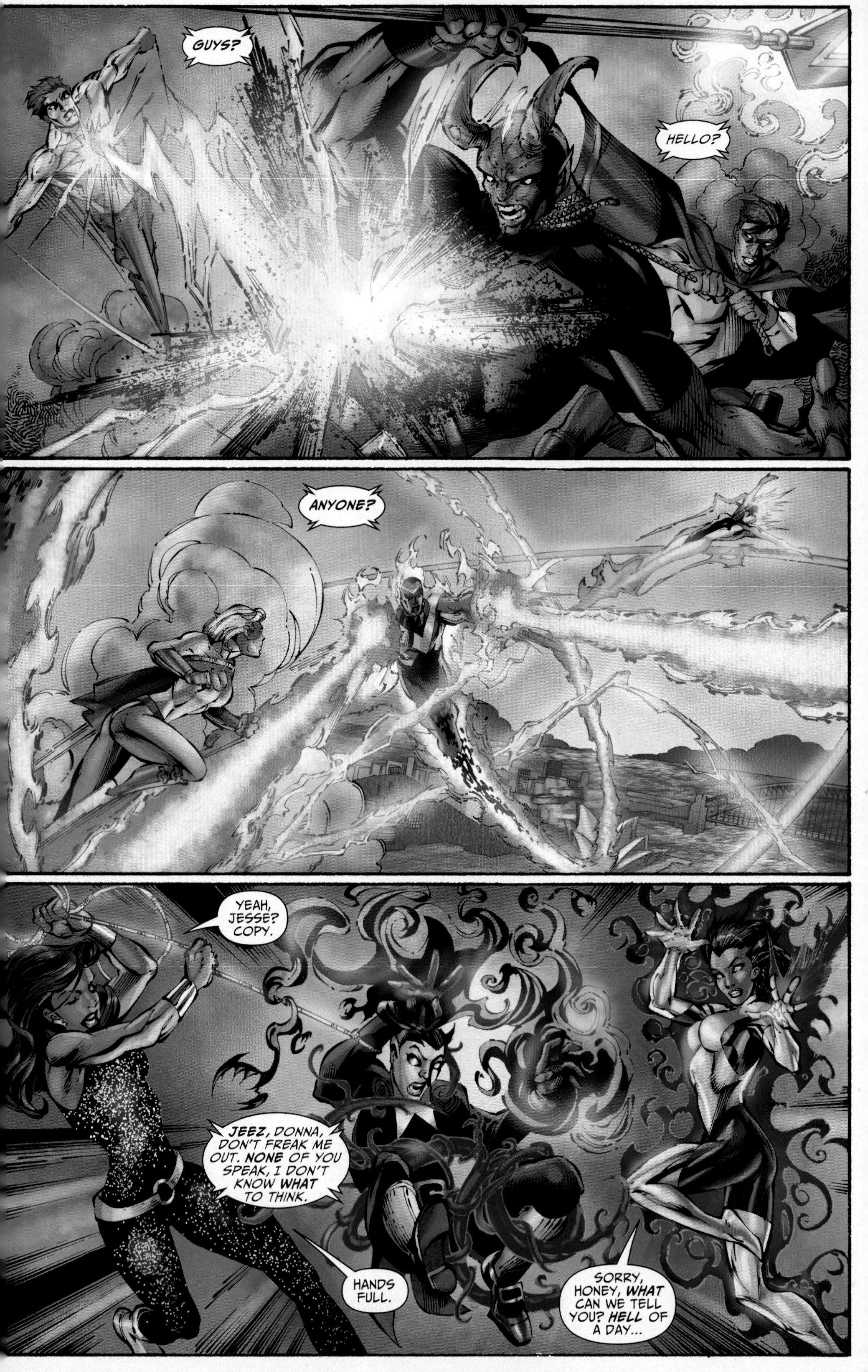
GUYS?
HELLO?
ANYONE?
YEAH, JESSE? COPY.
JEEZ, DONNA, DON'T FREAK ME OUT. NONE OF YOU SPEAK, I DON'T KNOW WHAT TO THINK.
HANDS FULL.
SORRY, HONEY, WHAT CAN WE TELL YOU? HELL OF A DAY...

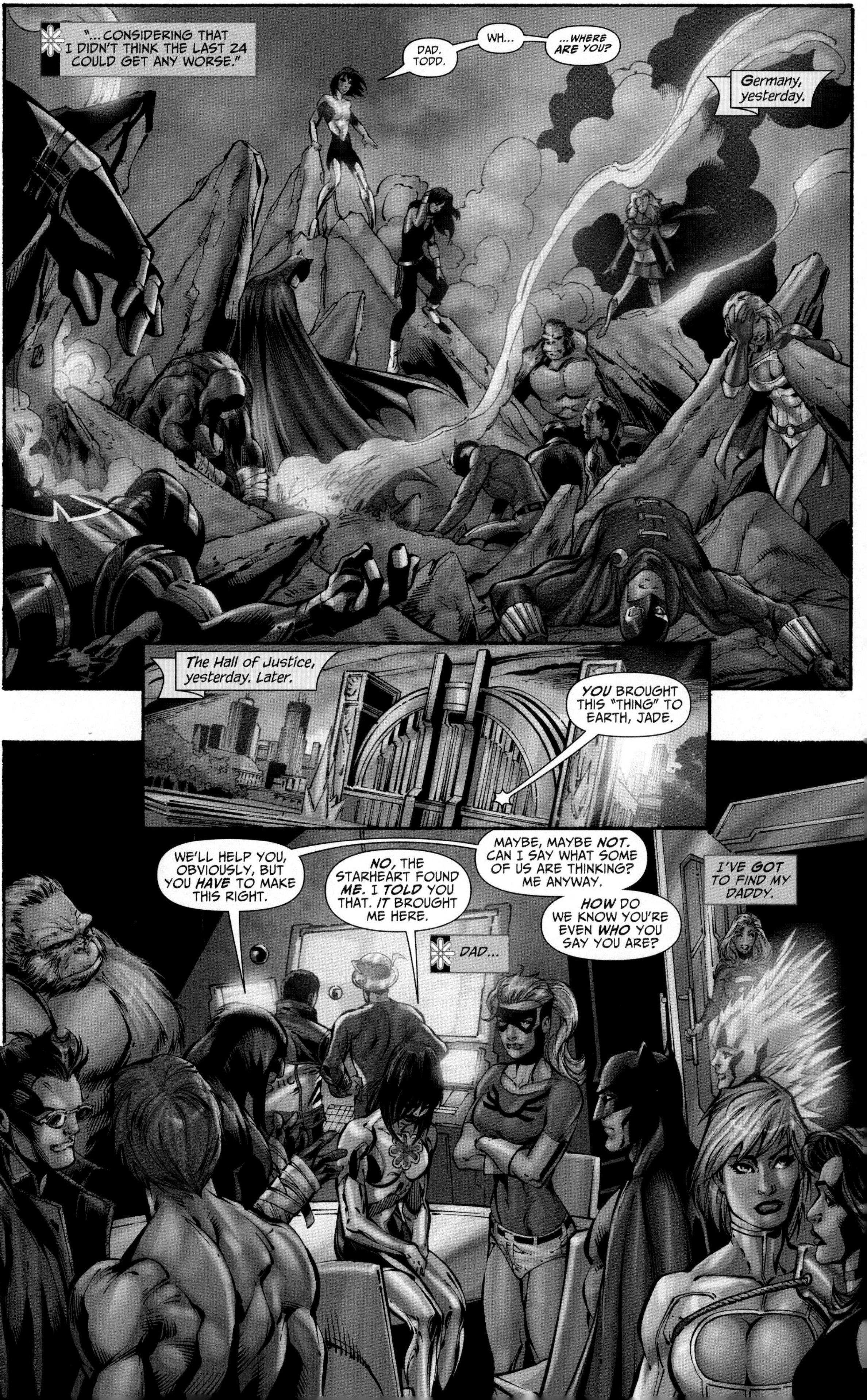
"...CONSIDERING THAT I DIDN'T THINK THE LAST 24 COULD GET ANY WORSE."
DAD. TODD.
WH...
...WHERE ARE YOU?
Germany, yesterday.
The Hall of Justice, yesterday. Later.
YOU BROUGHT THIS "THING" TO EARTH, JADE.
WE'LL HELP YOU, OBVIOUSLY, BUT YOU HAVE TO MAKE THIS RIGHT.
NO, THE STARHEART FOUND ME. I TOLD YOU THAT. IT BROUGHT ME HERE.
DAD...
MAYBE, MAYBE NOT. CAN I SAY WHAT SOME OF US ARE THINKING? ME ANYWAY.
HOW DO WE KNOW YOU'RE EVEN WHO YOU SAY YOU ARE?
I'VE GOT TO FIND MY DADDY.

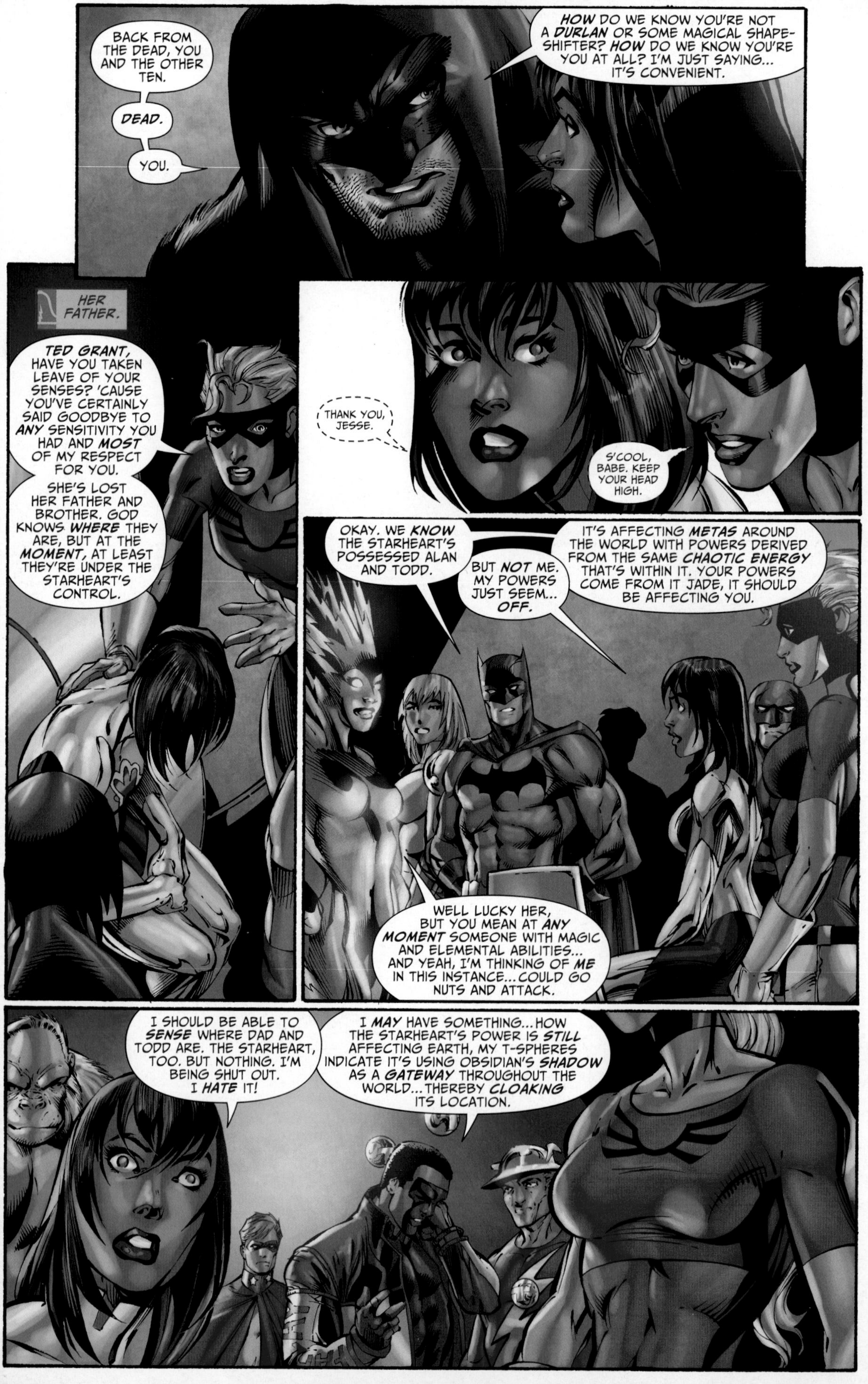
BACK FROM THE DEAD, YOU AND THE OTHER TEN.
DEAD.
YOU.
HOW DO WE KNOW YOU'RE NOT A DURLAN OR SOME MAGICAL SHAPE-SHIFTER? HOW DO WE KNOW YOU'RE YOU AT ALL? I'M JUST SAYING... IT'S CONVENIENT.
HER FATHER.
TED GRANT, HAVE YOU TAKEN LEAVE OF YOUR SENSES? 'CAUSE YOU'VE CERTAINLY SAID GOODBYE TO ANY SENSITIVITY YOU HAD AND MOST OF MY RESPECT FOR YOU.
SHE'S LOST HER FATHER AND BROTHER. GOD KNOWS WHERE THEY ARE, BUT AT THE MOMENT, AT LEAST THEY'RE UNDER THE STARHEART'S CONTROL.
THANK YOU, JESSE.
S'COOL, BABE. KEEP YOUR HEAD HIGH.
OKAY. WE KNOW THE STARHEART'S POSSESSED ALAN AND TODD.
BUT NOT ME. MY POWERS JUST SEEM... OFF.
IT'S AFFECTING METAS AROUND THE WORLD WITH POWERS DERIVED FROM THE SAME CHAOTIC ENERGY THAT'S WITHIN IT. YOUR POWERS COME FROM IT JADE, IT SHOULD BE AFFECTING YOU.
WELL LUCKY HER, BUT YOU MEAN AT ANY MOMENT SOMEONE WITH MAGIC AND ELEMENTAL ABILITIES... AND YEAH, I'M THINKING OF ME IN THIS INSTANCE... COULD GO NUTS AND ATTACK.
I SHOULD BE ABLE TO SENSE WHERE DAD AND TODD ARE. THE STARHEART, TOO. BUT NOTHING. I'M BEING SHUT OUT. I HATE IT!
I MAY HAVE SOMETHING... HOW THE STARHEART'S POWER IS STILL AFFECTING EARTH, MY T-SPHERES INDICATE IT'S USING OBSIDIAN'S SHADOW AS A GATEWAY THROUGHOUT THE WORLD... THEREBY CLOAKING ITS LOCATION.

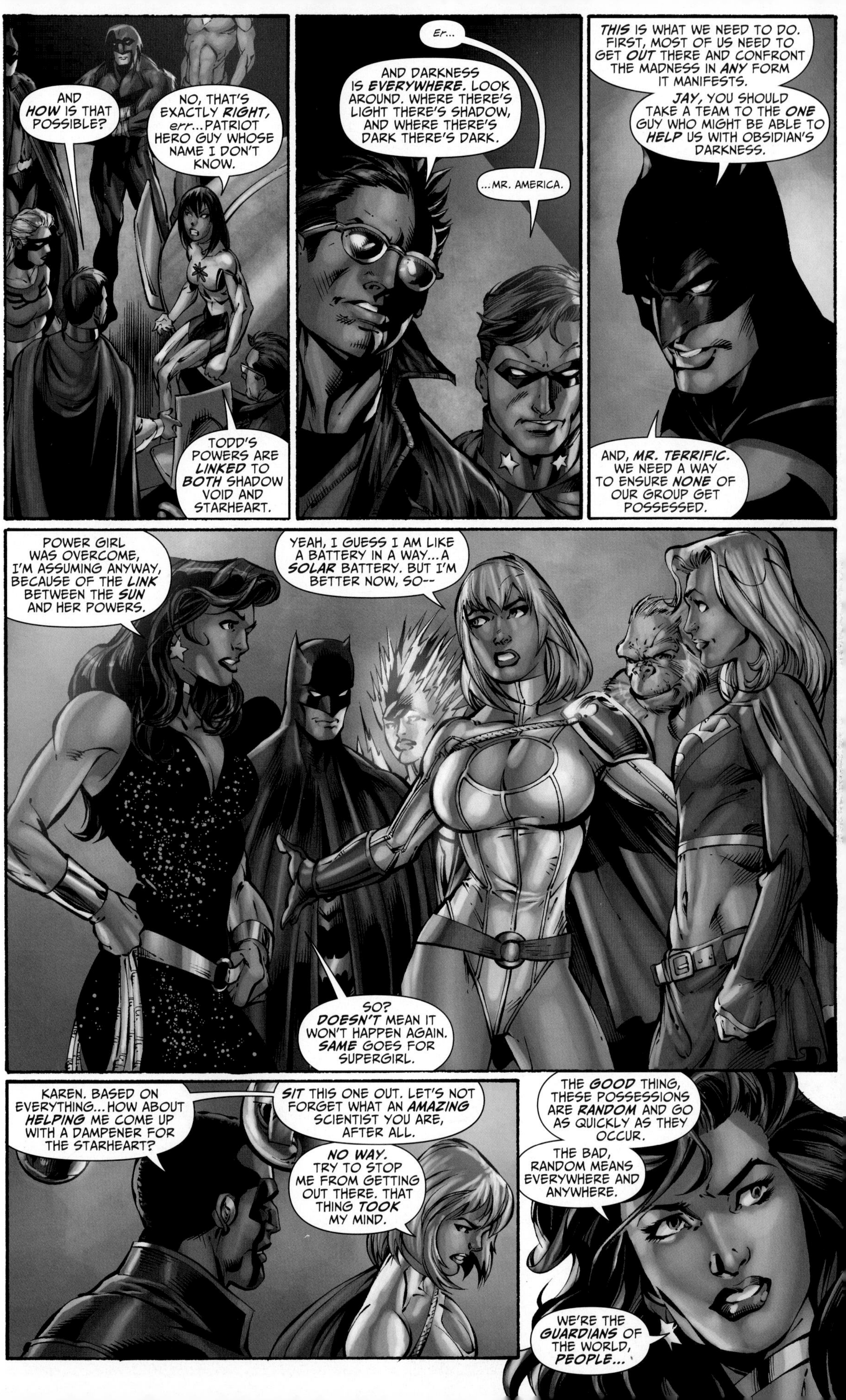
AND HOW IS THAT POSSIBLE?
NO, THAT'S EXACTLY RIGHT, err...PATRIOT HERO GUY WHOSE NAME I DON'T KNOW.
TODD'S POWERS ARE LINKED TO BOTH SHADOW VOID AND STARHEART.
AND DARKNESS IS EVERYWHERE. LOOK AROUND. WHERE THERE'S LIGHT THERE'S SHADOW, AND WHERE THERE'S DARK THERE'S DARK.
Er...
...MR. AMERICA.
THIS IS WHAT WE NEED TO DO. FIRST, MOST OF US NEED TO GET OUT THERE AND CONFRONT THE MADNESS IN ANY FORM IT MANIFESTS.
JAY, YOU SHOULD TAKE A TEAM TO THE ONE GUY WHO MIGHT BE ABLE TO HELP US WITH OBSIDIAN'S DARKNESS.
AND, MR. TERRIFIC. WE NEED A WAY TO ENSURE NONE OF OUR GROUP GET POSSESSED.
POWER GIRL WAS OVERCOME, I'M ASSUMING ANYWAY, BECAUSE OF THE LINK BETWEEN THE SUN AND HER POWERS.
YEAH, I GUESS I AM LIKE A BATTERY IN A WAY...A SOLAR BATTERY. BUT I'M BETTER NOW, SO--
SO? DOESN'T MEAN IT WON'T HAPPEN AGAIN. SAME GOES FOR SUPERGIRL.
KAREN. BASED ON EVERYTHING...HOW ABOUT HELPING ME COME UP WITH A DAMPENER FOR THE STARHEART?
SIT THIS ONE OUT. LET'S NOT FORGET WHAT AN AMAZING SCIENTIST YOU ARE, AFTER ALL.
NO WAY. TRY TO STOP ME FROM GETTING OUT THERE. THAT THING TOOK MY MIND.
THE GOOD THING, THESE POSSESSIONS ARE RANDOM AND GO AS QUICKLY AS THEY OCCUR.
THE BAD, RANDOM MEANS EVERYWHERE AND ANYWHERE.
WE'RE THE GUARDIANS OF THE WORLD, PEOPLE...

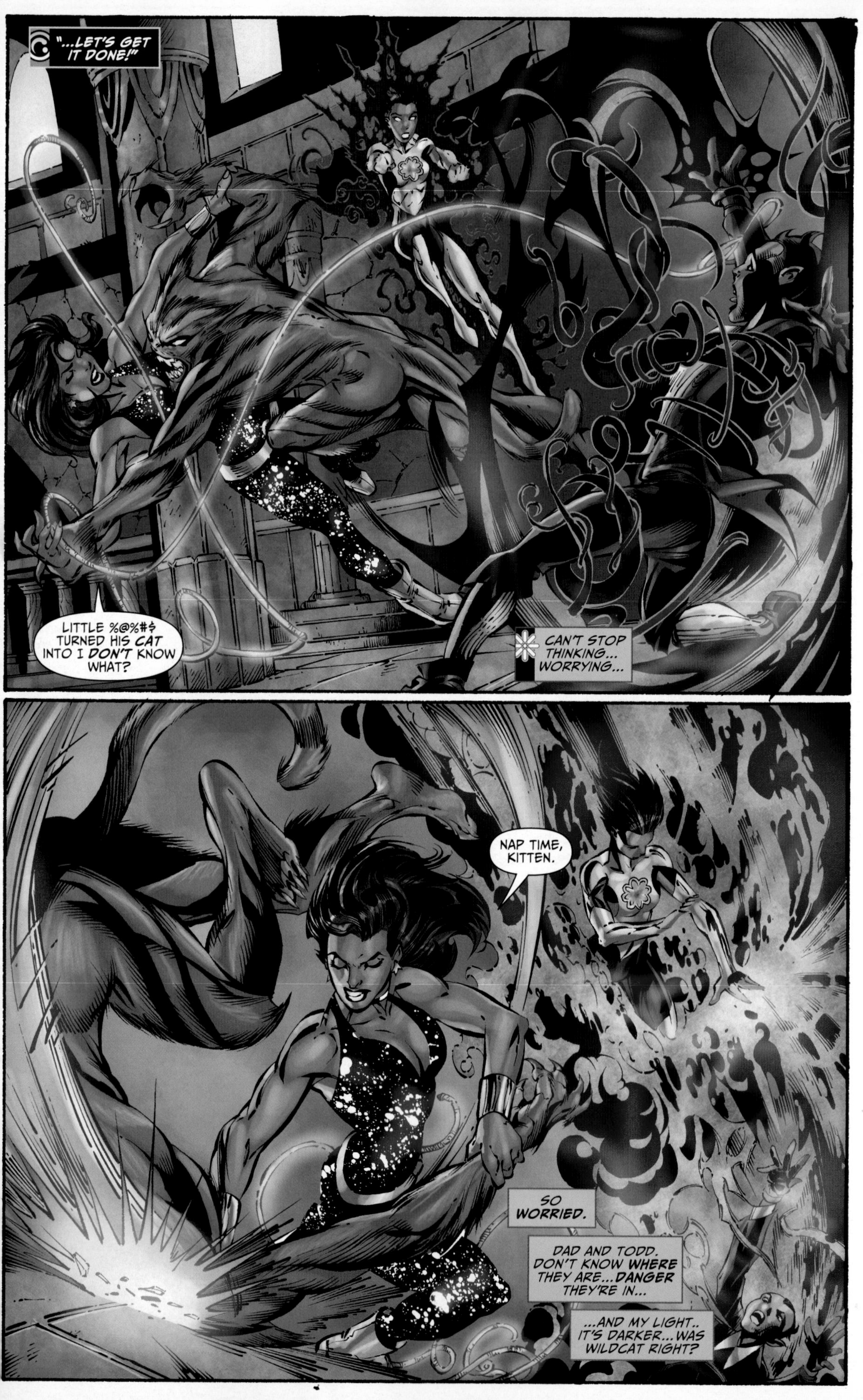
"...LET'S GET IT DONE!"
LITTLE %@%#$ TURNED HIS CAT INTO I DON'T KNOW WHAT?
CAN'T STOP THINKING... WORRYING...
NAP TIME, KITTEN.
SO WORRIED.
DAD AND TODD. DON'T KNOW WHERE THEY ARE...DANGER THEY'RE IN...
...AND MY LIGHT.. IT'S DARKER...WAS WILDCAT RIGHT?

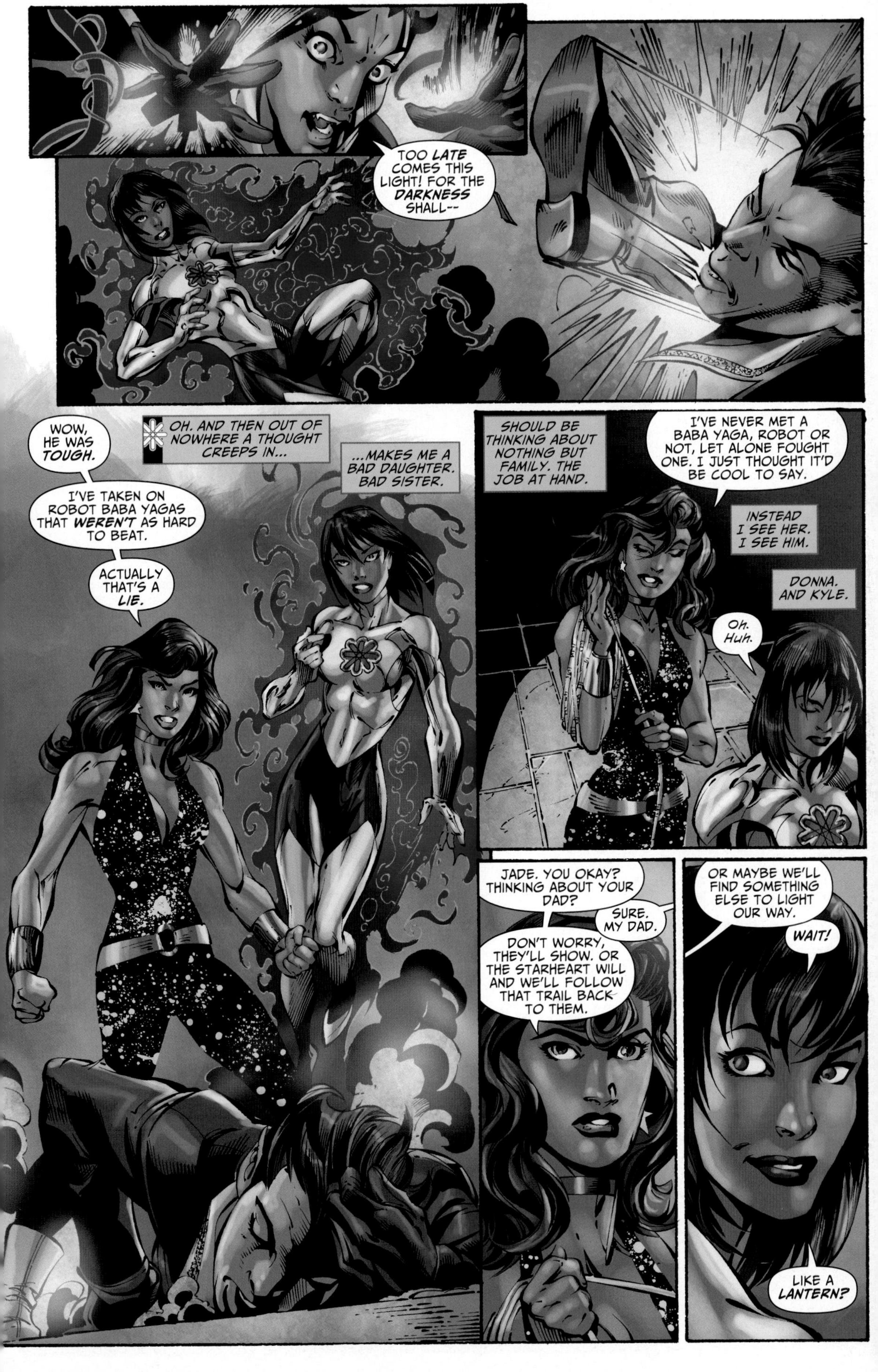
TOO LATE COMES THIS LIGHT! FOR THE DARKNESS SHALL--
WOW, HE WAS TOUGH.
OH. AND THEN OUT OF NOWHERE A THOUGHT CREEPS IN...
I'VE TAKEN ON ROBOT BABA YAGAS THAT WEREN'T AS HARD TO BEAT.
...MAKES ME A BAD DAUGHTER. BAD SISTER.
ACTUALLY THAT'S A LIE.
SHOULD BE THINKING ABOUT NOTHING BUT FAMILY. THE JOB AT HAND.
I'VE NEVER MET A BABA YAGA, ROBOT OR NOT, LET ALONE FOUGHT ONE. I JUST THOUGHT IT'D BE COOL TO SAY.
INSTEAD I SEE HER. I SEE HIM.
DONNA. AND KYLE.
Oh. Huh.
JADE. YOU OKAY? THINKING ABOUT YOUR DAD?
SURE. MY DAD.
DON'T WORRY, THEY'LL SHOW. OR THE STARHEART WILL AND WE'LL FOLLOW THAT TRAIL BACK TO THEM.
OR MAYBE WE'LL FIND SOMETHING ELSE TO LIGHT OUR WAY.
WAIT!
LIKE A LANTERN?

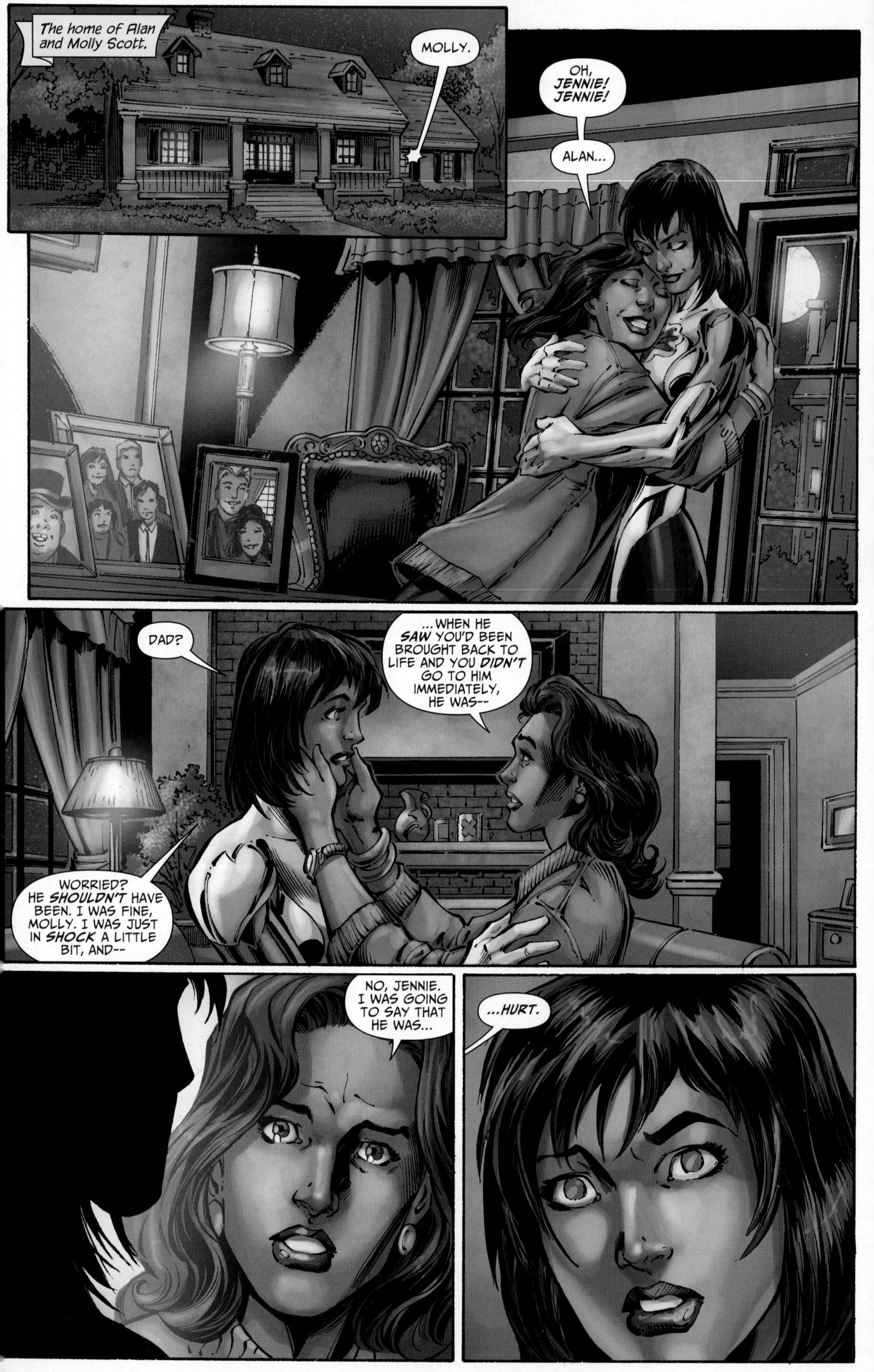
The home of Alan and Molly Scott.
MOLLY.
OH, JENNIE! JENNIE!
ALAN...
DAD?
...WHEN HE SAW YOU'D BEEN BROUGHT BACK TO LIFE AND YOU DIDN'T GO TO HIM IMMEDIATELY, HE WAS--
WORRIED? HE SHOULDN'T HAVE BEEN. I WAS FINE, MOLLY. I WAS JUST IN SHOCK A LITTLE BIT, AND--
NO, JENNIE. I WAS GOING TO SAY THAT HE WAS...
...HURT.

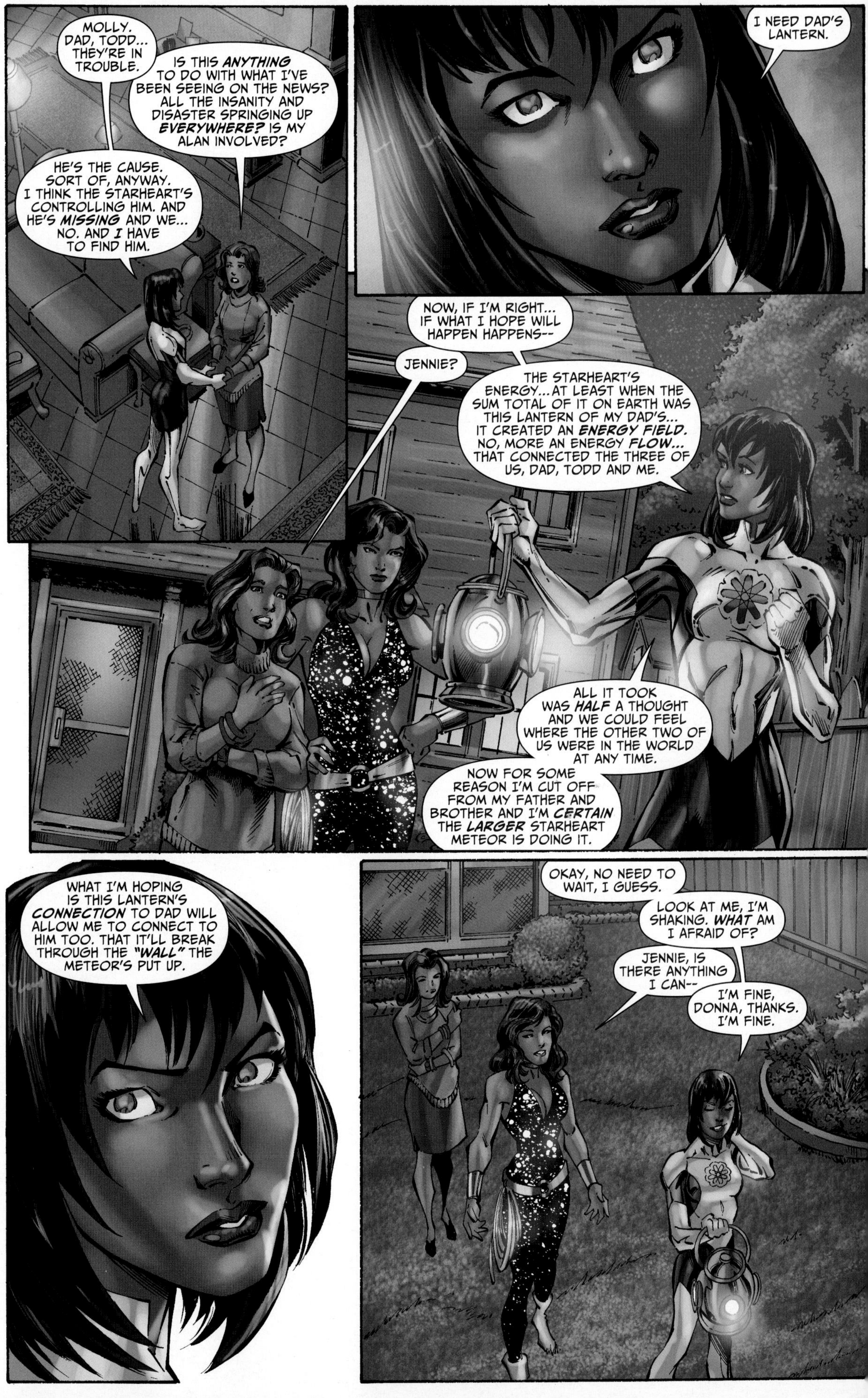
MOLLY. DAD, TODD... THEY'RE IN TROUBLE.
IS THIS ANYTHING TO DO WITH WHAT I'VE BEEN SEEING ON THE NEWS? ALL THE INSANITY AND DISASTER SPRINGING UP EVERYWHERE? IS MY ALAN INVOLVED?
HE'S THE CAUSE. SORT OF, ANYWAY. I THINK THE STARHEART'S CONTROLLING HIM. AND HE'S MISSING AND WE... NO. AND I HAVE TO FIND HIM.
I NEED DAD'S LANTERN.
NOW, IF I'M RIGHT... IF WHAT I HOPE WILL HAPPEN HAPPENS--
JENNIE?
THE STARHEART'S ENERGY...AT LEAST WHEN THE SUM TOTAL OF IT ON EARTH WAS THIS LANTERN OF MY DAD'S... IT CREATED AN ENERGY FIELD. NO, MORE AN ENERGY FLOW... THAT CONNECTED THE THREE OF US, DAD, TODD AND ME.
ALL IT TOOK WAS HALF A THOUGHT AND WE COULD FEEL WHERE THE OTHER TWO OF US WERE IN THE WORLD AT ANY TIME.
NOW FOR SOME REASON I'M CUT OFF FROM MY FATHER AND BROTHER AND I'M CERTAIN THE LARGER STARHEART METEOR IS DOING IT.
WHAT I'M HOPING IS THIS LANTERN'S CONNECTION TO DAD WILL ALLOW ME TO CONNECT TO HIM TOO. THAT IT'LL BREAK THROUGH THE "WALL" THE METEOR'S PUT UP.
OKAY, NO NEED TO WAIT, I GUESS.
LOOK AT ME, I'M SHAKING. WHAT AM I AFRAID OF?
JENNIE, IS THERE ANYTHING I CAN--
I'M FINE, DONNA, THANKS. I'M FINE.

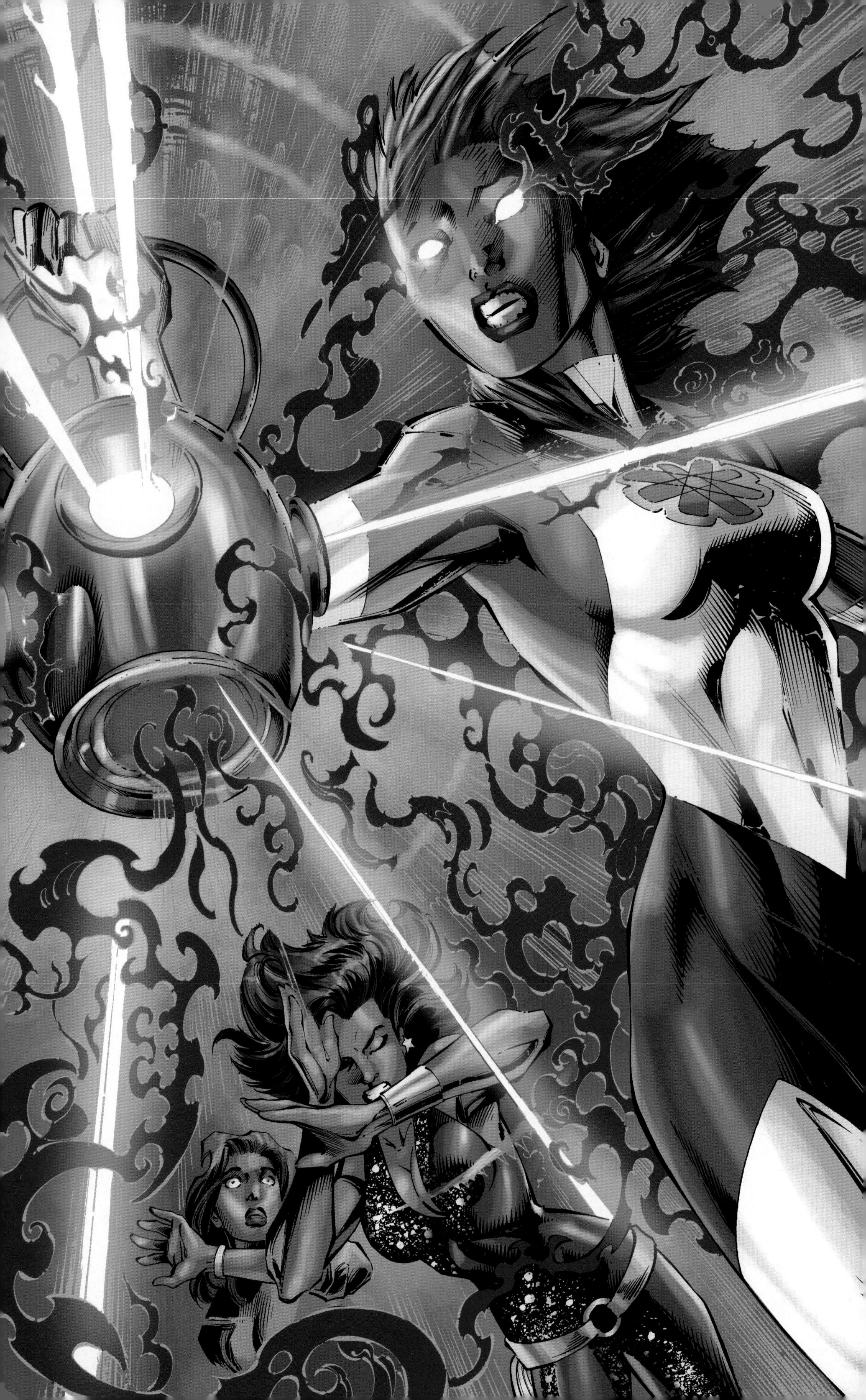

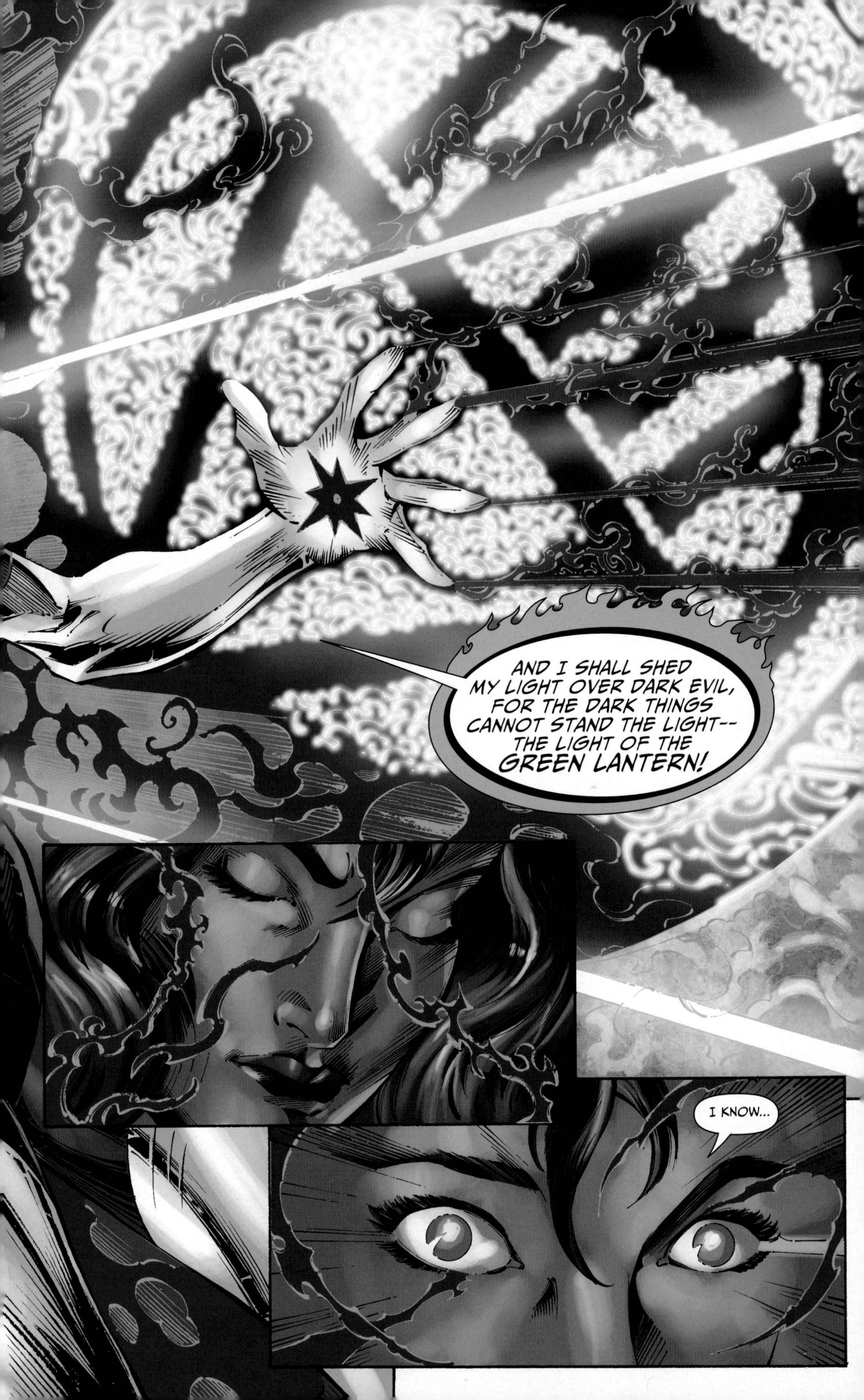
AND I SHALL SHED MY LIGHT OVER DARK EVIL, FOR THE DARK THINGS CANNOT STAND THE LIGHT-- THE LIGHT OF THE GREEN LANTERN!
I KNOW...

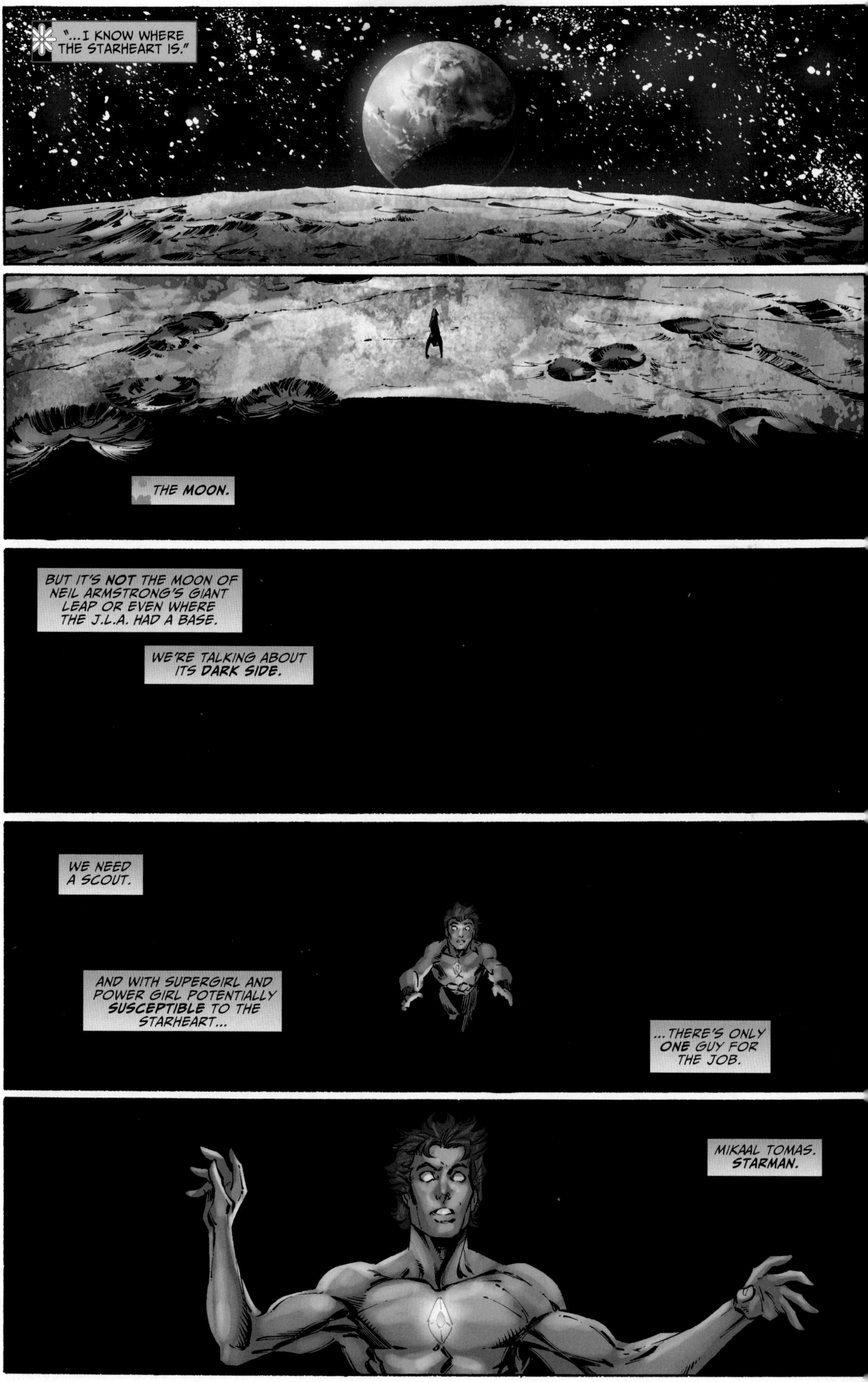
"...I KNOW WHERE THE STARHEART IS."
THE MOON.
BUT IT'S NOT THE MOON OF NEIL ARMSTRONG'S GIANT LEAP OR EVEN WHERE THE J.L.A. HAD A BASE.
WE'RE TALKING ABOUT ITS DARK SIDE.
WE NEED A SCOUT.
AND WITH SUPERGIRL AND POWER GIRL POTENTIALLY SUSCEPTIBLE TO THE STARHEART...
...THERE'S ONLY ONE GUY FOR THE JOB.
MIKAAL TOMAS. STARMAN.

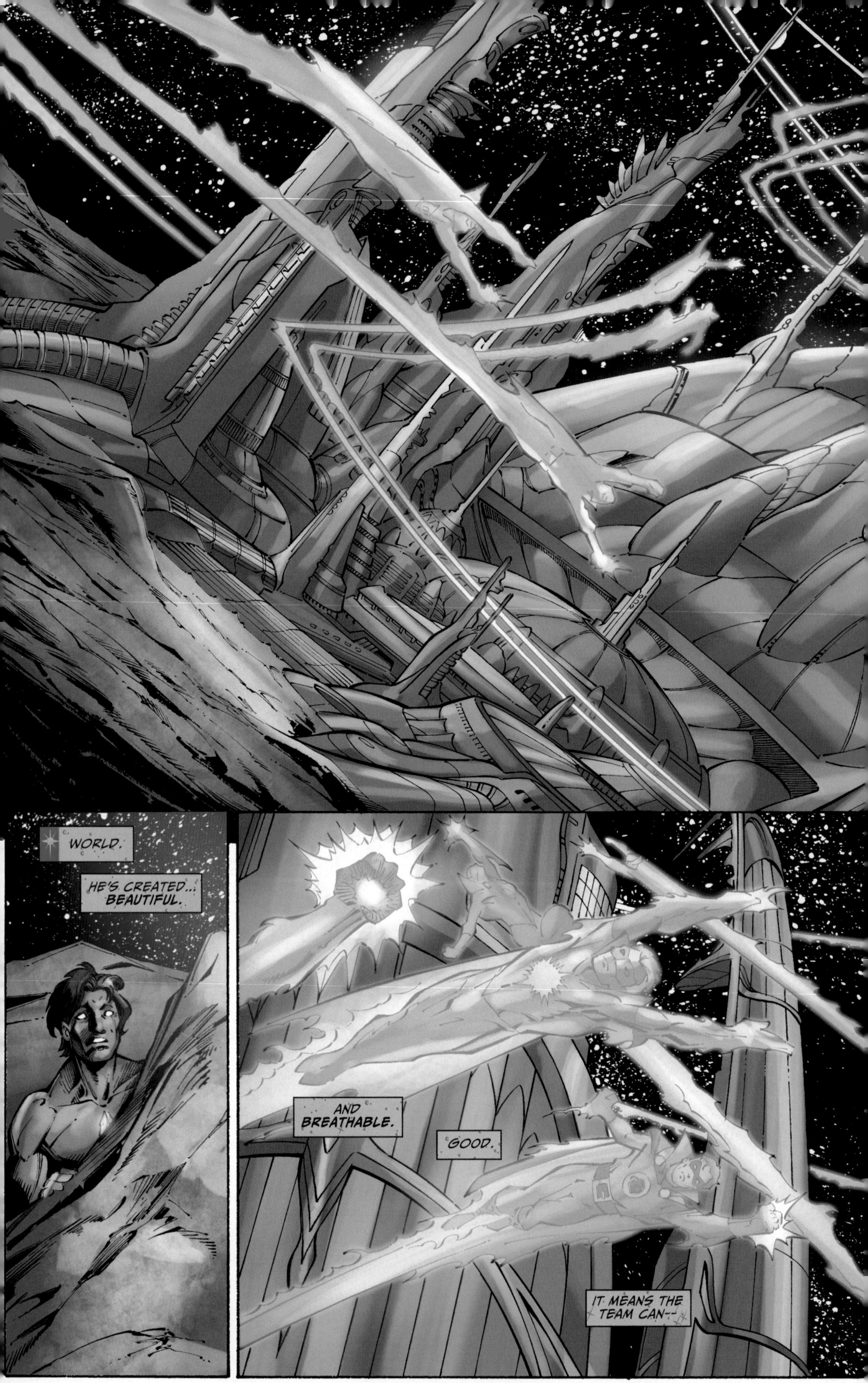
WORLD.
HE'S CREATED... BEAUTIFUL.
AND BREATHABLE.
GOOD.
IT MEANS THE TEAM CAN--

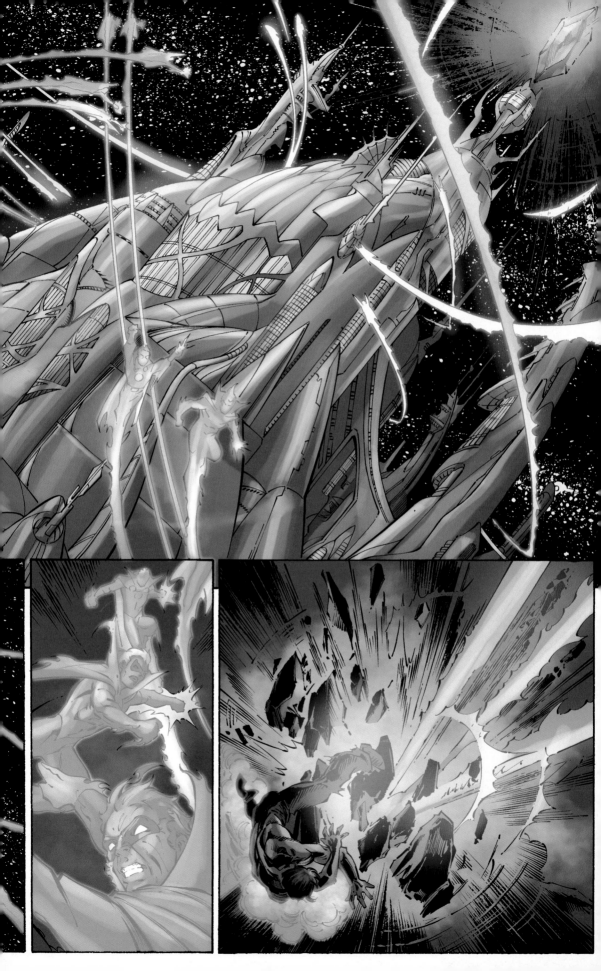

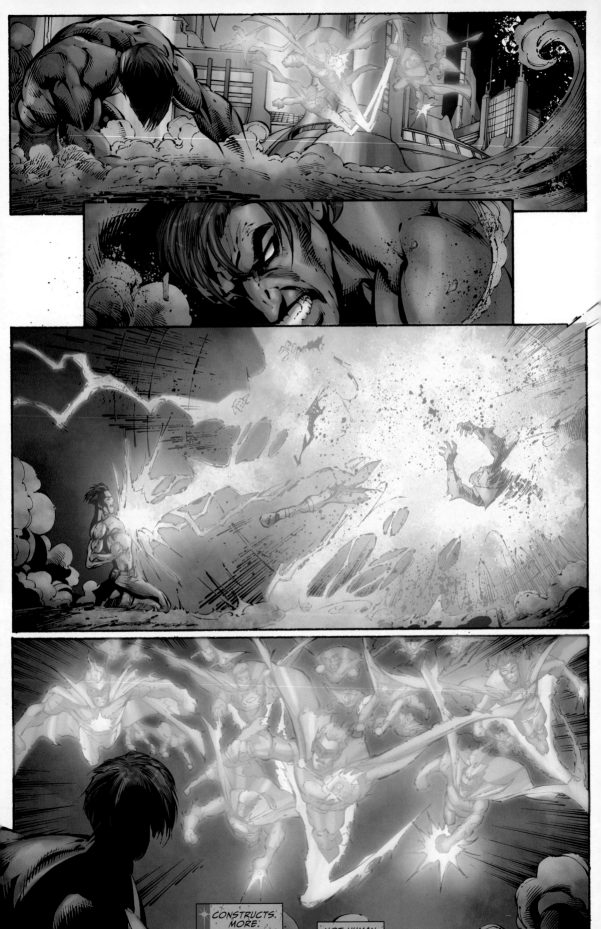

CONSTRUCTS. MORE.

NOT HUMAN. LIVING.

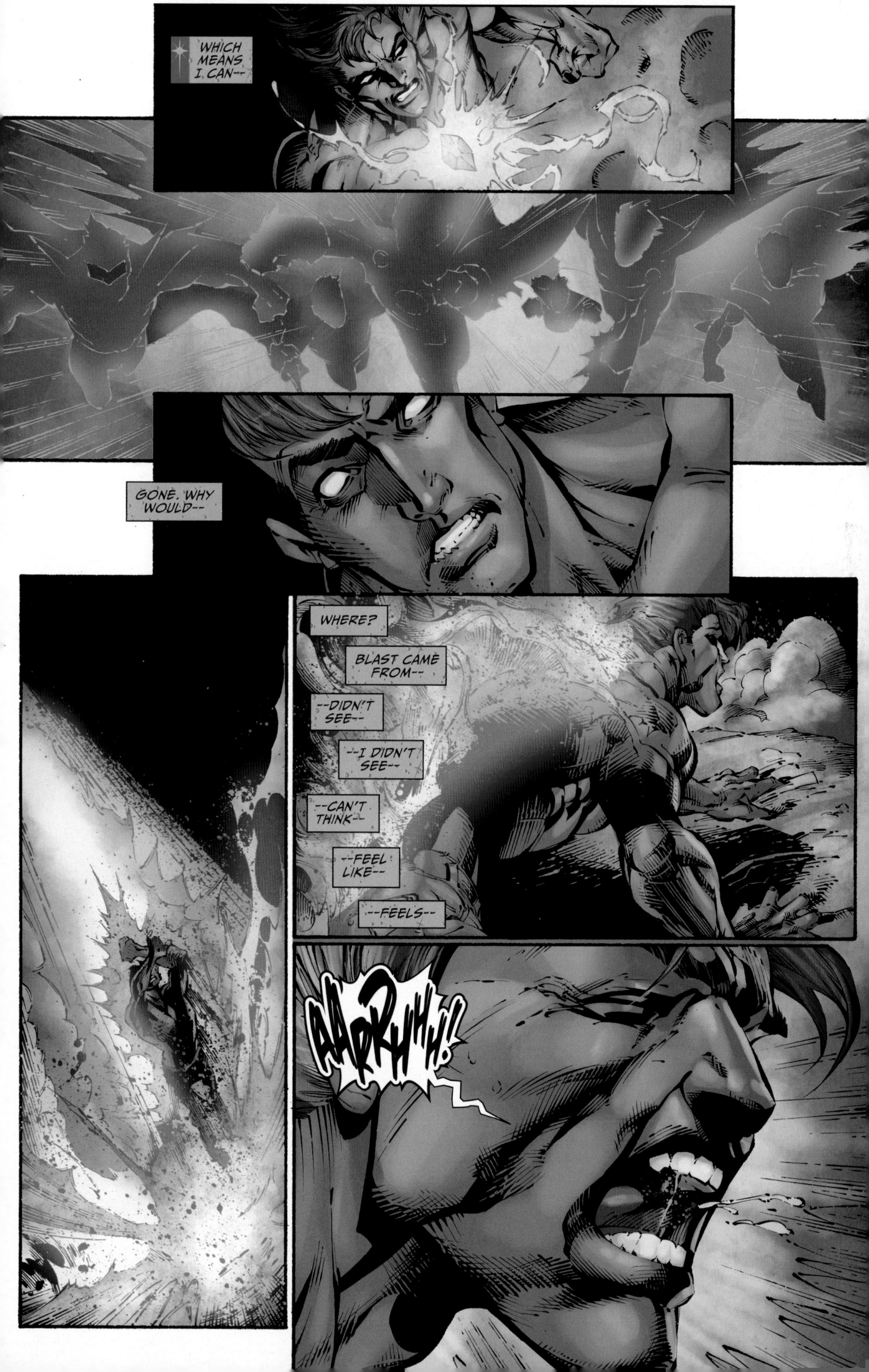
WHICH MEANS I CAN--
GONE. WHY WOULD--
WHERE?
BLAST CAME FROM--
--DIDN'T SEE--
--I DIDN'T SEE--
--CAN'T THINK--
--FEEL LIKE--
--FEELS--
AARRHHH!

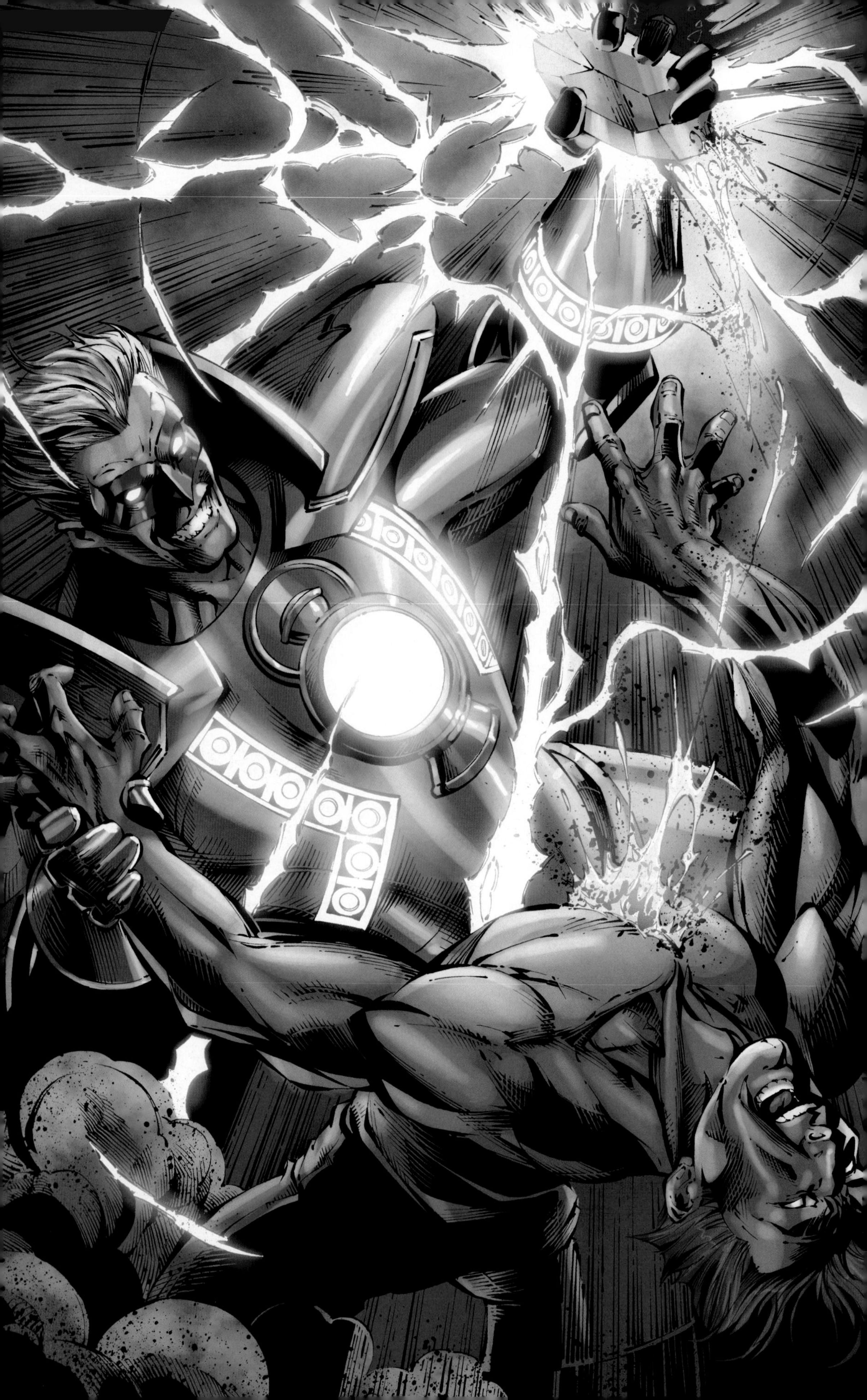

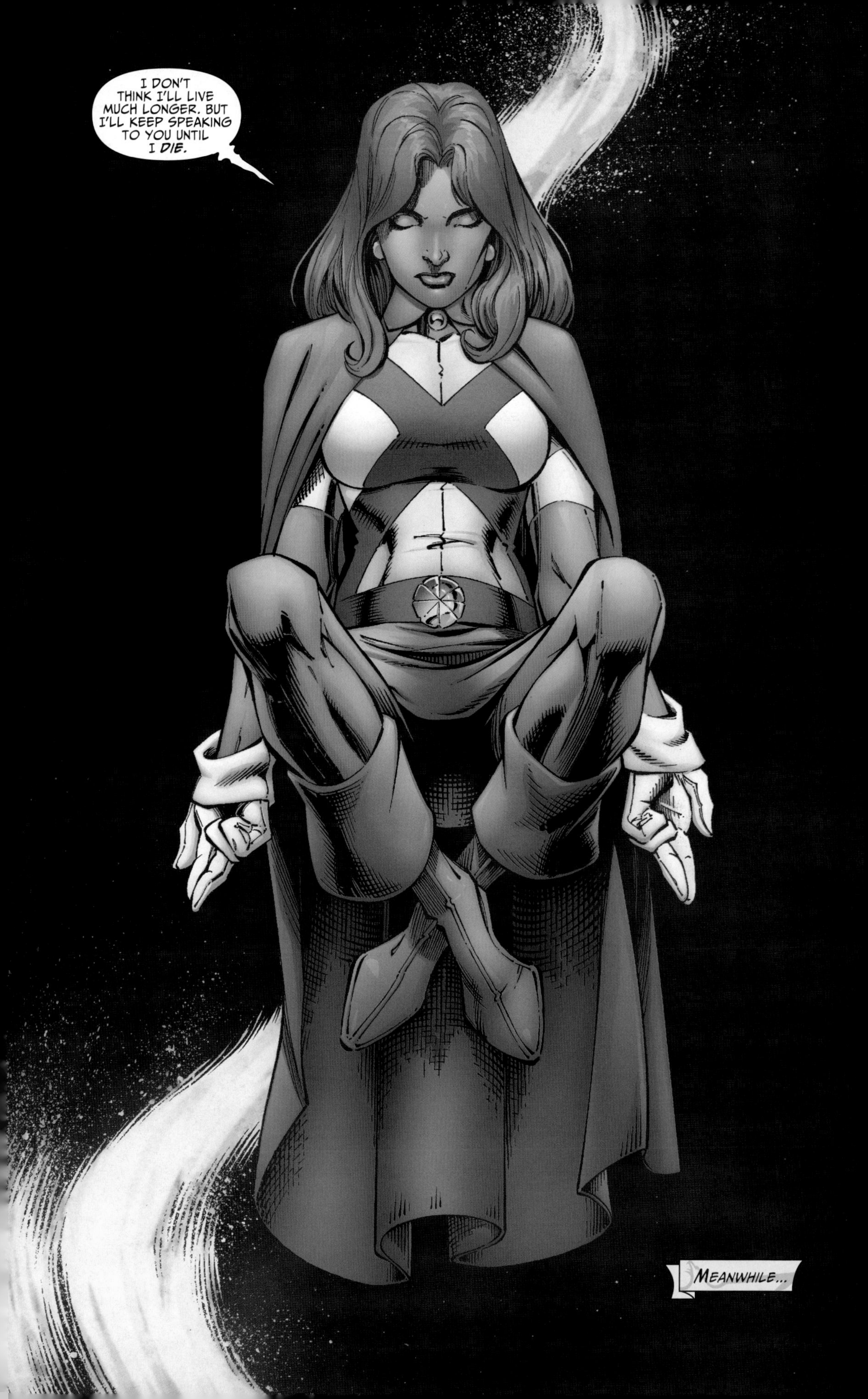
I DON'T THINK I'LL LIVE MUCH LONGER. BUT I'LL KEEP SPEAKING TO YOU UNTIL I *DIE*.
MEANWHILE...

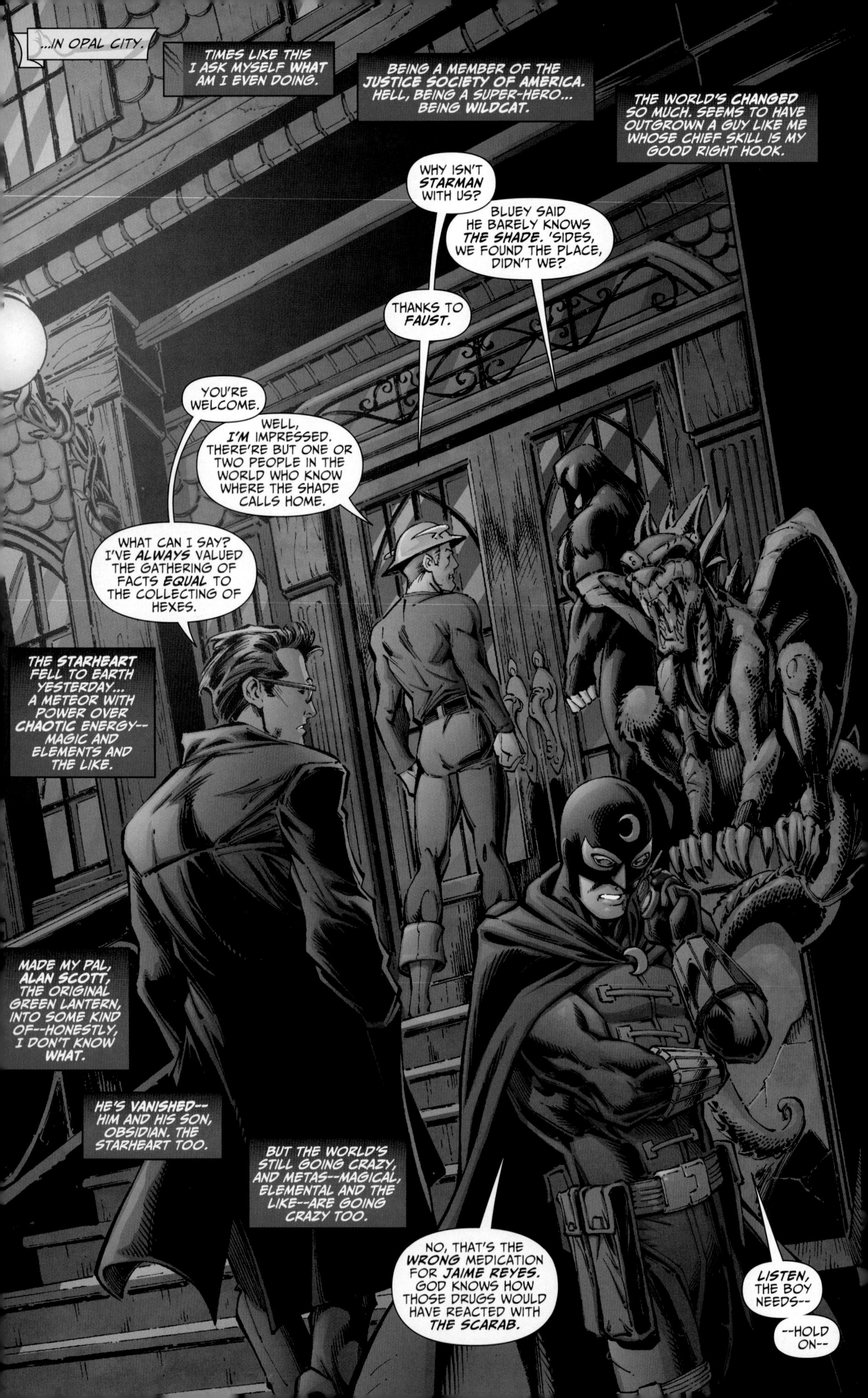
...IN OPAL CITY.
TIMES LIKE THIS I ASK MYSELF WHAT AM I EVEN DOING.
BEING A MEMBER OF THE JUSTICE SOCIETY OF AMERICA. HELL, BEING A SUPER-HERO... BEING WILDCAT.
THE WORLD'S CHANGED SO MUCH. SEEMS TO HAVE OUTGROWN A GUY LIKE ME WHOSE CHIEF SKILL IS MY GOOD RIGHT HOOK.
WHY ISN'T STARMAN WITH US?
BLUEY SAID HE BARELY KNOWS THE SHADE. 'SIDES, WE FOUND THE PLACE, DIDN'T WE?
THANKS TO FAUST.
YOU'RE WELCOME.
WELL, I'M IMPRESSED. THERE'RE BUT ONE OR TWO PEOPLE IN THE WORLD WHO KNOW WHERE THE SHADE CALLS HOME.
WHAT CAN I SAY? I'VE ALWAYS VALUED THE GATHERING OF FACTS EQUAL TO THE COLLECTING OF HEXES.
THE STARHEART FELL TO EARTH YESTERDAY... A METEOR WITH POWER OVER CHAOTIC ENERGY-- MAGIC AND ELEMENTS AND THE LIKE.
MADE MY PAL, ALAN SCOTT, THE ORIGINAL GREEN LANTERN, INTO SOME KIND OF--HONESTLY, I DON'T KNOW WHAT.
HE'S VANISHED-- HIM AND HIS SON, OBSIDIAN. THE STARHEART TOO.
BUT THE WORLD'S STILL GOING CRAZY, AND METAS--MAGICAL, ELEMENTAL AND THE LIKE--ARE GOING CRAZY TOO.
NO, THAT'S THE WRONG MEDICATION FOR JAIME REYES. GOD KNOWS HOW THOSE DRUGS WOULD HAVE REACTED WITH THE SCARAB.
LISTEN, THE BOY NEEDS--
--HOLD ON--

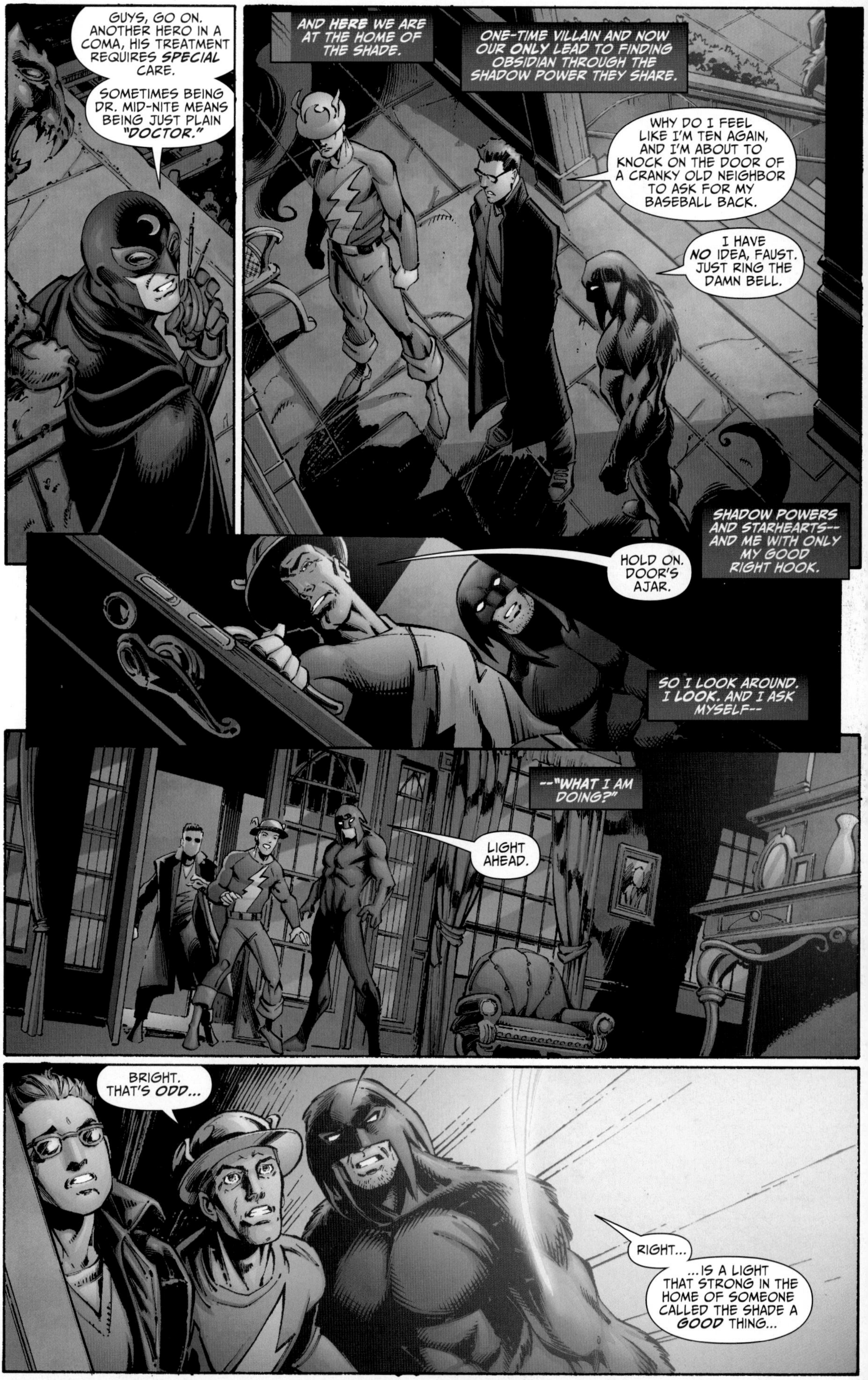
GUYS, GO ON. ANOTHER HERO IN A COMA, HIS TREATMENT REQUIRES SPECIAL CARE.
SOMETIMES BEING DR. MID-NITE MEANS BEING JUST PLAIN "DOCTOR."
AND HERE WE ARE AT THE HOME OF THE SHADE.
ONE-TIME VILLAIN AND NOW OUR ONLY LEAD TO FINDING OBSIDIAN THROUGH THE SHADOW POWER THEY SHARE.
WHY DO I FEEL LIKE I'M TEN AGAIN, AND I'M ABOUT TO KNOCK ON THE DOOR OF A CRANKY OLD NEIGHBOR TO ASK FOR MY BASEBALL BACK.
I HAVE NO IDEA, FAUST. JUST RING THE DAMN BELL.
SHADOW POWERS AND STARHEARTS-- AND ME WITH ONLY MY GOOD RIGHT HOOK.
HOLD ON. DOOR'S AJAR.
SO I LOOK AROUND. I LOOK. AND I ASK MYSELF--
--"WHAT I AM DOING?"
LIGHT AHEAD.
BRIGHT. THAT'S ODD...
RIGHT...
...IS A LIGHT THAT STRONG IN THE HOME OF SOMEONE CALLED THE SHADE A GOOD THING...

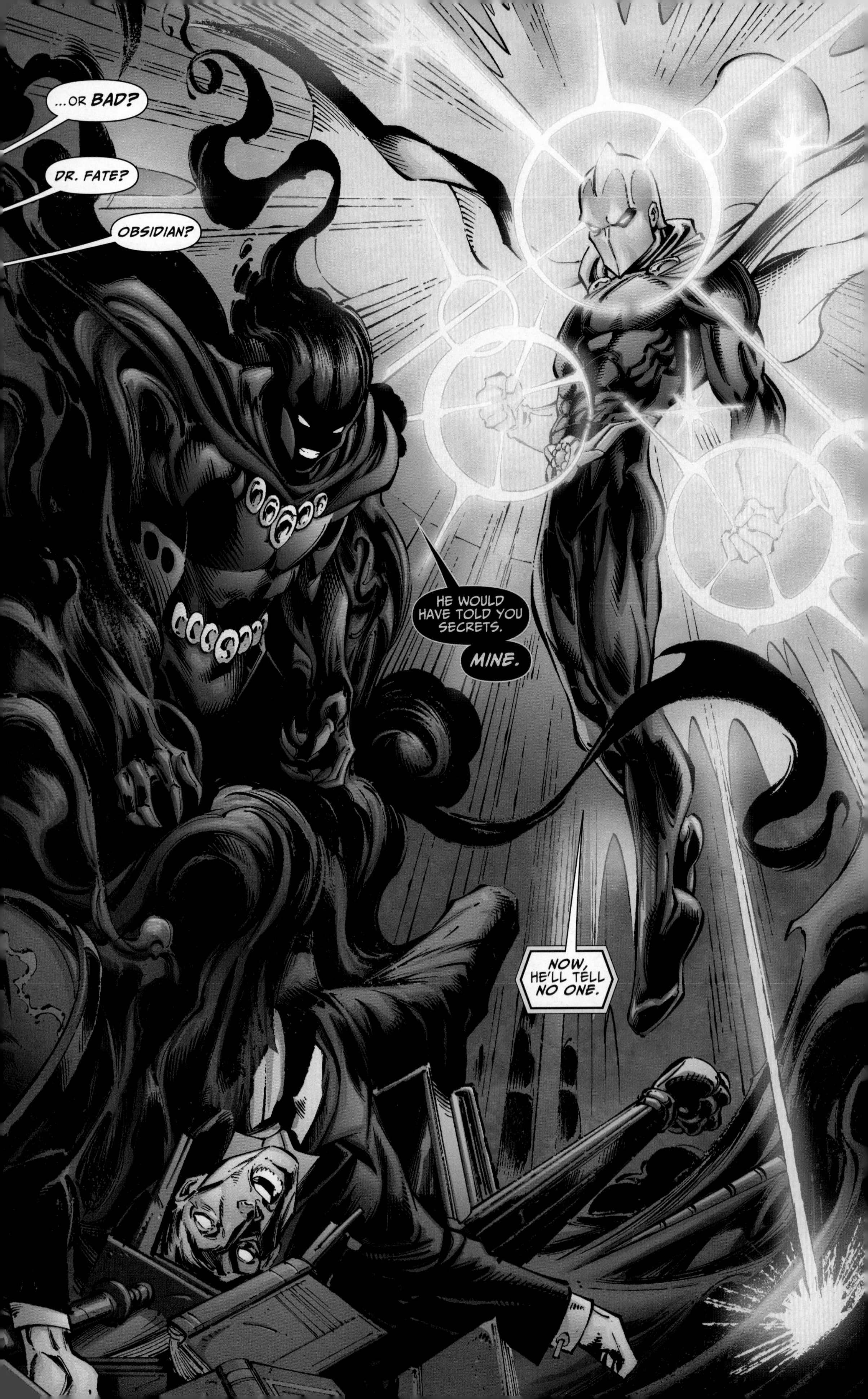
...OR BAD?
DR. FATE?
OBSIDIAN?
HE WOULD HAVE TOLD YOU SECRETS.
MINE.
NOW, HE'LL TELL NO ONE.

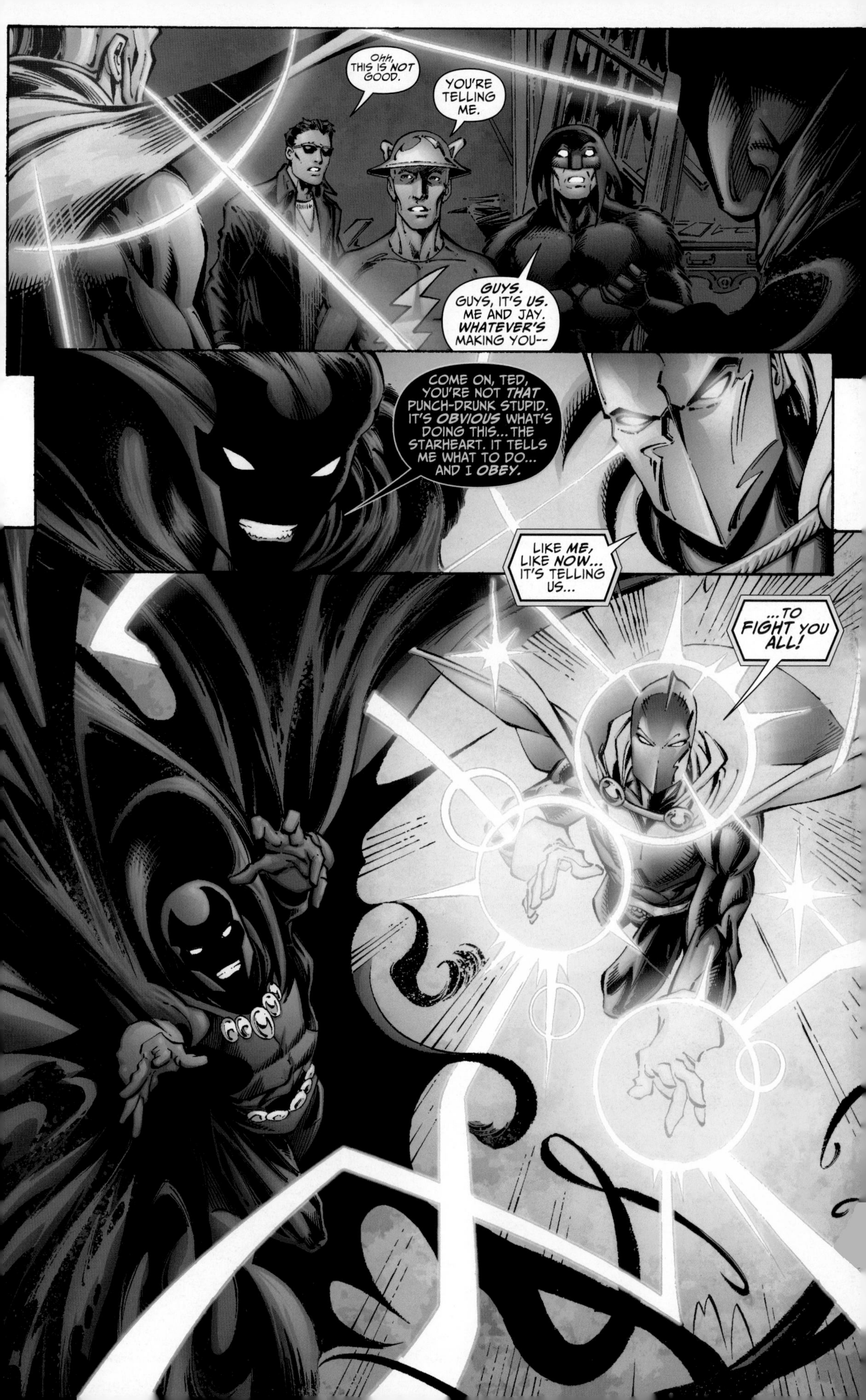

OHH, THIS IS NOT GOOD.
YOU'RE TELLING ME.
GUYS. GUYS, IT'S US. ME AND JAY. WHATEVER'S MAKING YOU--
COME ON, TED, YOU'RE NOT THAT PUNCH-DRUNK STUPID. IT'S OBVIOUS WHAT'S DOING THIS...THE STARHEART. IT TELLS ME WHAT TO DO... AND I OBEY.
LIKE ME, LIKE NOW... IT'S TELLING US...
...TO FIGHT YOU ALL!

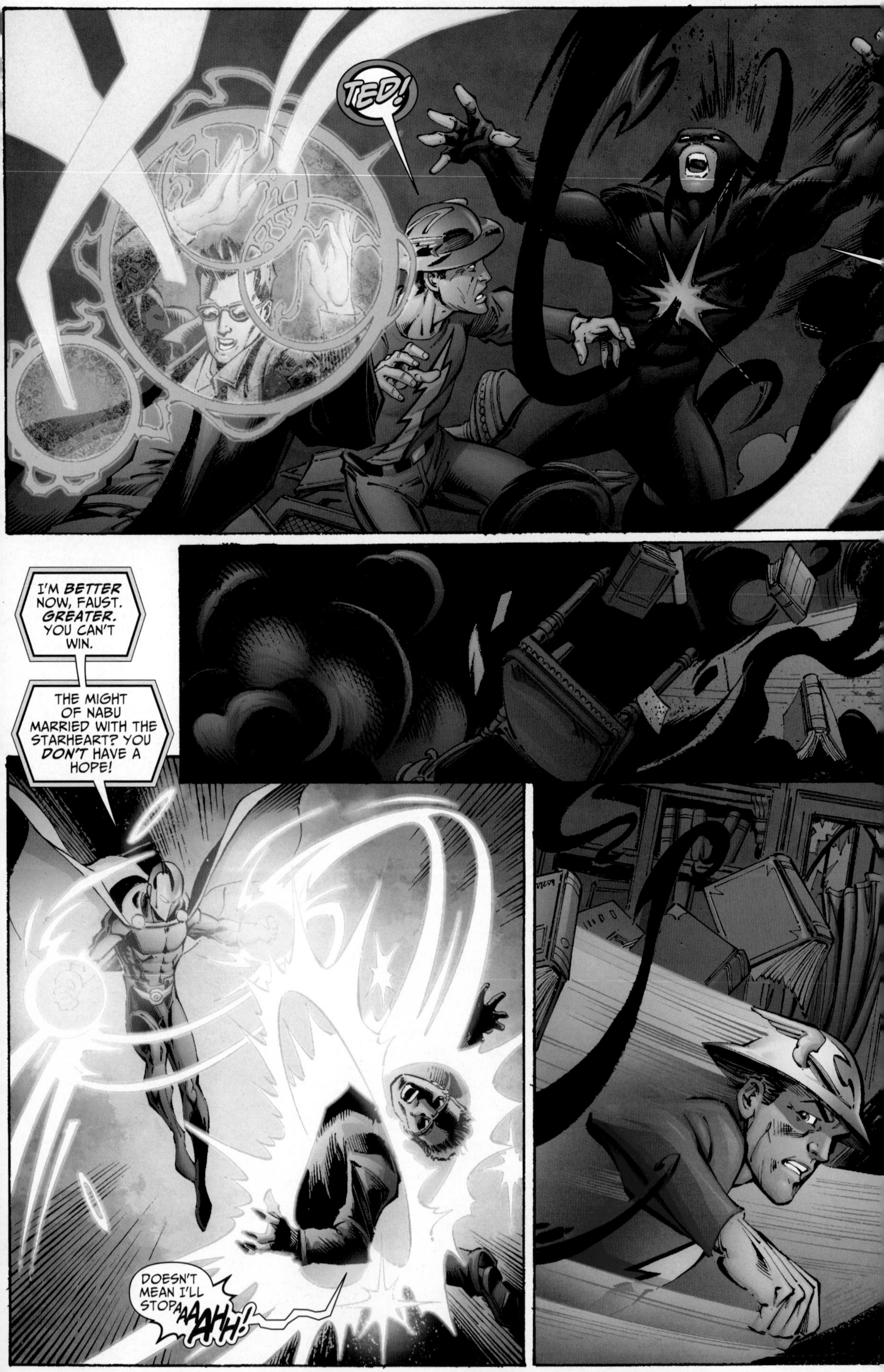
TED!
I'M BETTER NOW, FAUST. GREATER. YOU CAN'T WIN.
THE MIGHT OF NABU MARRIED WITH THE STARHEART? YOU DON'T HAVE A HOPE!
DOESN'T MEAN I'LL STOPAAAAHH!

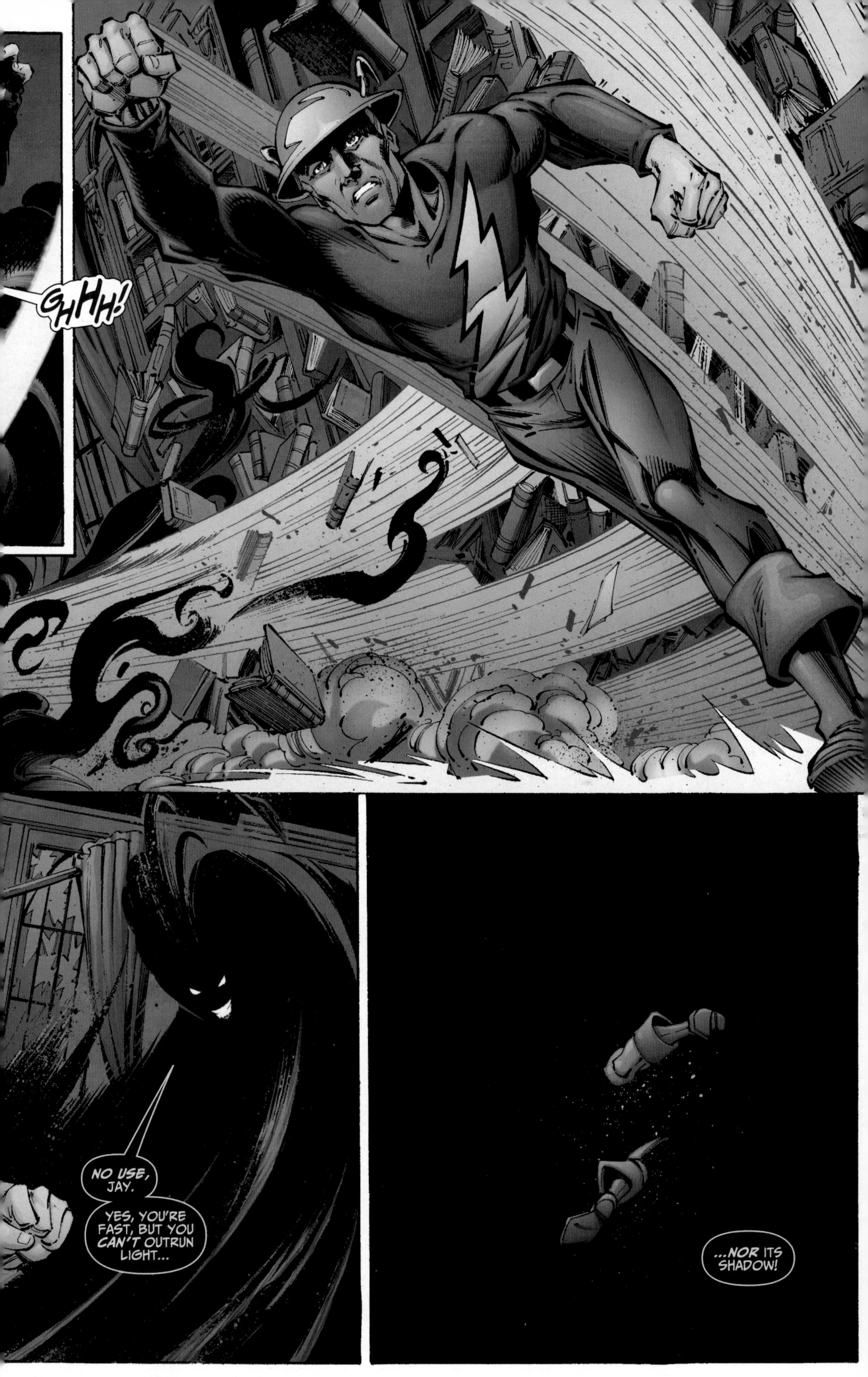
GHHH!
NO USE, JAY.
YES, YOU'RE FAST, BUT YOU CAN'T OUTRUN LIGHT...
...NOR ITS SHADOW!

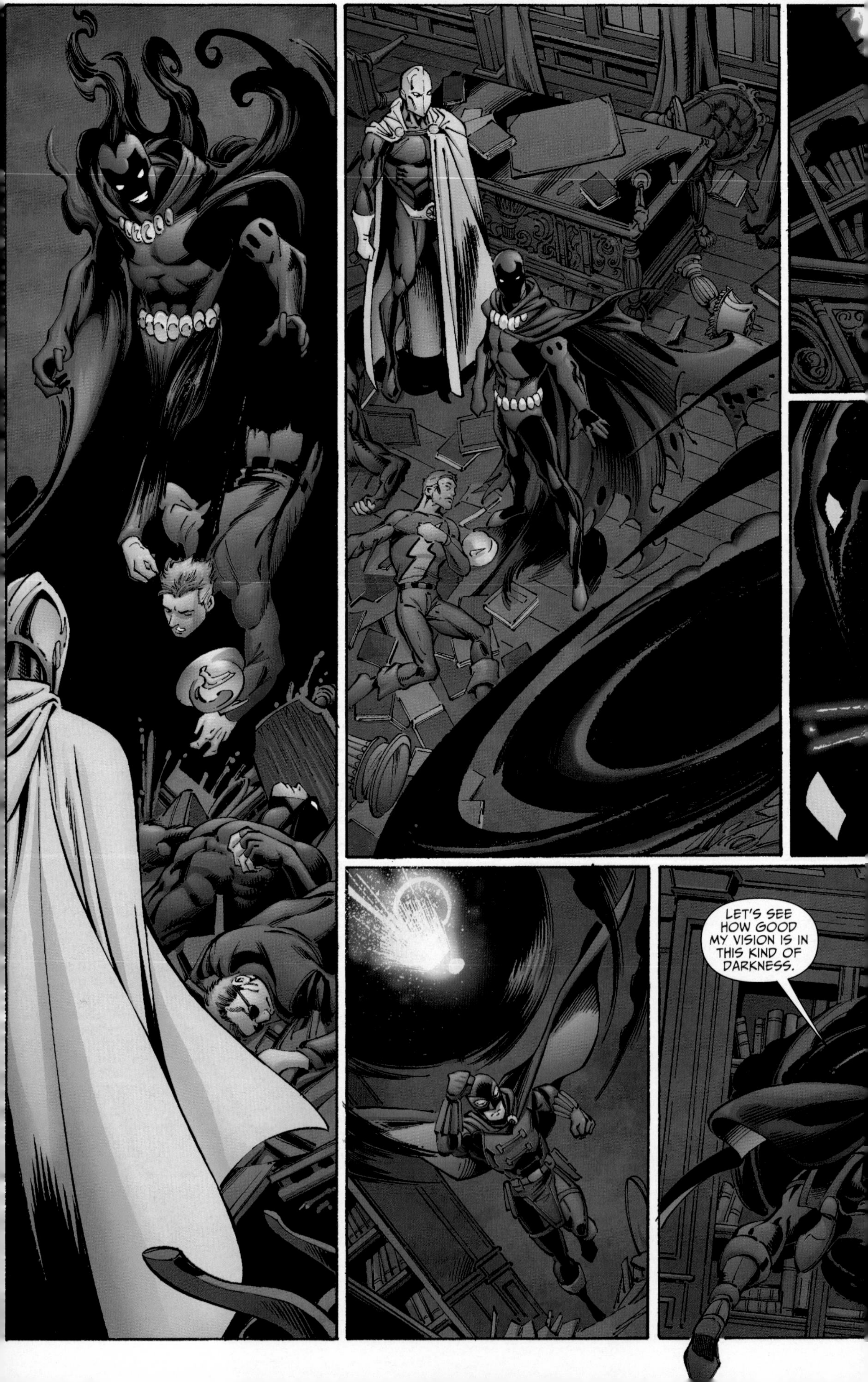
LET'S SEE HOW GOOD MY VISION IS IN THIS KIND OF DARKNESS.

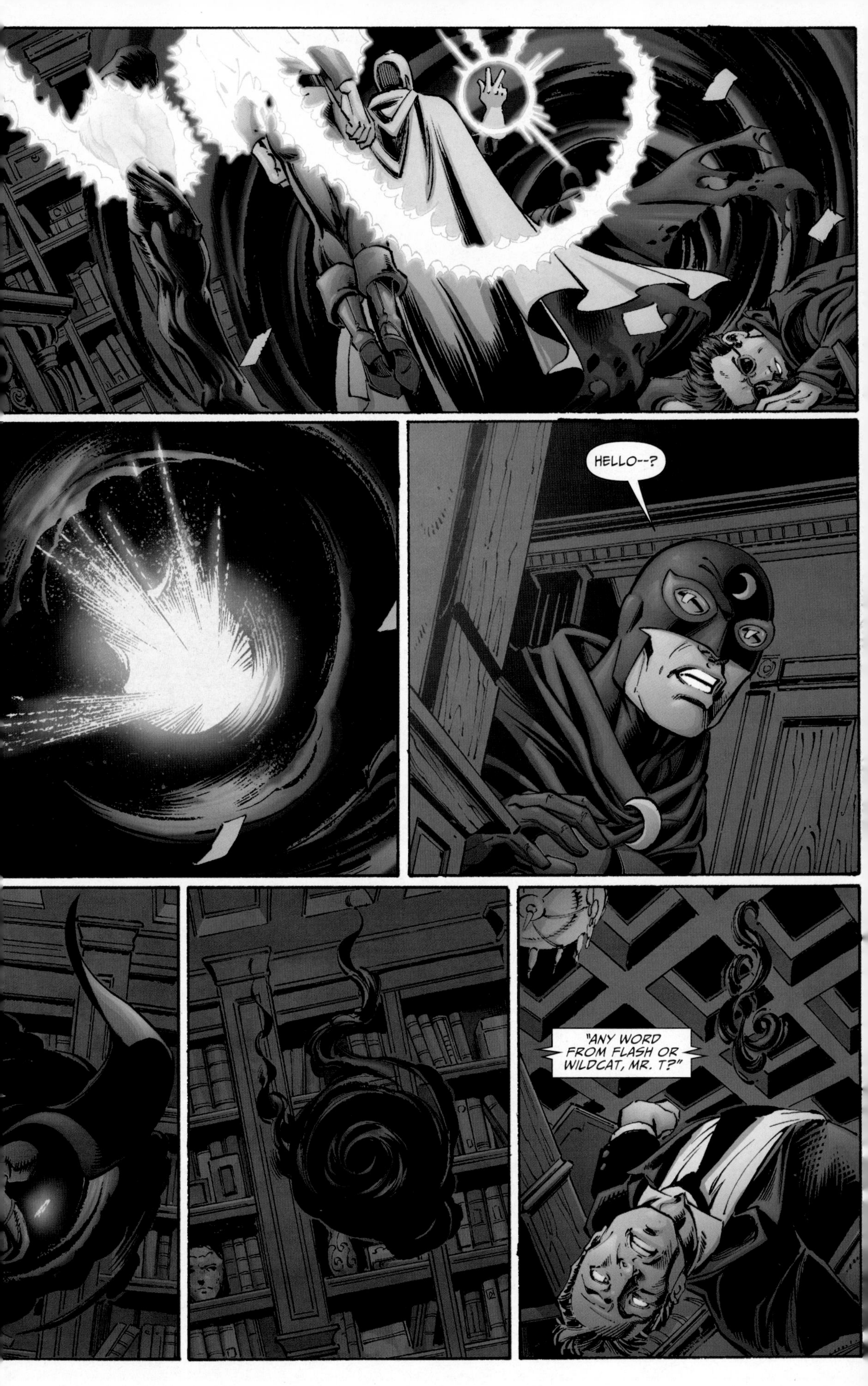
HELLO--?
"ANY WORD FROM FLASH OR WILDCAT, MR. T?"

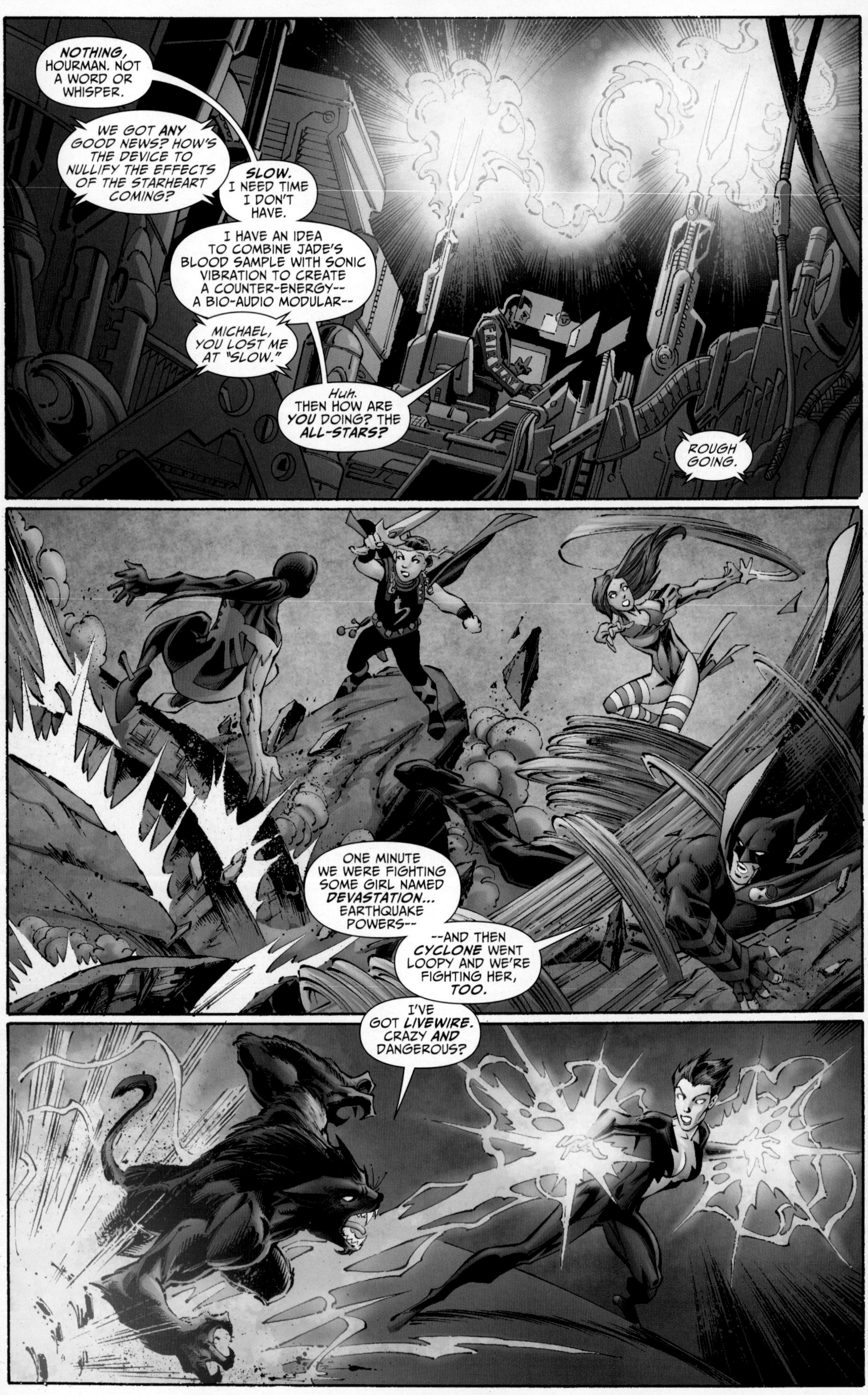
NOTHING, HOURMAN. NOT A WORD OR WHISPER.
WE GOT ANY GOOD NEWS? HOW'S THE DEVICE TO NULLIFY THE EFFECTS OF THE STARHEART COMING?
SLOW. I NEED TIME I DON'T HAVE.
I HAVE AN IDEA TO COMBINE JADE'S BLOOD SAMPLE WITH SONIC VIBRATION TO CREATE A COUNTER-ENERGY-- A BIO-AUDIO MODULAR--
MICHAEL, YOU LOST ME AT "SLOW."
Huh. THEN HOW ARE YOU DOING? THE ALL-STARS?
ROUGH GOING.
ONE MINUTE WE WERE FIGHTING SOME GIRL NAMED DEVASTATION... EARTHQUAKE POWERS--
--AND THEN CYCLONE WENT LOOPY AND WE'RE FIGHTING HER, TOO.
I'VE GOT LIVEWIRE. CRAZY AND DANGEROUS?

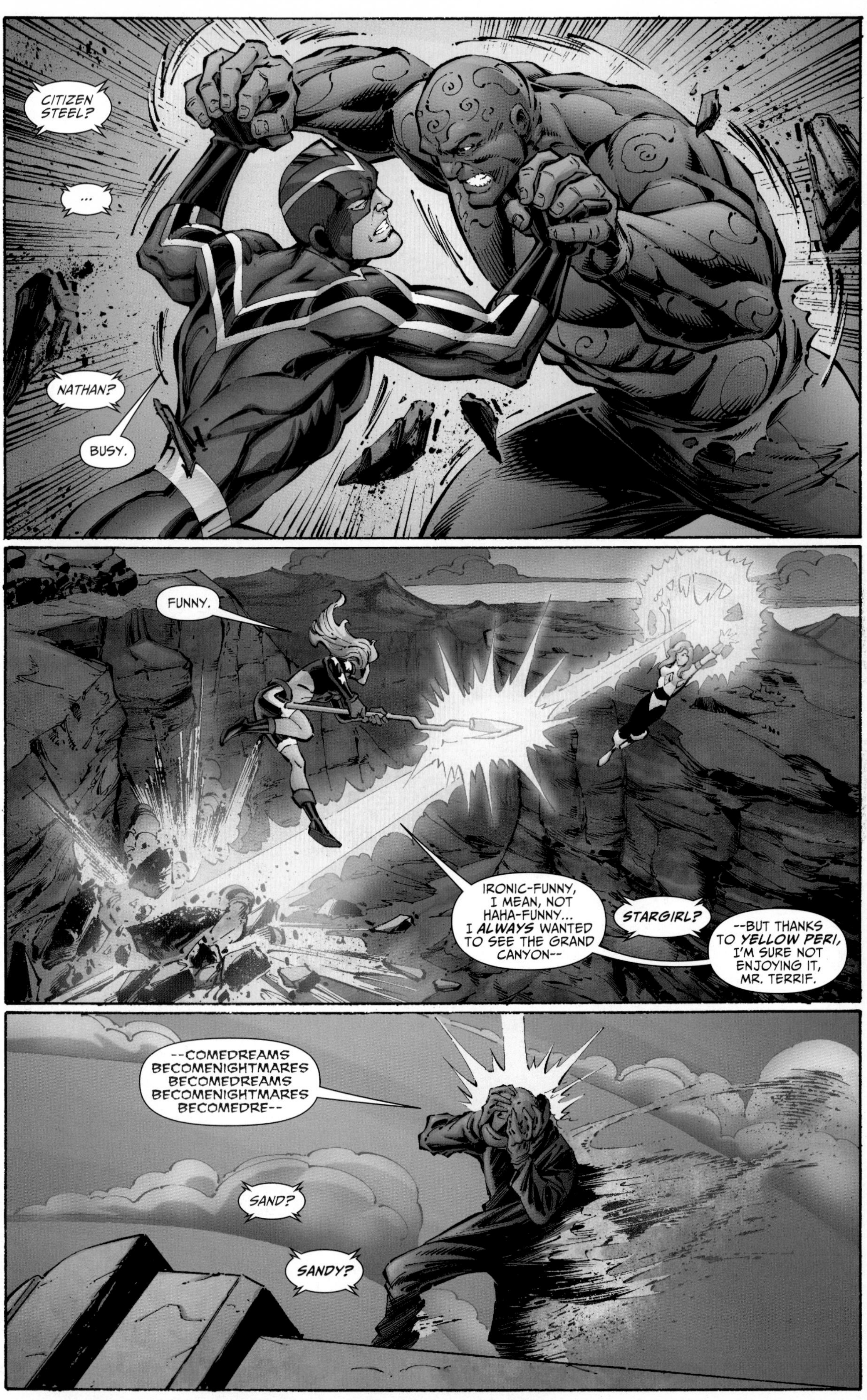
CITIZEN STEEL?
...
NATHAN?
BUSY.
FUNNY.
IRONIC-FUNNY, I MEAN, NOT HAHA-FUNNY... I ALWAYS WANTED TO SEE THE GRAND CANYON--
STARGIRL?
--BUT THANKS TO YELLOW PERI, I'M SURE NOT ENJOYING IT, MR. TERRIF.
--COMEDREAMS BECOMENIGHTMARES BECOMEDREAMS BECOMENIGHTMARES BECOMEDRE--
SAND?
SANDY?

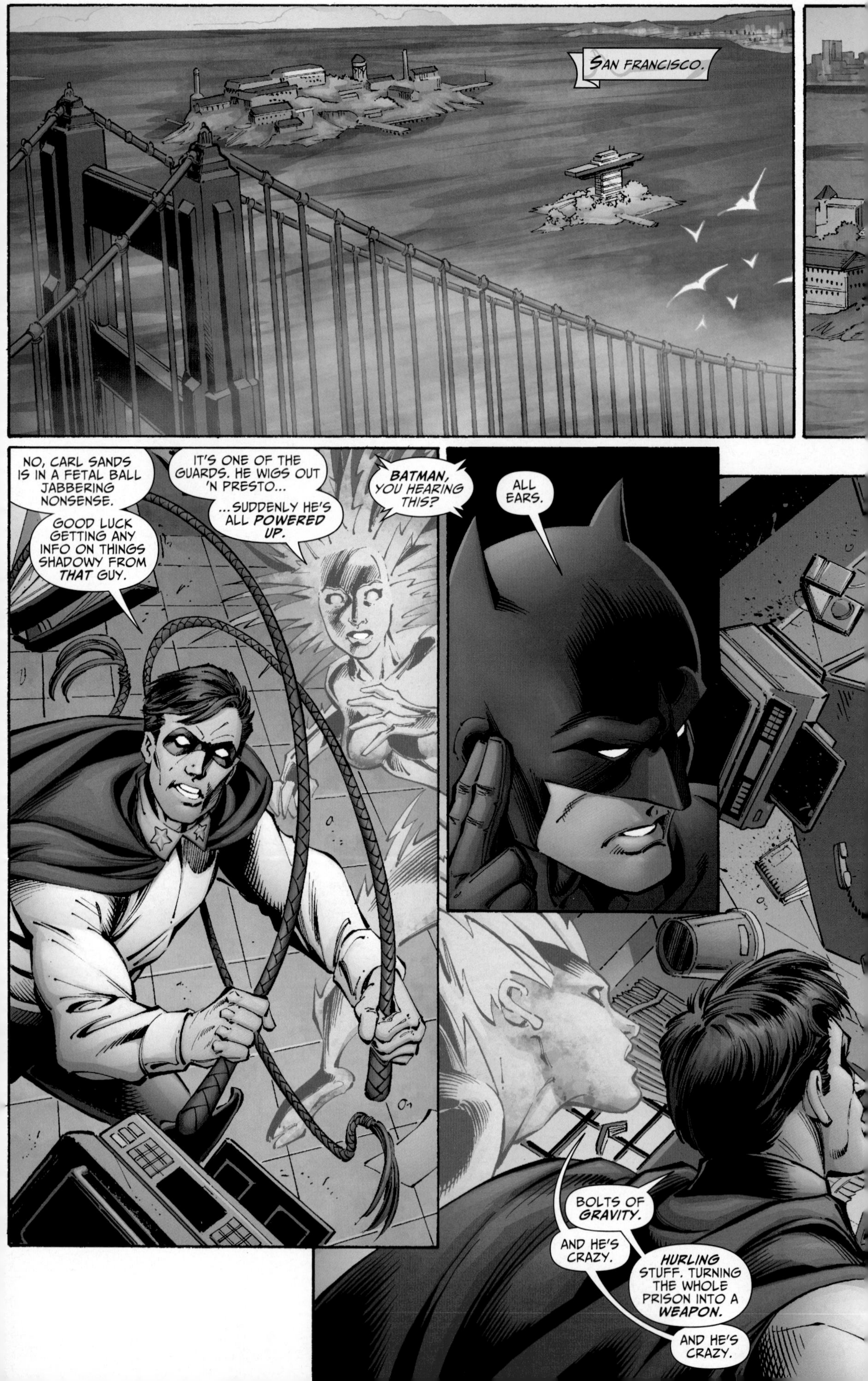
SAN FRANCISCO.
NO, CARL SANDS IS IN A FETAL BALL JABBERING NONSENSE.
GOOD LUCK GETTING ANY INFO ON THINGS SHADOWY FROM THAT GUY.
IT'S ONE OF THE GUARDS. HE WIGS OUT 'N PRESTO...
...SUDDENLY HE'S ALL POWERED UP.
BATMAN, YOU HEARING THIS?
ALL EARS.
BOLTS OF GRAVITY.
AND HE'S CRAZY.
HURLING STUFF. TURNING THE WHOLE PRISON INTO A WEAPON.
AND HE'S CRAZY.

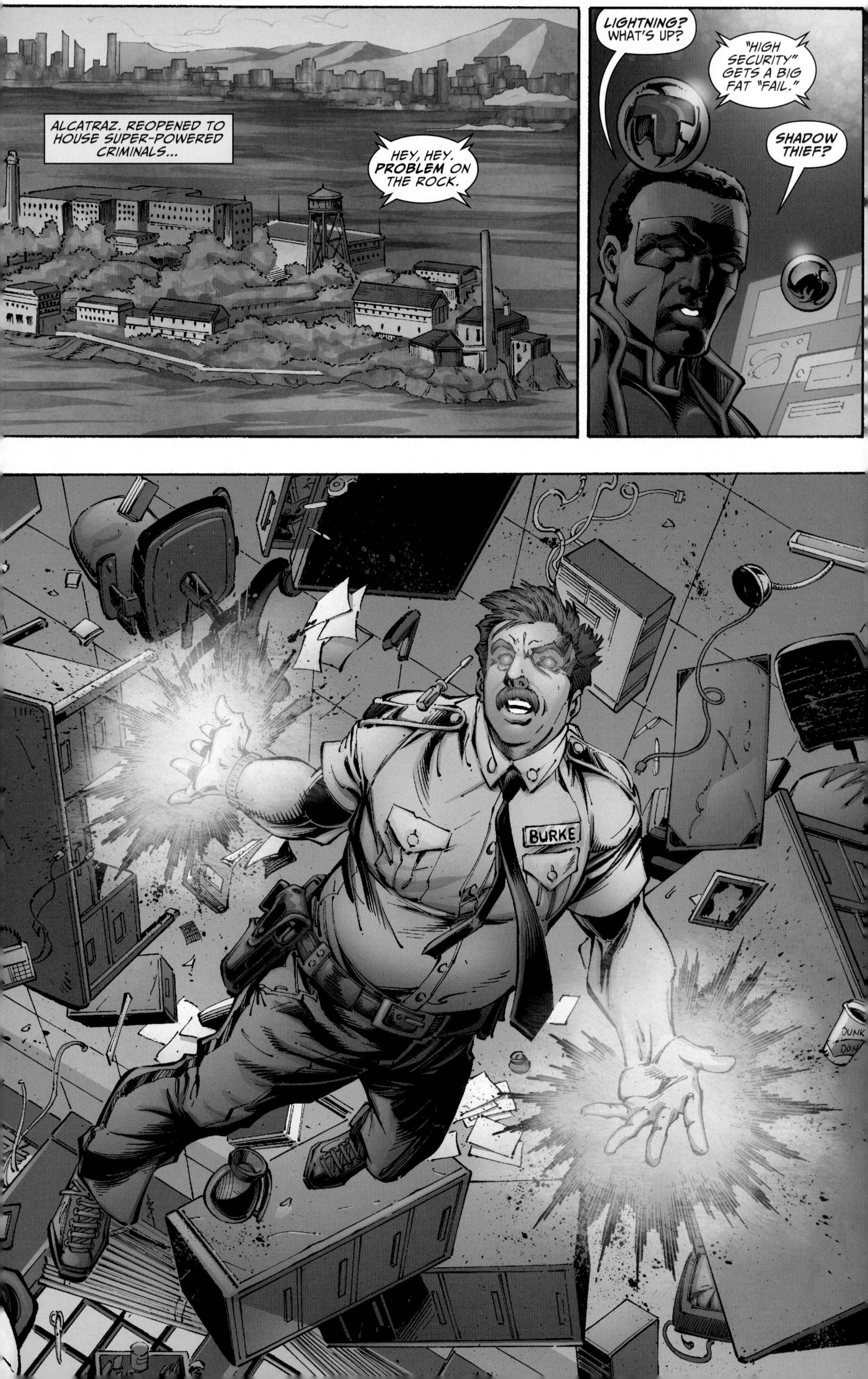
ALCATRAZ. REOPENED TO HOUSE SUPER-POWERED CRIMINALS...
HEY, HEY. **PROBLEM** ON THE ROCK.
LIGHTNING? WHAT'S UP?
"HIGH SECURITY" GETS A BIG FAT "FAIL."
SHADOW THIEF?
BURKE
DUNK DON

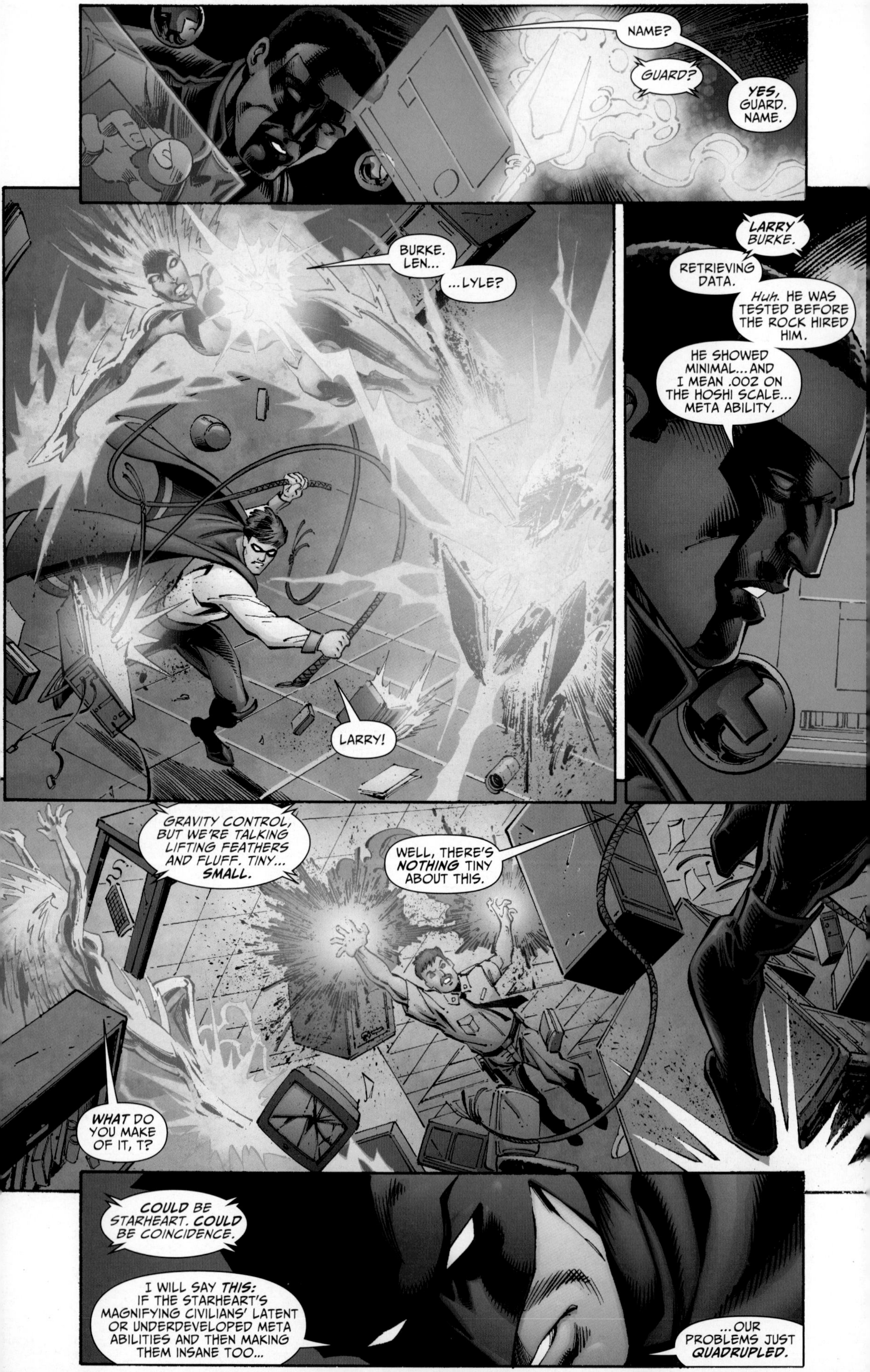
NAME?
GUARD?
YES, GUARD. NAME.
BURKE. LEN...
...LYLE?
LARRY!
LARRY BURKE.
RETRIEVING DATA.
Huh. HE WAS TESTED BEFORE THE ROCK HIRED HIM.
HE SHOWED MINIMAL... AND I MEAN .002 ON THE HOSHI SCALE... META ABILITY.
GRAVITY CONTROL, BUT WE'RE TALKING LIFTING FEATHERS AND FLUFF. TINY... SMALL.
WELL, THERE'S NOTHING TINY ABOUT THIS.
WHAT DO YOU MAKE OF IT, T?
COULD BE STARHEART. COULD BE COINCIDENCE.
I WILL SAY THIS: IF THE STARHEART'S MAGNIFYING CIVILIANS' LATENT OR UNDERDEVELOPED META ABILITIES AND THEN MAKING THEM INSANE TOO...
...OUR PROBLEMS JUST QUADRUPLED.

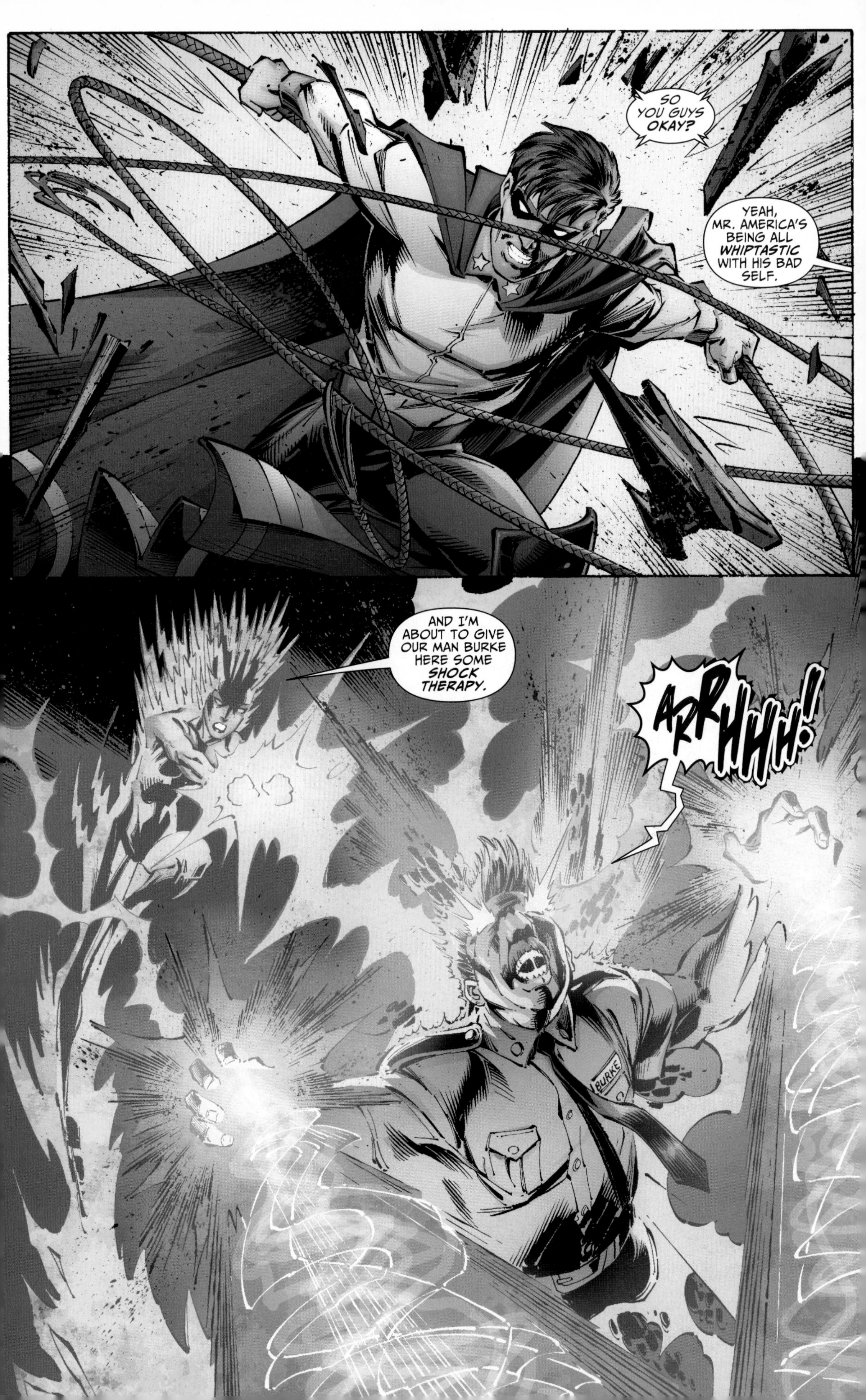
SO YOU GUYS OKAY?
YEAH, MR. AMERICA'S BEING ALL WHIPTASTIC WITH HIS BAD SELF.
AND I'M ABOUT TO GIVE OUR MAN BURKE HERE SOME SHOCK THERAPY.
ARRHHHH!!
BURKE

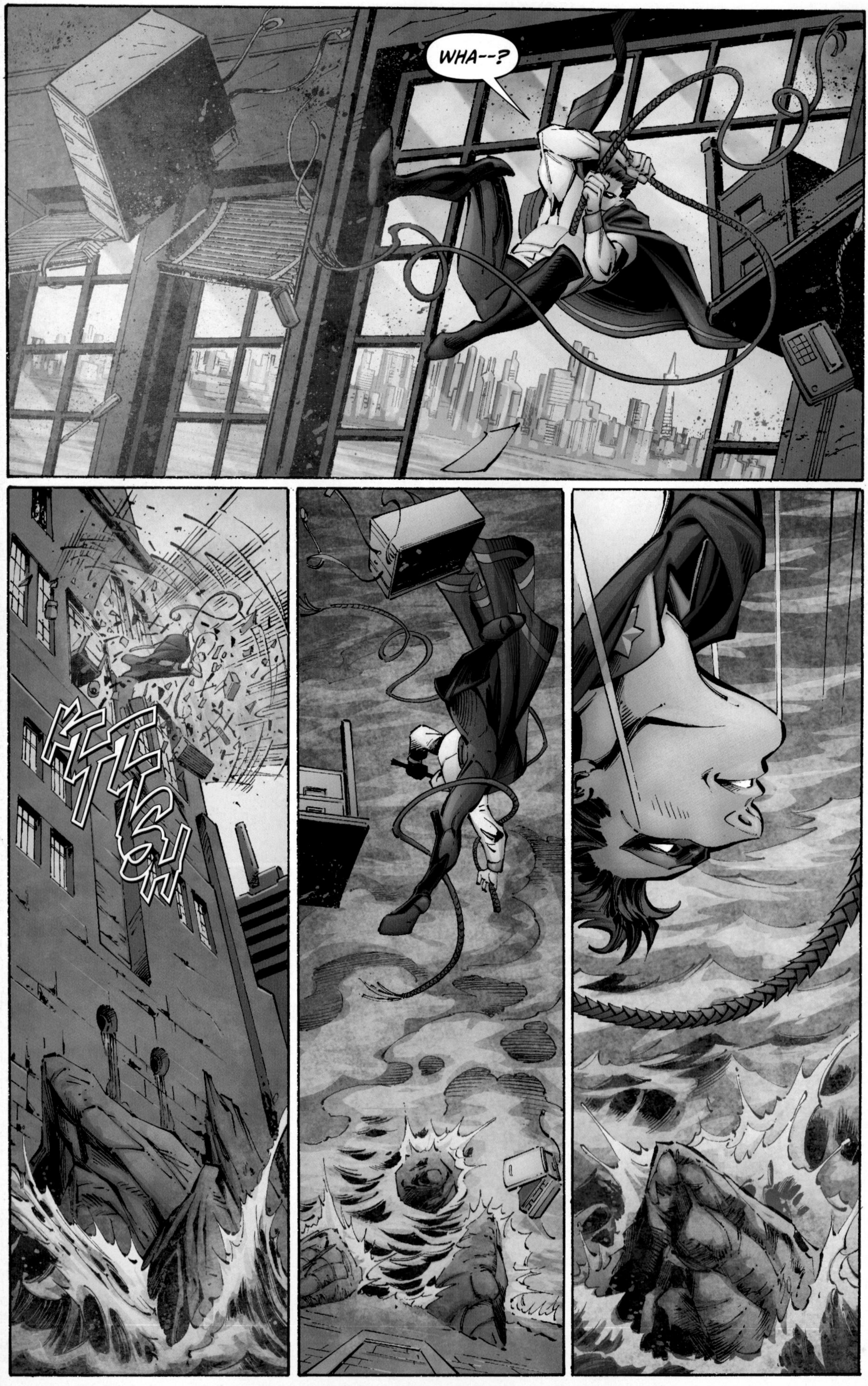
WHA--?
KRSSH

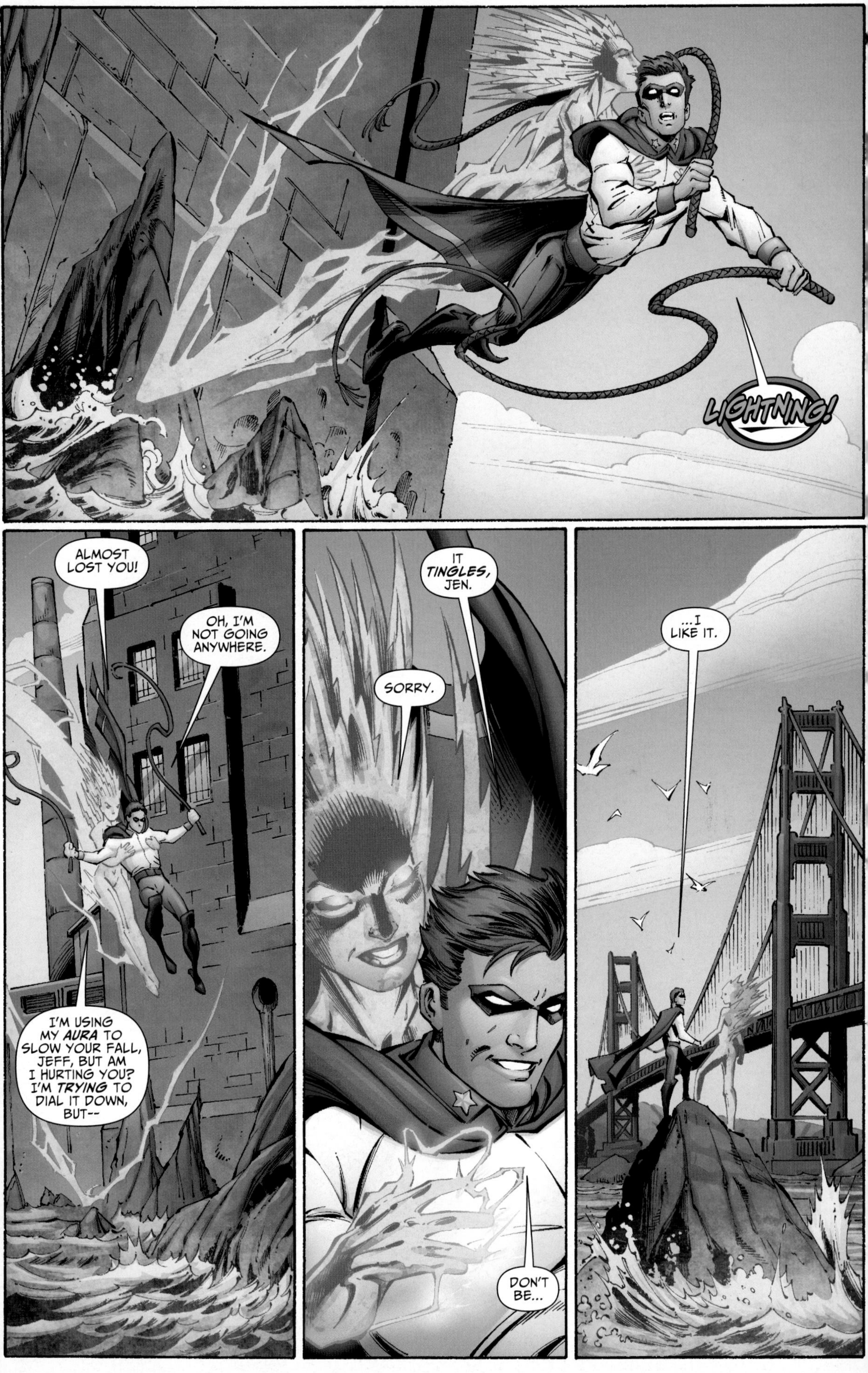
LIGHTNING!
ALMOST LOST YOU!
OH, I'M NOT GOING ANYWHERE.
I'M USING MY *AURA* TO SLOW YOUR FALL, JEFF, BUT AM I HURTING YOU? I'M *TRYING* TO DIAL IT DOWN, BUT--
IT *TINGLES,* JEN.
SORRY.
DON'T BE...
...I LIKE IT.

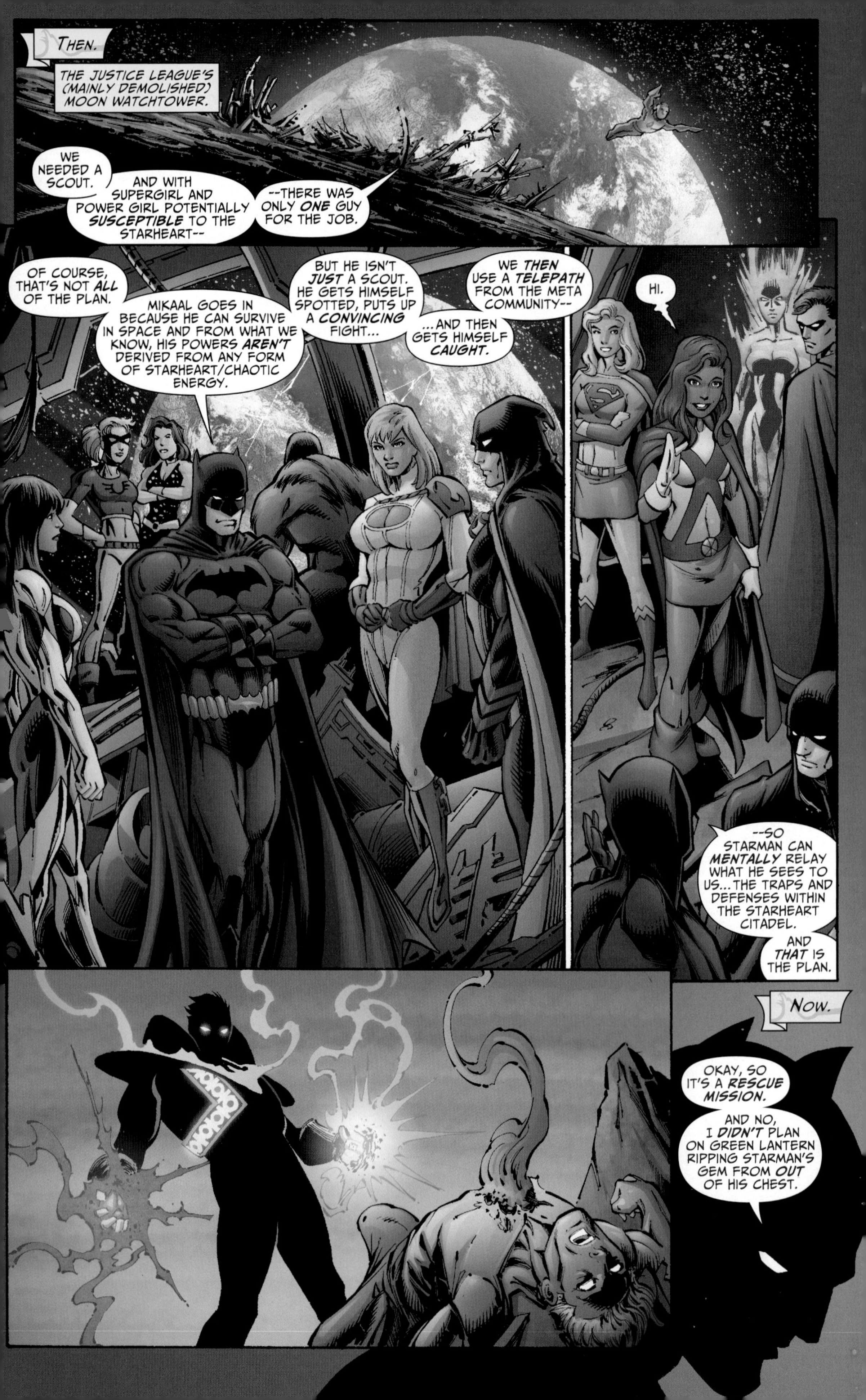
THEN.
THE JUSTICE LEAGUE'S (MAINLY DEMOLISHED) MOON WATCHTOWER.
WE NEEDED A SCOUT.
AND WITH SUPERGIRL AND POWER GIRL POTENTIALLY SUSCEPTIBLE TO THE STARHEART--
--THERE WAS ONLY ONE GUY FOR THE JOB.
OF COURSE, THAT'S NOT ALL OF THE PLAN.
MIKAAL GOES IN BECAUSE HE CAN SURVIVE IN SPACE AND FROM WHAT WE KNOW, HIS POWERS AREN'T DERIVED FROM ANY FORM OF STARHEART/CHAOTIC ENERGY.
BUT HE ISN'T JUST A SCOUT. HE GETS HIMSELF SPOTTED, PUTS UP A CONVINCING FIGHT...
...AND THEN GETS HIMSELF CAUGHT.
WE THEN USE A TELEPATH FROM THE META COMMUNITY--
HI.
--SO STARMAN CAN MENTALLY RELAY WHAT HE SEES TO US...THE TRAPS AND DEFENSES WITHIN THE STARHEART CITADEL.
AND THAT IS THE PLAN.
NOW.
OKAY, SO IT'S A RESCUE MISSION.
AND NO, I DIDN'T PLAN ON GREEN LANTERN RIPPING STARMAN'S GEM FROM OUT OF HIS CHEST.

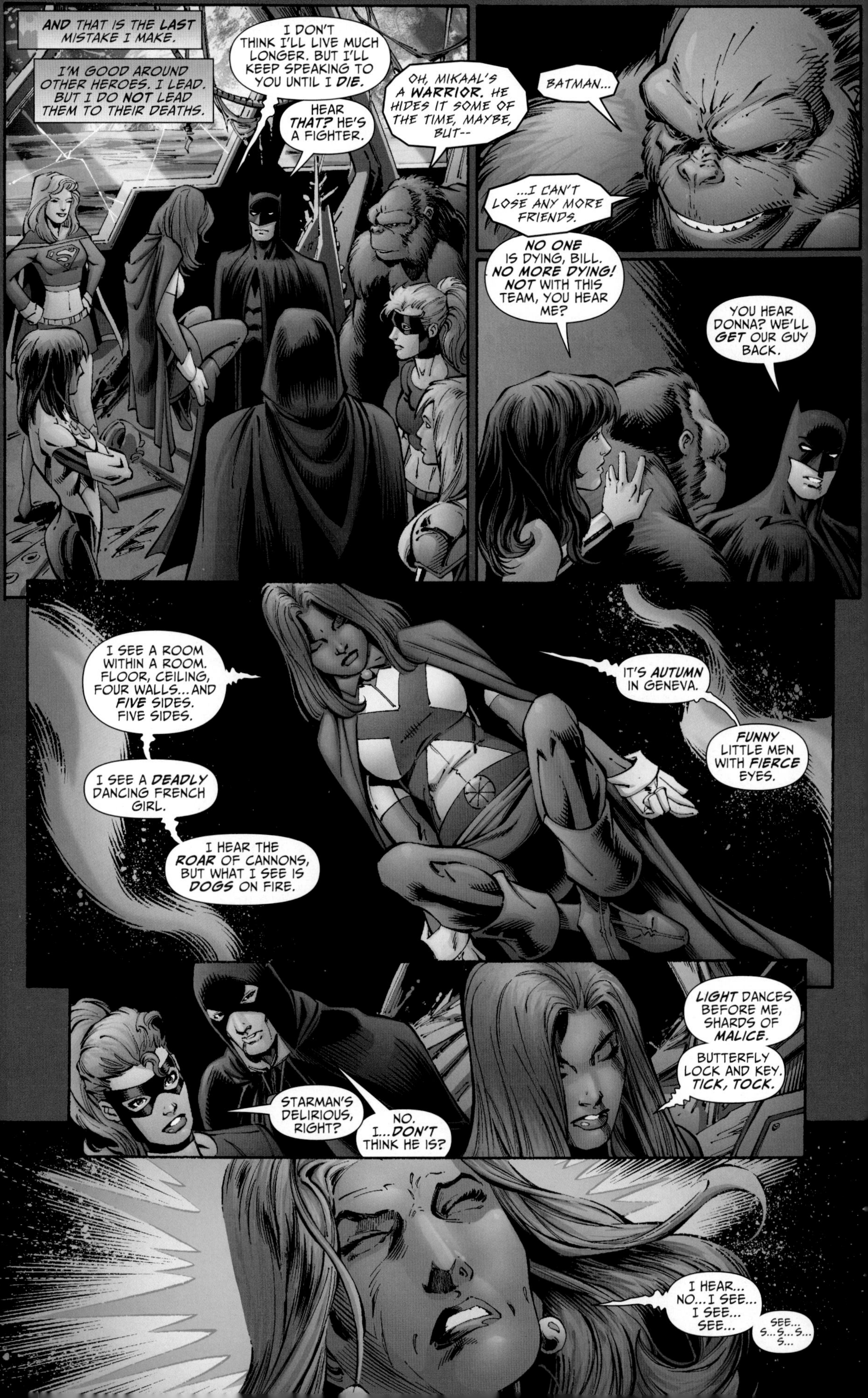
AND THAT IS THE LAST MISTAKE I MAKE.
I'M GOOD AROUND OTHER HEROES. I LEAD. BUT I DO NOT LEAD THEM TO THEIR DEATHS.
I DON'T THINK I'LL LIVE MUCH LONGER. BUT I'LL KEEP SPEAKING TO YOU UNTIL I DIE.
HEAR THAT? HE'S A FIGHTER.
OH, MIKAAL'S A WARRIOR. HE HIDES IT SOME OF THE TIME, MAYBE, BUT--
BATMAN...
...I CAN'T LOSE ANY MORE FRIENDS.
NO ONE IS DYING, BILL. NO MORE DYING! NOT WITH THIS TEAM, YOU HEAR ME?
YOU HEAR DONNA? WE'LL GET OUR GUY BACK.
I SEE A ROOM WITHIN A ROOM. FLOOR, CEILING, FOUR WALLS...AND FIVE SIDES. FIVE SIDES.
I SEE A DEADLY DANCING FRENCH GIRL.
I HEAR THE ROAR OF CANNONS, BUT WHAT I SEE IS DOGS ON FIRE.
IT'S AUTUMN IN GENEVA.
FUNNY LITTLE MEN WITH FIERCE EYES.
STARMAN'S DELIRIOUS, RIGHT?
NO. I...DON'T THINK HE IS?
LIGHT DANCES BEFORE ME, SHARDS OF MALICE.
BUTTERFLY LOCK AND KEY. TICK, TOCK.
I HEAR... NO...I SEE... I SEE... SEE...
SEE... S...S...S... S...

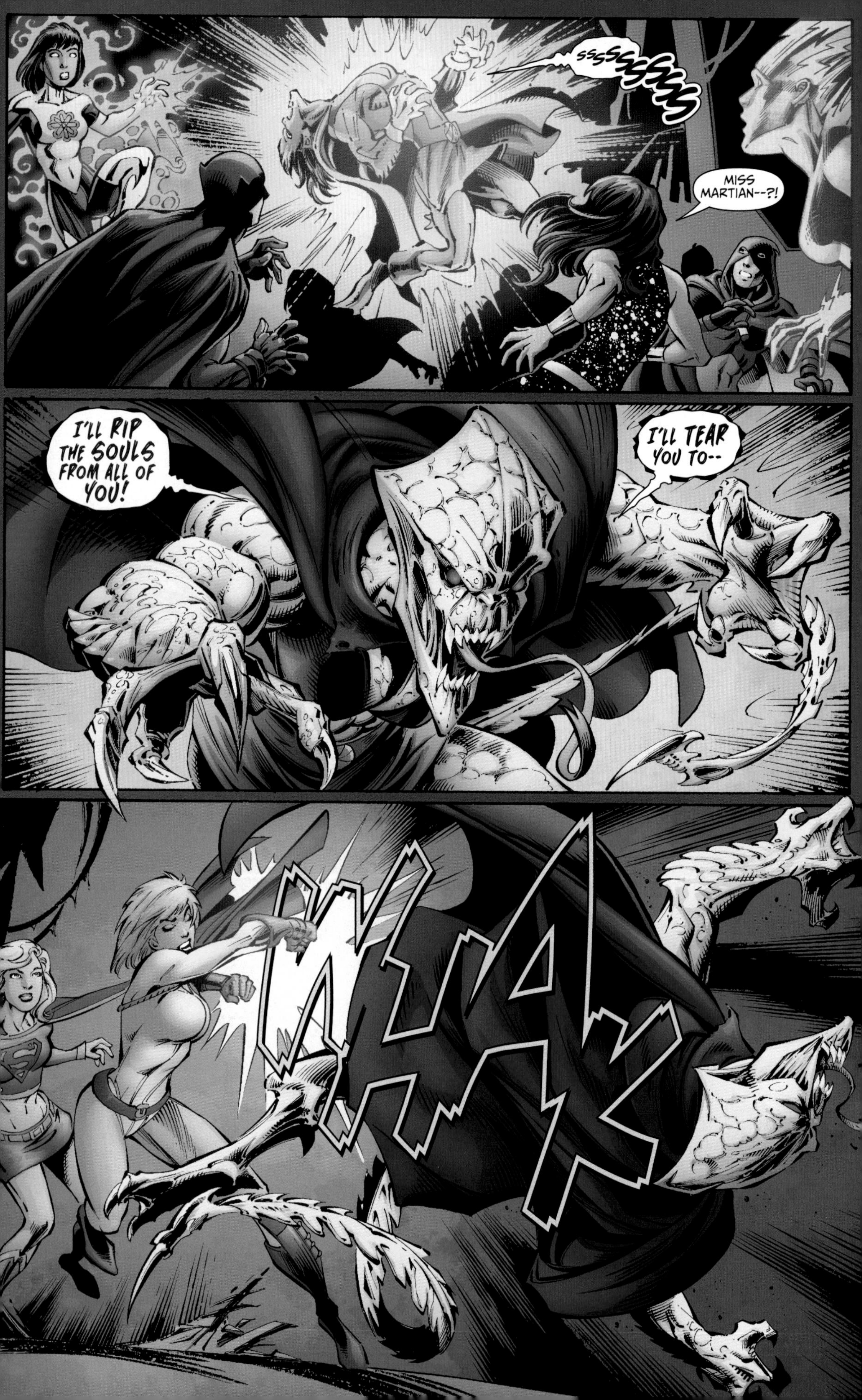
SSSSSSSSSS
MISS MARTIAN--?!
I'LL RIP THE SOULS FROM ALL OF YOU!
I'LL TEAR YOU TO--
WHAM

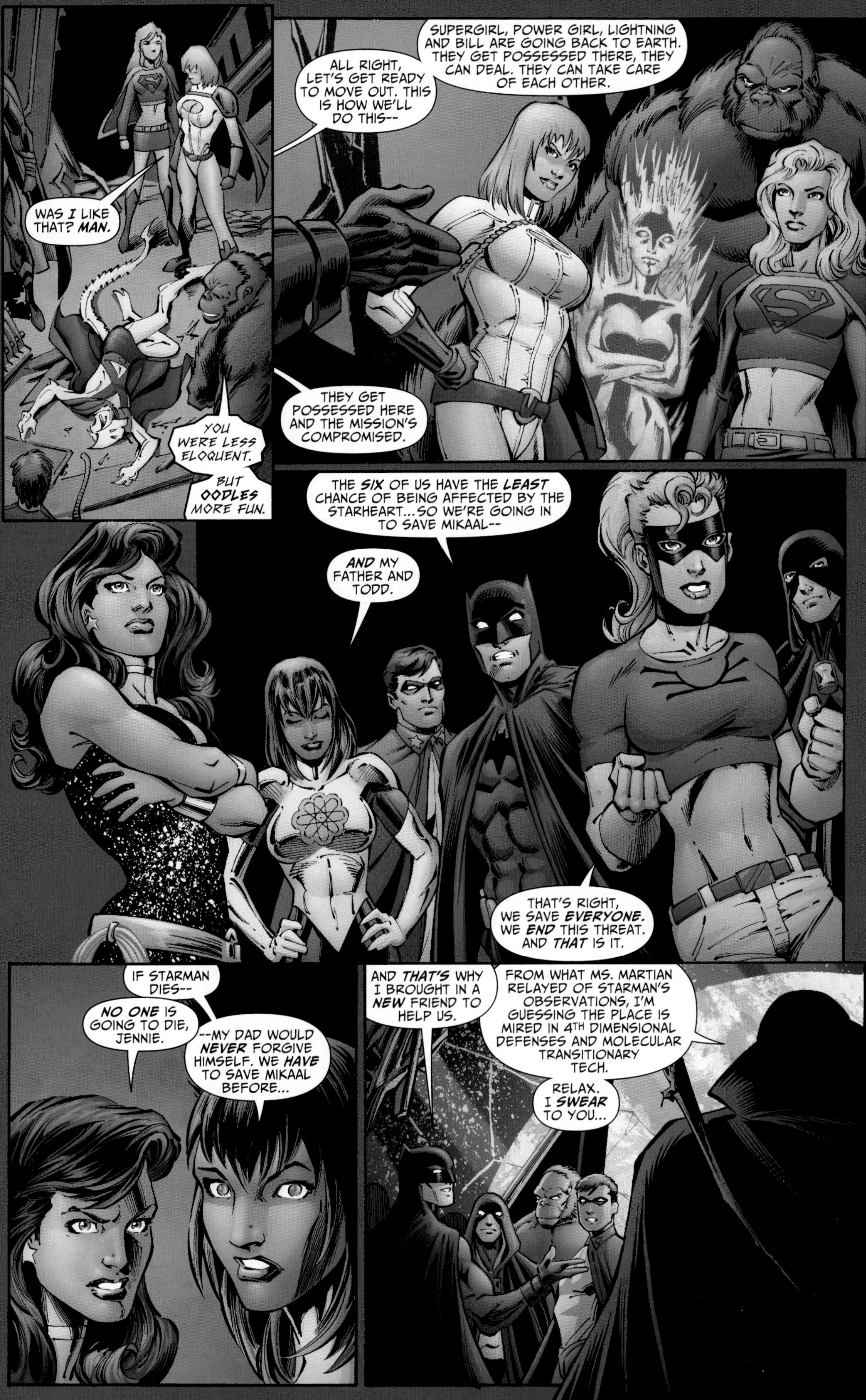
WAS I LIKE THAT? MAN.
YOU WERE LESS ELOQUENT.
BUT OODLES MORE FUN.
ALL RIGHT, LET'S GET READY TO MOVE OUT. THIS IS HOW WE'LL DO THIS--
SUPERGIRL, POWER GIRL, LIGHTNING AND BILL ARE GOING BACK TO EARTH. THEY GET POSSESSED THERE, THEY CAN DEAL. THEY CAN TAKE CARE OF EACH OTHER.
THEY GET POSSESSED HERE AND THE MISSION'S COMPROMISED.
THE SIX OF US HAVE THE LEAST CHANCE OF BEING AFFECTED BY THE STARHEART...SO WE'RE GOING IN TO SAVE MIKAAL--
AND MY FATHER AND TODD.
THAT'S RIGHT, WE SAVE EVERYONE. WE END THIS THREAT. AND THAT IS IT.
IF STARMAN DIES--
NO ONE IS GOING TO DIE, JENNIE.
--MY DAD WOULD NEVER FORGIVE HIMSELF. WE HAVE TO SAVE MIKAAL BEFORE...
AND THAT'S WHY I BROUGHT IN A NEW FRIEND TO HELP US.
FROM WHAT MS. MARTIAN RELAYED OF STARMAN'S OBSERVATIONS, I'M GUESSING THE PLACE IS MIRED IN 4TH DIMENSIONAL DEFENSES AND MOLECULAR TRANSITIONARY TECH.
RELAX. I SWEAR TO YOU...

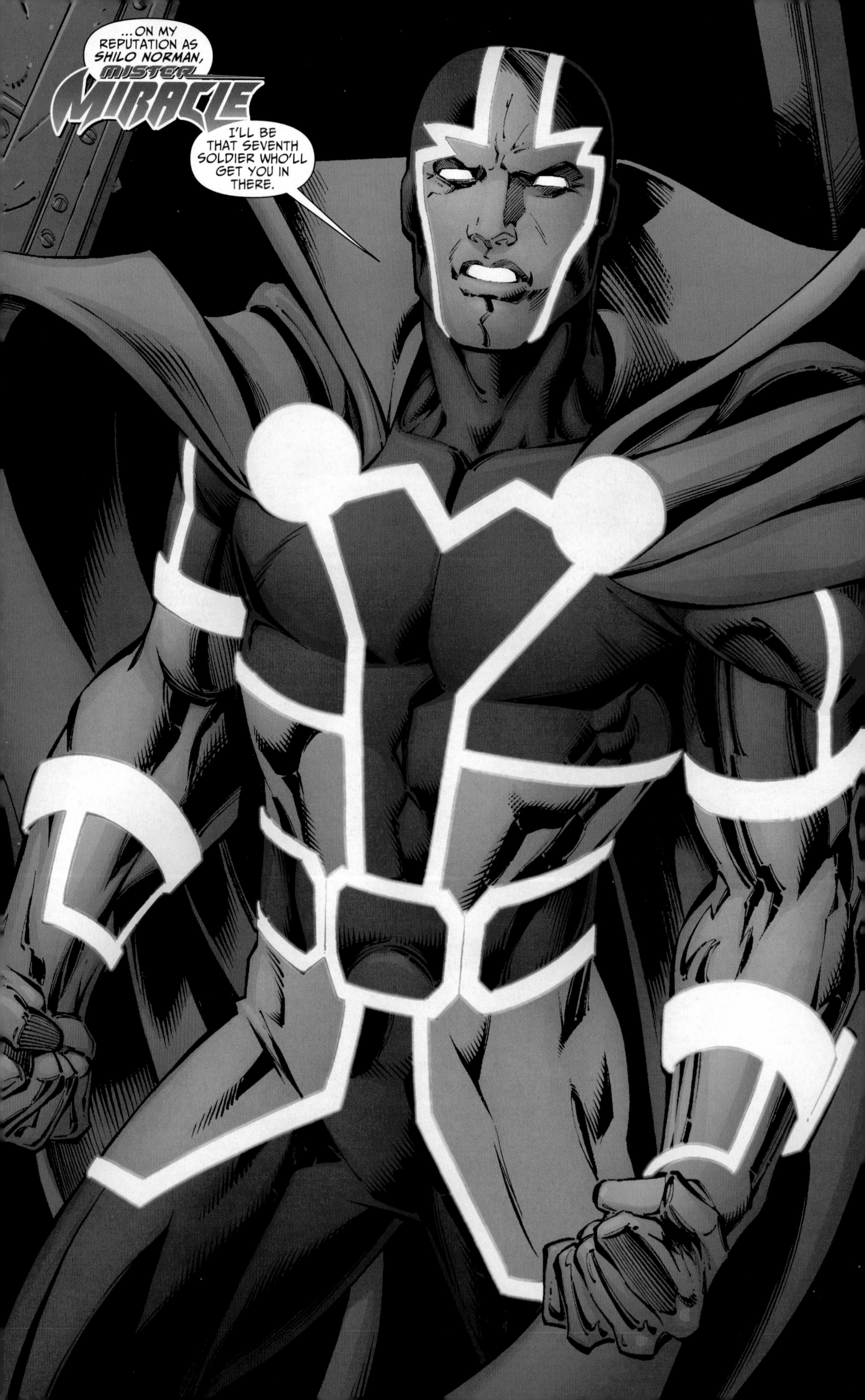
...ON MY REPUTATION AS SHILO NORMAN,
MISTER MIRACLE
I'LL BE THAT SEVENTH SOLDIER WHO'LL GET YOU IN THERE.

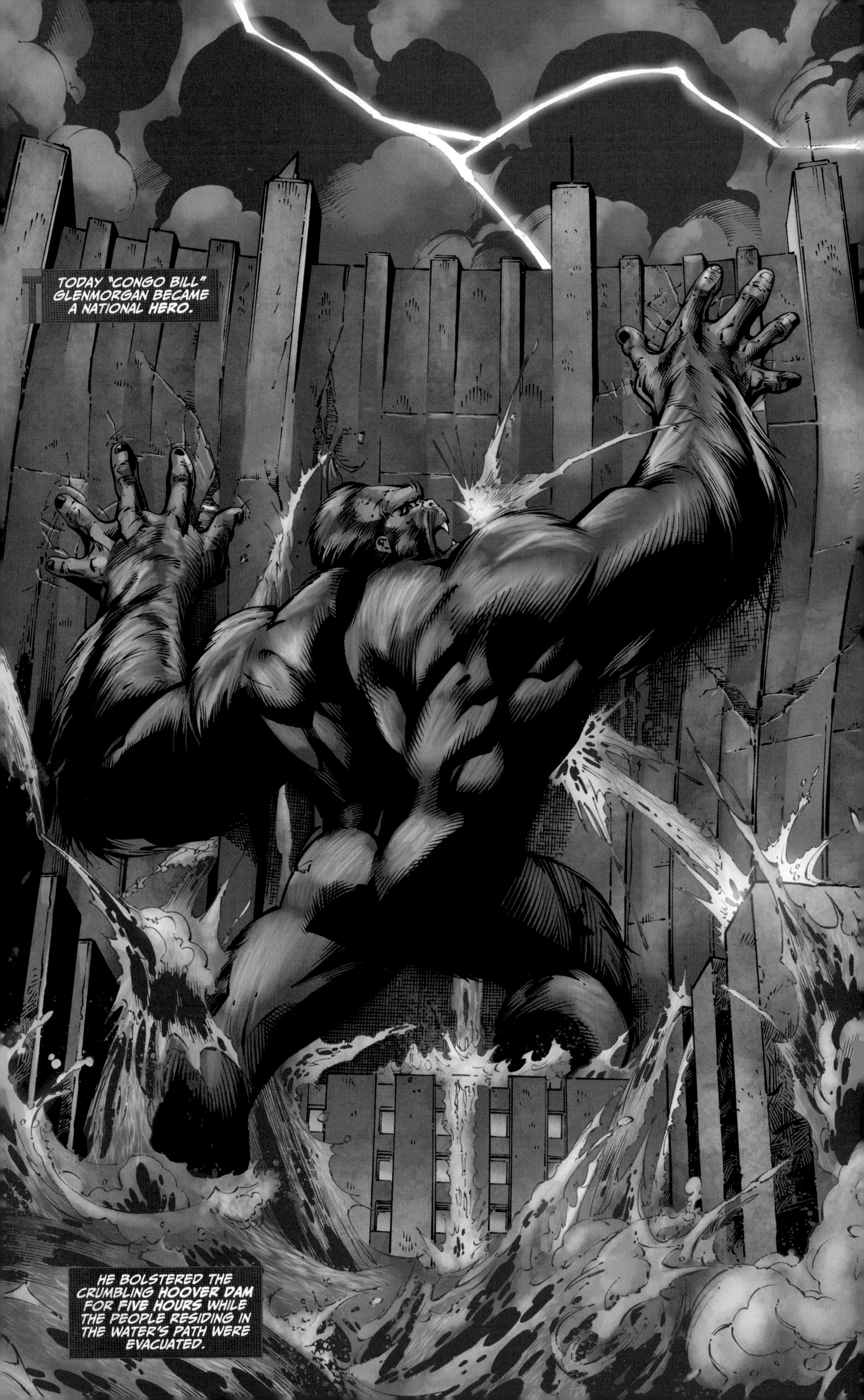
TODAY "CONGO BILL" GLENMORGAN BECAME A NATIONAL HERO.
HE BOLSTERED THE CRUMBLING HOOVER DAM FOR FIVE HOURS WHILE THE PEOPLE RESIDING IN THE WATER'S PATH WERE EVACUATED.

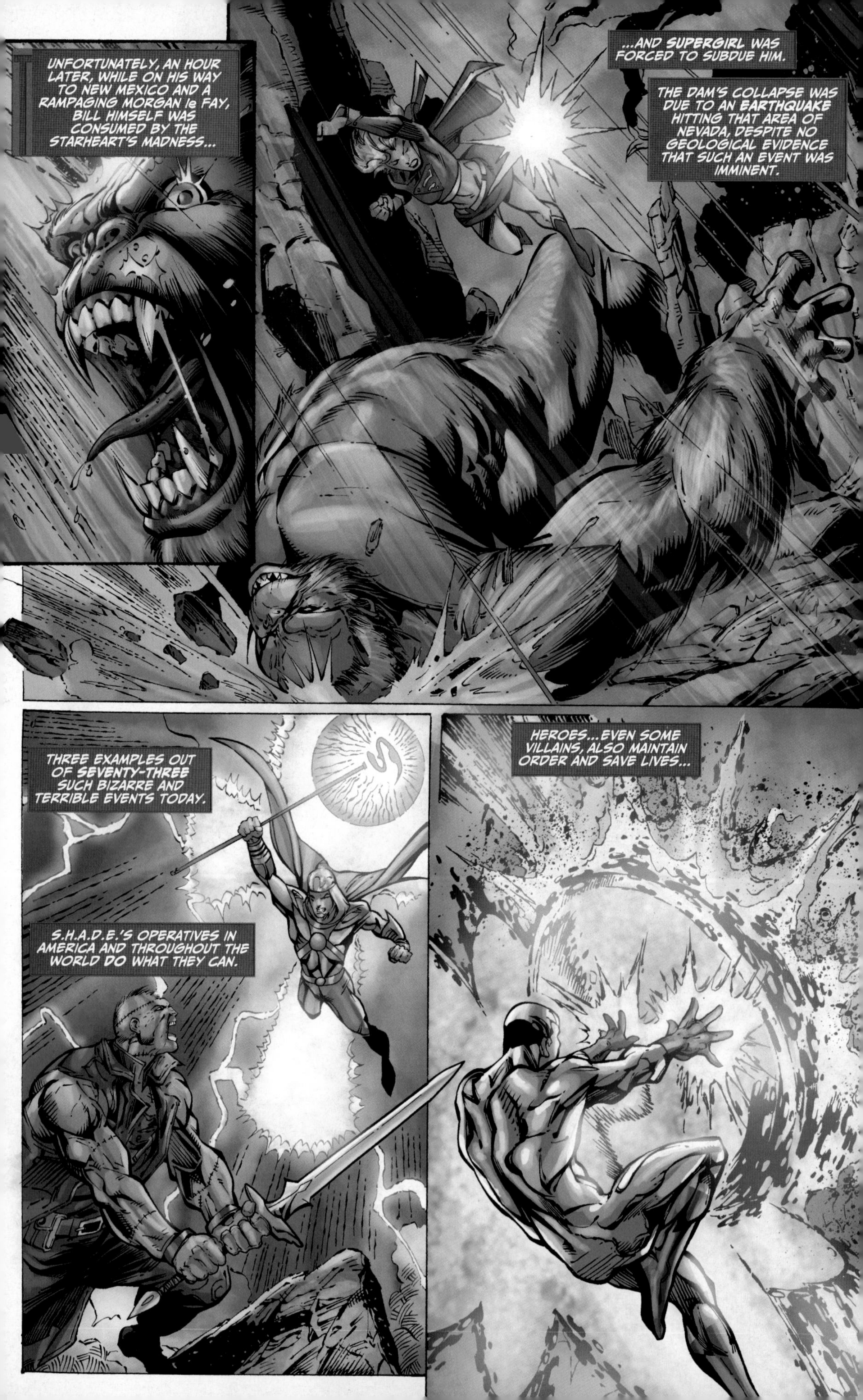
UNFORTUNATELY, AN HOUR LATER, WHILE ON HIS WAY TO NEW MEXICO AND A RAMPAGING MORGAN le FAY, BILL HIMSELF WAS CONSUMED BY THE STARHEART'S MADNESS...
...AND SUPERGIRL WAS FORCED TO SUBDUE HIM.
THE DAM'S COLLAPSE WAS DUE TO AN EARTHQUAKE HITTING THAT AREA OF NEVADA, DESPITE NO GEOLOGICAL EVIDENCE THAT SUCH AN EVENT WAS IMMINENT.
THREE EXAMPLES OUT OF SEVENTY-THREE SUCH BIZARRE AND TERRIBLE EVENTS TODAY.
S.H.A.D.E.'S OPERATIVES IN AMERICA AND THROUGHOUT THE WORLD DO WHAT THEY CAN.
HEROES...EVEN SOME VILLAINS, ALSO MAINTAIN ORDER AND SAVE LIVES...

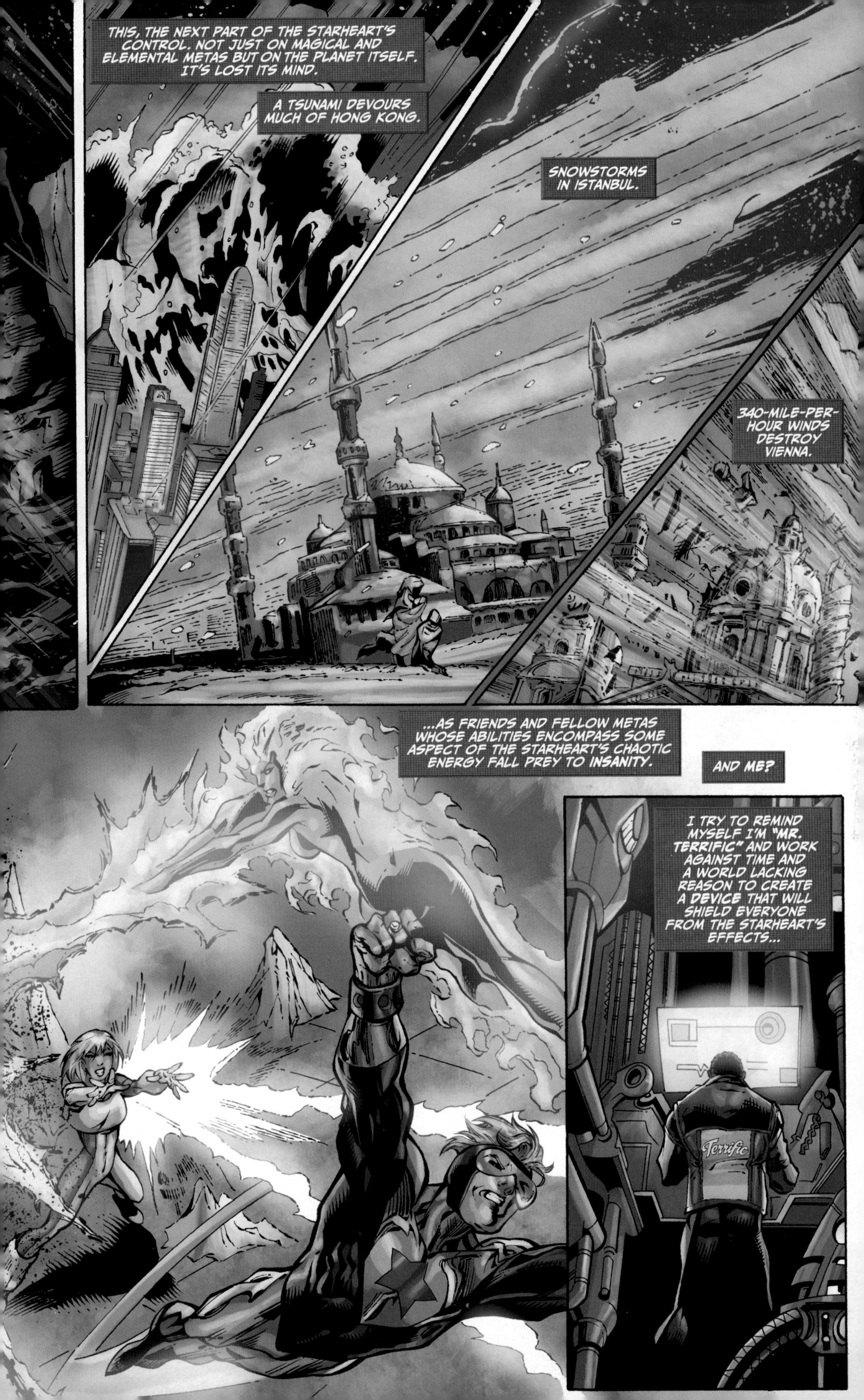
THIS, THE NEXT PART OF THE STARHEART'S CONTROL. NOT JUST ON MAGICAL AND ELEMENTAL METAS BUT ON THE PLANET ITSELF. IT'S LOST ITS MIND.
A TSUNAMI DEVOURS MUCH OF HONG KONG.
SNOWSTORMS IN ISTANBUL.
340-MILE-PER-HOUR WINDS DESTROY VIENNA.
...AS FRIENDS AND FELLOW METAS WHOSE ABILITIES ENCOMPASS SOME ASPECT OF THE STARHEART'S CHAOTIC ENERGY FALL PREY TO INSANITY.
AND ME?
I TRY TO REMIND MYSELF I'M "MR. TERRIFIC" AND WORK AGAINST TIME AND A WORLD LACKING REASON TO CREATE A DEVICE THAT WILL SHIELD EVERYONE FROM THE STARHEART'S EFFECTS...
Terrific

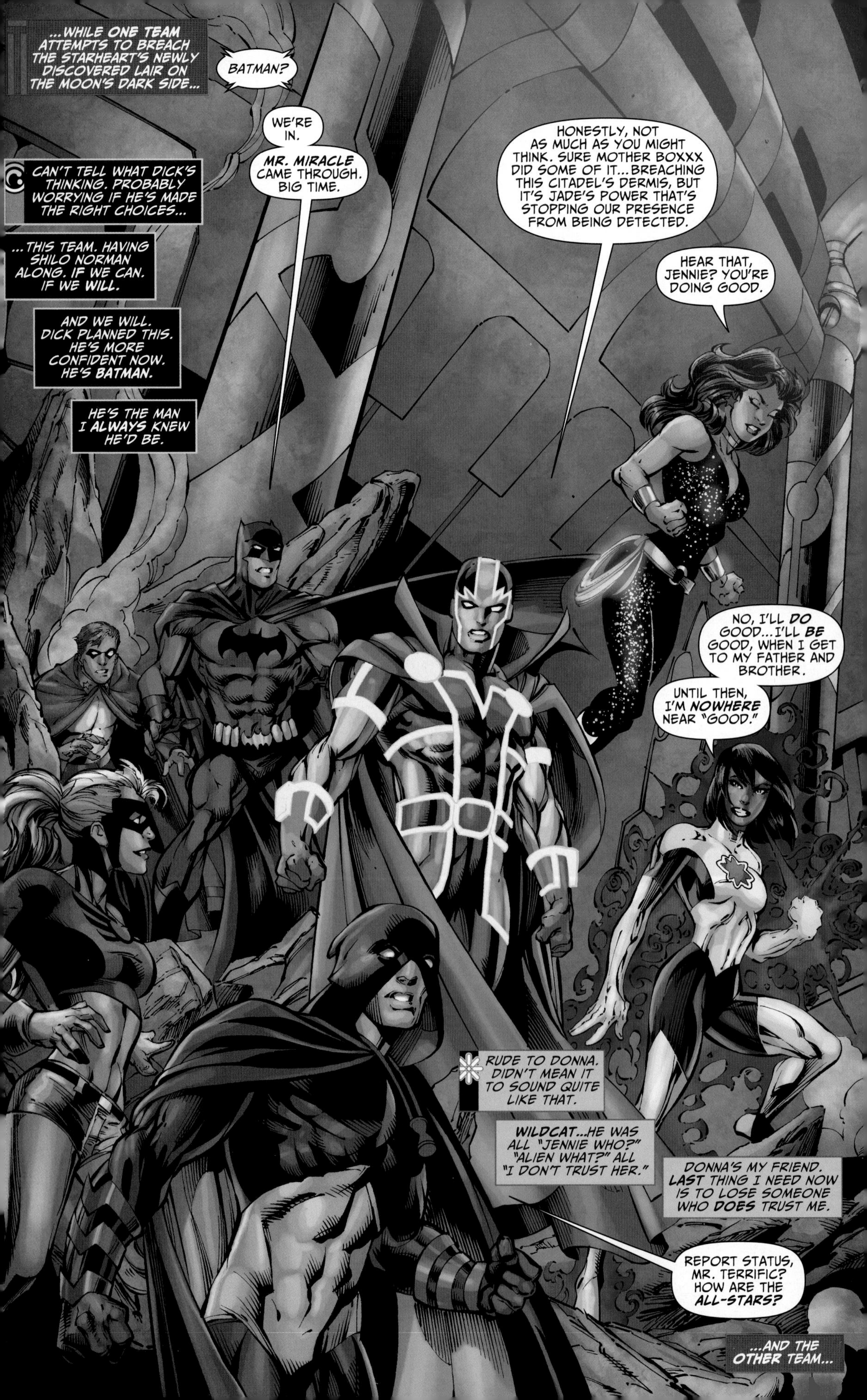
...WHILE ONE TEAM ATTEMPTS TO BREACH THE STARHEART'S NEWLY DISCOVERED LAIR ON THE MOON'S DARK SIDE...
BATMAN?
WE'RE IN.
MR. MIRACLE CAME THROUGH. BIG TIME.
CAN'T TELL WHAT DICK'S THINKING. PROBABLY WORRYING IF HE'S MADE THE RIGHT CHOICES...
...THIS TEAM. HAVING SHILO NORMAN ALONG. IF WE CAN. IF WE WILL.
AND WE WILL. DICK PLANNED THIS. HE'S MORE CONFIDENT NOW. HE'S BATMAN.
HE'S THE MAN I ALWAYS KNEW HE'D BE.
HONESTLY, NOT AS MUCH AS YOU MIGHT THINK. SURE MOTHER BOXXX DID SOME OF IT...BREACHING THIS CITADEL'S DERMIS, BUT IT'S JADE'S POWER THAT'S STOPPING OUR PRESENCE FROM BEING DETECTED.
HEAR THAT, JENNIE? YOU'RE DOING GOOD.
NO, I'LL DO GOOD...I'LL BE GOOD, WHEN I GET TO MY FATHER AND BROTHER.
UNTIL THEN, I'M NOWHERE NEAR "GOOD."
RUDE TO DONNA. DIDN'T MEAN IT TO SOUND QUITE LIKE THAT.
WILDCAT...HE WAS ALL "JENNIE WHO?" "ALIEN WHAT?" ALL "I DON'T TRUST HER."
DONNA'S MY FRIEND. LAST THING I NEED NOW IS TO LOSE SOMEONE WHO DOES TRUST ME.
REPORT STATUS, MR. TERRIFIC? HOW ARE THE ALL-STARS?
...AND THE OTHER TEAM...

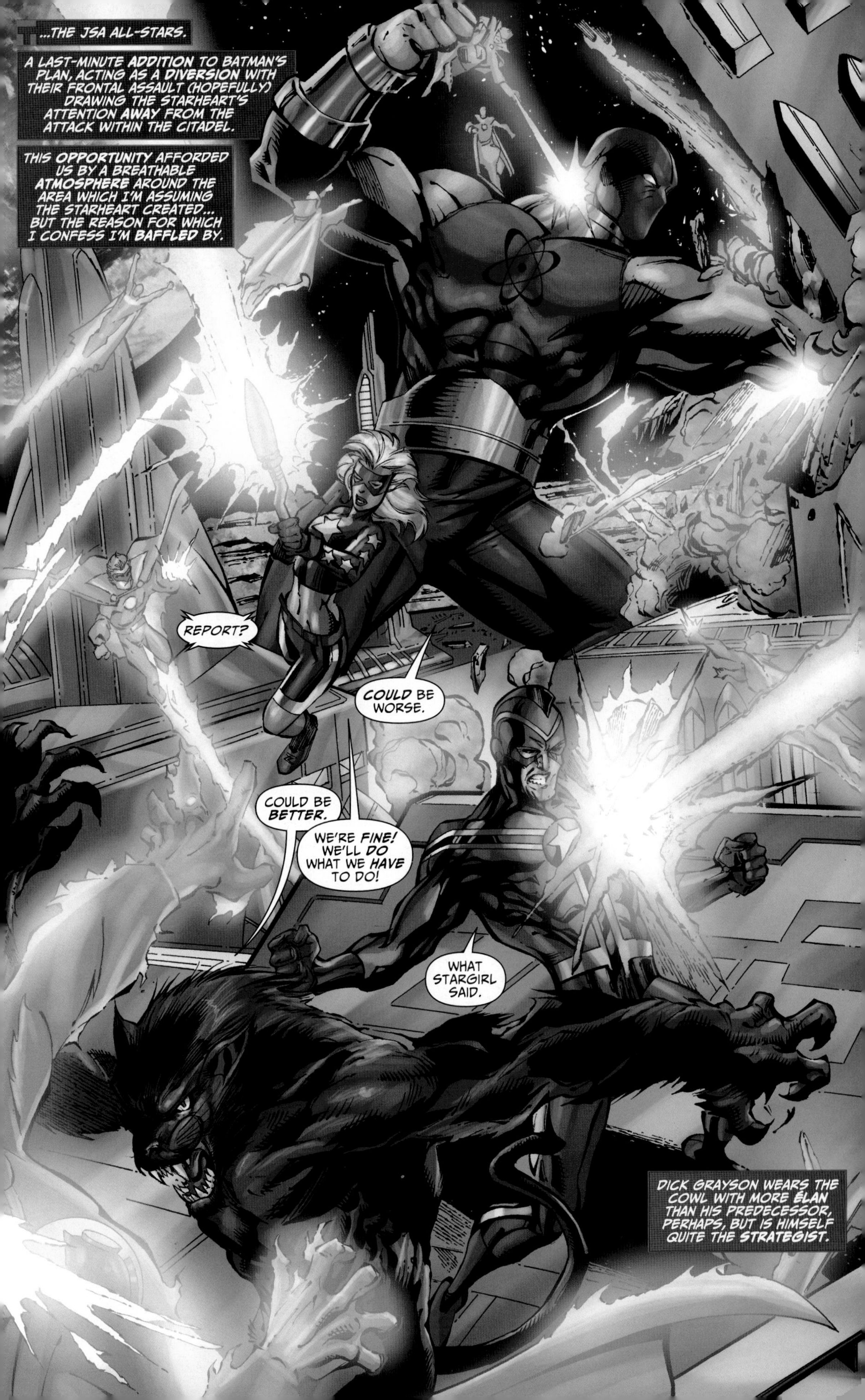
...THE JSA ALL-STARS.
A LAST-MINUTE ADDITION TO BATMAN'S PLAN, ACTING AS A DIVERSION WITH THEIR FRONTAL ASSAULT (HOPEFULLY) DRAWING THE STARHEART'S ATTENTION AWAY FROM THE ATTACK WITHIN THE CITADEL.
THIS OPPORTUNITY AFFORDED US BY A BREATHABLE ATMOSPHERE AROUND THE AREA WHICH I'M ASSUMING THE STARHEART CREATED... BUT THE REASON FOR WHICH I CONFESS I'M BAFFLED BY.
REPORT?
COULD BE WORSE.
COULD BE BETTER.
WE'RE FINE! WE'LL DO WHAT WE HAVE TO DO!
WHAT STARGIRL SAID.
DICK GRAYSON WEARS THE COWL WITH MORE ÉLAN THAN HIS PREDECESSOR, PERHAPS, BUT IS HIMSELF QUITE THE STRATEGIST.

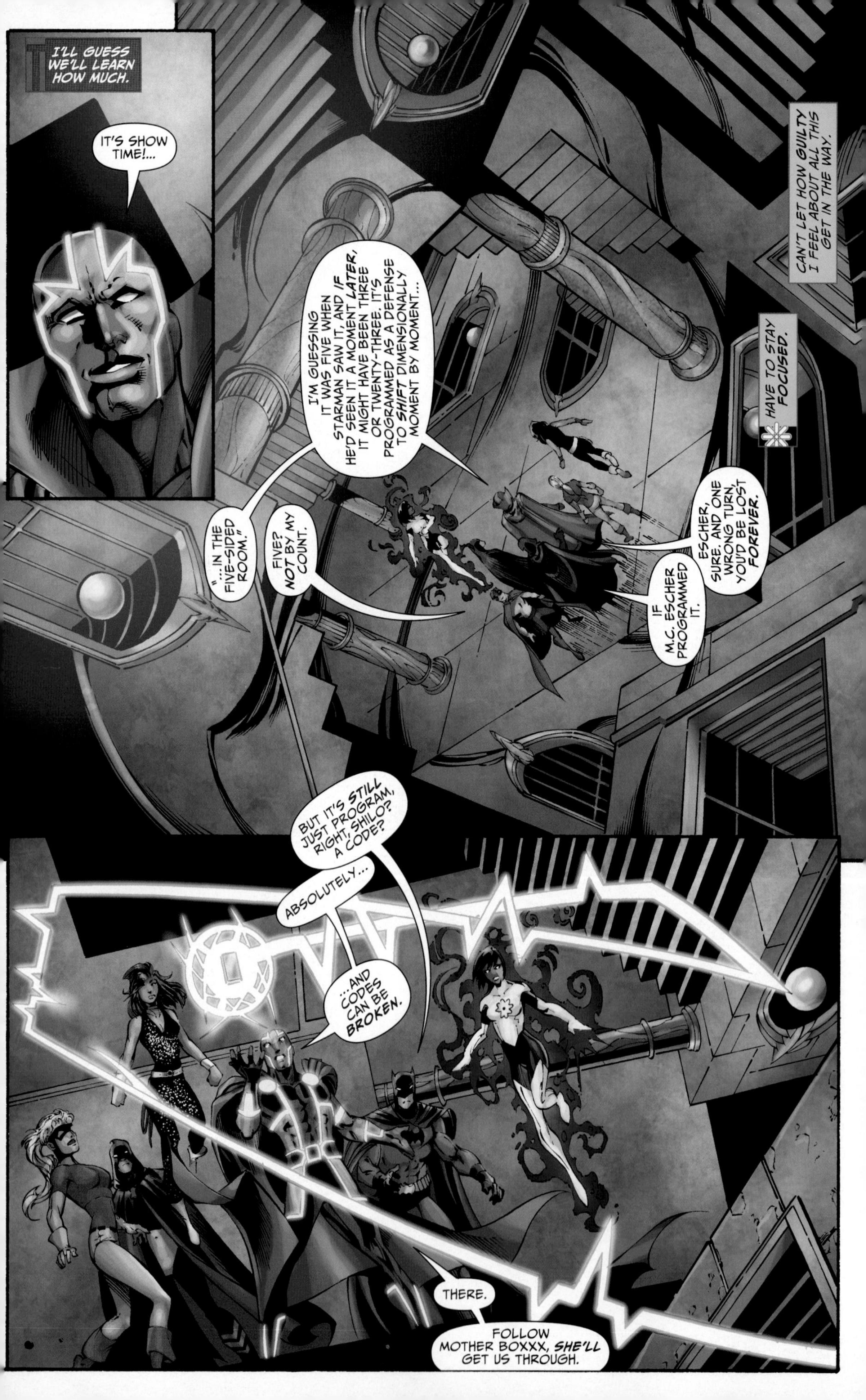
I'LL GUESS WE'LL LEARN HOW MUCH.
IT'S SHOW TIME!...
CAN'T LET HOW GUILTY I FEEL ABOUT ALL THIS GET IN THE WAY.
HAVE TO STAY FOCUSED.
I'M GUESSING IT WAS FIVE WHEN STARMAN SAW IT, AND IF HE'D SEEN IT A MOMENT LATER, IT MIGHT HAVE BEEN THREE OR TWENTY-THREE. IT'S PROGRAMMED AS A DEFENSE TO SHIFT DIMENSIONALLY MOMENT BY MOMENT...
"...IN THE FIVE-SIDED ROOM."
FIVE? NOT BY MY COUNT.
ESCHER, SURE. AND ONE WRONG TURN, YOU'D BE LOST FOREVER.
IF M.C. ESCHER PROGRAMMED IT.
BUT IT'S STILL JUST PROGRAM, RIGHT, SHILO? A CODE?
ABSOLUTELY...
...AND CODES CAN BE BROKEN.
THERE.
FOLLOW MOTHER BOXXX, SHE'LL GET US THROUGH.

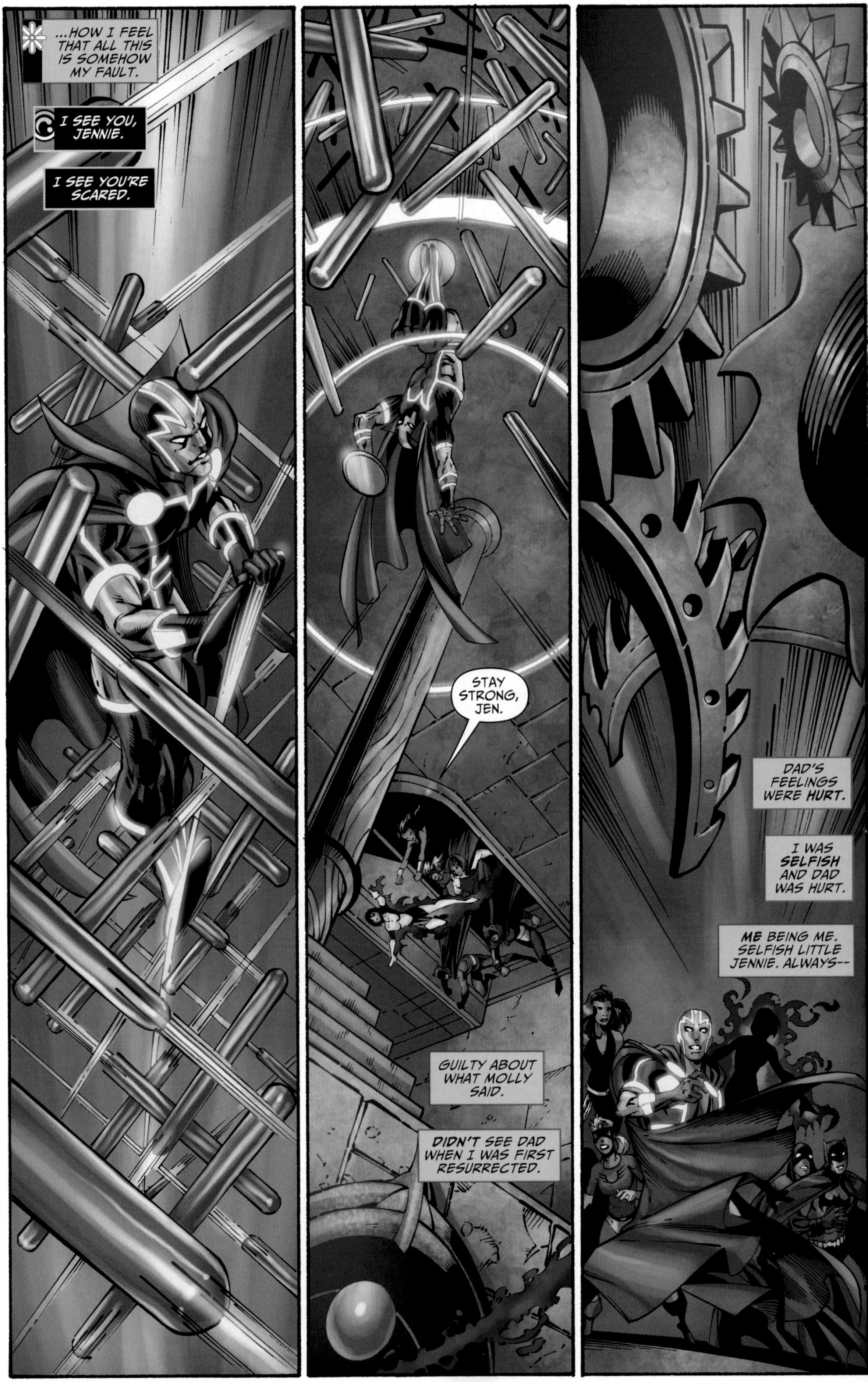
...HOW I FEEL THAT ALL THIS IS SOMEHOW MY FAULT.
I SEE YOU, JENNIE.
I SEE YOU'RE SCARED.
STAY STRONG, JEN.
GUILTY ABOUT WHAT MOLLY SAID.
DIDN'T SEE DAD WHEN I WAS FIRST RESURRECTED.
DAD'S FEELINGS WERE HURT.
I WAS SELFISH AND DAD WAS HURT.
ME BEING ME. SELFISH LITTLE JENNIE. ALWAYS--

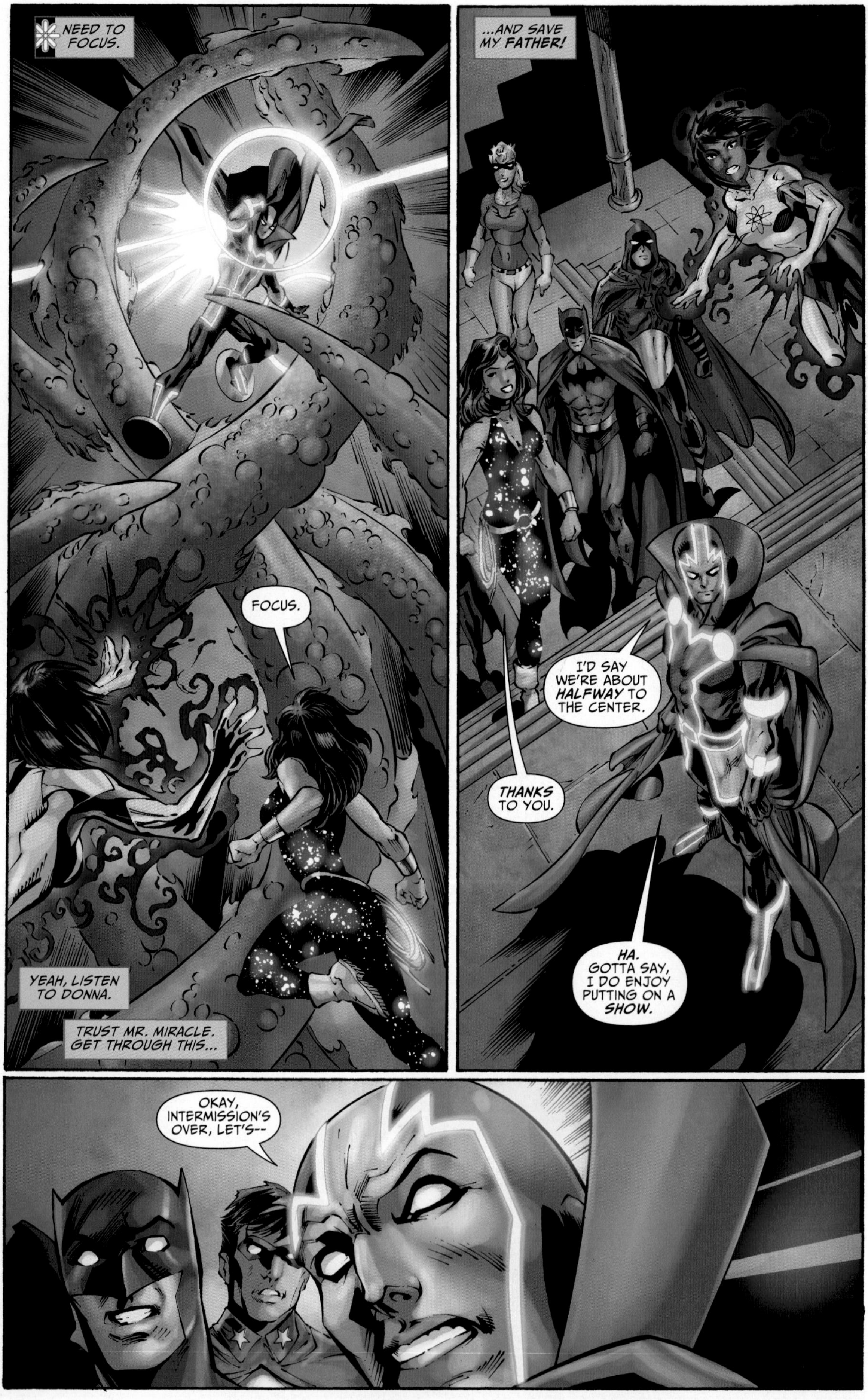
NEED TO FOCUS.
FOCUS.
YEAH, LISTEN TO DONNA.
TRUST MR. MIRACLE. GET THROUGH THIS...
...AND SAVE MY FATHER!
I'D SAY WE'RE ABOUT HALFWAY TO THE CENTER.
THANKS TO YOU.
HA. GOTTA SAY, I DO ENJOY PUTTING ON A SHOW.
OKAY, INTERMISSION'S OVER, LET'S--

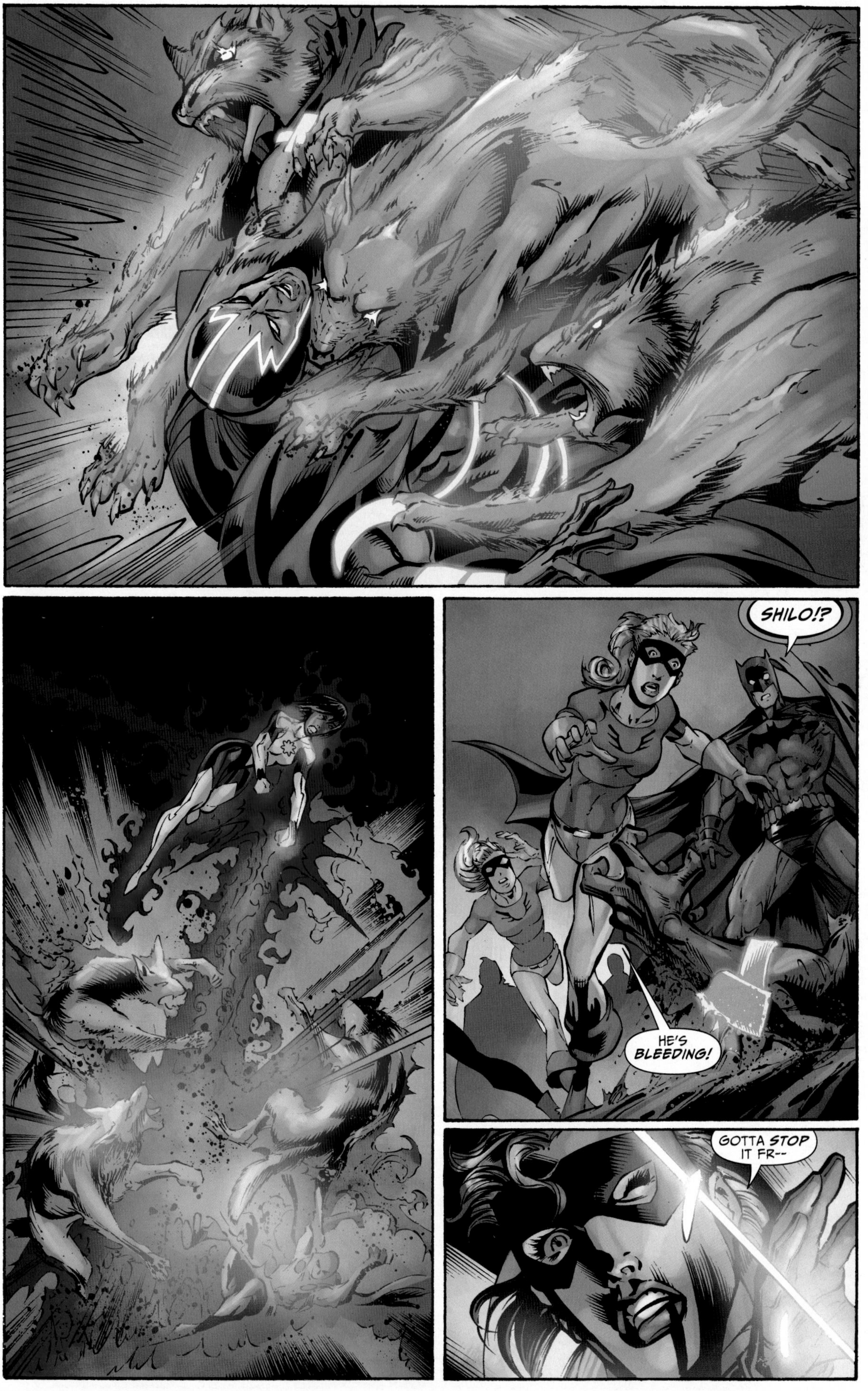
SHILO!?
HE'S BLEEDING!
GOTTA STOP IT FR--

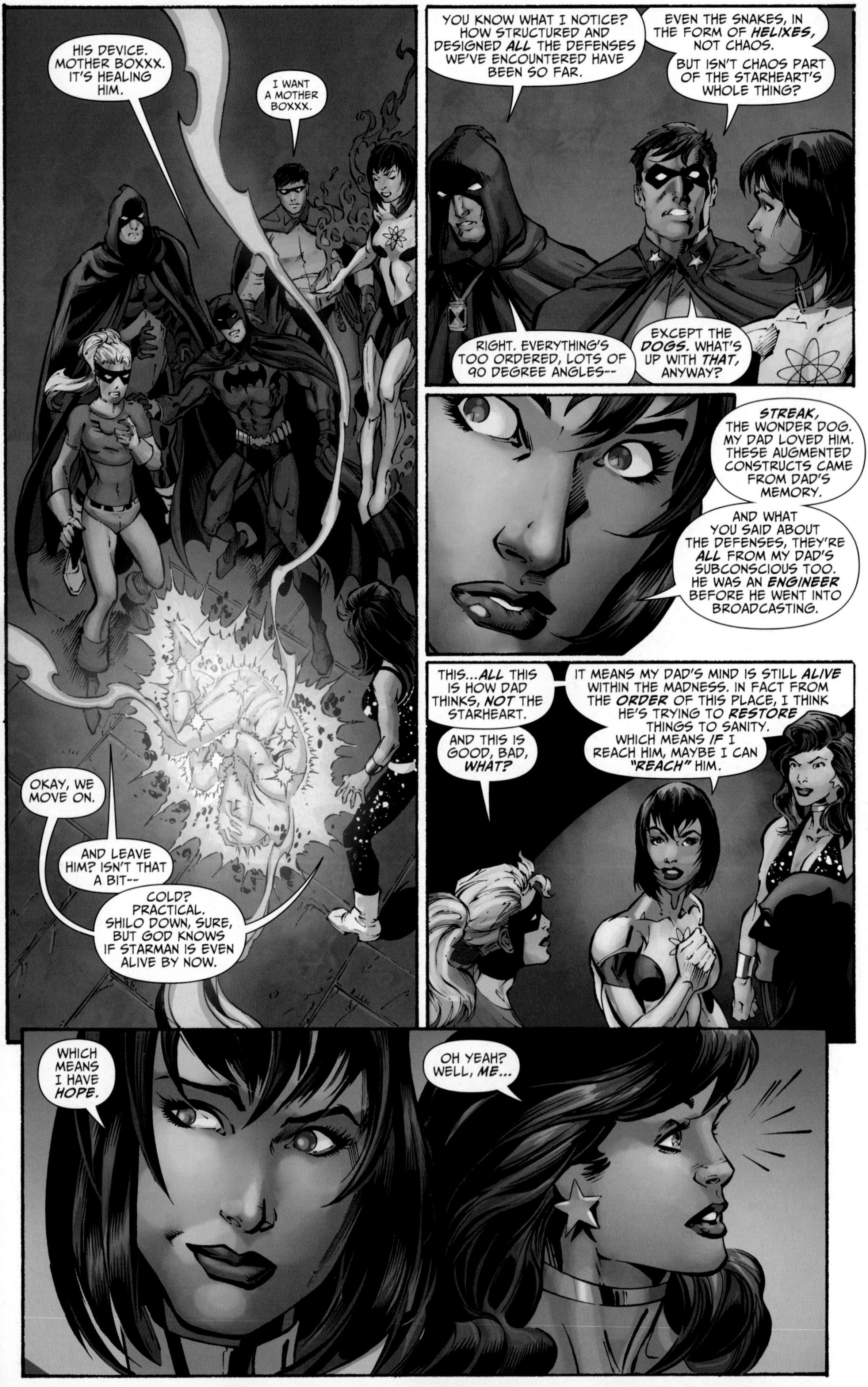
HIS DEVICE. MOTHER BOXXX. IT'S HEALING HIM.
I WANT A MOTHER BOXXX.
OKAY, WE MOVE ON.
AND LEAVE HIM? ISN'T THAT A BIT--
COLD? PRACTICAL. SHILO DOWN, SURE, BUT GOD KNOWS IF STARMAN IS EVEN ALIVE BY NOW.
YOU KNOW WHAT I NOTICE? HOW STRUCTURED AND DESIGNED ALL THE DEFENSES WE'VE ENCOUNTERED HAVE BEEN SO FAR.
EVEN THE SNAKES, IN THE FORM OF HELIXES, NOT CHAOS.
BUT ISN'T CHAOS PART OF THE STARHEART'S WHOLE THING?
RIGHT. EVERYTHING'S TOO ORDERED, LOTS OF 90 DEGREE ANGLES--
EXCEPT THE DOGS. WHAT'S UP WITH THAT, ANYWAY?
STREAK, THE WONDER DOG. MY DAD LOVED HIM. THESE AUGMENTED CONSTRUCTS CAME FROM DAD'S MEMORY.
AND WHAT YOU SAID ABOUT THE DEFENSES, THEY'RE ALL FROM MY DAD'S SUBCONSCIOUS TOO. HE WAS AN ENGINEER BEFORE HE WENT INTO BROADCASTING.
THIS...ALL THIS IS HOW DAD THINKS, NOT THE STARHEART.
AND THIS IS GOOD, BAD, WHAT?
IT MEANS MY DAD'S MIND IS STILL ALIVE WITHIN THE MADNESS. IN FACT FROM THE ORDER OF THIS PLACE, I THINK HE'S TRYING TO RESTORE THINGS TO SANITY.
WHICH MEANS IF I REACH HIM, MAYBE I CAN "REACH" HIM.
WHICH MEANS I HAVE HOPE.
OH YEAH? WELL, ME...

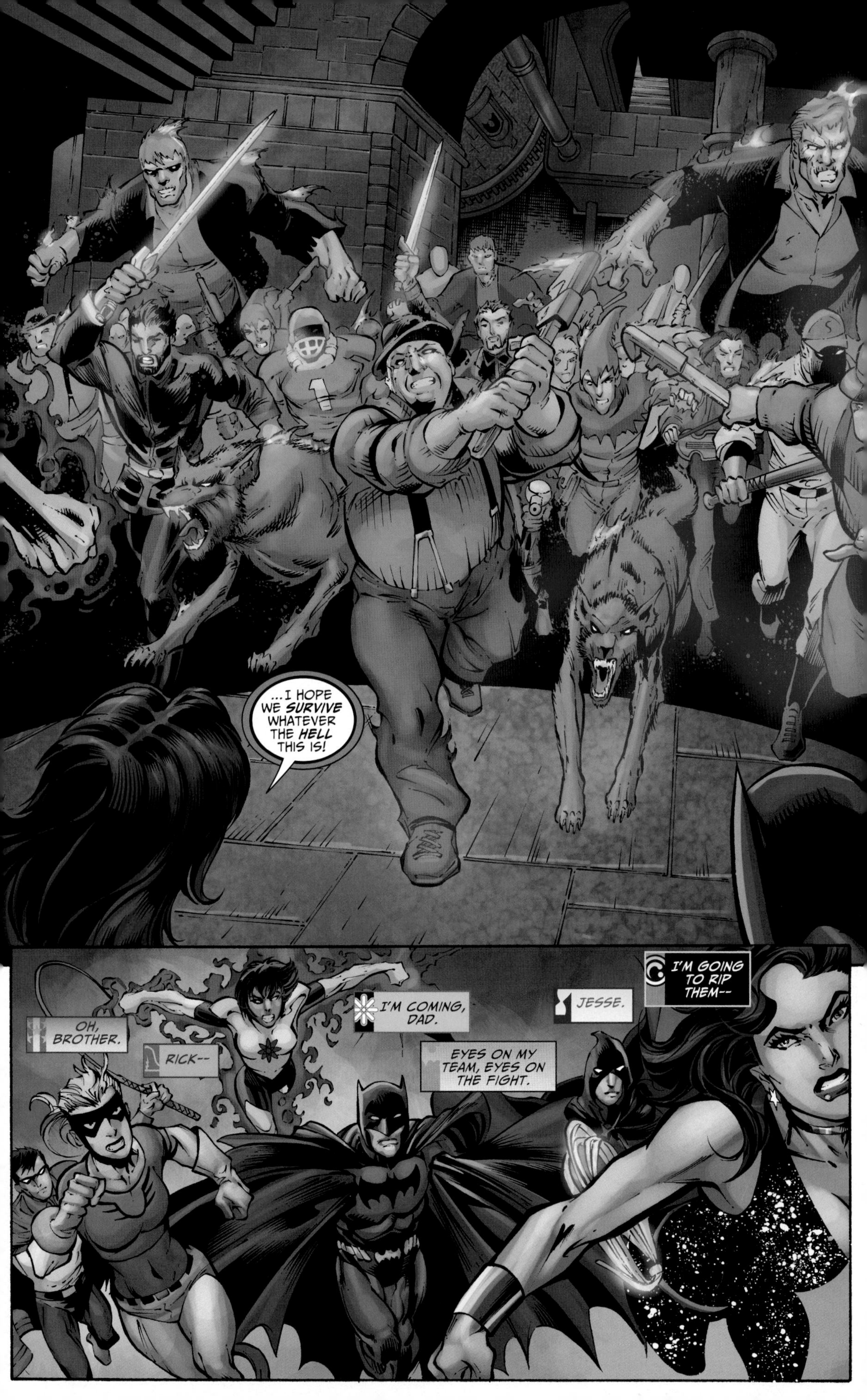
...I HOPE WE SURVIVE WHATEVER THE HELL THIS IS!
OH, BROTHER.
RICK--
I'M COMING, DAD.
EYES ON MY TEAM, EYES ON THE FIGHT.
JESSE.
I'M GOING TO RIP THEM--

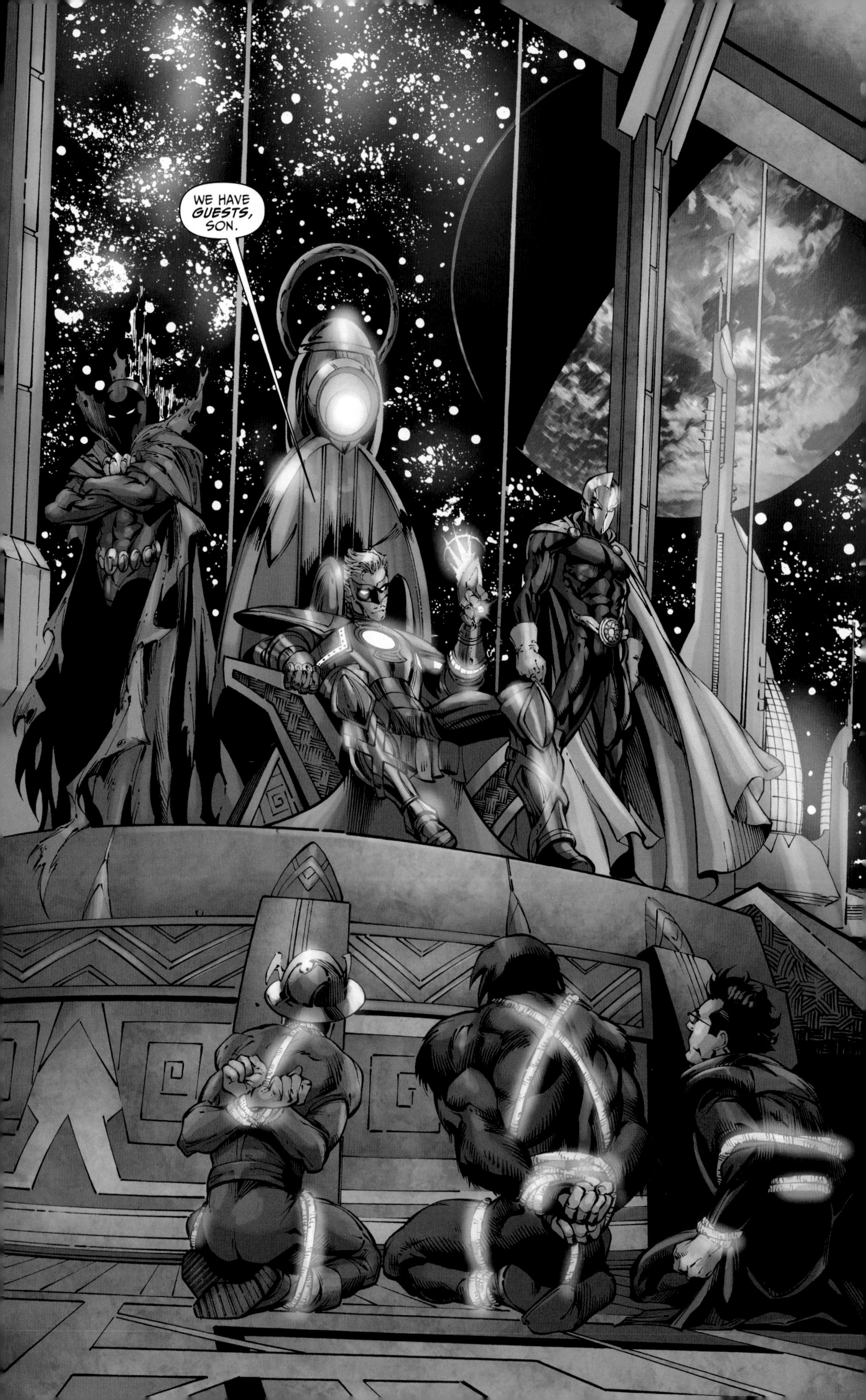
WE HAVE GUESTS, SON.

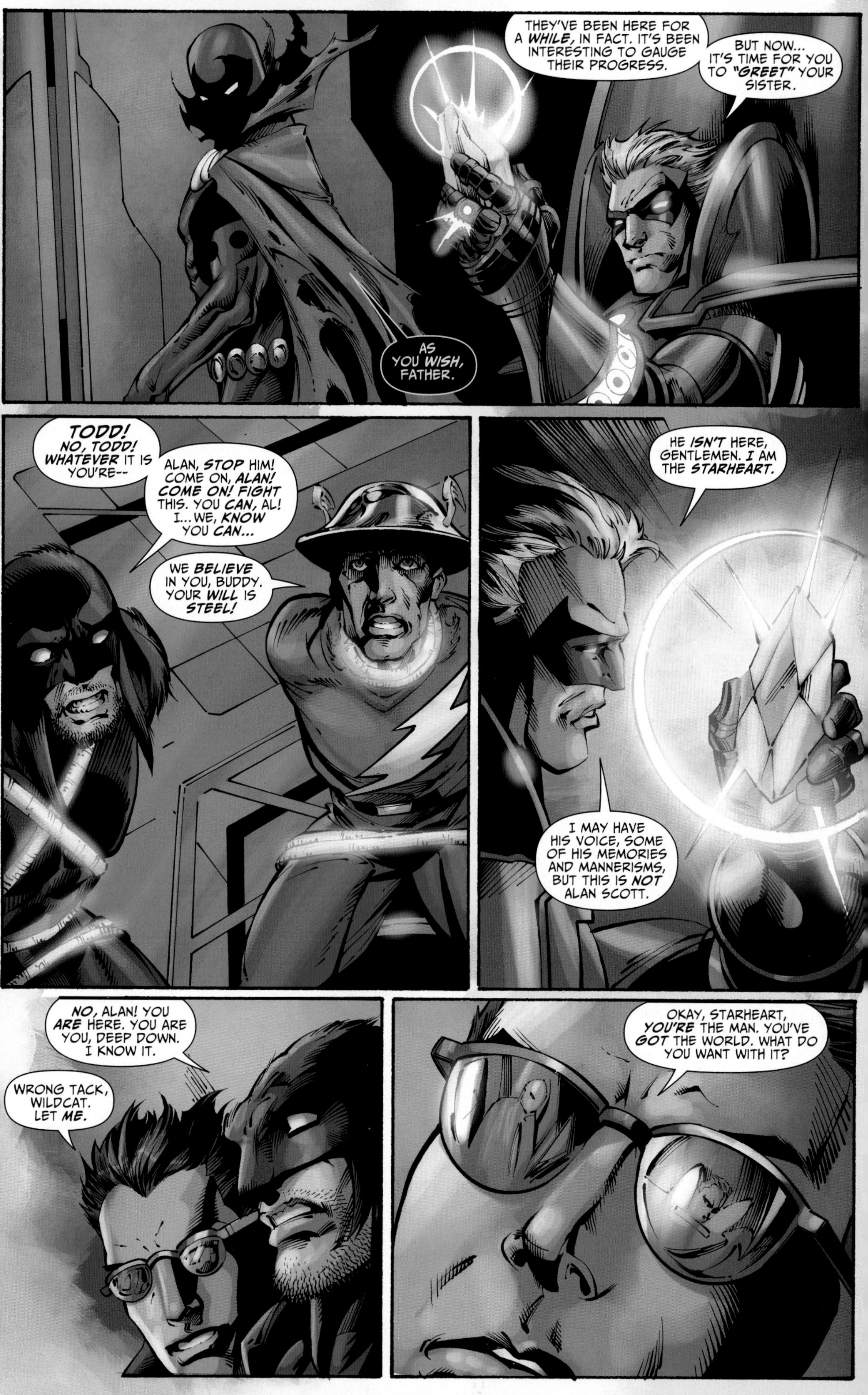

THEY'VE BEEN HERE FOR A WHILE, IN FACT. IT'S BEEN INTERESTING TO GAUGE THEIR PROGRESS.
BUT NOW... IT'S TIME FOR YOU TO "GREET" YOUR SISTER.
AS YOU WISH, FATHER.
TODD! NO, TODD! WHATEVER IT IS YOU'RE--
ALAN, STOP HIM! COME ON, ALAN! COME ON! FIGHT THIS. YOU CAN, AL! I...WE, KNOW YOU CAN...
WE BELIEVE IN YOU, BUDDY. YOUR WILL IS STEEL!
HE ISN'T HERE, GENTLEMEN. I AM THE STARHEART.
I MAY HAVE HIS VOICE, SOME OF HIS MEMORIES AND MANNERISMS, BUT THIS IS NOT ALAN SCOTT.
NO, ALAN! YOU ARE HERE. YOU ARE YOU, DEEP DOWN. I KNOW IT.
WRONG TACK, WILDCAT. LET ME.
OKAY, STARHEART, YOU'RE THE MAN. YOU'VE GOT THE WORLD. WHAT DO YOU WANT WITH IT?

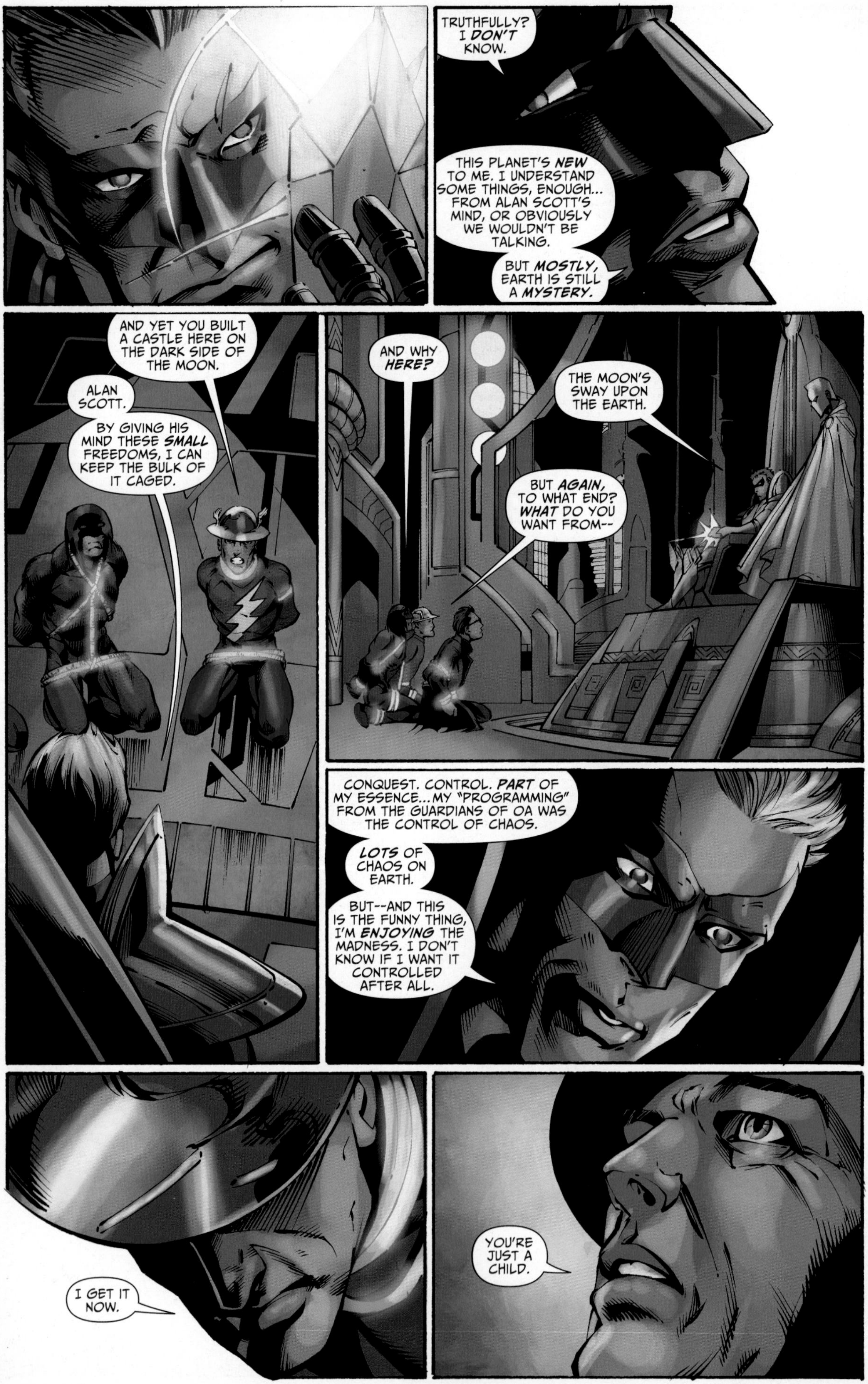
TRUTHFULLY? I DON'T KNOW.
THIS PLANET'S NEW TO ME. I UNDERSTAND SOME THINGS, ENOUGH... FROM ALAN SCOTT'S MIND, OR OBVIOUSLY WE WOULDN'T BE TALKING.
BUT MOSTLY, EARTH IS STILL A MYSTERY.
AND YET YOU BUILT A CASTLE HERE ON THE DARK SIDE OF THE MOON.
ALAN SCOTT.
BY GIVING HIS MIND THESE SMALL FREEDOMS, I CAN KEEP THE BULK OF IT CAGED.
AND WHY HERE?
THE MOON'S SWAY UPON THE EARTH.
BUT AGAIN, TO WHAT END? WHAT DO YOU WANT FROM--
CONQUEST. CONTROL. PART OF MY ESSENCE... MY "PROGRAMMING" FROM THE GUARDIANS OF OA WAS THE CONTROL OF CHAOS.
LOTS OF CHAOS ON EARTH.
BUT--AND THIS IS THE FUNNY THING, I'M ENJOYING THE MADNESS. I DON'T KNOW IF I WANT IT CONTROLLED AFTER ALL.
I GET IT NOW.
YOU'RE JUST A CHILD.

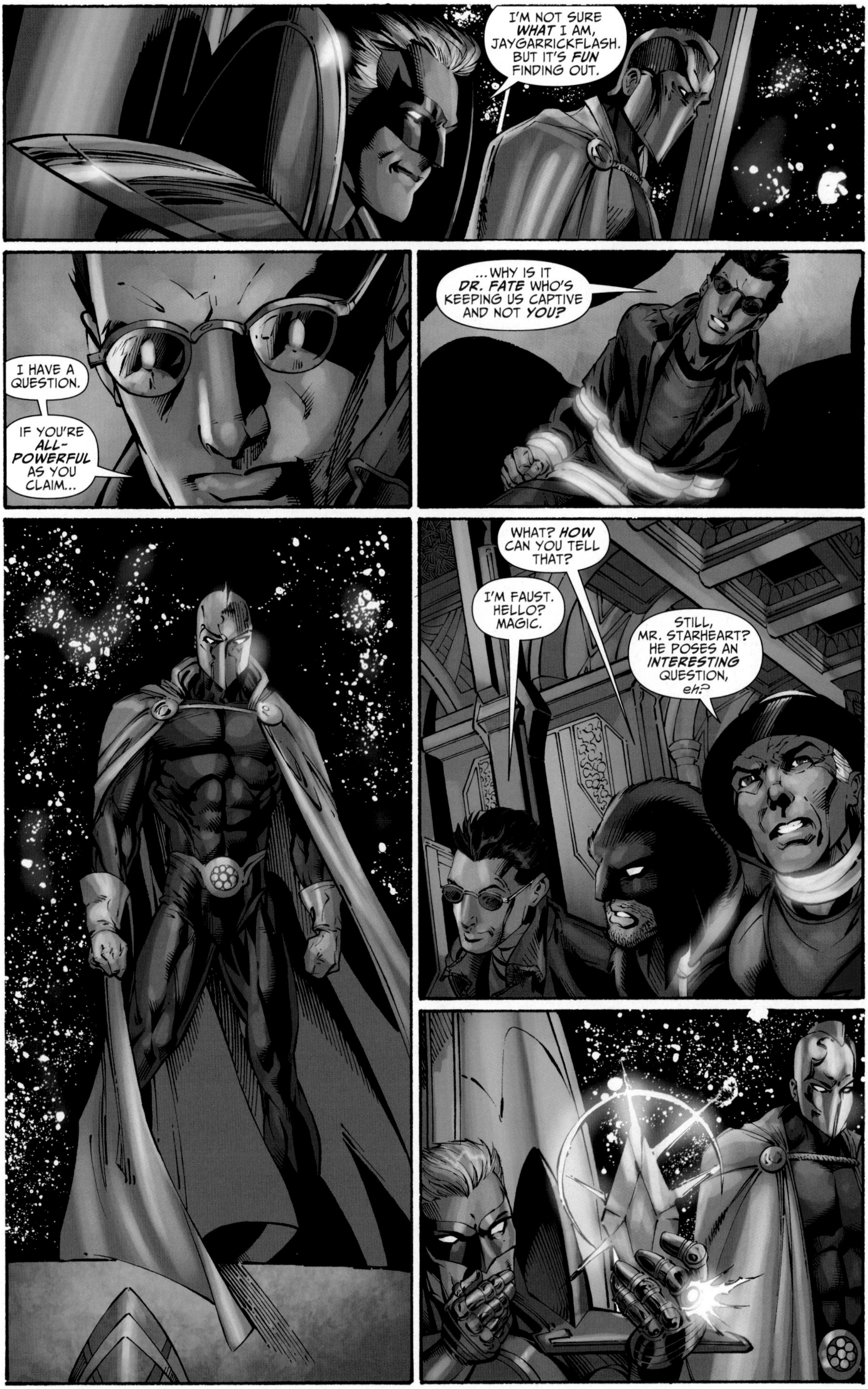
I'M NOT SURE *WHAT* I AM, JAYGARRICKFLASH. BUT IT'S *FUN* FINDING OUT.
I HAVE A QUESTION.
IF YOU'RE *ALL-POWERFUL* AS YOU CLAIM...
...WHY IS IT *DR. FATE* WHO'S KEEPING US CAPTIVE AND NOT *YOU?*
WHAT? *HOW* CAN YOU TELL THAT?
I'M FAUST. HELLO? MAGIC.
STILL, MR. STARHEART? HE POSES AN *INTERESTING* QUESTION, *eh?*

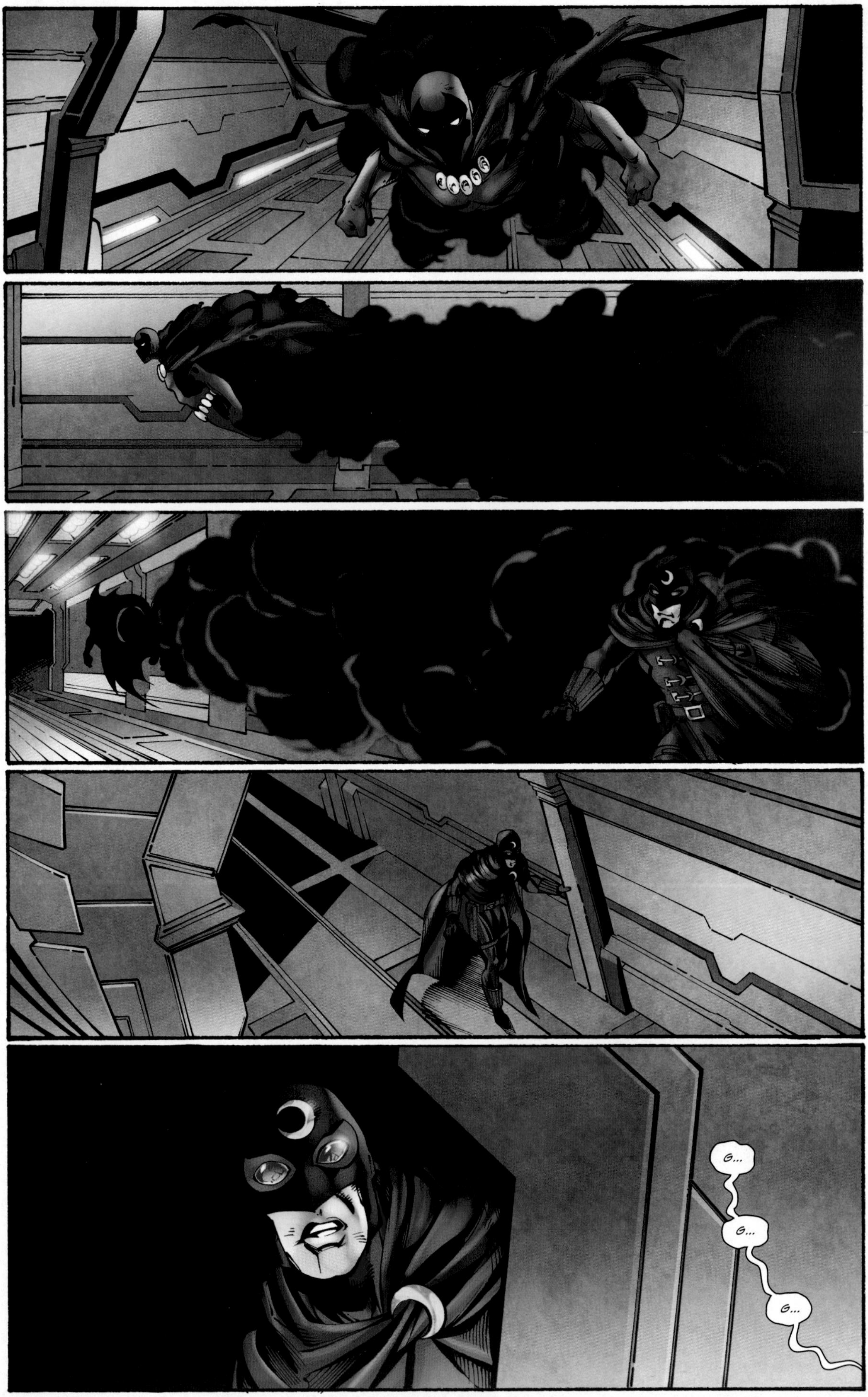
G...
G...
G...

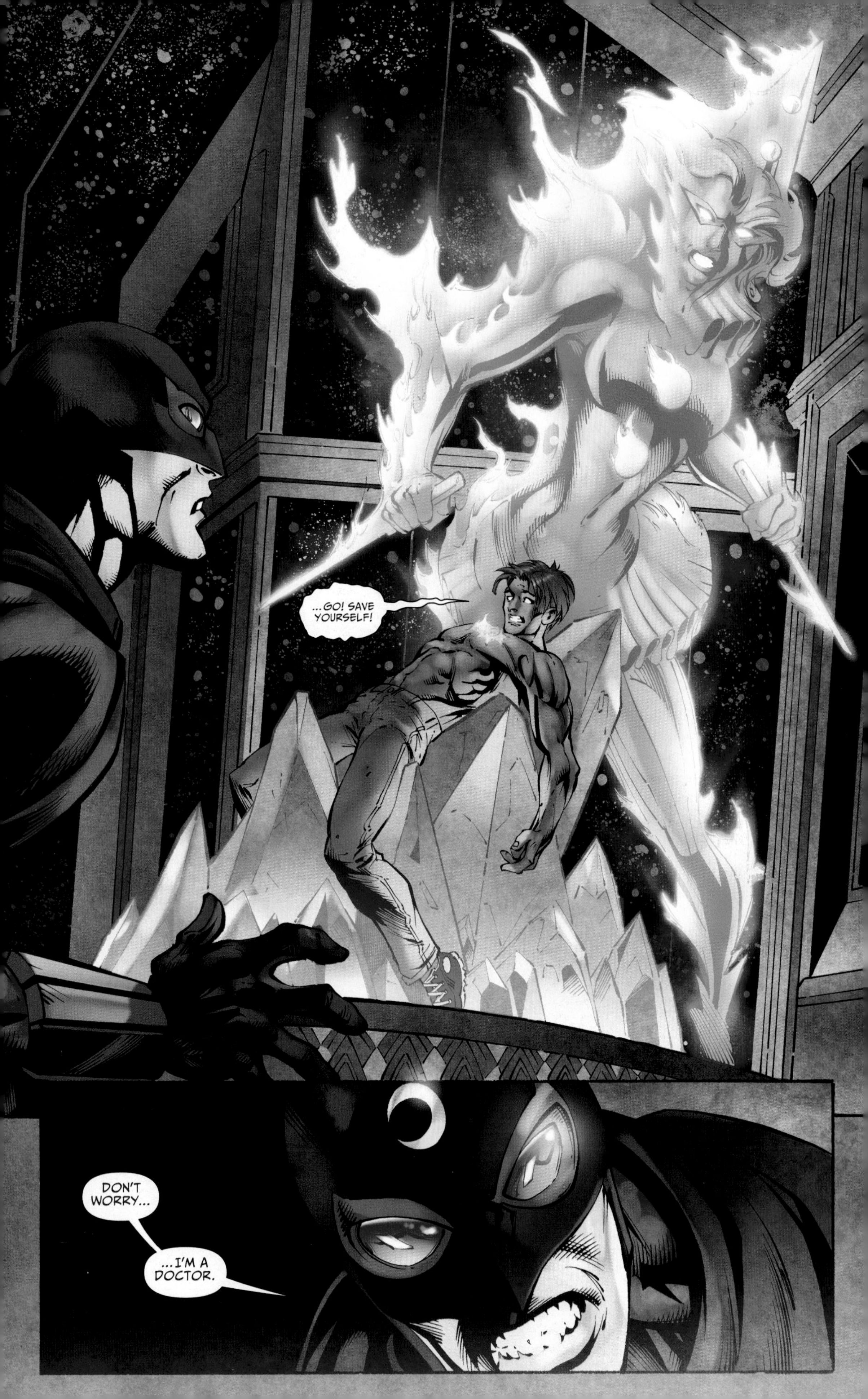
...GO! SAVE YOURSELF!
DON'T WORRY...
...I'M A DOCTOR.

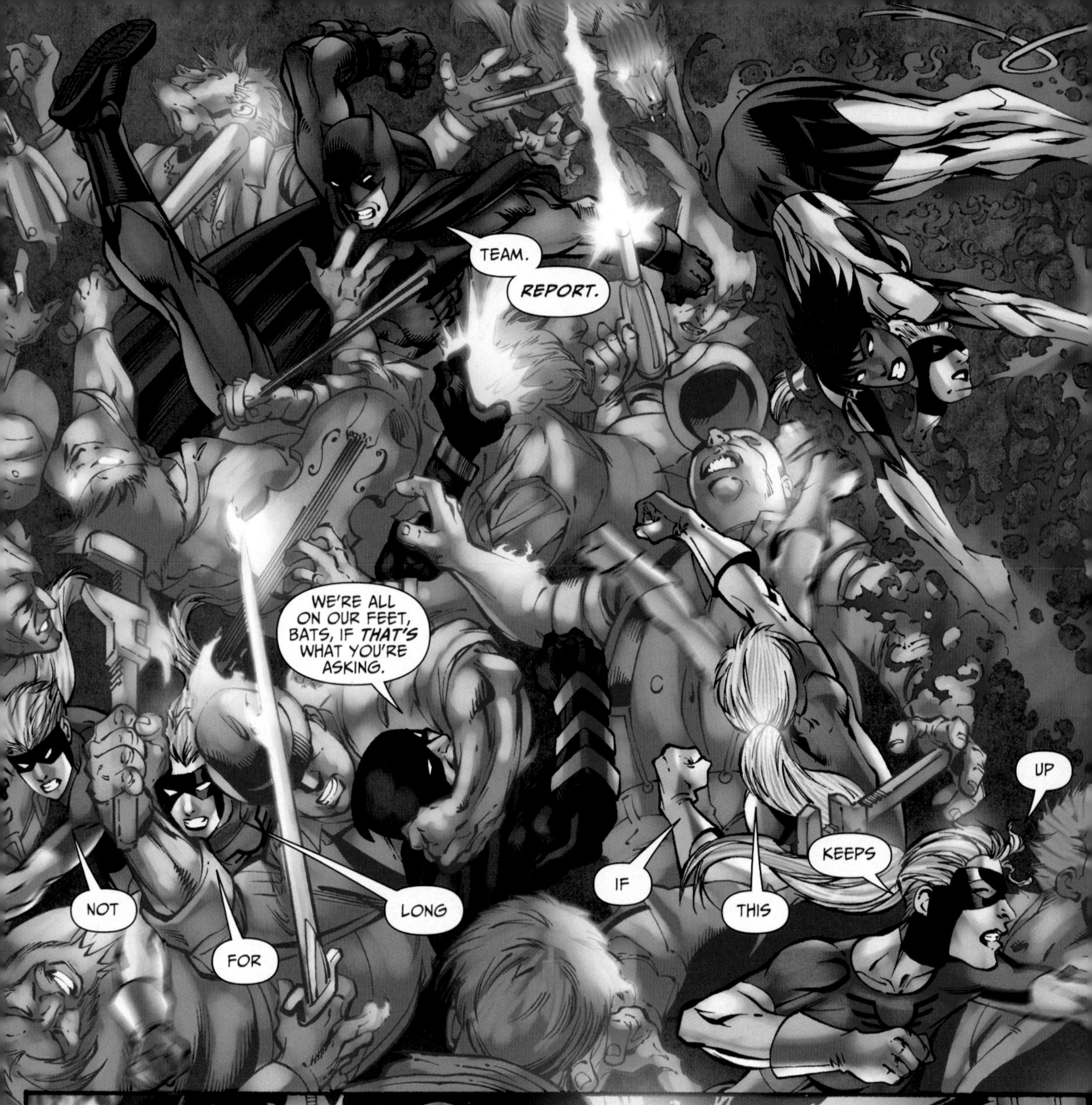
TEAM.
REPORT.
WE'RE ALL ON OUR FEET, BATS, IF THAT'S WHAT YOU'RE ASKING.
NOT
FOR
LONG
IF
THIS
KEEPS
UP

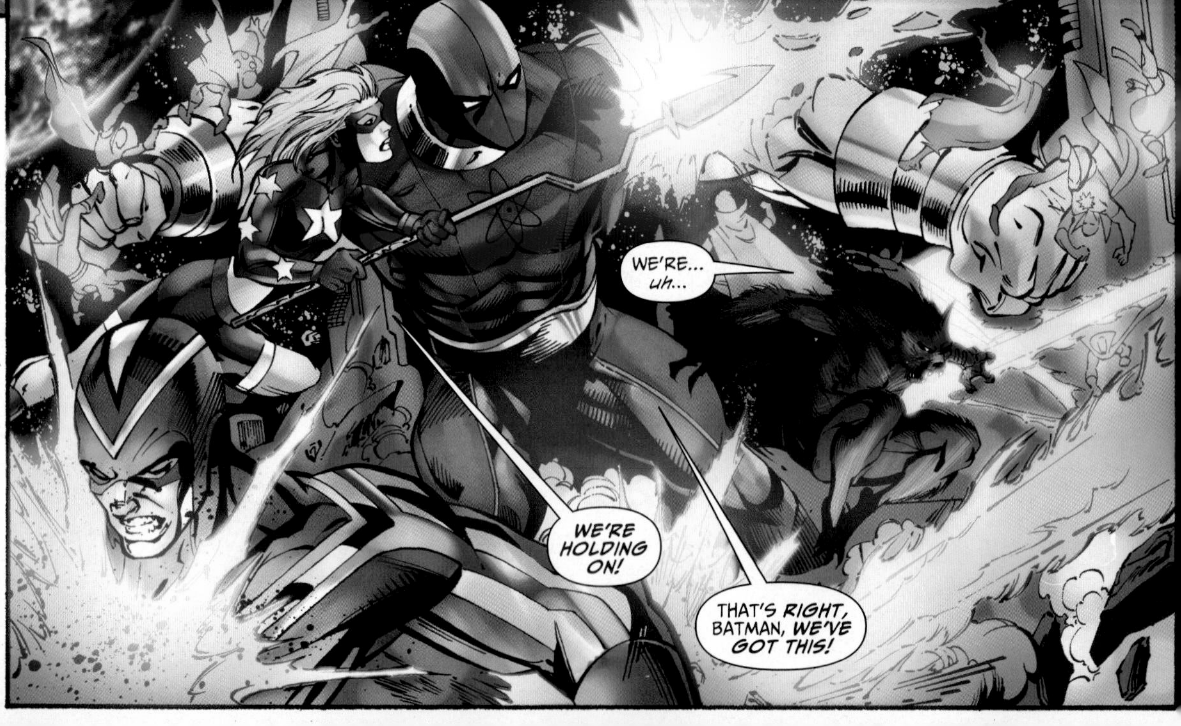
WE'RE... uh...
WE'RE HOLDING ON!
THAT'S RIGHT, BATMAN, WE'VE GOT THIS!

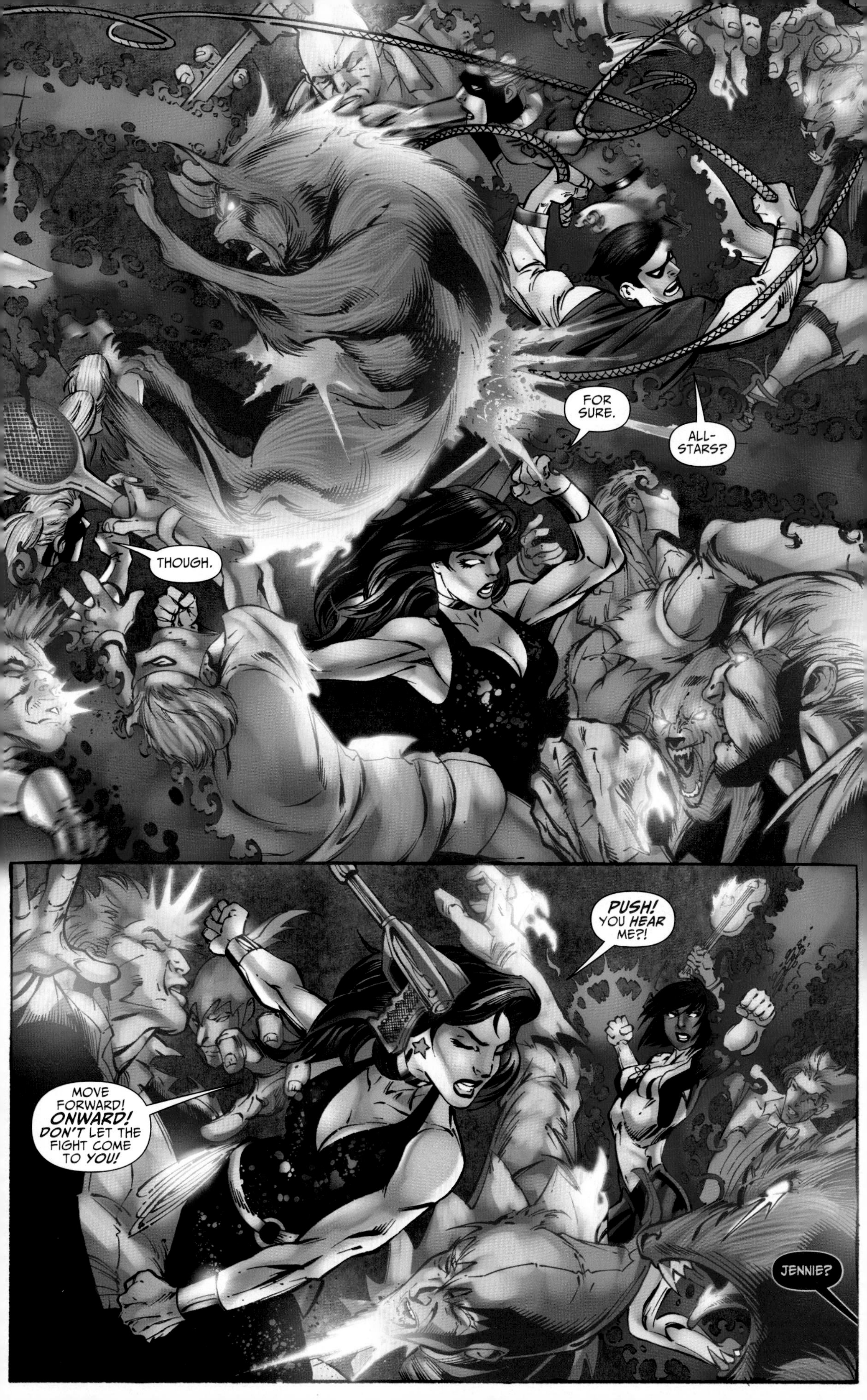
FOR SURE.
ALL-STARS?
THOUGH.
PUSH! YOU HEAR ME?!
MOVE FORWARD! ONWARD! DON'T LET THE FIGHT COME TO YOU!
JENNIE?

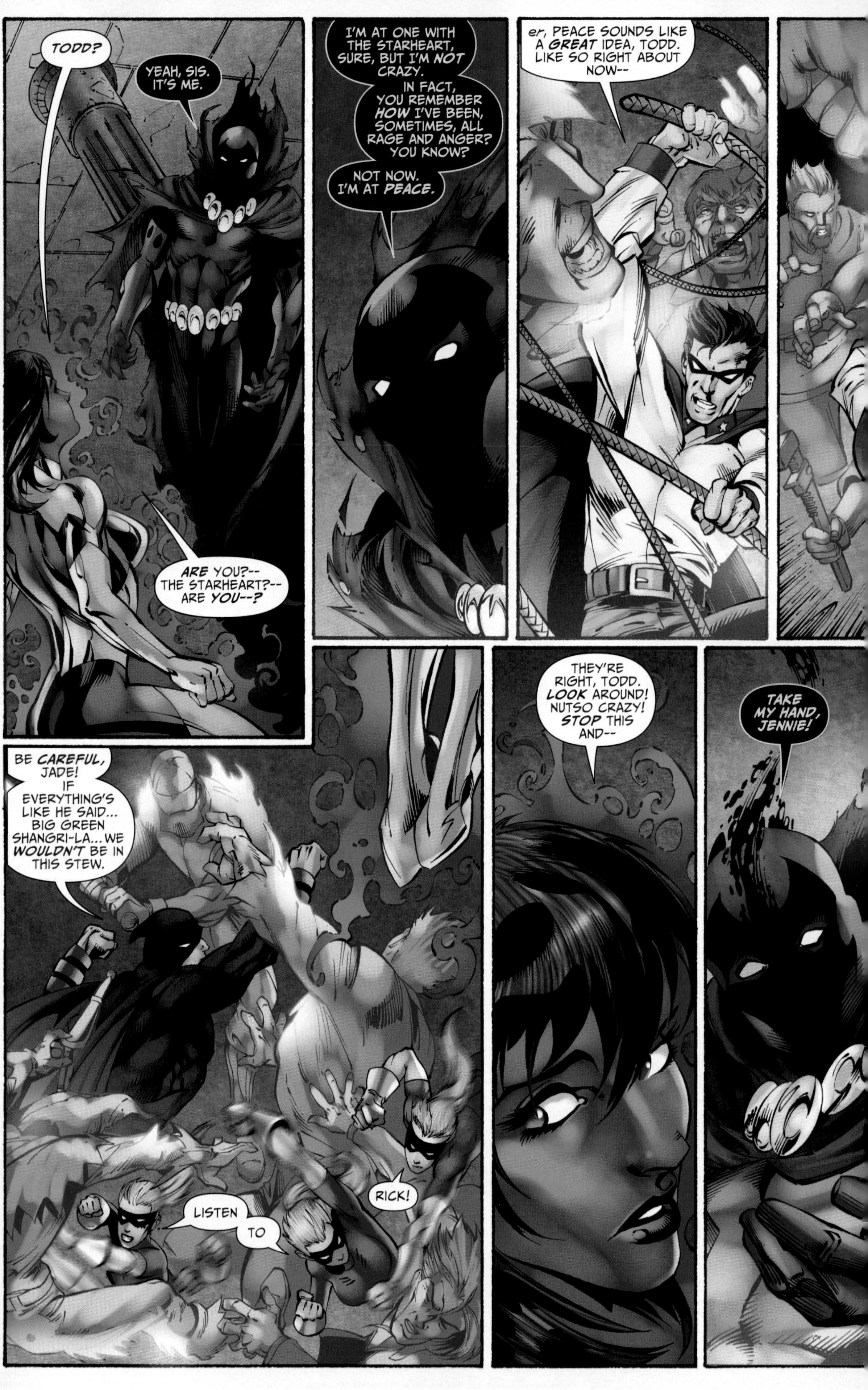
TODD?
YEAH, SIS. IT'S ME.
ARE YOU?-- THE STARHEART?-- ARE YOU--?
I'M AT ONE WITH THE STARHEART, SURE, BUT I'M NOT CRAZY.
IN FACT, YOU REMEMBER HOW I'VE BEEN, SOMETIMES, ALL RAGE AND ANGER? YOU KNOW?
NOT NOW. I'M AT PEACE.
er, PEACE SOUNDS LIKE A GREAT IDEA, TODD. LIKE SO RIGHT ABOUT NOW--
BE CAREFUL, JADE! IF EVERYTHING'S LIKE HE SAID... BIG GREEN SHANGRI-LA... WE WOULDN'T BE IN THIS STEW.
RICK!
LISTEN
TO
THEY'RE RIGHT, TODD. LOOK AROUND! NUTSO CRAZY! STOP THIS AND--
TAKE MY HAND, JENNIE!

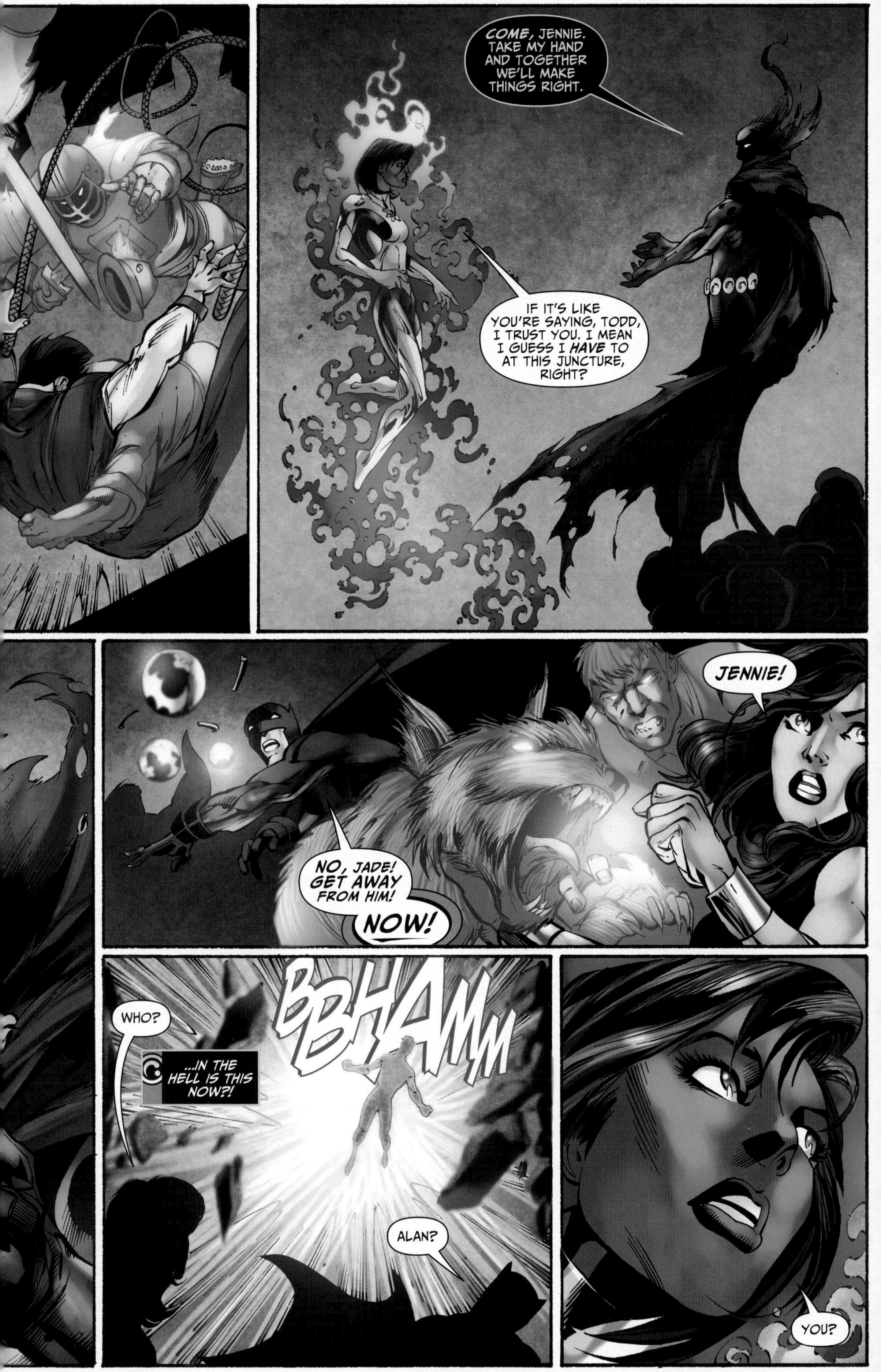

COME, JENNIE. TAKE MY HAND AND TOGETHER WE'LL MAKE THINGS RIGHT.
IF IT'S LIKE YOU'RE SAYING, TODD, I TRUST YOU. I MEAN I GUESS I HAVE TO AT THIS JUNCTURE, RIGHT?
JENNIE!
NO, JADE! GET AWAY FROM HIM!
NOW!
BBHAMM
WHO?
...IN THE HELL IS THIS NOW?!
ALAN?
YOU?

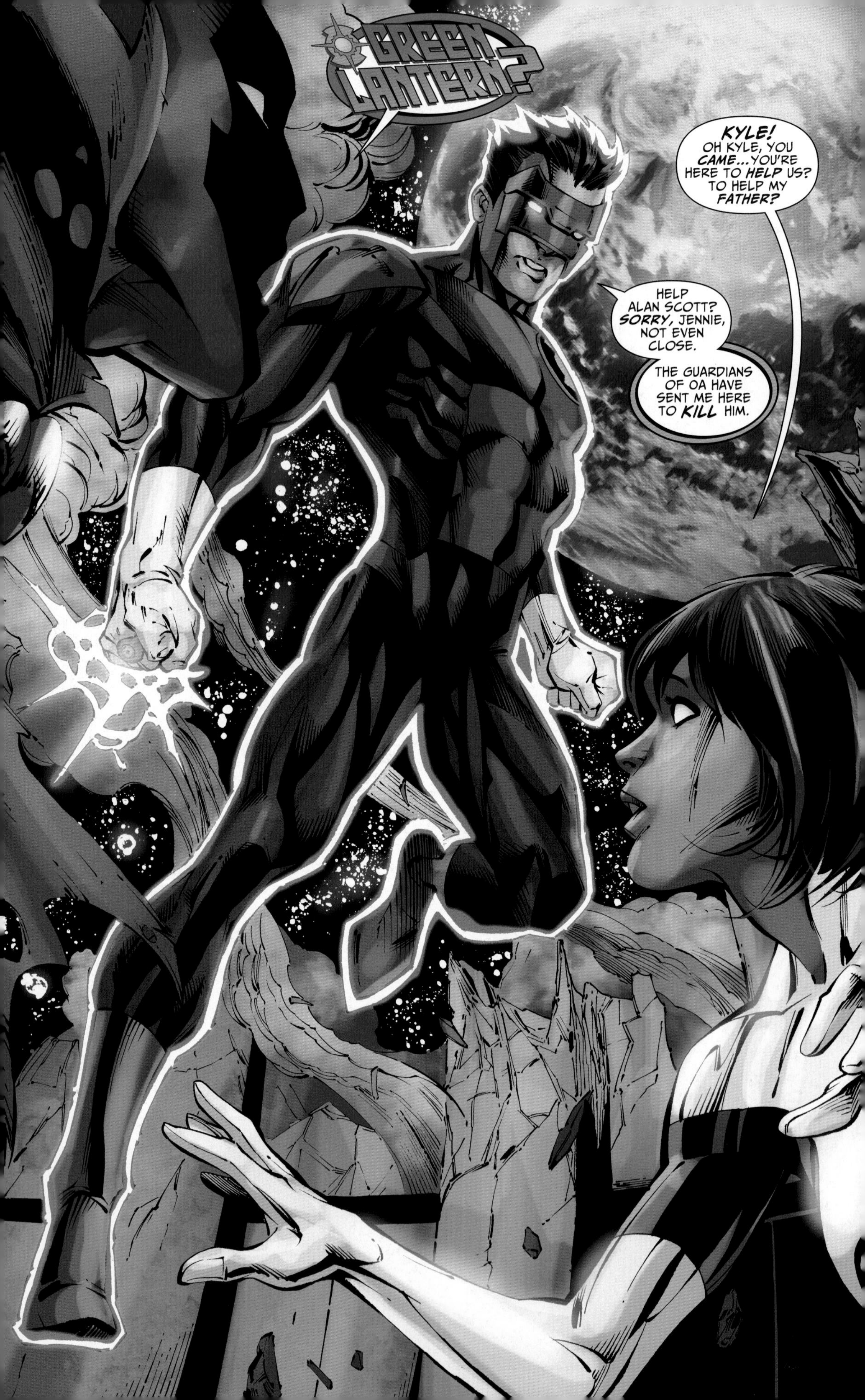
GREEN LANTERN?
KYLE! OH KYLE, YOU CAME...YOU'RE HERE TO HELP US? TO HELP MY FATHER?
HELP ALAN SCOTT? SORRY, JENNIE, NOT EVEN CLOSE.
THE GUARDIANS OF OA HAVE SENT ME HERE TO KILL HIM.

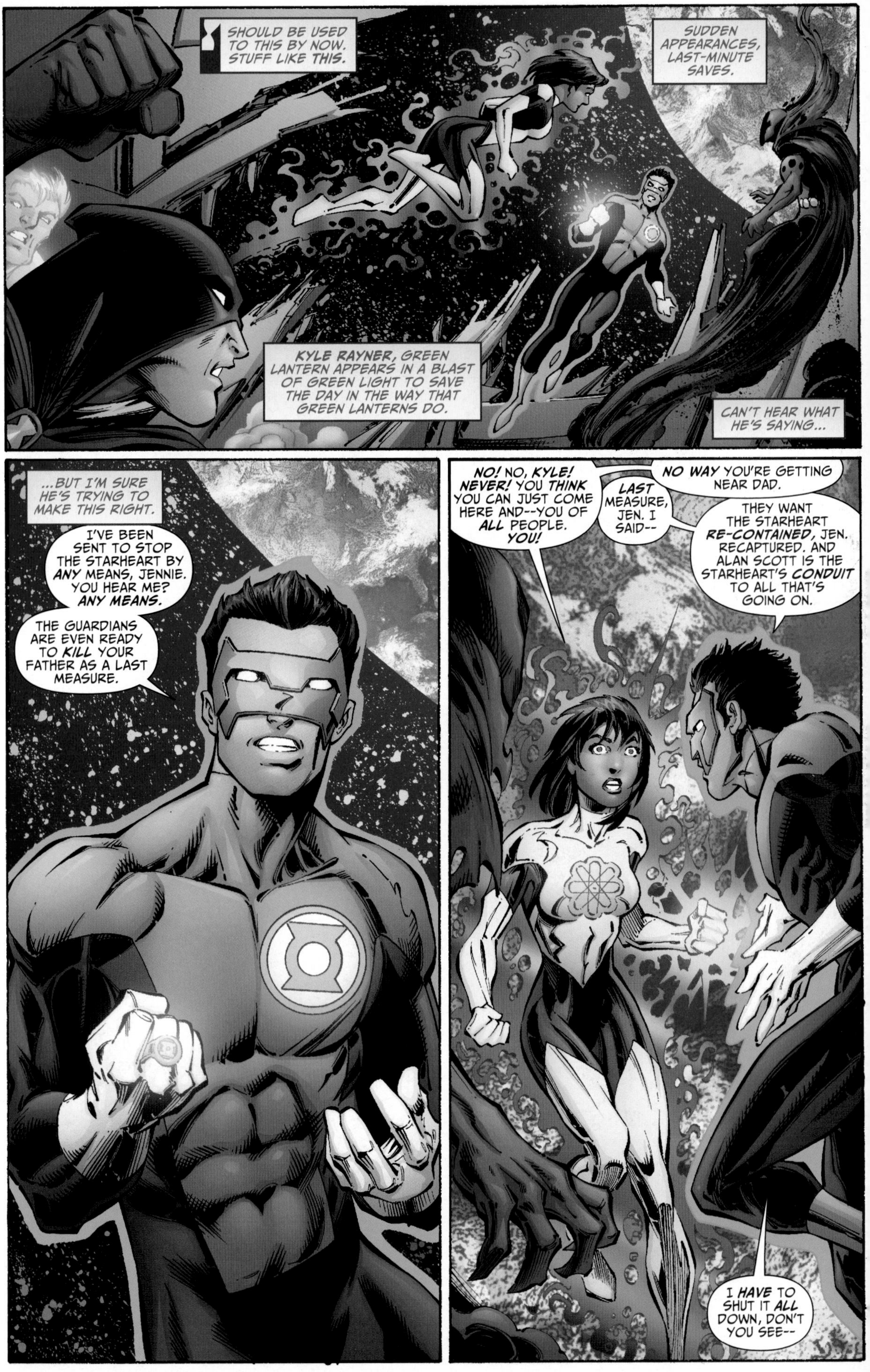
SHOULD BE USED TO THIS BY NOW. STUFF LIKE THIS.
SUDDEN APPEARANCES, LAST-MINUTE SAVES.
KYLE RAYNER, GREEN LANTERN APPEARS IN A BLAST OF GREEN LIGHT TO SAVE THE DAY IN THE WAY THAT GREEN LANTERNS DO.
CAN'T HEAR WHAT HE'S SAYING...
...BUT I'M SURE HE'S TRYING TO MAKE THIS RIGHT.
I'VE BEEN SENT TO STOP THE STARHEART BY ANY MEANS, JENNIE. YOU HEAR ME? ANY MEANS.
THE GUARDIANS ARE EVEN READY TO KILL YOUR FATHER AS A LAST MEASURE.
NO! NO, KYLE! NEVER! YOU THINK YOU CAN JUST COME HERE AND--YOU OF ALL PEOPLE. YOU!
LAST MEASURE, JEN. I SAID--
NO WAY YOU'RE GETTING NEAR DAD.
THEY WANT THE STARHEART RE-CONTAINED, JEN. RECAPTURED. AND ALAN SCOTT IS THE STARHEART'S CONDUIT TO ALL THAT'S GOING ON.
I HAVE TO SHUT IT ALL DOWN, DON'T YOU SEE--

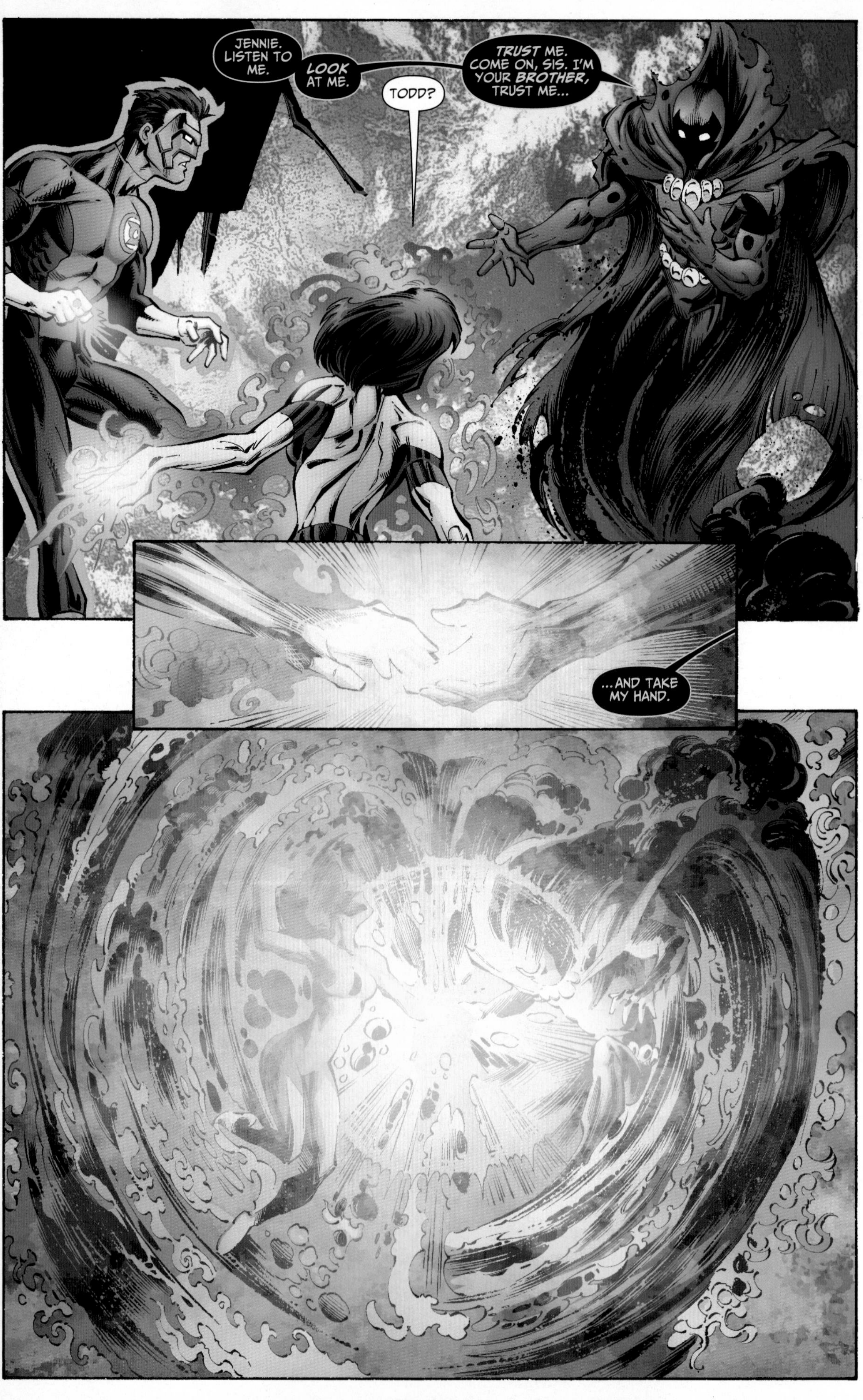
JENNIE. LISTEN TO ME.
LOOK AT ME.
TODD?
TRUST ME. COME ON, SIS. I'M YOUR BROTHER, TRUST ME...
...AND TAKE MY HAND.

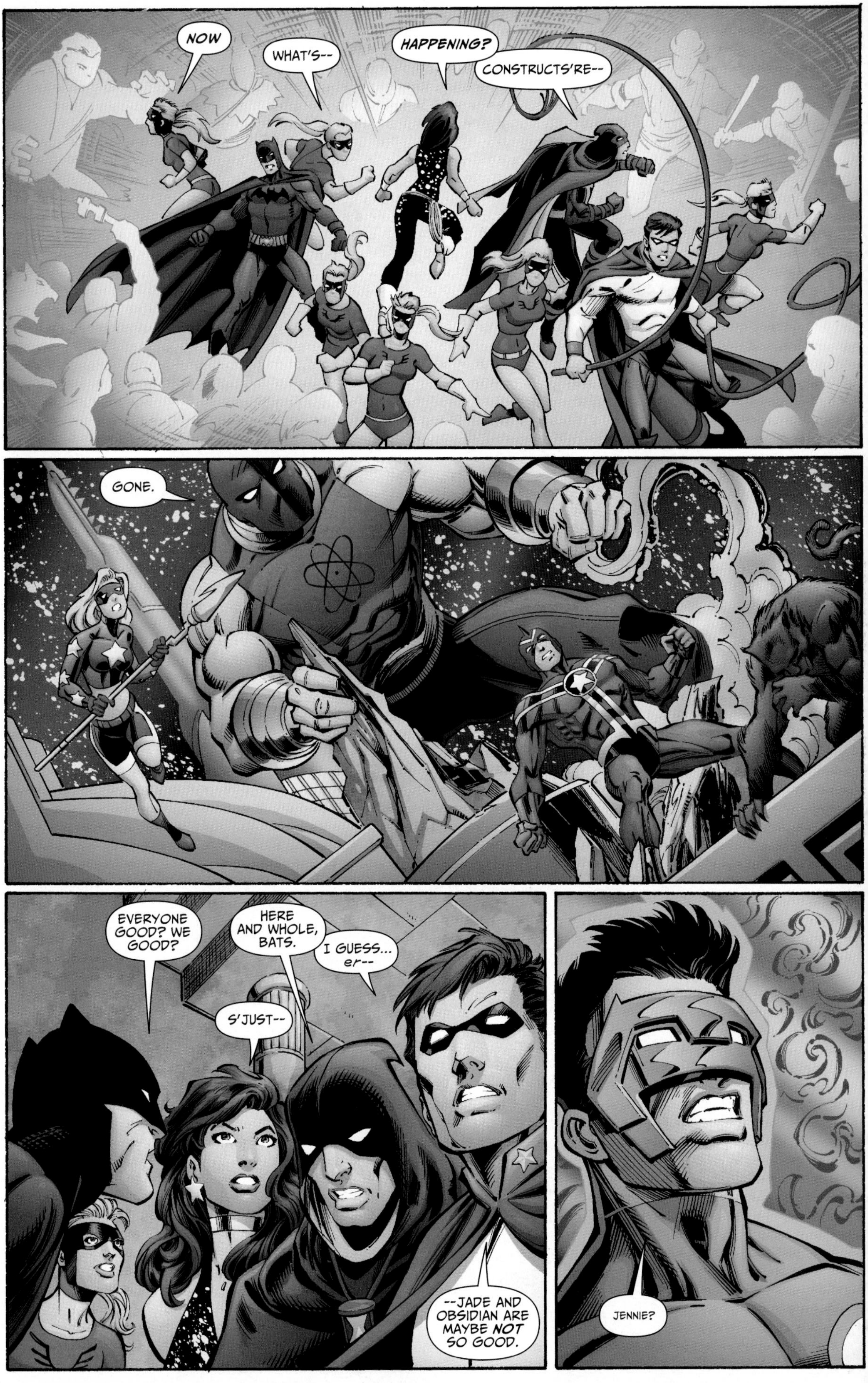
NOW
WHAT'S--
HAPPENING?
CONSTRUCTS'RE--
GONE.
EVERYONE GOOD? WE GOOD?
HERE AND WHOLE, BATS.
I GUESS... er--
S'JUST--
--JADE AND OBSIDIAN ARE MAYBE NOT SO GOOD.
JENNIE?

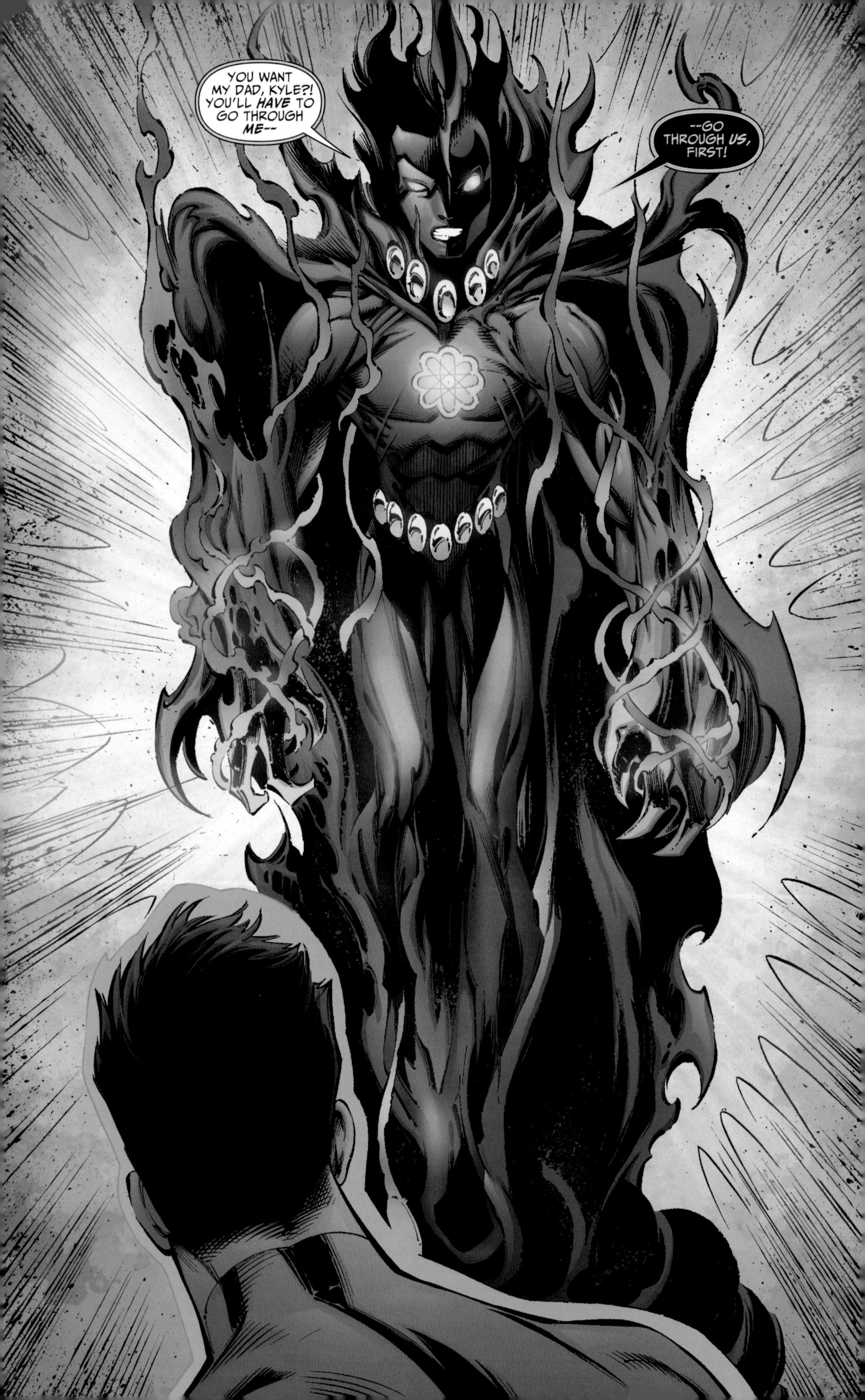
YOU WANT MY DAD, KYLE?! YOU'LL HAVE TO GO THROUGH ME--
--GO THROUGH US, FIRST!

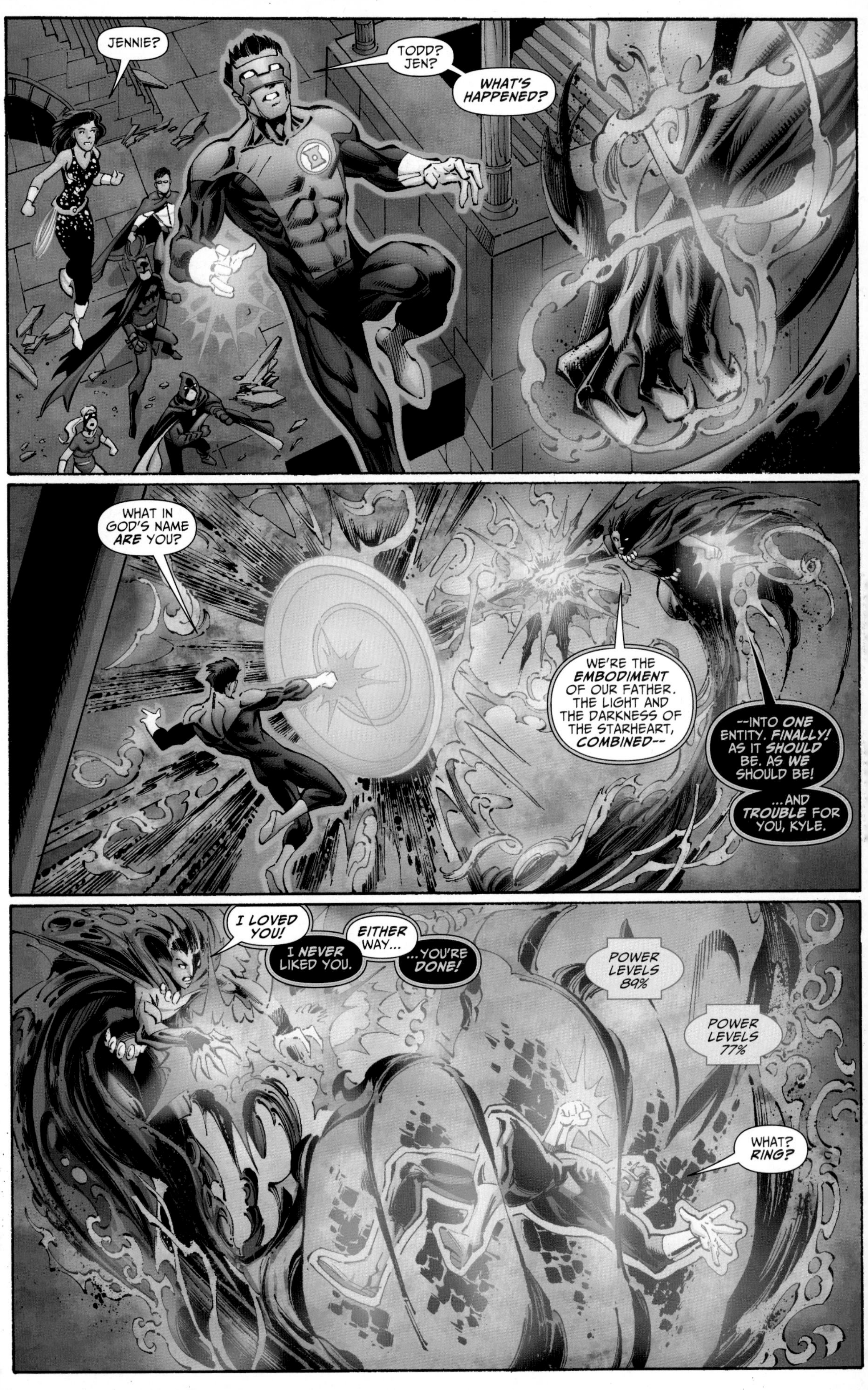
JENNIE?
TODD? JEN?
WHAT'S HAPPENED?
WHAT IN GOD'S NAME ARE YOU?
WE'RE THE EMBODIMENT OF OUR FATHER. THE LIGHT AND THE DARKNESS OF THE STARHEART, COMBINED--
--INTO ONE ENTITY. FINALLY! AS IT SHOULD BE. AS WE SHOULD BE!
...AND TROUBLE FOR YOU, KYLE.
I LOVED YOU!
I NEVER LIKED YOU.
EITHER WAY...
...YOU'RE DONE!
POWER LEVELS 89%
POWER LEVELS 77%
WHAT? RING?

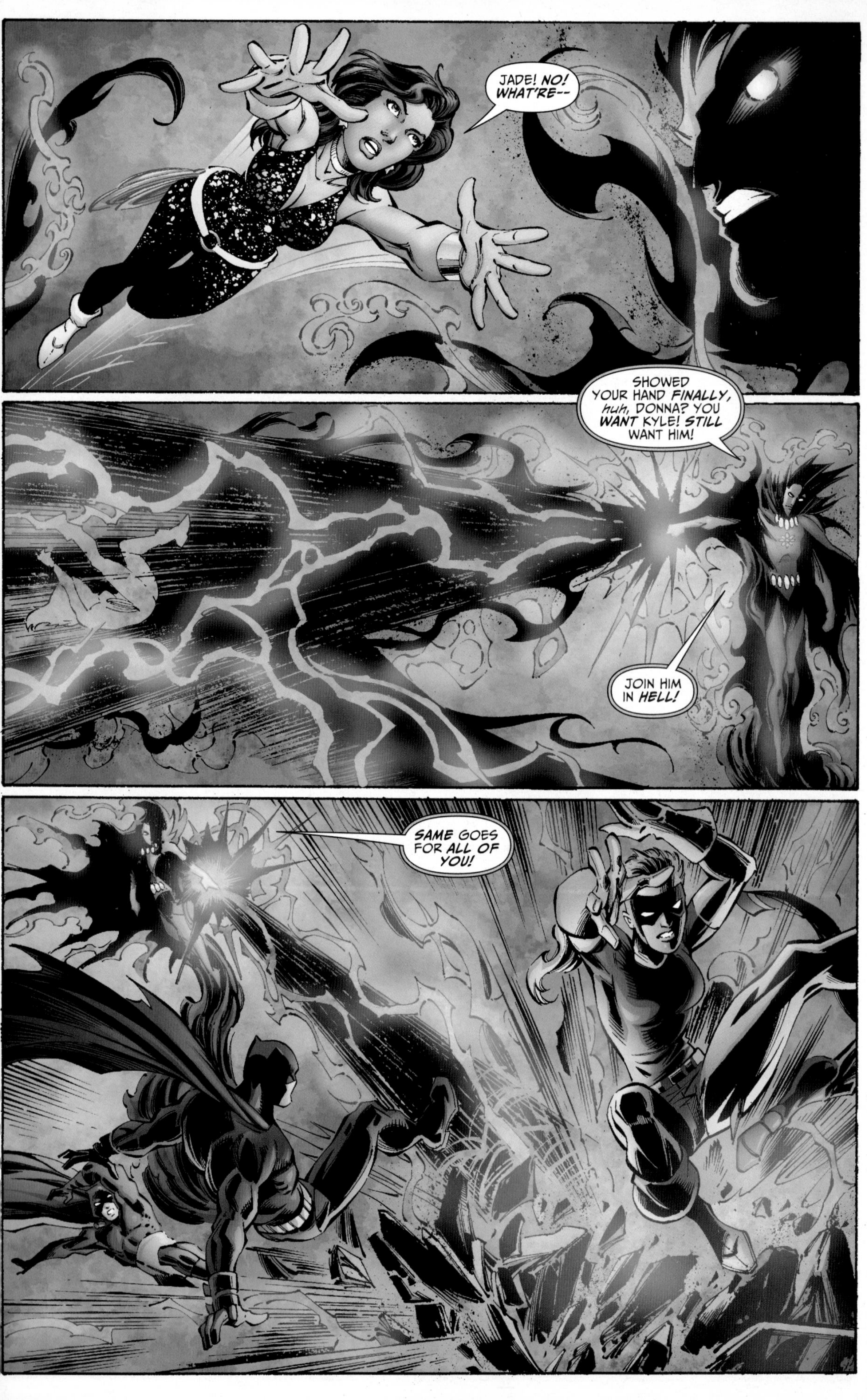
JADE! NO! WHAT'RE--
SHOWED YOUR HAND FINALLY, huh, DONNA? YOU WANT KYLE! STILL WANT HIM!
JOIN HIM IN HELL!
SAME GOES FOR ALL OF YOU!

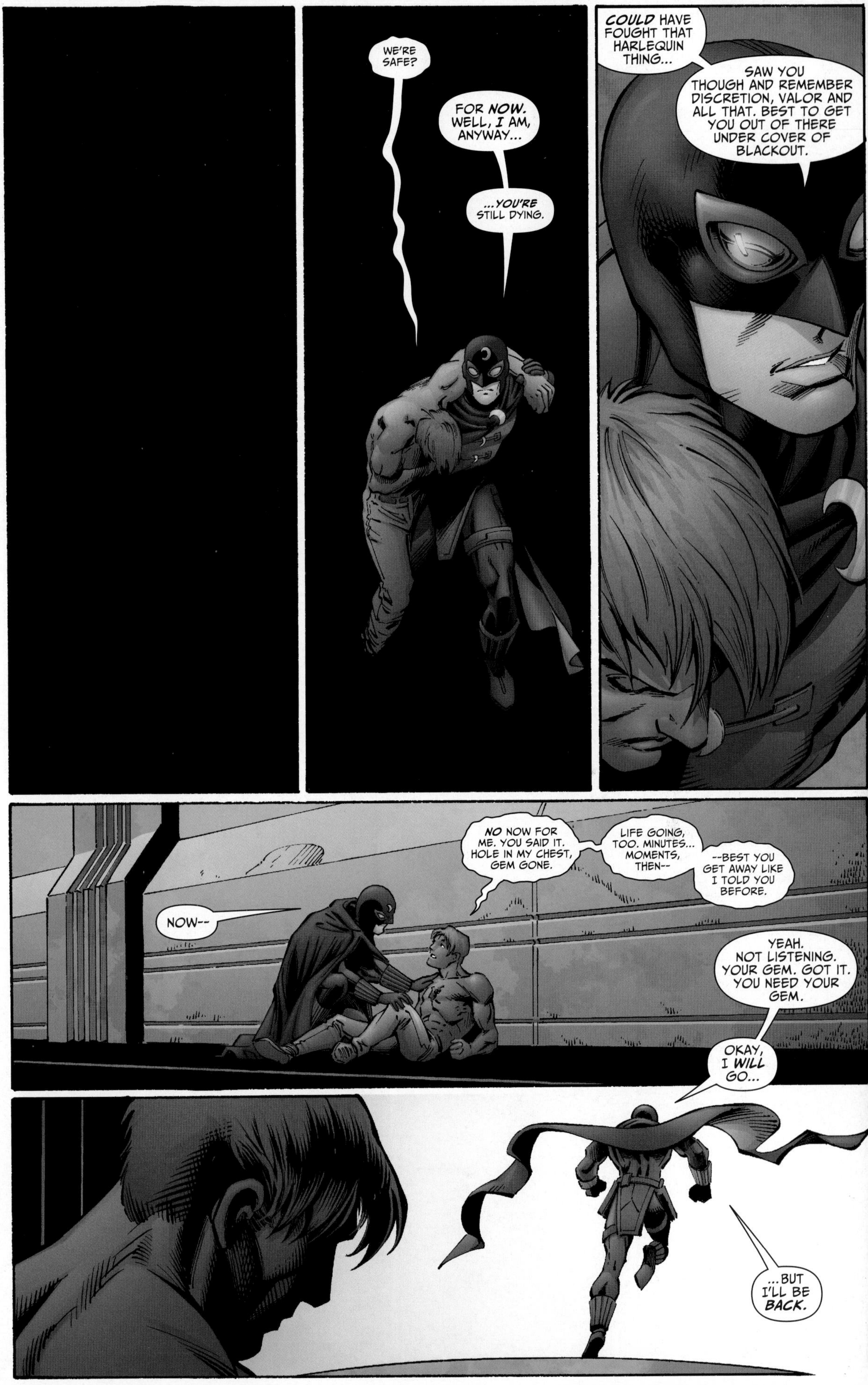

WE'RE SAFE?
FOR *NOW.* WELL, *I* AM, ANYWAY...
...*YOU'RE* STILL DYING.
COULD HAVE FOUGHT THAT HARLEQUIN THING...
SAW YOU THOUGH AND REMEMBER DISCRETION, VALOR AND ALL THAT. BEST TO GET YOU OUT OF THERE UNDER COVER OF BLACKOUT.
NOW--
NO NOW FOR ME. YOU SAID IT. HOLE IN MY CHEST, GEM GONE.
LIFE GOING, TOO. MINUTES... MOMENTS, THEN--
--BEST YOU GET AWAY LIKE I TOLD YOU BEFORE.
YEAH. NOT LISTENING. YOUR GEM. GOT IT. YOU NEED YOUR GEM.
OKAY, I *WILL* GO...
...BUT I'LL BE *BACK.*

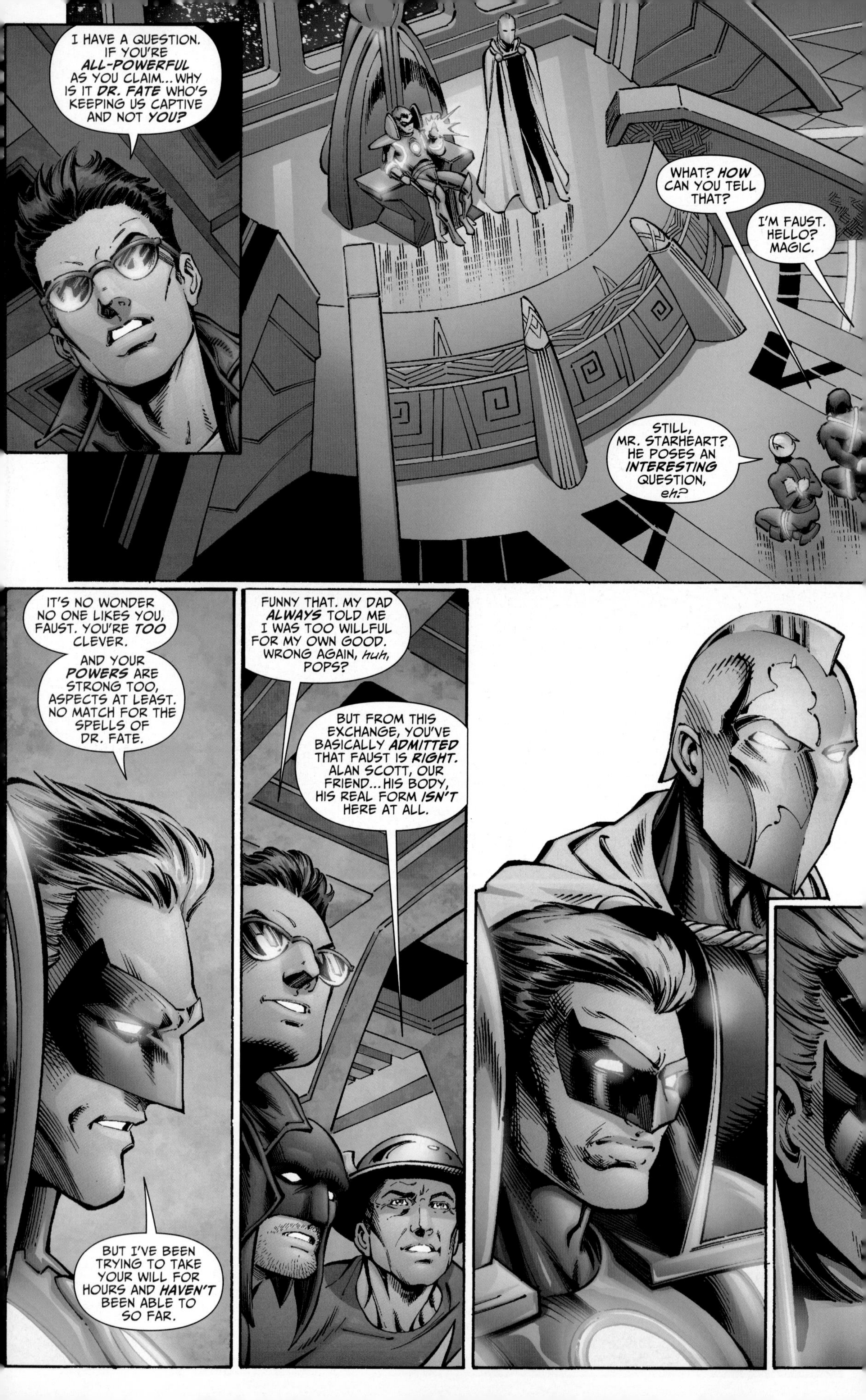
I HAVE A QUESTION. IF YOU'RE ALL-POWERFUL AS YOU CLAIM... WHY IS IT DR. FATE WHO'S KEEPING US CAPTIVE AND NOT YOU?
WHAT? HOW CAN YOU TELL THAT?
I'M FAUST. HELLO? MAGIC.
STILL, MR. STARHEART? HE POSES AN INTERESTING QUESTION, eh?
IT'S NO WONDER NO ONE LIKES YOU, FAUST. YOU'RE TOO CLEVER.
AND YOUR POWERS ARE STRONG TOO, ASPECTS AT LEAST. NO MATCH FOR THE SPELLS OF DR. FATE.
BUT I'VE BEEN TRYING TO TAKE YOUR WILL FOR HOURS AND HAVEN'T BEEN ABLE TO SO FAR.
FUNNY THAT. MY DAD ALWAYS TOLD ME I WAS TOO WILLFUL FOR MY OWN GOOD. WRONG AGAIN, huh, POPS?
BUT FROM THIS EXCHANGE, YOU'VE BASICALLY ADMITTED THAT FAUST IS RIGHT. ALAN SCOTT, OUR FRIEND... HIS BODY, HIS REAL FORM ISN'T HERE AT ALL.

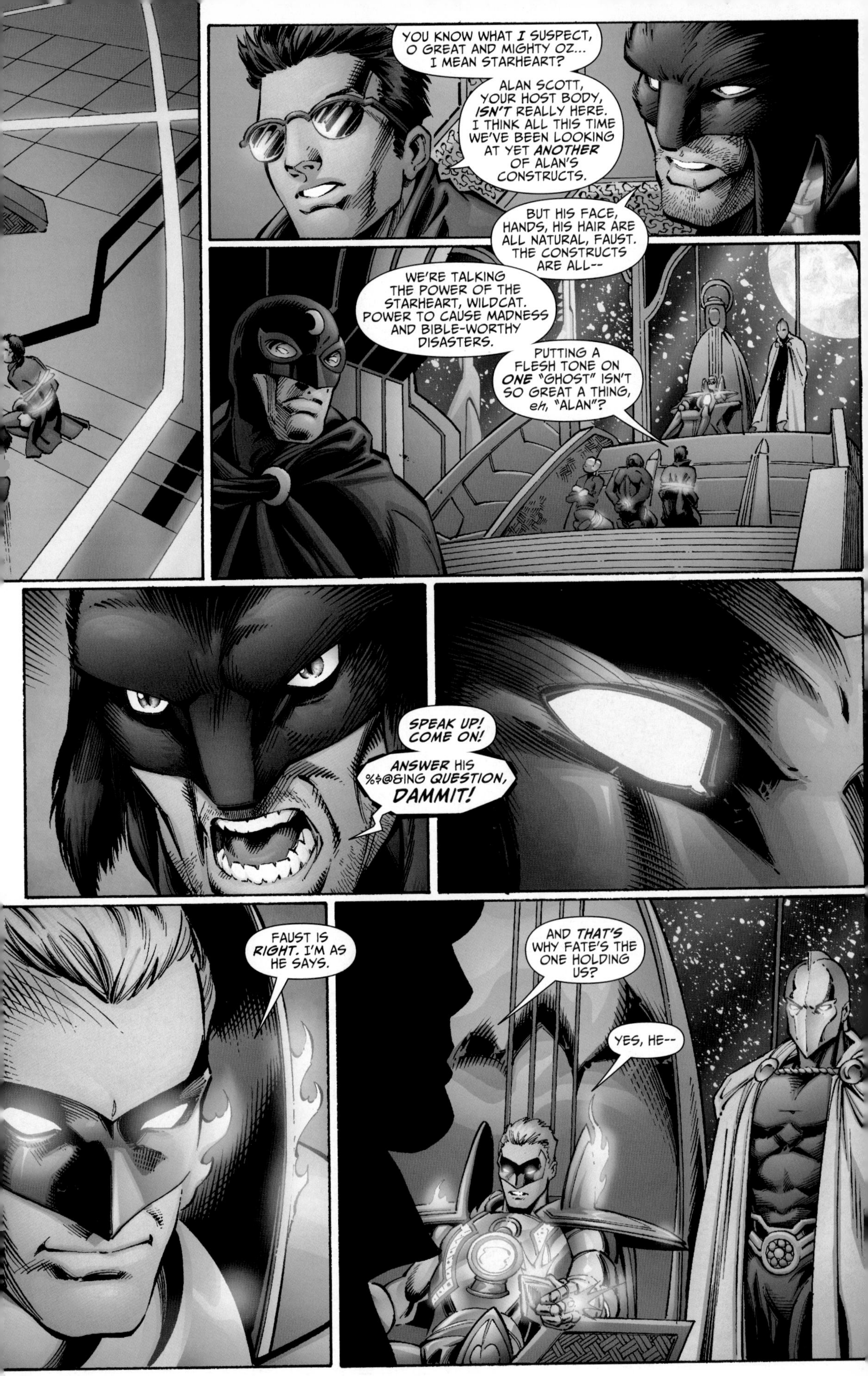

YOU KNOW WHAT *I* SUSPECT, O GREAT AND MIGHTY OZ... I MEAN STARHEART?
ALAN SCOTT, YOUR HOST BODY, ***ISN'T*** REALLY HERE. I THINK ALL THIS TIME WE'VE BEEN LOOKING AT YET ***ANOTHER*** OF ALAN'S CONSTRUCTS.
BUT HIS FACE, HANDS, HIS HAIR ARE ALL NATURAL, FAUST. THE CONSTRUCTS ARE ALL--
WE'RE TALKING THE POWER OF THE STARHEART, WILDCAT. POWER TO CAUSE MADNESS AND BIBLE-WORTHY DISASTERS.
PUTTING A FLESH TONE ON ***ONE*** "GHOST" ISN'T SO GREAT A THING, *eh*, "ALAN"?
SPEAK UP! COME ON!
ANSWER HIS %$@&ING ***QUESTION, DAMMIT!***
FAUST IS ***RIGHT***. I'M AS HE SAYS.
AND ***THAT'S*** WHY FATE'S THE ONE HOLDING US?
YES, HE--

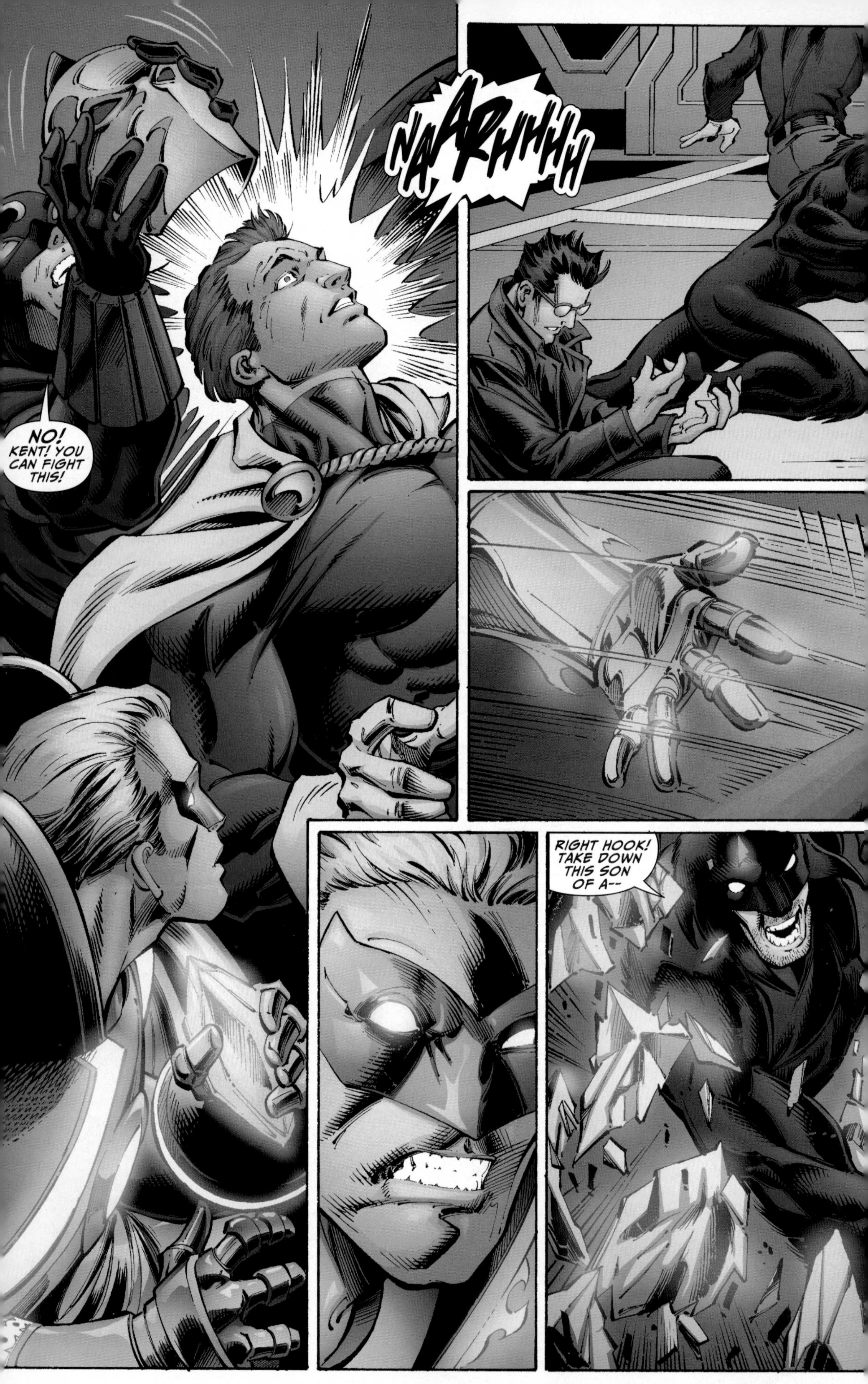
NAARHHHH
NO! KENT! YOU CAN FIGHT THIS!
RIGHT HOOK! TAKE DOWN THIS SON OF A--

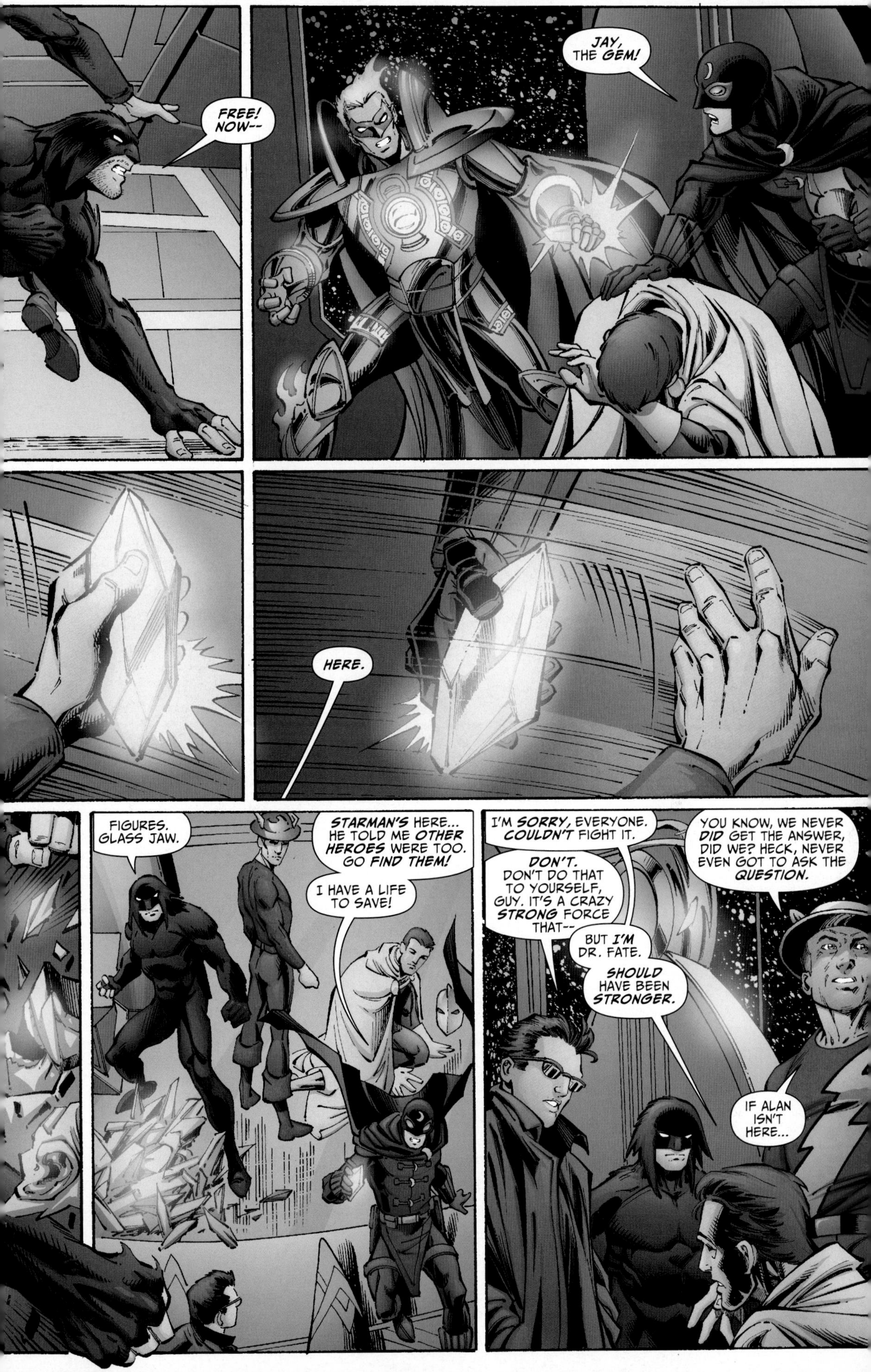
FREE! NOW--
JAY, THE GEM!
HERE.
FIGURES. GLASS JAW.
STARMAN'S HERE... HE TOLD ME OTHER HEROES WERE TOO. GO FIND THEM!
I HAVE A LIFE TO SAVE!
I'M SORRY, EVERYONE. COULDN'T FIGHT IT.
DON'T. DON'T DO THAT TO YOURSELF, GUY. IT'S A CRAZY STRONG FORCE THAT--
BUT I'M DR. FATE.
SHOULD HAVE BEEN STRONGER.
YOU KNOW, WE NEVER DID GET THE ANSWER, DID WE? HECK, NEVER EVEN GOT TO ASK THE QUESTION.
IF ALAN ISN'T HERE...

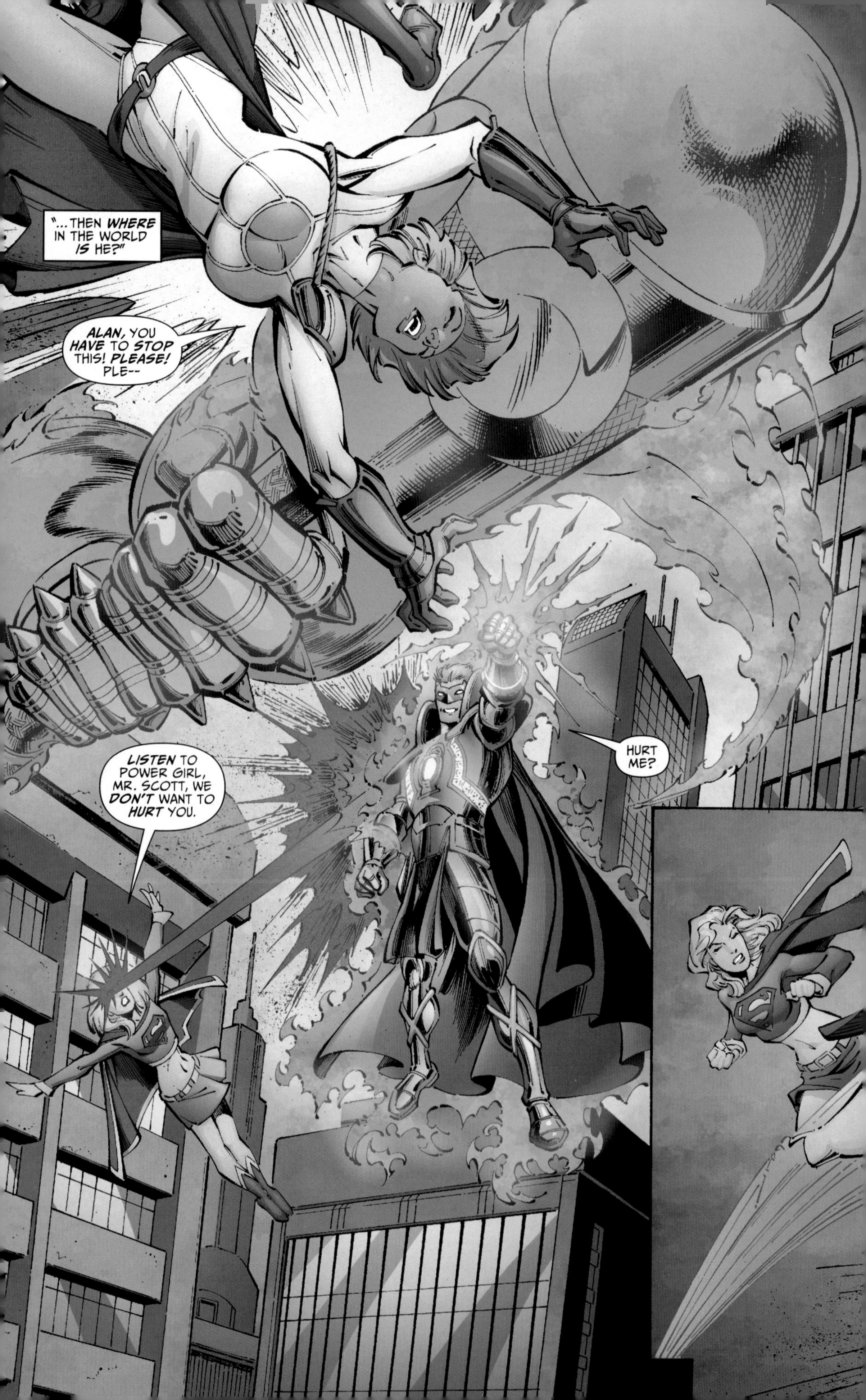
"...THEN WHERE IN THE WORLD IS HE?"
ALAN, YOU HAVE TO STOP THIS! PLEASE! PLE--
LISTEN TO POWER GIRL, MR. SCOTT, WE DON'T WANT TO HURT YOU.
HURT ME?

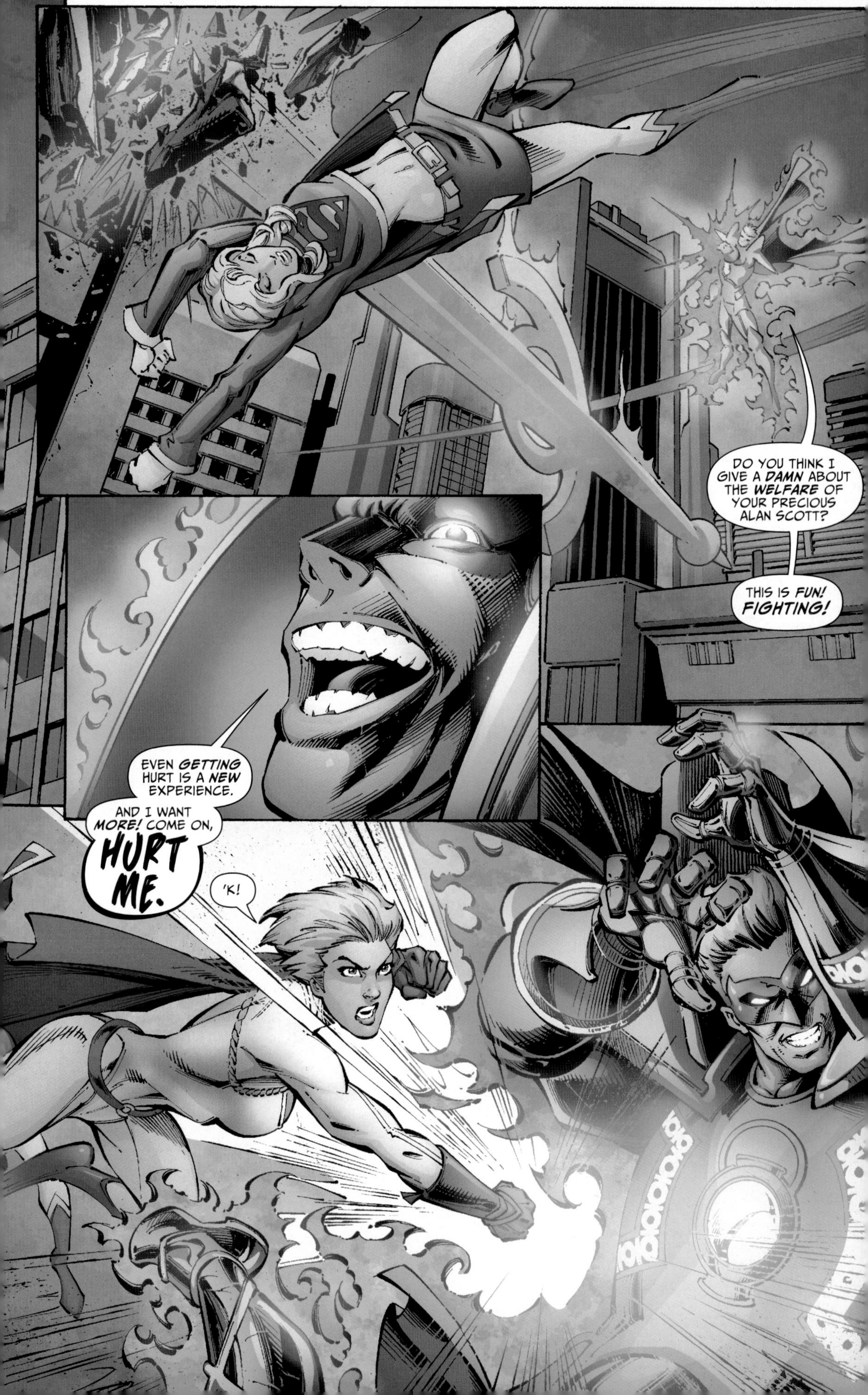
DO YOU THINK I GIVE A DAMN ABOUT THE WELFARE OF YOUR PRECIOUS ALAN SCOTT?
THIS IS FUN! FIGHTING!
EVEN GETTING HURT IS A NEW EXPERIENCE.
AND I WANT MORE! COME ON, HURT ME.
'K!

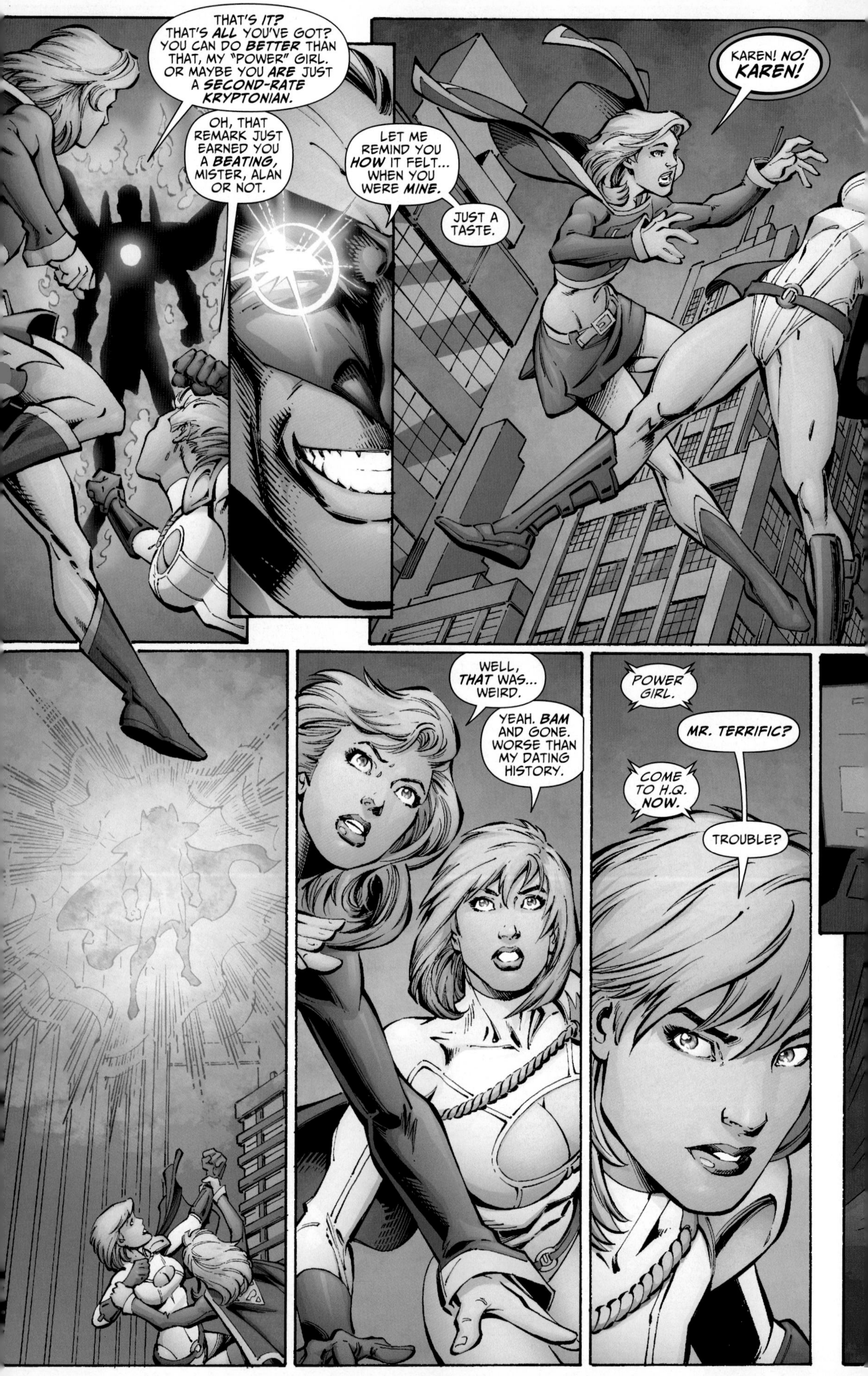
THAT'S IT? THAT'S ALL YOU'VE GOT? YOU CAN DO BETTER THAN THAT, MY "POWER" GIRL. OR MAYBE YOU ARE JUST A SECOND-RATE KRYPTONIAN.
OH, THAT REMARK JUST EARNED YOU A BEATING, MISTER, ALAN OR NOT.
LET ME REMIND YOU HOW IT FELT... WHEN YOU WERE MINE.
JUST A TASTE.
KAREN! NO! KAREN!
WELL, THAT WAS... WEIRD.
YEAH. BAM AND GONE. WORSE THAN MY DATING HISTORY.
POWER GIRL.
MR. TERRIFIC?
COME TO H.Q. NOW.
TROUBLE?

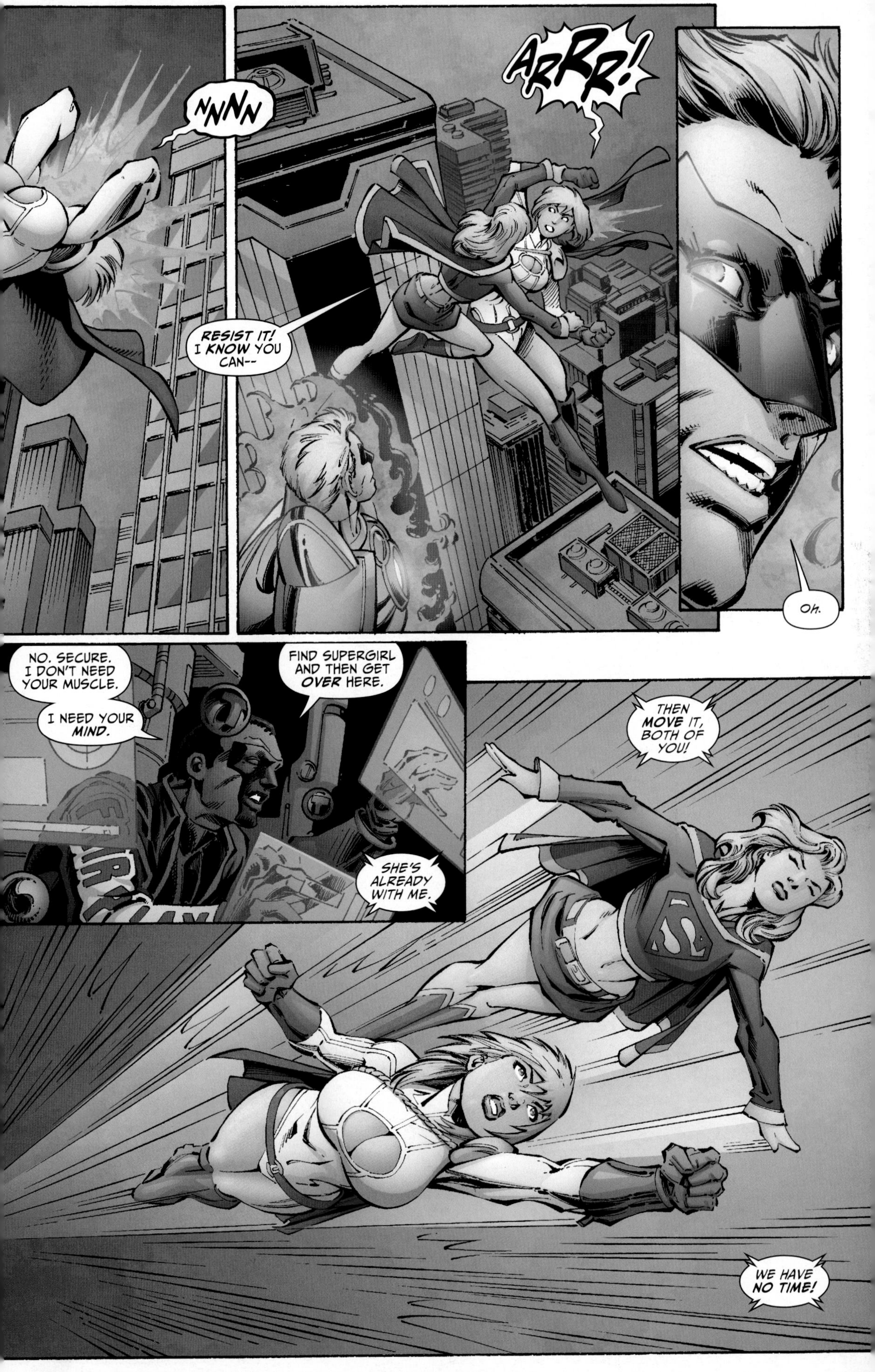
NNNN
RESIST IT! I KNOW YOU CAN--
ARRR!
Oh.
NO. SECURE. I DON'T NEED YOUR MUSCLE.
I NEED YOUR MIND.
FIND SUPERGIRL AND THEN GET OVER HERE.
SHE'S ALREADY WITH ME.
THEN MOVE IT, BOTH OF YOU!
WE HAVE NO TIME!

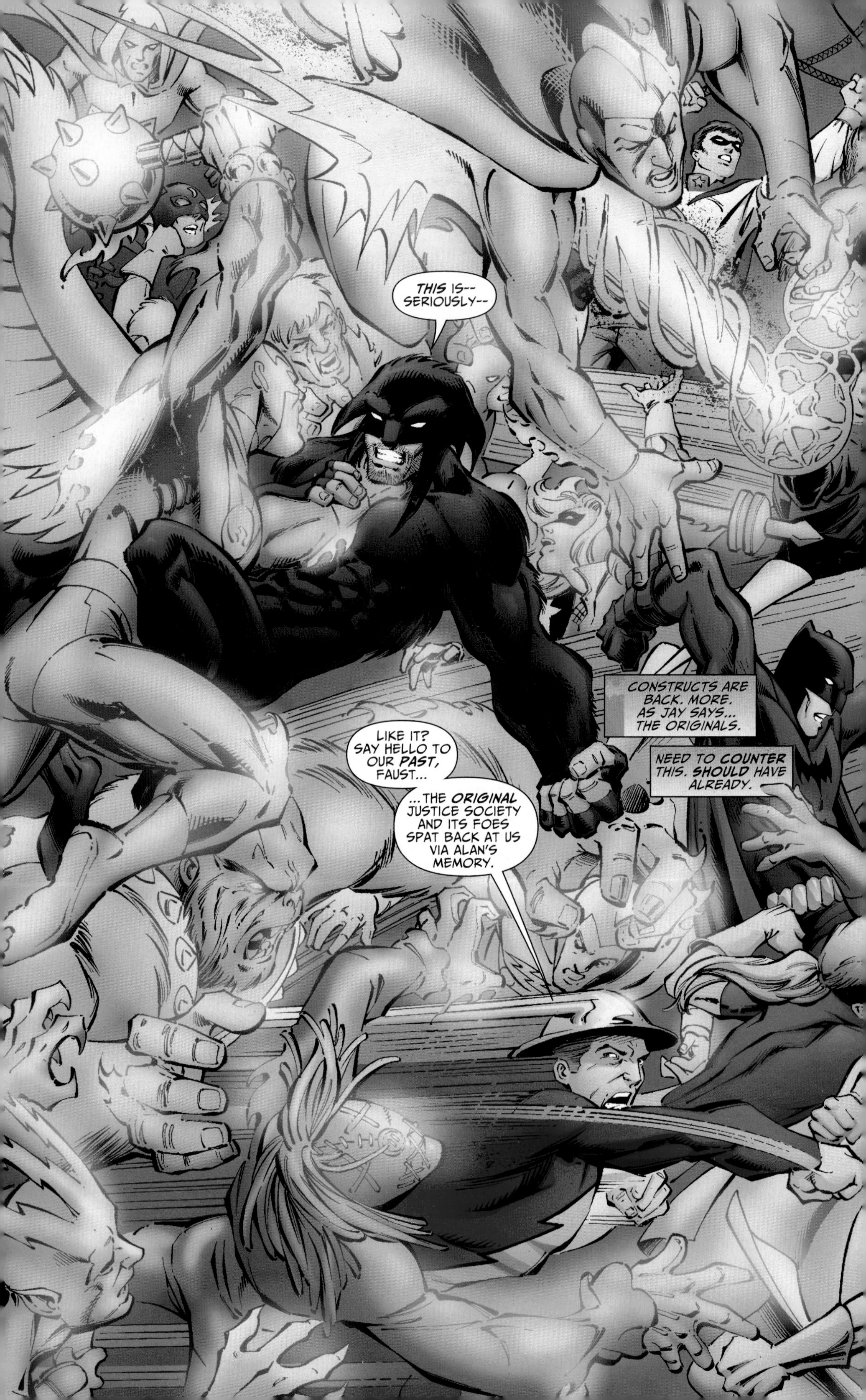
THIS IS-- SERIOUSLY--
CONSTRUCTS ARE BACK. MORE. AS JAY SAYS... THE ORIGINALS.
NEED TO COUNTER THIS. SHOULD HAVE ALREADY.
LIKE IT? SAY HELLO TO OUR PAST, FAUST...
...THE ORIGINAL JUSTICE SOCIETY AND ITS FOES SPAT BACK AT US VIA ALAN'S MEMORY.

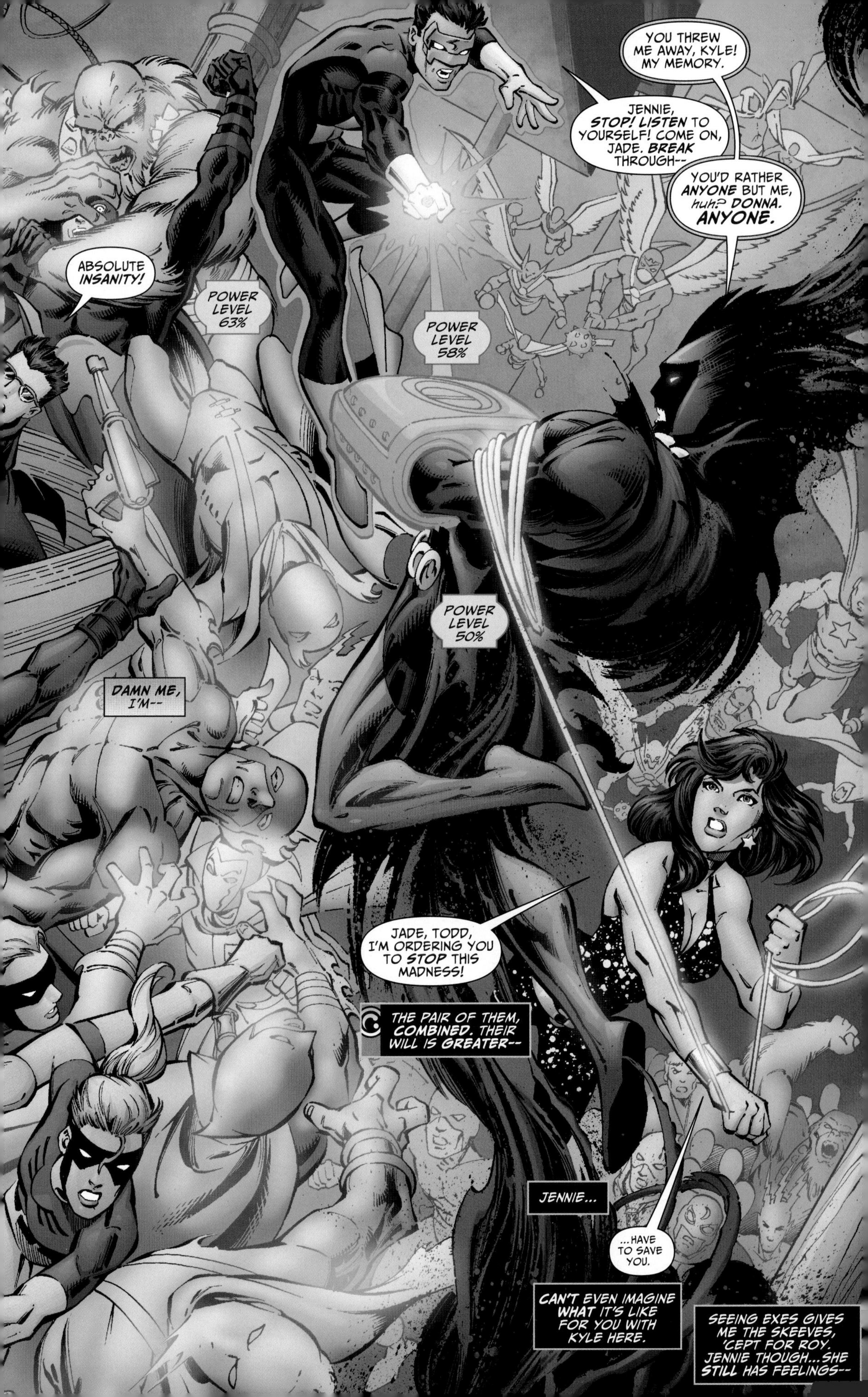

YOU THREW ME AWAY, KYLE! MY MEMORY.
JENNIE, STOP! LISTEN TO YOURSELF! COME ON, JADE. BREAK THROUGH--
YOU'D RATHER ANYONE BUT ME, huh? DONNA. ANYONE.
ABSOLUTE INSANITY!
POWER LEVEL 63%
POWER LEVEL 58%
POWER LEVEL 50%
DAMN ME, I'M--
JADE, TODD, I'M ORDERING YOU TO STOP THIS MADNESS!
THE PAIR OF THEM, COMBINED. THEIR WILL IS GREATER--
JENNIE...
...HAVE TO SAVE YOU.
CAN'T EVEN IMAGINE WHAT IT'S LIKE FOR YOU WITH KYLE HERE.
SEEING EXES GIVES ME THE SKEEVES, 'CEPT FOR ROY. JENNIE THOUGH...SHE STILL HAS FEELINGS--

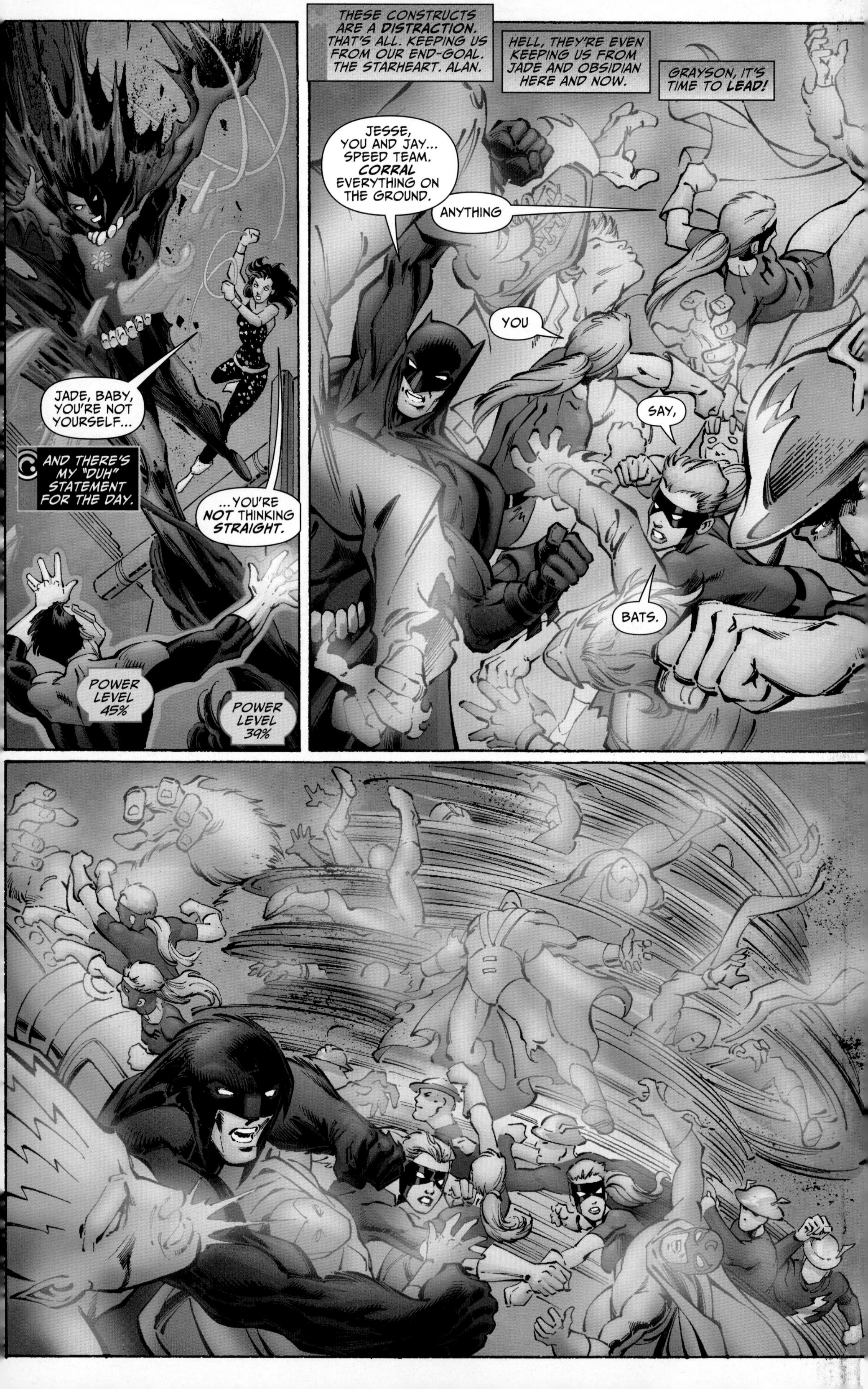
JADE, BABY, YOU'RE NOT YOURSELF...
AND THERE'S MY "DUH" STATEMENT FOR THE DAY.
...YOU'RE NOT THINKING STRAIGHT.
POWER LEVEL 45%
POWER LEVEL 39%
THESE CONSTRUCTS ARE A DISTRACTION. THAT'S ALL. KEEPING US FROM OUR END-GOAL. THE STARHEART. ALAN.
HELL, THEY'RE EVEN KEEPING US FROM JADE AND OBSIDIAN HERE AND NOW.
GRAYSON, IT'S TIME TO LEAD!
JESSE, YOU AND JAY... SPEED TEAM. CORRAL EVERYTHING ON THE GROUND.
ANYTHING
YOU
SAY,
BATS.

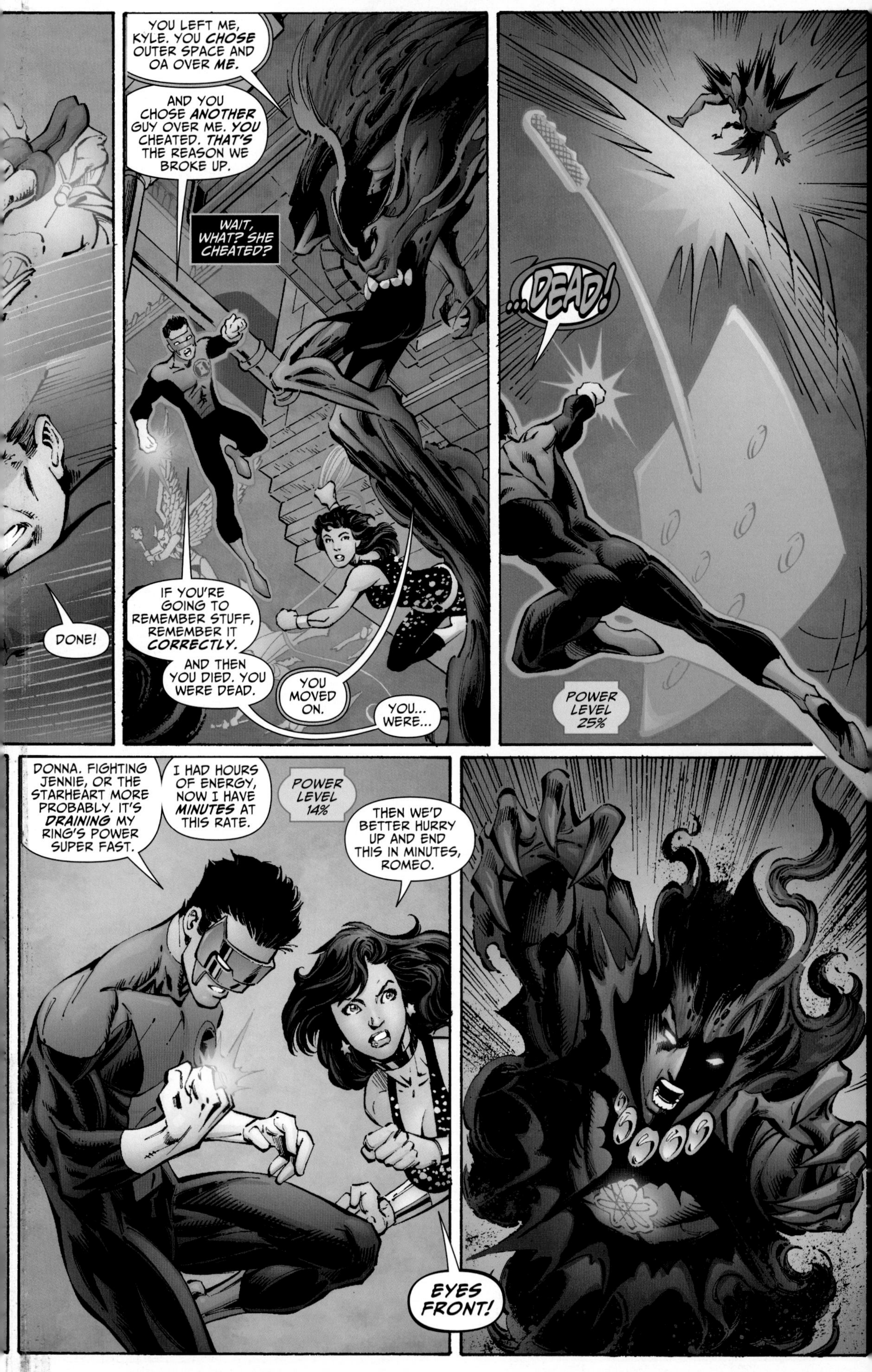
YOU LEFT ME, KYLE. YOU CHOSE OUTER SPACE AND OA OVER ME.
AND YOU CHOSE ANOTHER GUY OVER ME. YOU CHEATED. THAT'S THE REASON WE BROKE UP.
WAIT, WHAT? SHE CHEATED?
IF YOU'RE GOING TO REMEMBER STUFF, REMEMBER IT CORRECTLY.
AND THEN YOU DIED. YOU WERE DEAD.
YOU MOVED ON.
YOU... WERE...
DONE!
...DEAD!
POWER LEVEL 25%
DONNA. FIGHTING JENNIE, OR THE STARHEART MORE PROBABLY. IT'S DRAINING MY RING'S POWER SUPER FAST.
I HAD HOURS OF ENERGY, NOW I HAVE MINUTES AT THIS RATE.
POWER LEVEL 14%
THEN WE'D BETTER HURRY UP AND END THIS IN MINUTES, ROMEO.
EYES FRONT!

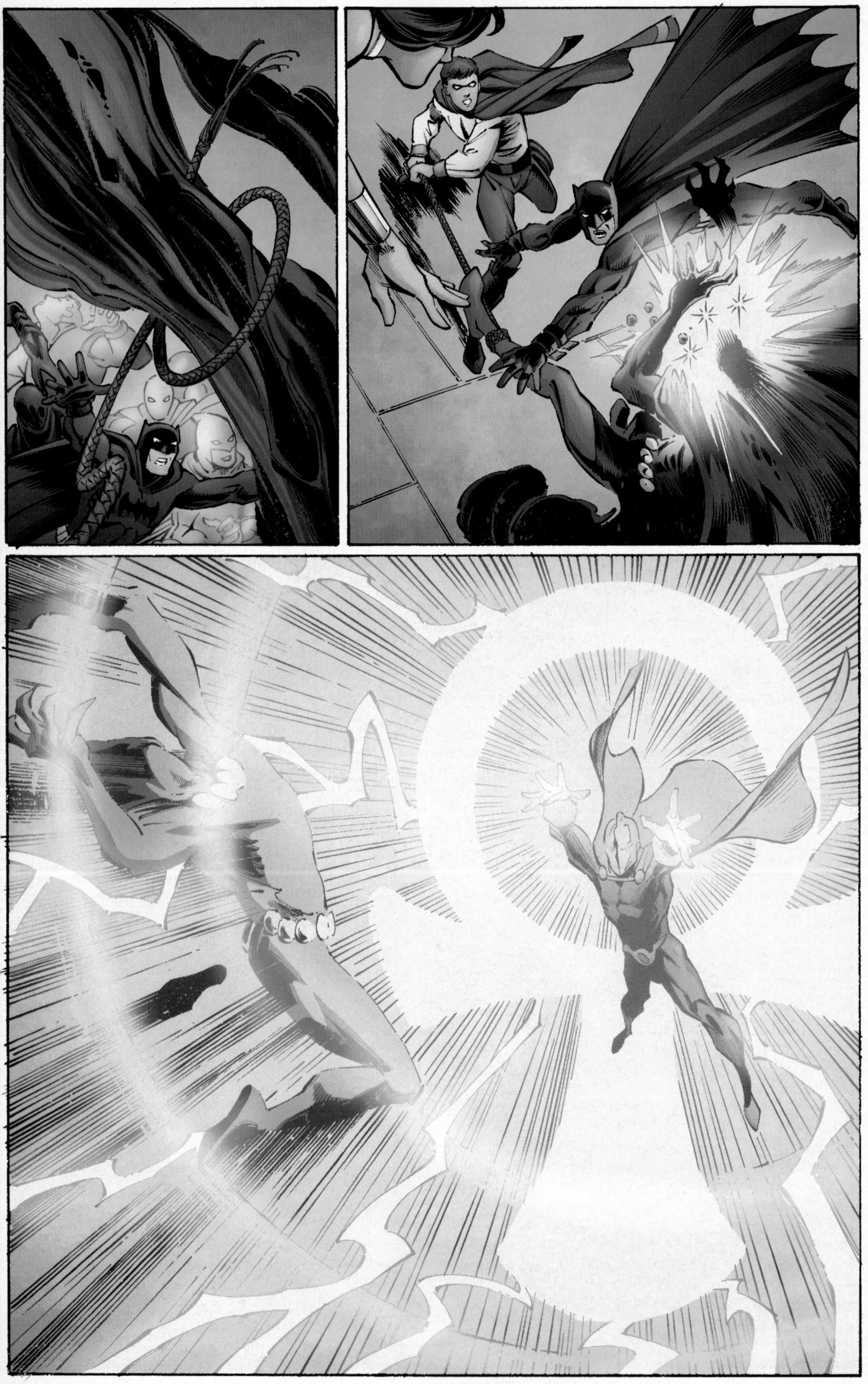

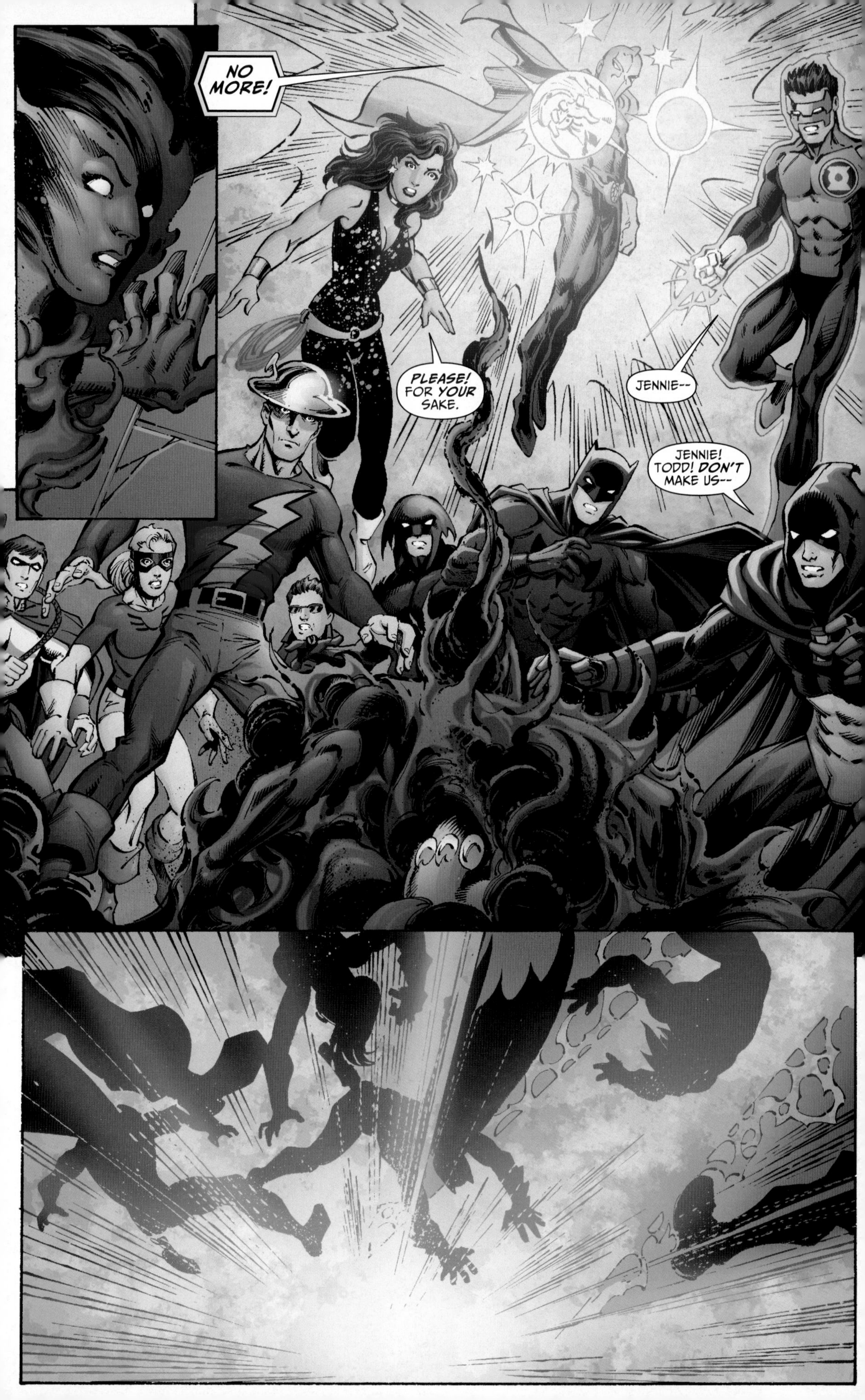
NO MORE!
PLEASE! FOR YOUR SAKE.
JENNIE--
JENNIE! TODD! DON'T MAKE US--

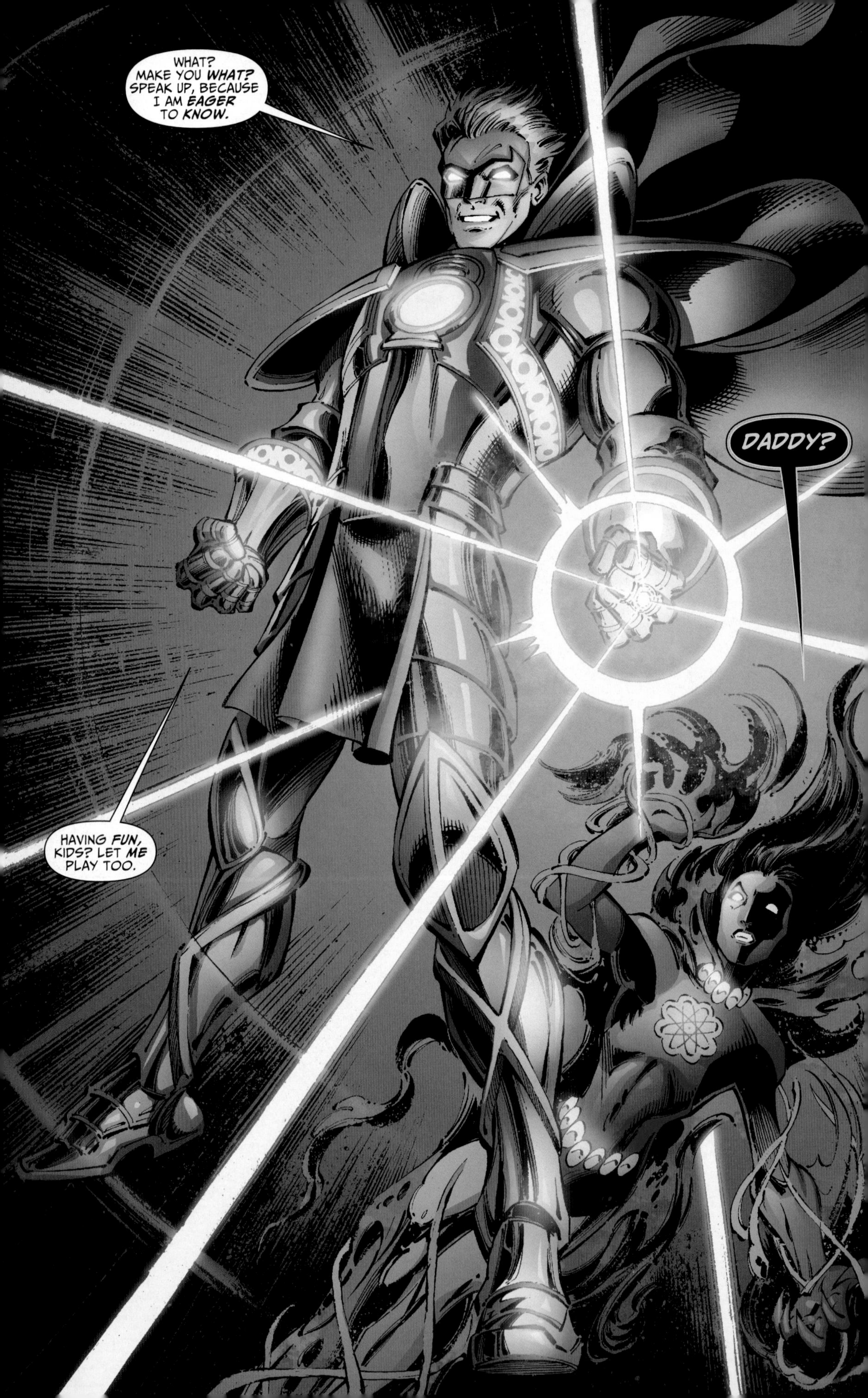
WHAT? MAKE YOU WHAT? SPEAK UP, BECAUSE I AM EAGER TO KNOW.
DADDY?
HAVING FUN, KIDS? LET ME PLAY TOO.

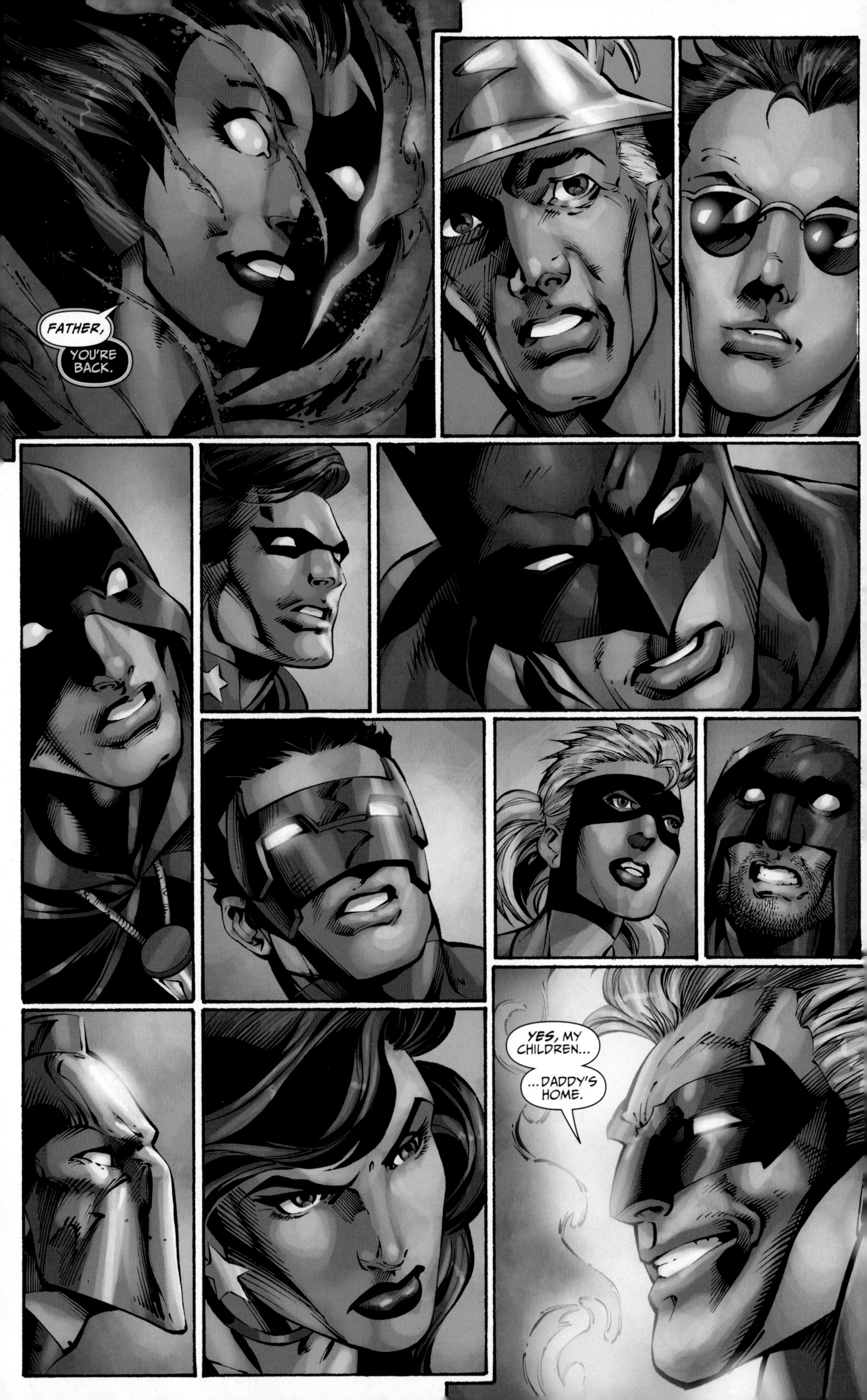
FATHER,
YOU'RE BACK.
YES, MY CHILDREN...
...DADDY'S HOME.

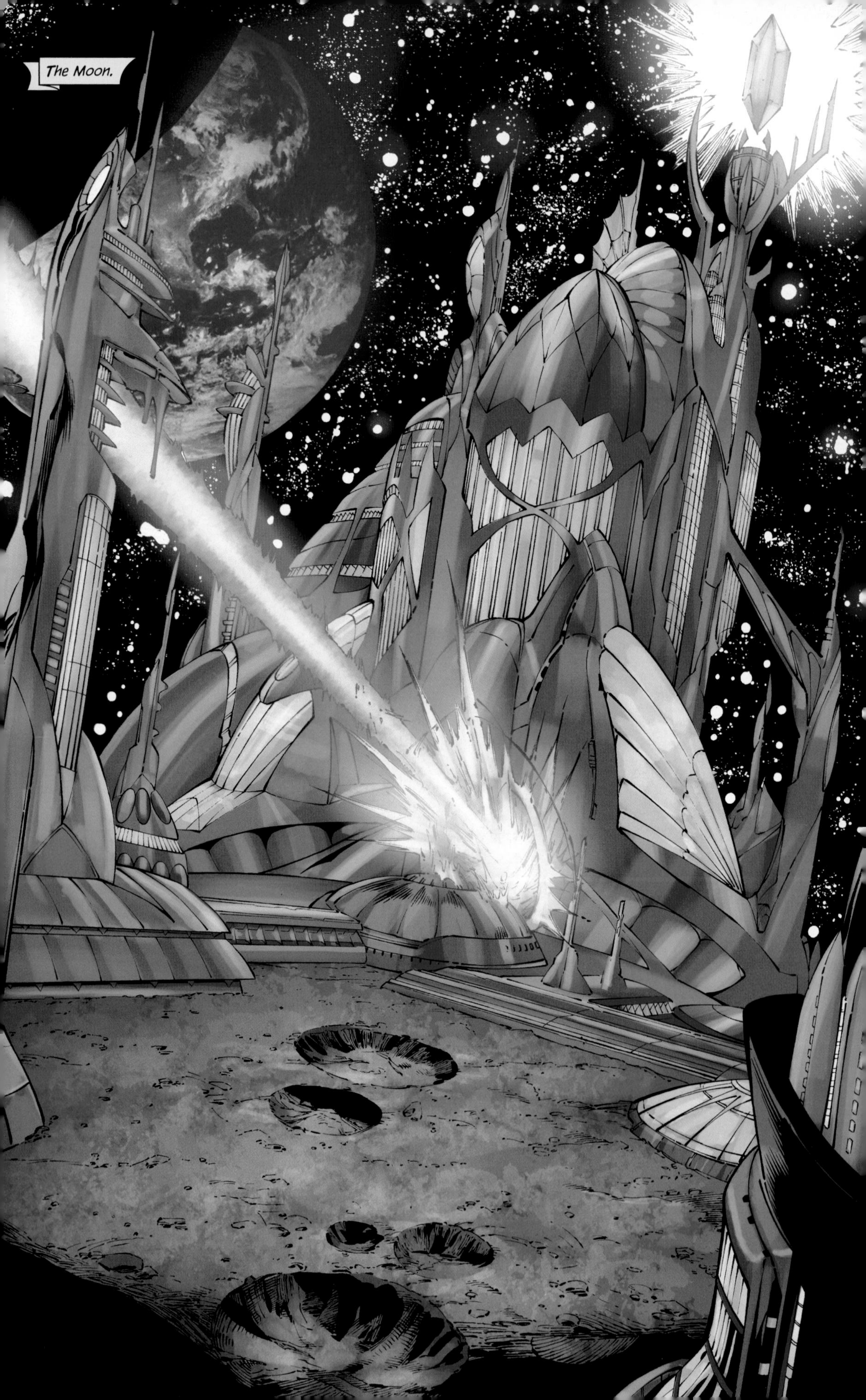
The Moon.

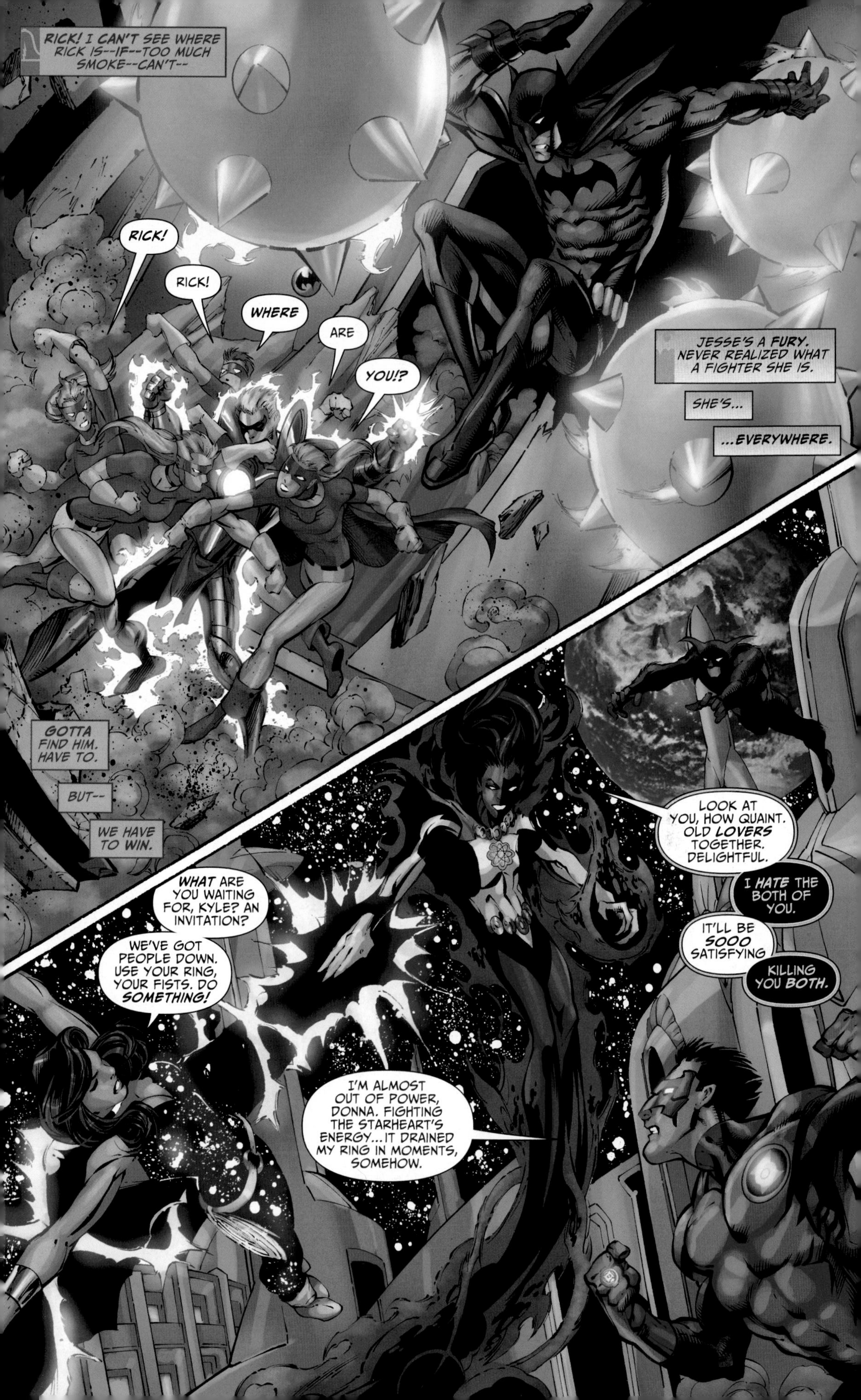
RICK! I CAN'T SEE WHERE RICK IS--IF--TOO MUCH SMOKE--CAN'T--
RICK!
RICK!
WHERE
ARE
YOU!?
JESSE'S A FURY. NEVER REALIZED WHAT A FIGHTER SHE IS.
SHE'S...
...EVERYWHERE.
GOTTA FIND HIM. HAVE TO.
BUT--
WE HAVE TO WIN.
LOOK AT YOU, HOW QUAINT. OLD LOVERS TOGETHER. DELIGHTFUL.
I HATE THE BOTH OF YOU.
IT'LL BE SOOO SATISFYING
KILLING YOU BOTH.
WHAT ARE YOU WAITING FOR, KYLE? AN INVITATION?
WE'VE GOT PEOPLE DOWN. USE YOUR RING, YOUR FISTS. DO SOMETHING!
I'M ALMOST OUT OF POWER, DONNA. FIGHTING THE STARHEART'S ENERGY...IT DRAINED MY RING IN MOMENTS, SOMEHOW.

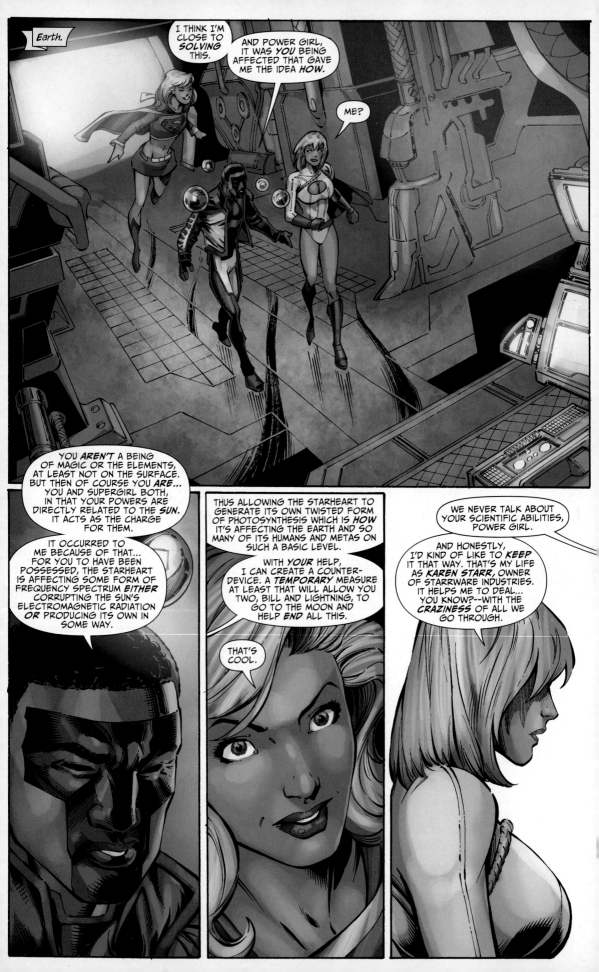

Earth.

I THINK I'M CLOSE TO *SOLVING* THIS.

AND POWER GIRL, IT WAS *YOU* BEING AFFECTED THAT GAVE ME THE IDEA *HOW.*

ME?

YOU *AREN'T* A BEING OF MAGIC OR THE ELEMENTS, AT LEAST NOT ON THE SURFACE. BUT THEN OF COURSE YOU *ARE...* YOU AND SUPERGIRL BOTH, IN THAT YOUR POWERS ARE DIRECTLY RELATED TO THE *SUN.* IT ACTS AS THE CHARGE FOR THEM.

IT OCCURRED TO ME BECAUSE OF THAT... FOR YOU TO HAVE BEEN POSSESSED, THE STARHEART IS AFFECTING SOME FORM OF FREQUENCY SPECTRUM *EITHER* CORRUPTING THE SUN'S ELECTROMAGNETIC RADIATION *OR* PRODUCING ITS OWN IN SOME WAY.

THUS ALLOWING THE STARHEART TO GENERATE ITS OWN TWISTED FORM OF PHOTOSYNTHESIS WHICH IS *HOW* IT'S AFFECTING THE EARTH AND SO MANY OF ITS HUMANS AND METAS ON SUCH A BASIC LEVEL.

WITH *YOUR* HELP, I CAN CREATE A COUNTER-DEVICE. A *TEMPORARY* MEASURE AT LEAST THAT WILL ALLOW YOU TWO, BILL AND LIGHTNING, TO GO TO THE MOON AND HELP *END* ALL THIS.

THAT'S COOL.

WE NEVER TALK ABOUT YOUR SCIENTIFIC ABILITIES, POWER GIRL.

AND HONESTLY, I'D KIND OF LIKE TO *KEEP* IT THAT WAY. THAT'S MY LIFE AS *KAREN STARR,* OWNER OF STARRWARE INDUSTRIES. IT HELPS ME TO DEAL... YOU KNOW?--WITH THE *CRAZINESS* OF ALL WE GO THROUGH.

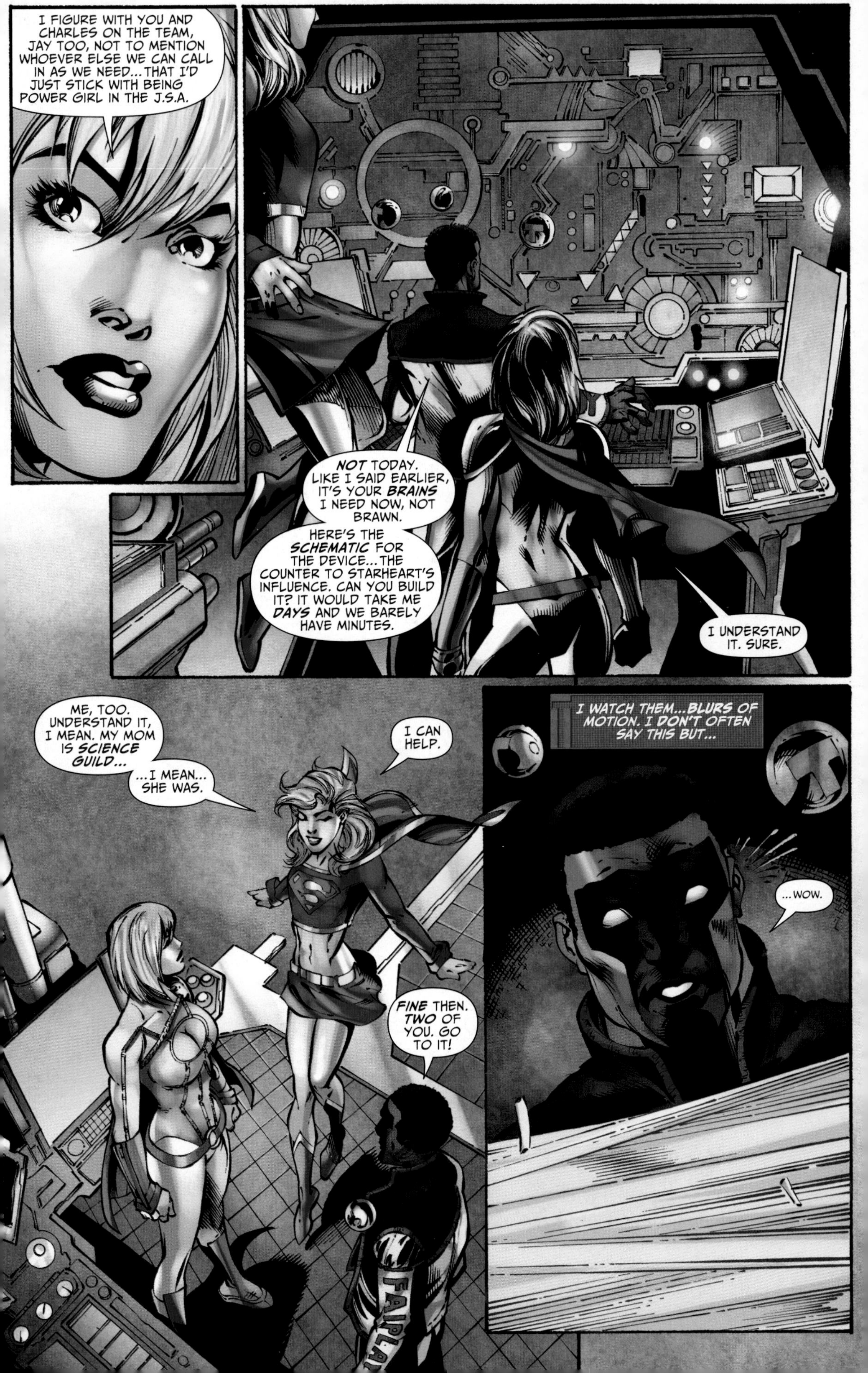

I FIGURE WITH YOU AND CHARLES ON THE TEAM, JAY TOO, NOT TO MENTION WHOEVER ELSE WE CAN CALL IN AS WE NEED... THAT I'D JUST STICK WITH BEING POWER GIRL IN THE J.S.A.
NOT TODAY. LIKE I SAID EARLIER, IT'S YOUR BRAINS I NEED NOW, NOT BRAWN.
HERE'S THE SCHEMATIC FOR THE DEVICE... THE COUNTER TO STARHEART'S INFLUENCE. CAN YOU BUILD IT? IT WOULD TAKE ME DAYS AND WE BARELY HAVE MINUTES.
I UNDERSTAND IT. SURE.
ME, TOO. UNDERSTAND IT, I MEAN. MY MOM IS SCIENCE GUILD...
...I MEAN... SHE WAS.
I CAN HELP.
FINE THEN. TWO OF YOU. GO TO IT!
I WATCH THEM... BLURS OF MOTION. I DON'T OFTEN SAY THIS BUT...
...WOW.

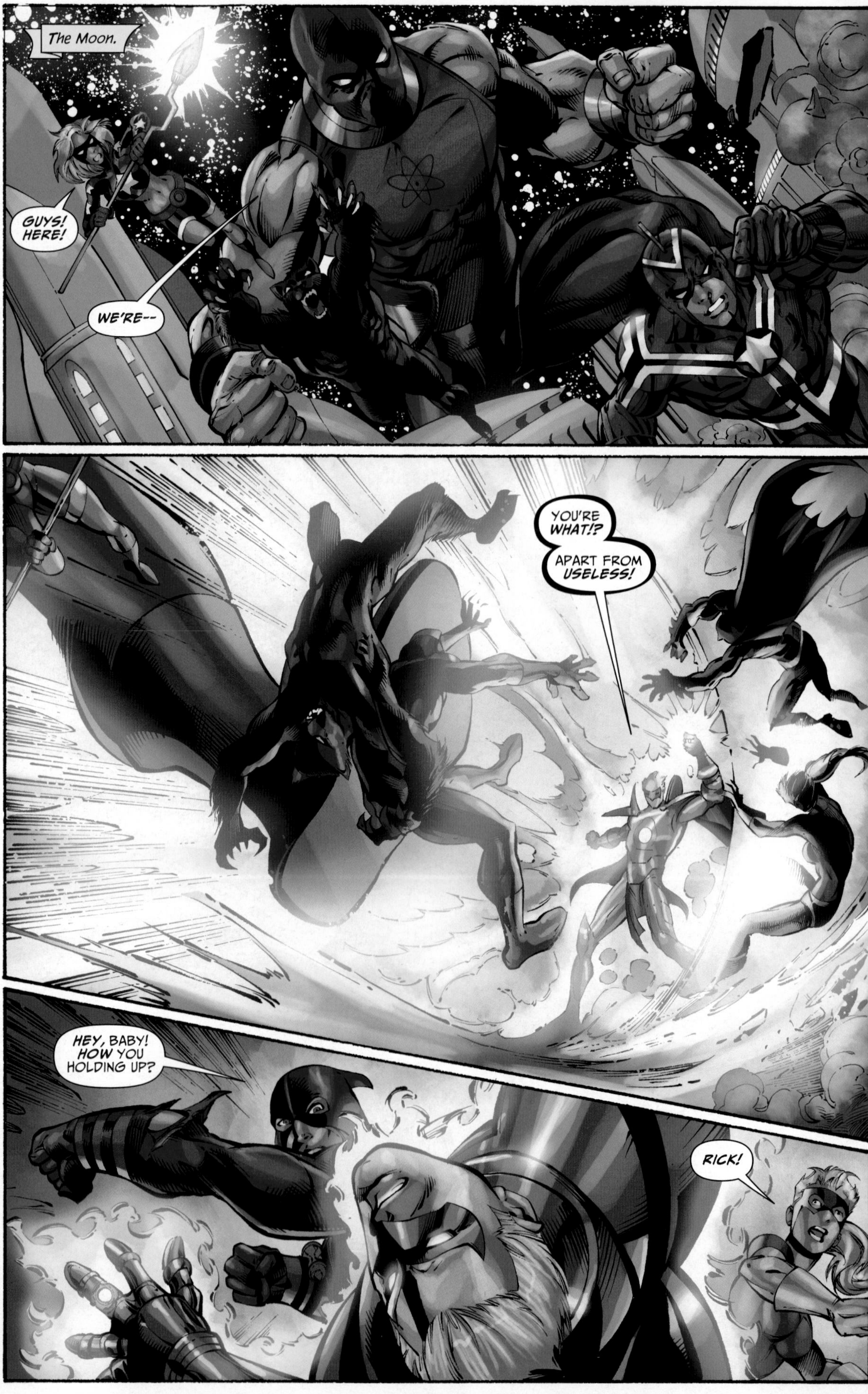
The Moon.
GUYS! HERE!
WE'RE--
YOU'RE WHAT!?
APART FROM USELESS!
HEY, BABY! HOW YOU HOLDING UP?
RICK!

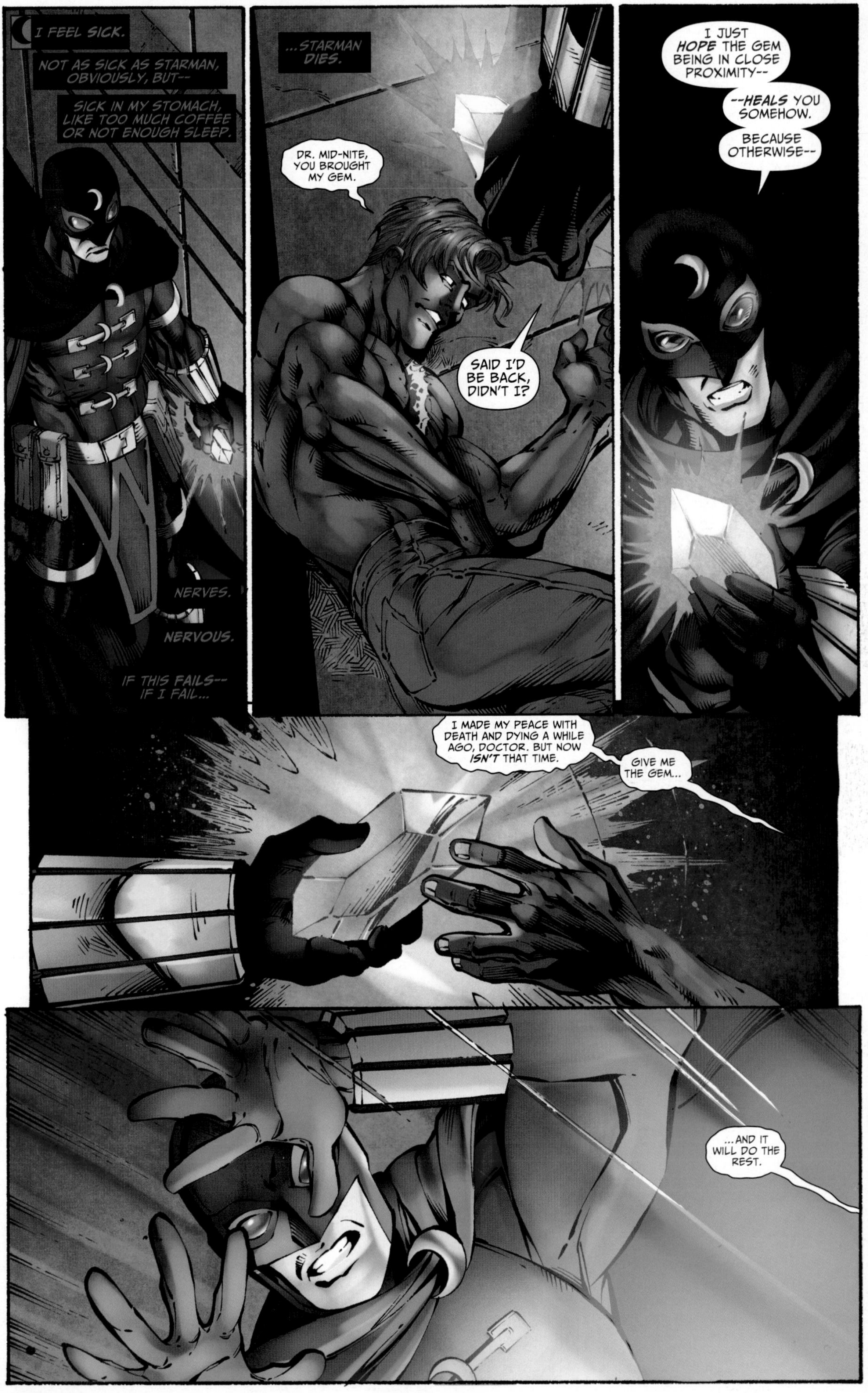

I FEEL SICK.
NOT AS SICK AS STARMAN, OBVIOUSLY, BUT--
SICK IN MY STOMACH, LIKE TOO MUCH COFFEE OR NOT ENOUGH SLEEP.
NERVES.
NERVOUS.
IF THIS FAILS-- IF I FAIL...
...STARMAN DIES.
DR. MID-NITE, YOU BROUGHT MY GEM.
SAID I'D BE BACK, DIDN'T I?
I JUST HOPE THE GEM BEING IN CLOSE PROXIMITY--
--HEALS YOU SOMEHOW.
BECAUSE OTHERWISE--
I MADE MY PEACE WITH DEATH AND DYING A WHILE AGO, DOCTOR. BUT NOW ISN'T THAT TIME.
GIVE ME THE GEM...
...AND IT WILL DO THE REST.

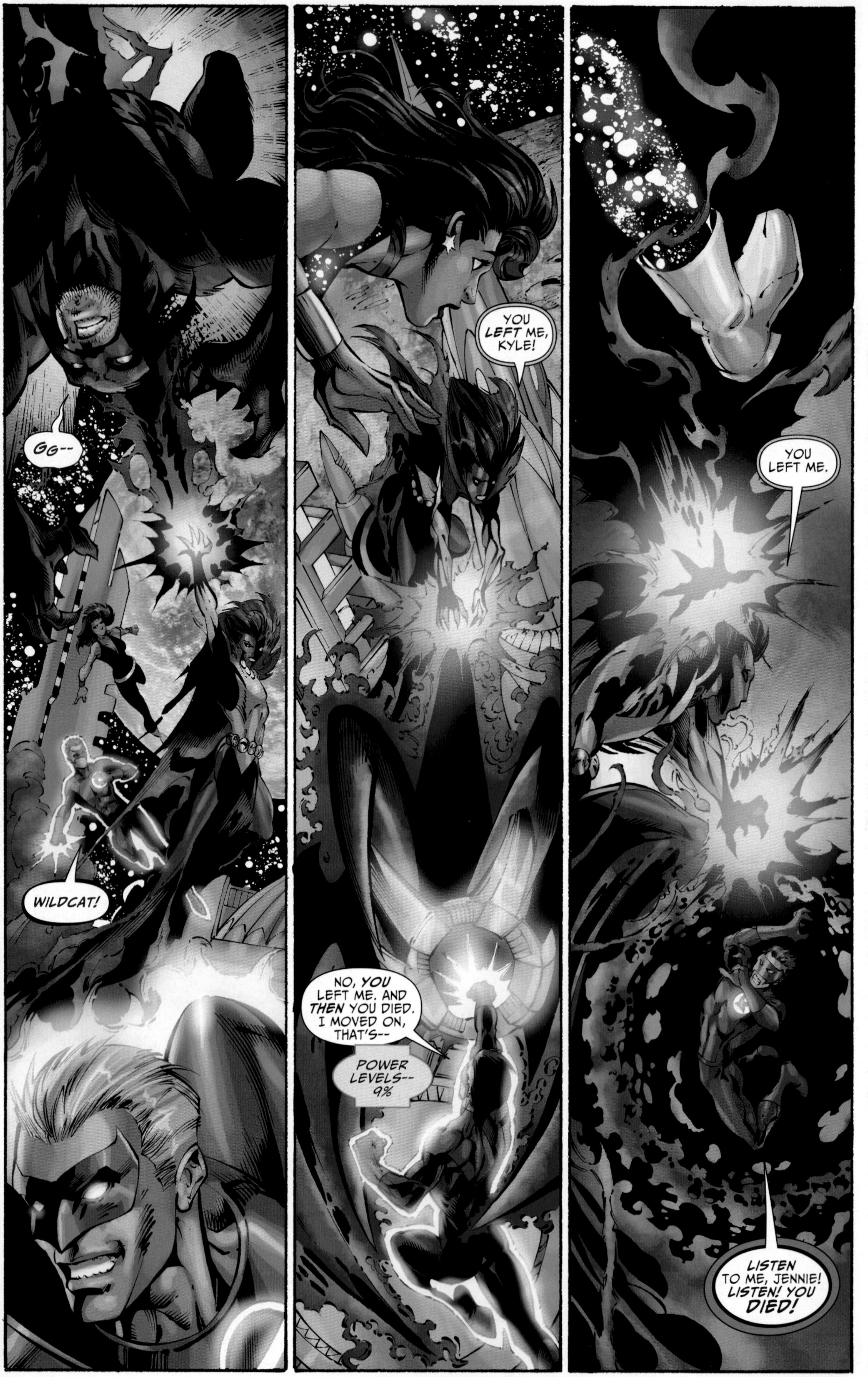
GG--
WILDCAT!
YOU LEFT ME, KYLE!
NO, YOU LEFT ME. AND THEN YOU DIED. I MOVED ON, THAT'S--
POWER LEVELS-- 9%
YOU LEFT ME.
LISTEN TO ME, JENNIE! LISTEN! YOU DIED!

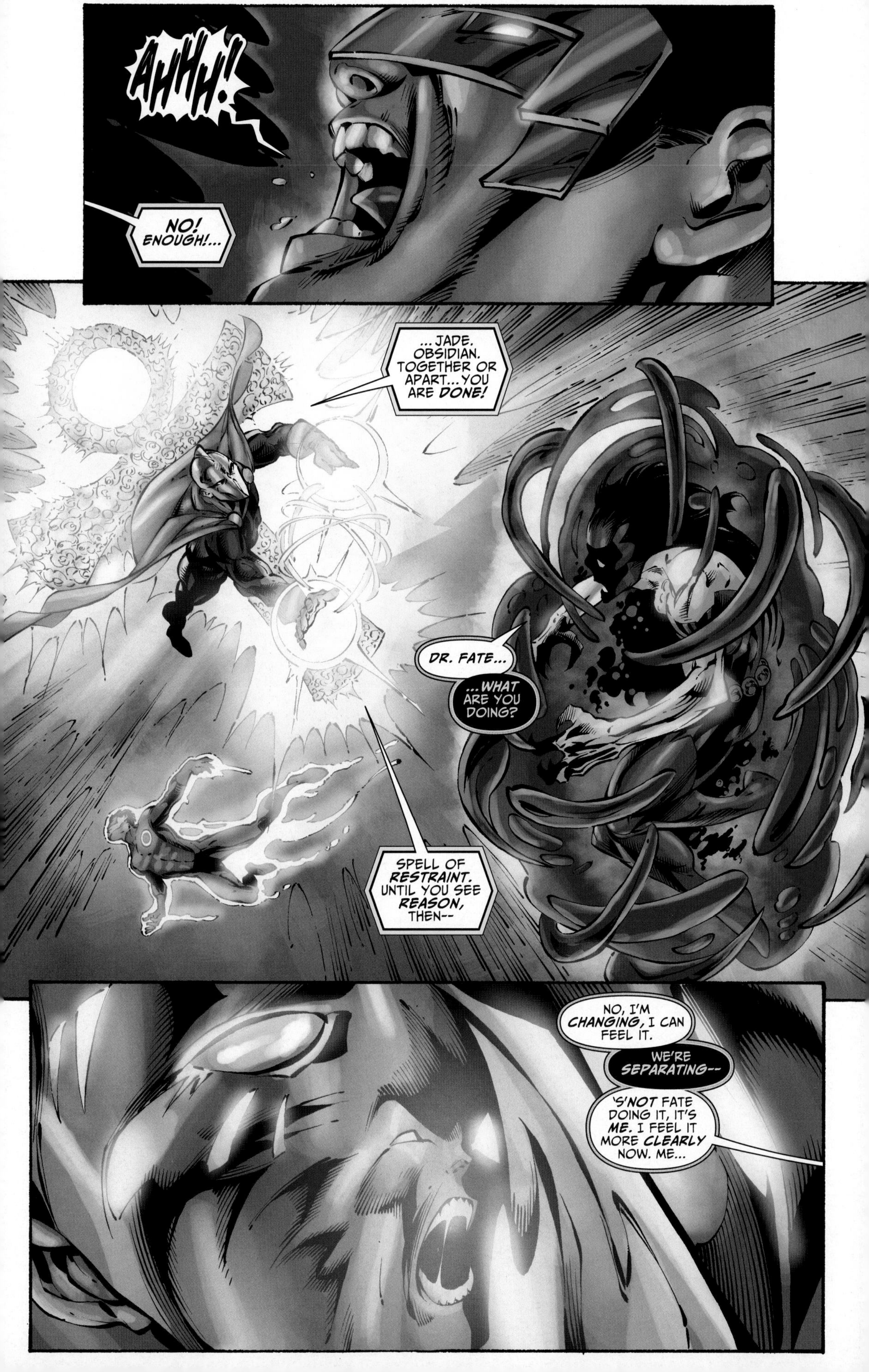
AHHH!
NO! ENOUGH!...
...JADE. OBSIDIAN. TOGETHER OR APART...YOU ARE DONE!
DR. FATE...
...WHAT ARE YOU DOING?
SPELL OF RESTRAINT. UNTIL YOU SEE REASON, THEN--
NO, I'M CHANGING, I CAN FEEL IT.
WE'RE SEPARATING--
'S'NOT FATE DOING IT, IT'S ME. I FEEL IT MORE CLEARLY NOW. ME...

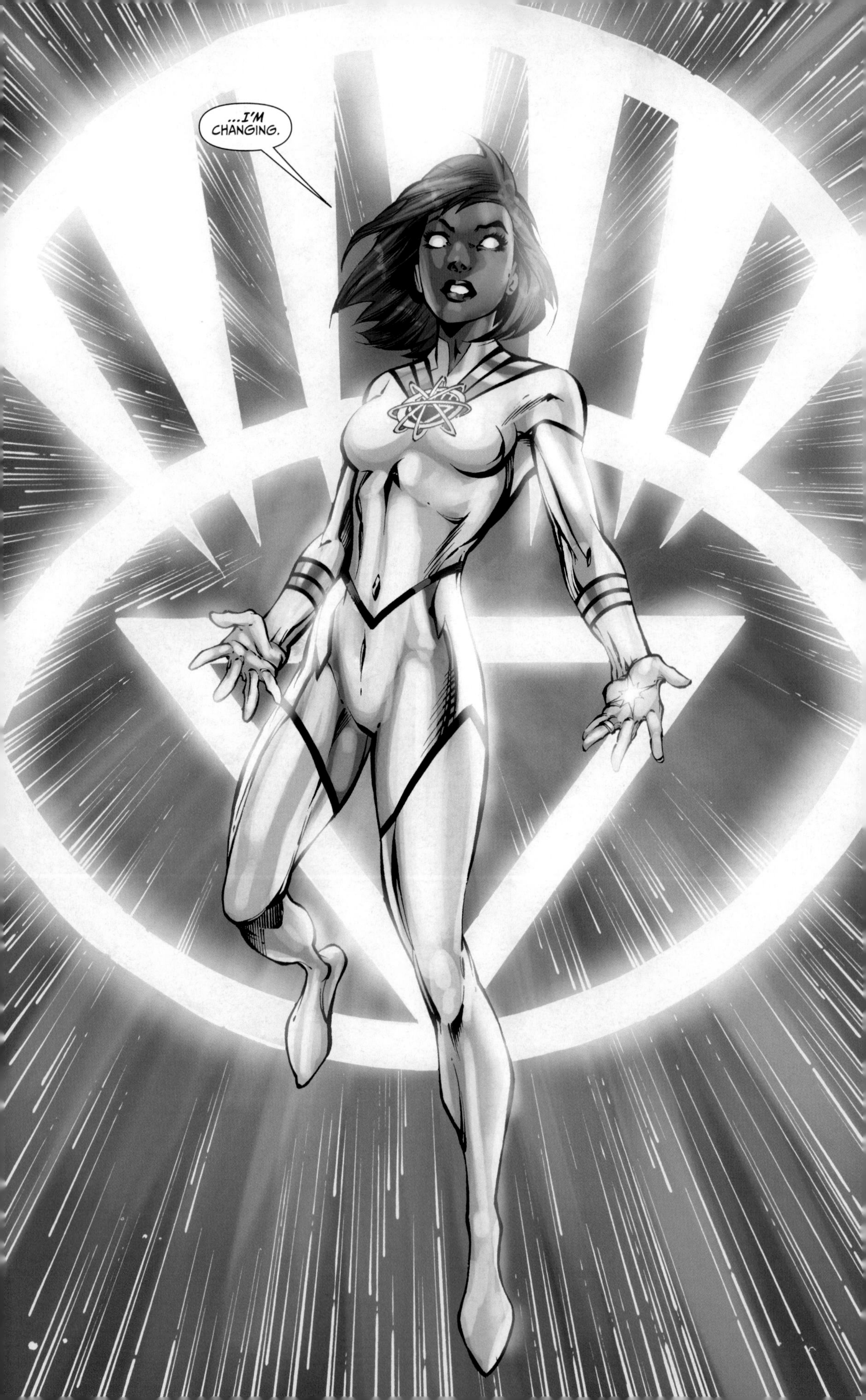
...I'M CHANGING.

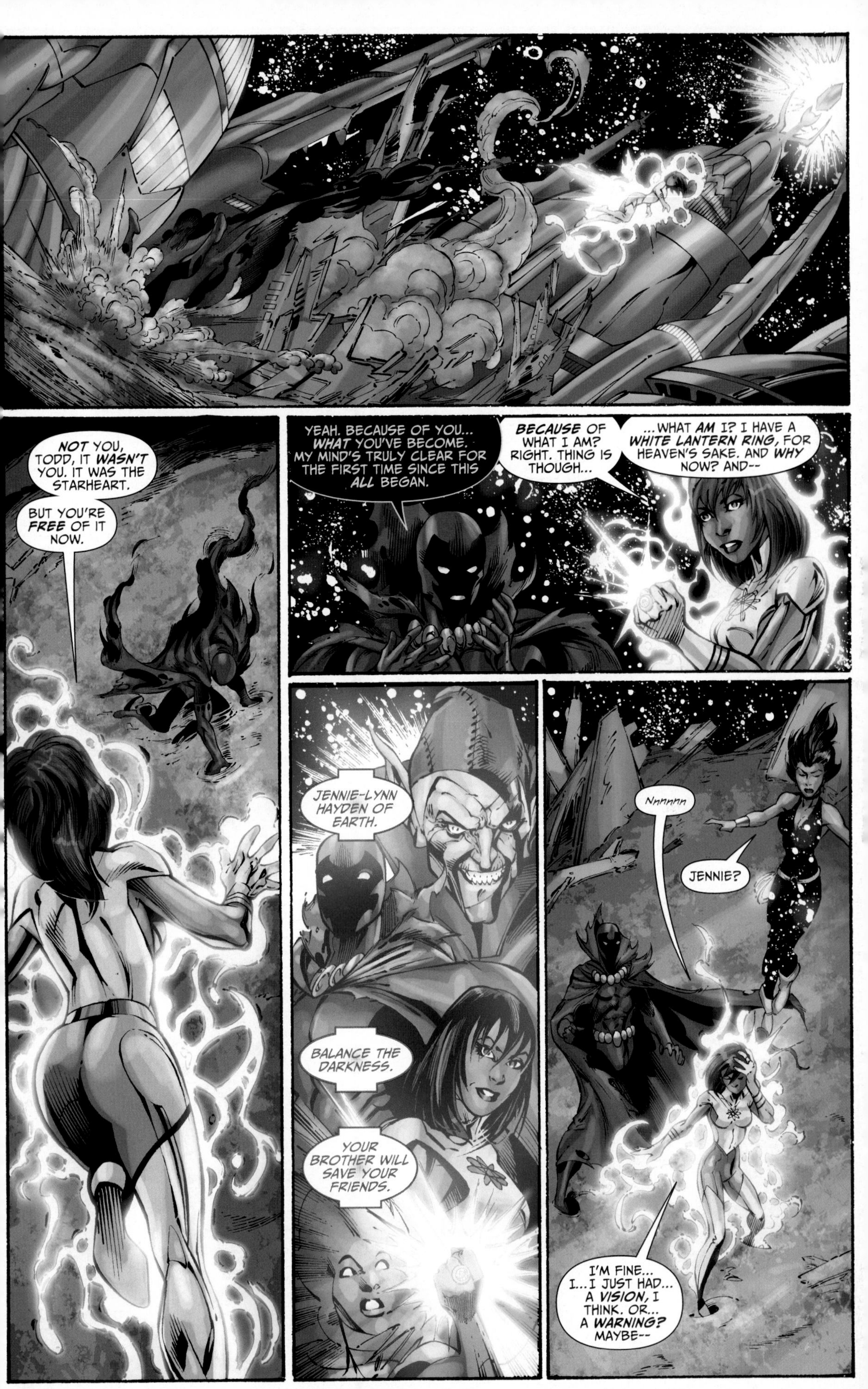
NOT YOU, TODD, IT WASN'T YOU. IT WAS THE STARHEART.
BUT YOU'RE FREE OF IT NOW.
YEAH. BECAUSE OF YOU... WHAT YOU'VE BECOME. MY MIND'S TRULY CLEAR FOR THE FIRST TIME SINCE THIS ALL BEGAN.
BECAUSE OF WHAT I AM? RIGHT. THING IS THOUGH...
...WHAT AM I? I HAVE A WHITE LANTERN RING, FOR HEAVEN'S SAKE. AND WHY NOW? AND--
JENNIE-LYNN HAYDEN OF EARTH.
BALANCE THE DARKNESS.
YOUR BROTHER WILL SAVE YOUR FRIENDS.
Nnnnnn
JENNIE?
I'M FINE... I...I JUST HAD... A VISION, I THINK. OR... A WARNING? MAYBE--

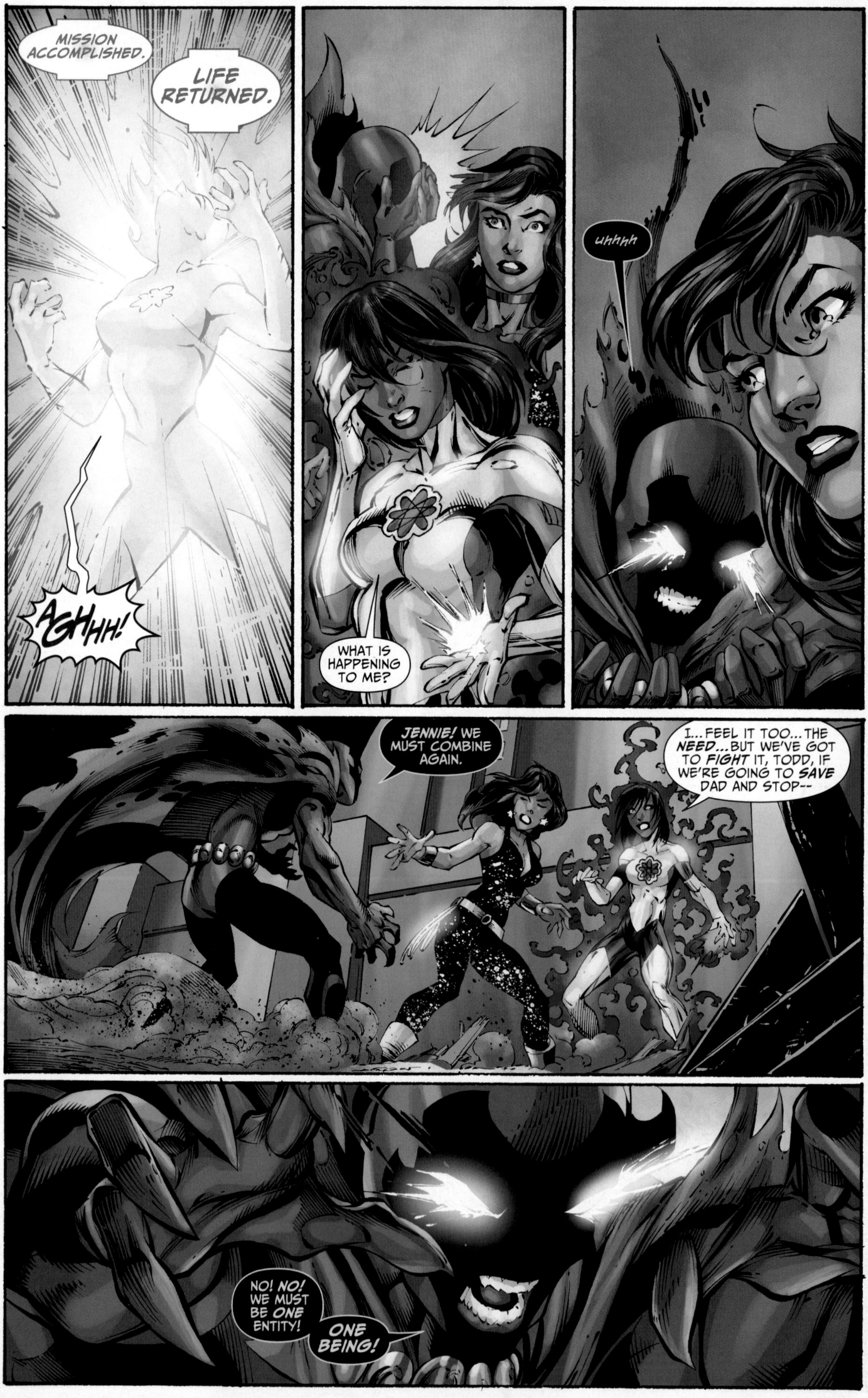
MISSION ACCOMPLISHED.
LIFE RETURNED.
AGHHH!
WHAT IS HAPPENING TO ME?
uhhhh
JENNIE! WE MUST COMBINE AGAIN.
I...FEEL IT TOO...THE NEED...BUT WE'VE GOT TO FIGHT IT, TODD, IF WE'RE GOING TO SAVE DAD AND STOP--
NO! NO! WE MUST BE ONE ENTITY!
ONE BEING!

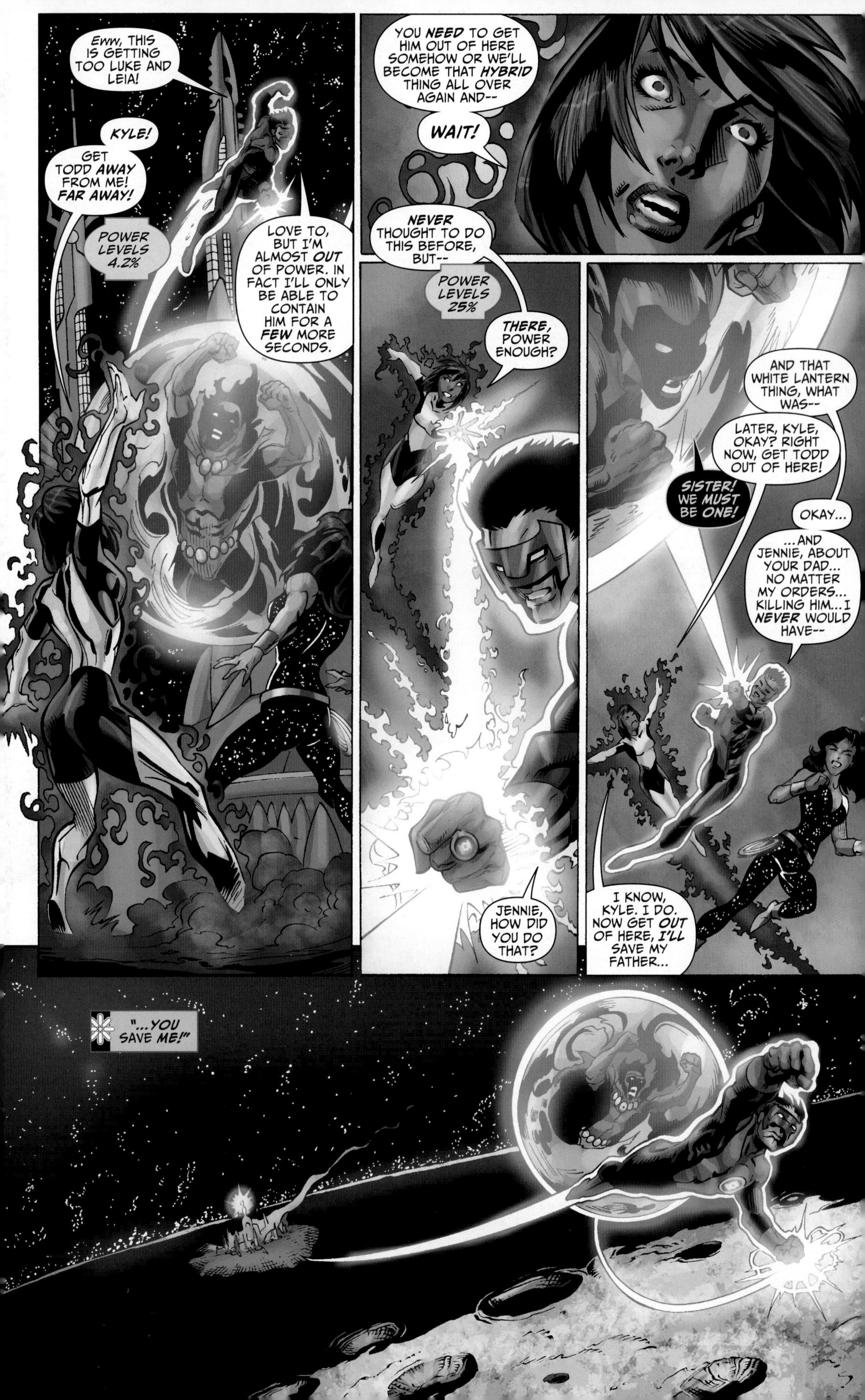

EWW, THIS IS GETTING TOO LUKE AND LEIA!
KYLE!
GET TODD AWAY FROM ME! FAR AWAY!
POWER LEVELS 4.2%
LOVE TO, BUT I'M ALMOST OUT OF POWER. IN FACT I'LL ONLY BE ABLE TO CONTAIN HIM FOR A FEW MORE SECONDS.
YOU NEED TO GET HIM OUT OF HERE SOMEHOW OR WE'LL BECOME THAT HYBRID THING ALL OVER AGAIN AND--
WAIT!
NEVER THOUGHT TO DO THIS BEFORE, BUT--
POWER LEVELS 25%
THERE, POWER ENOUGH?
JENNIE, HOW DID YOU DO THAT?
AND THAT WHITE LANTERN THING, WHAT WAS--
LATER, KYLE, OKAY? RIGHT NOW, GET TODD OUT OF HERE!
SISTER! WE MUST BE ONE!
OKAY...
...AND JENNIE, ABOUT YOUR DAD... NO MATTER MY ORDERS... KILLING HIM... I NEVER WOULD HAVE--
I KNOW, KYLE. I DO. NOW GET OUT OF HERE, I'LL SAVE MY FATHER...
"...YOU SAVE ME!"

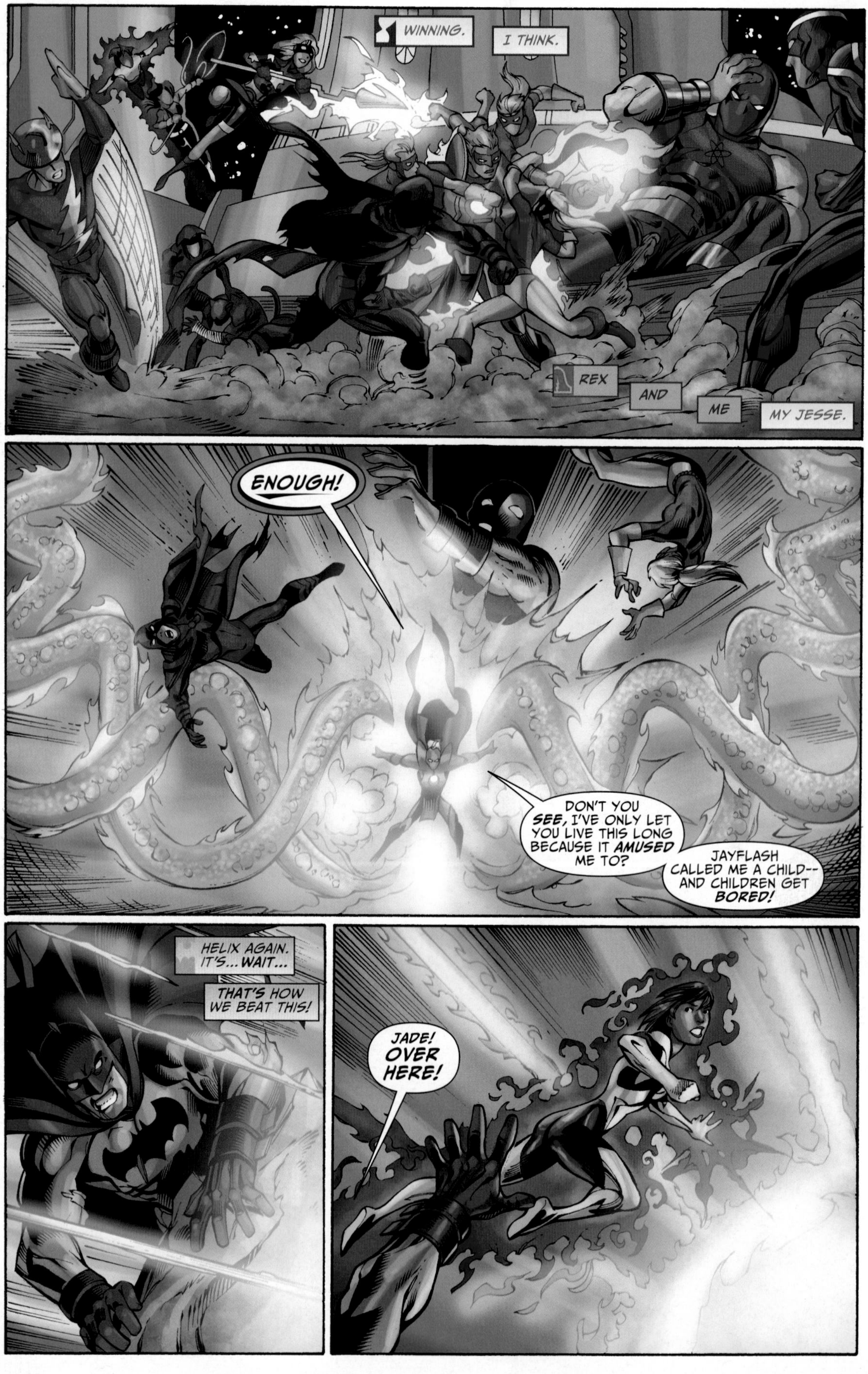
WINNING.
I THINK.
REX
AND
ME
MY JESSE.
ENOUGH!
DON'T YOU SEE, I'VE ONLY LET YOU LIVE THIS LONG BECAUSE IT AMUSED ME TO?
JAYFLASH CALLED ME A CHILD-- AND CHILDREN GET BORED!
HELIX AGAIN. IT'S... WAIT...
THAT'S HOW WE BEAT THIS!
JADE! OVER HERE!

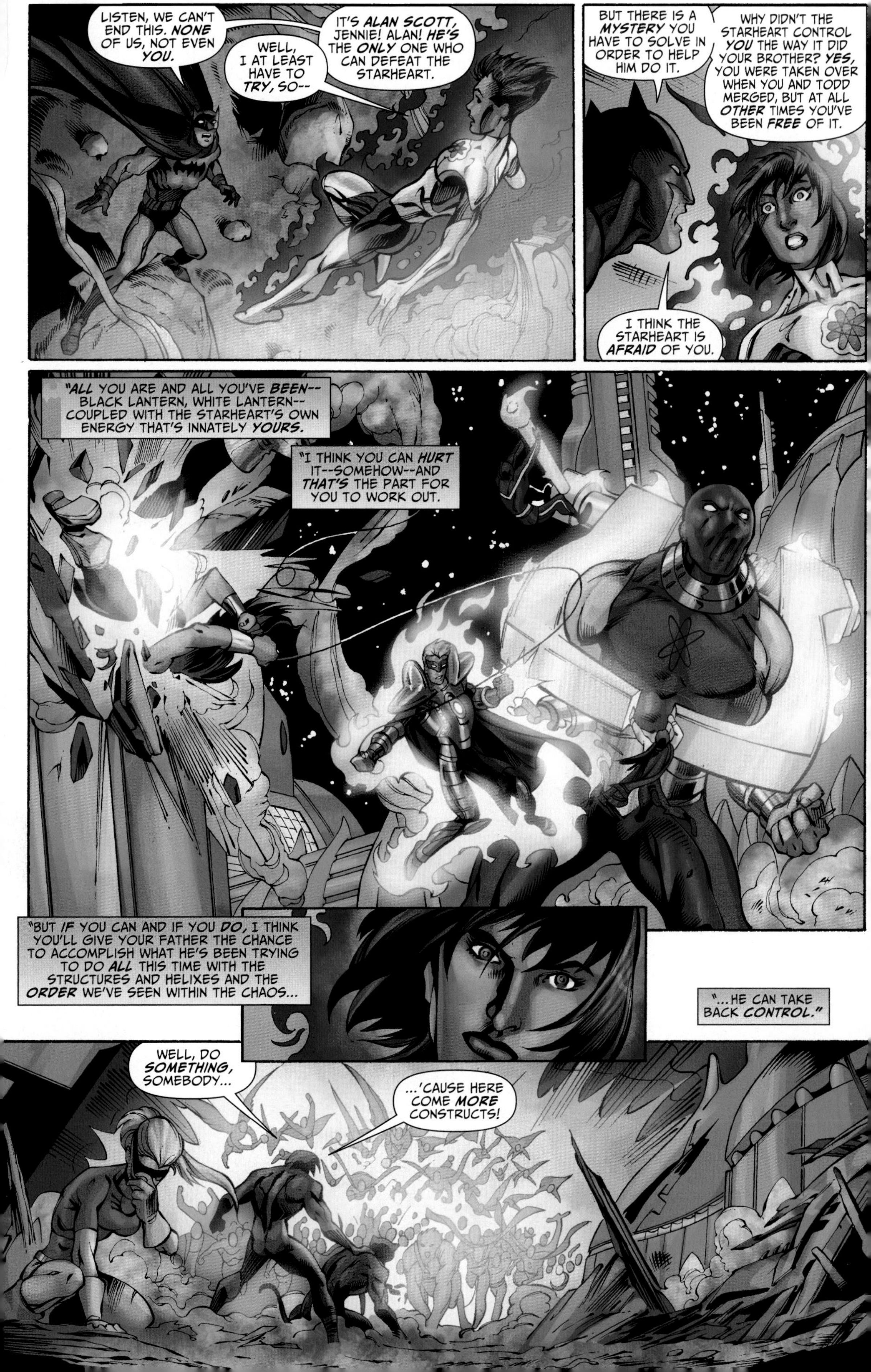
LISTEN, WE CAN'T END THIS. NONE OF US, NOT EVEN YOU.
WELL, I AT LEAST HAVE TO TRY, SO--
IT'S ALAN SCOTT, JENNIE! ALAN! HE'S THE ONLY ONE WHO CAN DEFEAT THE STARHEART.
BUT THERE IS A MYSTERY YOU HAVE TO SOLVE IN ORDER TO HELP HIM DO IT.
WHY DIDN'T THE STARHEART CONTROL YOU THE WAY IT DID YOUR BROTHER? YES, YOU WERE TAKEN OVER WHEN YOU AND TODD MERGED, BUT AT ALL OTHER TIMES YOU'VE BEEN FREE OF IT.
I THINK THE STARHEART IS AFRAID OF YOU.
"ALL YOU ARE AND ALL YOU'VE BEEN-- BLACK LANTERN, WHITE LANTERN-- COUPLED WITH THE STARHEART'S OWN ENERGY THAT'S INNATELY YOURS.
"I THINK YOU CAN HURT IT--SOMEHOW--AND THAT'S THE PART FOR YOU TO WORK OUT.
"BUT IF YOU CAN AND IF YOU DO, I THINK YOU'LL GIVE YOUR FATHER THE CHANCE TO ACCOMPLISH WHAT HE'S BEEN TRYING TO DO ALL THIS TIME WITH THE STRUCTURES AND HELIXES AND THE ORDER WE'VE SEEN WITHIN THE CHAOS...
"...HE CAN TAKE BACK CONTROL."
WELL, DO SOMETHING, SOMEBODY...
...'CAUSE HERE COME MORE CONSTRUCTS!

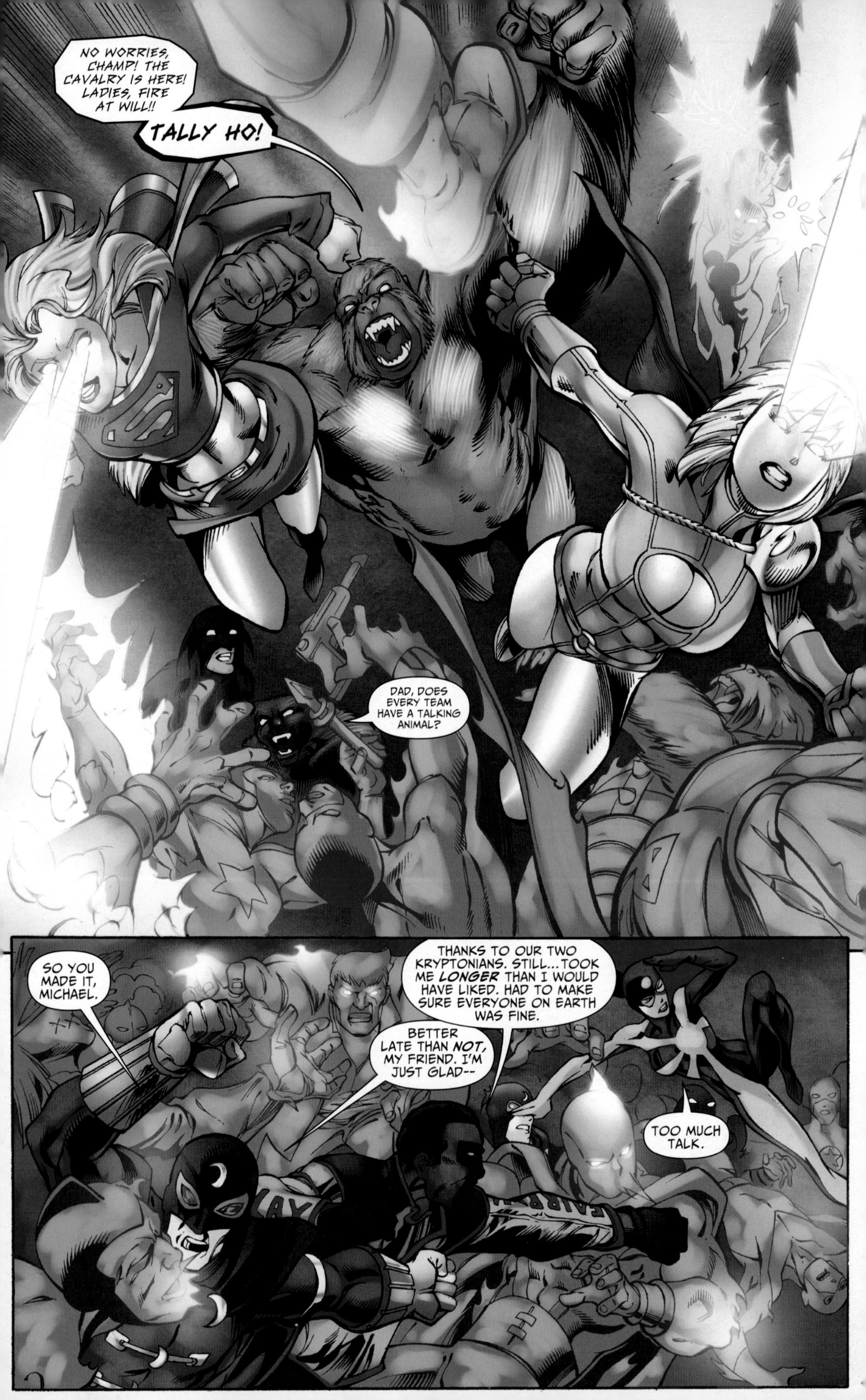
NO WORRIES, CHAMP! THE CAVALRY IS HERE! LADIES, FIRE AT WILL!!
TALLY HO!
DAD, DOES EVERY TEAM HAVE A TALKING ANIMAL?
SO YOU MADE IT, MICHAEL.
THANKS TO OUR TWO KRYPTONIANS. STILL... TOOK ME LONGER THAN I WOULD HAVE LIKED. HAD TO MAKE SURE EVERYONE ON EARTH WAS FINE.
BETTER LATE THAN NOT, MY FRIEND. I'M JUST GLAD--
TOO MUCH TALK.

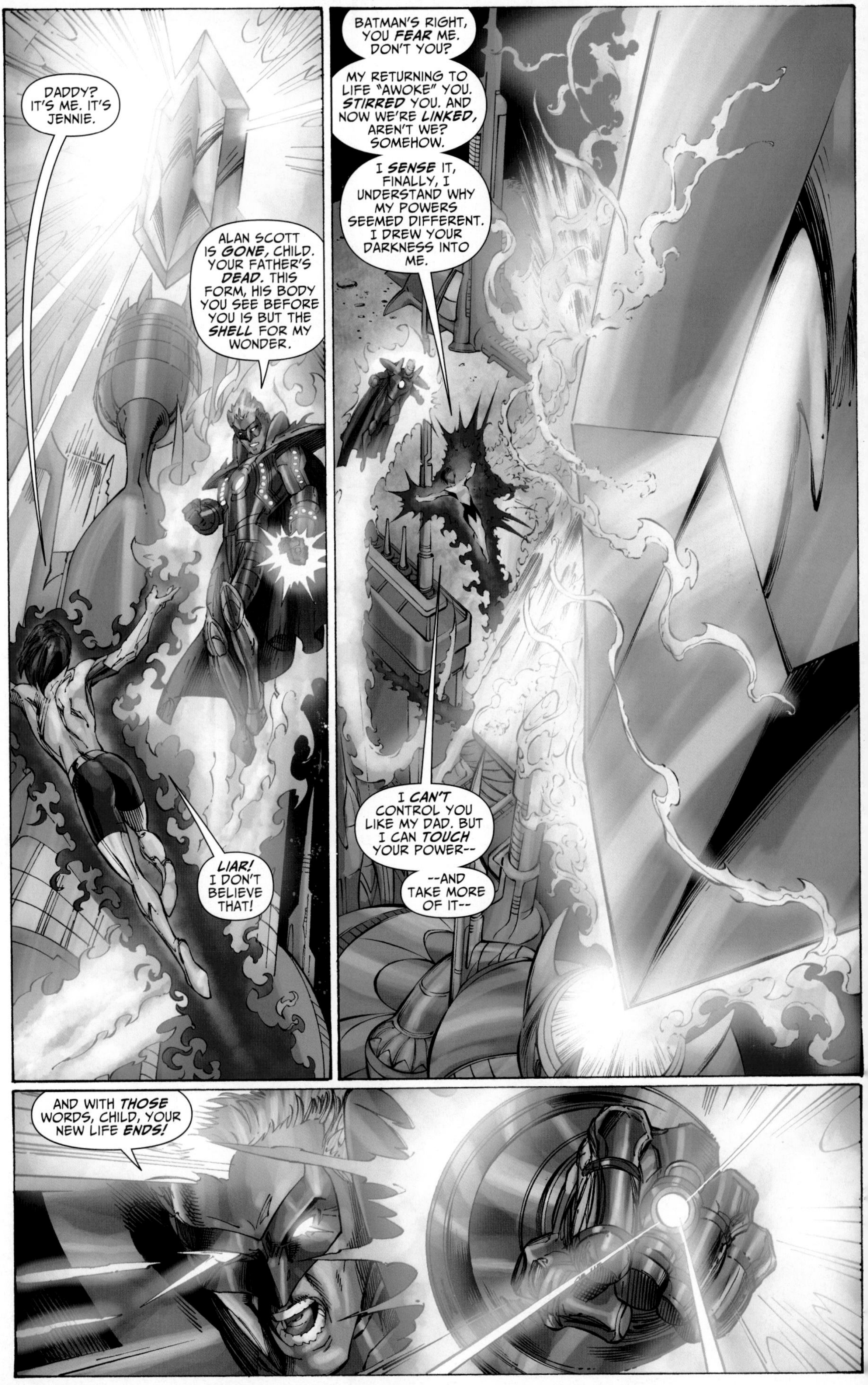
DADDY? IT'S ME. IT'S JENNIE.
ALAN SCOTT IS GONE, CHILD. YOUR FATHER'S DEAD. THIS FORM, HIS BODY YOU SEE BEFORE YOU IS BUT THE SHELL FOR MY WONDER.
LIAR! I DON'T BELIEVE THAT!
BATMAN'S RIGHT, YOU FEAR ME. DON'T YOU?
MY RETURNING TO LIFE "AWOKE" YOU. STIRRED YOU. AND NOW WE'RE LINKED, AREN'T WE? SOMEHOW.
I SENSE IT, FINALLY, I UNDERSTAND WHY MY POWERS SEEMED DIFFERENT. I DREW YOUR DARKNESS INTO ME.
I CAN'T CONTROL YOU LIKE MY DAD. BUT I CAN TOUCH YOUR POWER--
--AND TAKE MORE OF IT--
AND WITH THOSE WORDS, CHILD, YOUR NEW LIFE ENDS!

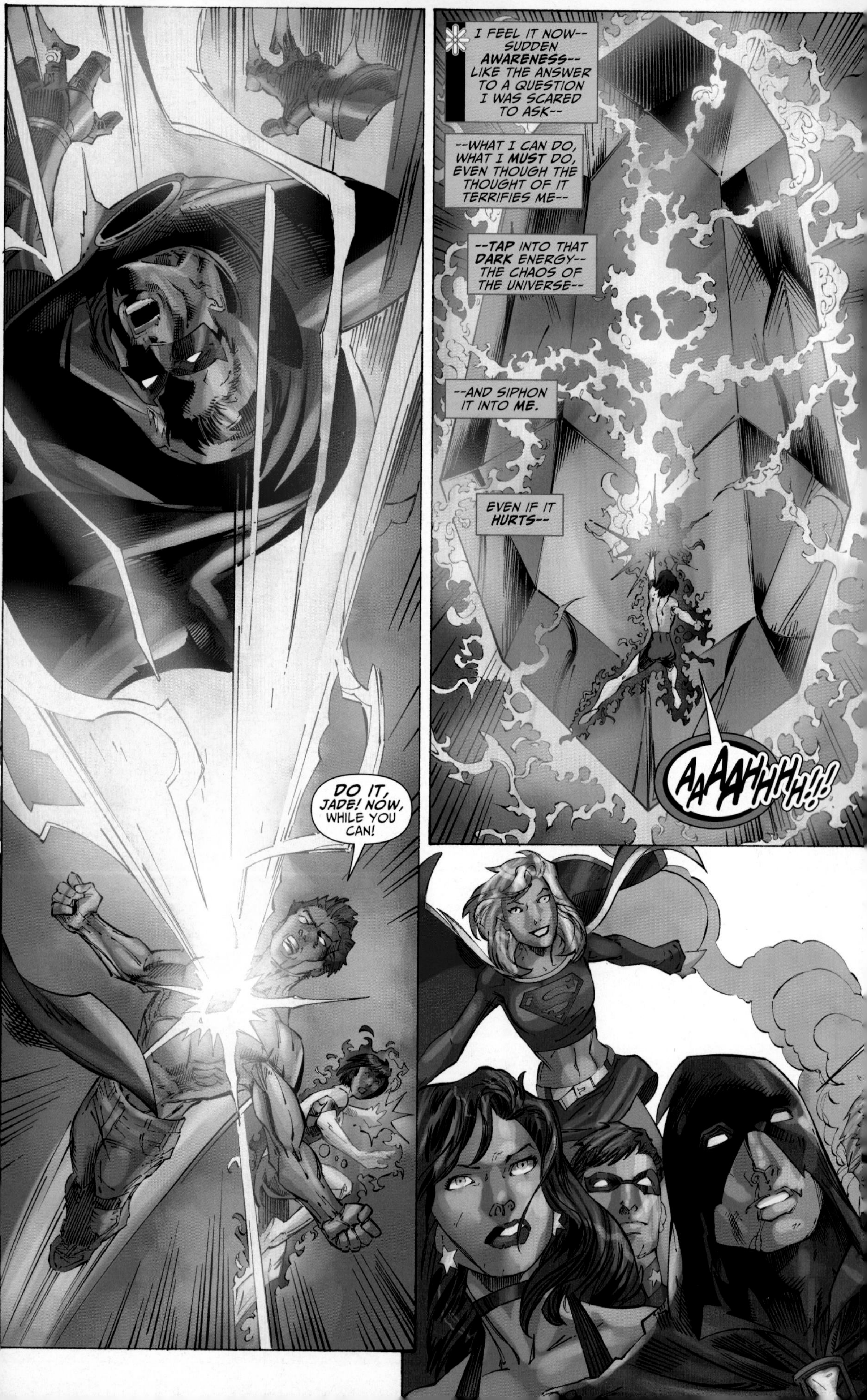
I FEEL IT NOW-- SUDDEN AWARENESS-- LIKE THE ANSWER TO A QUESTION I WAS SCARED TO ASK--
--WHAT I CAN DO, WHAT I MUST DO, EVEN THOUGH THE THOUGHT OF IT TERRIFIES ME--
--TAP INTO THAT DARK ENERGY-- THE CHAOS OF THE UNIVERSE--
--AND SIPHON IT INTO ME.
EVEN IF IT HURTS--
AAAAHHHH!!!
DO IT, JADE! NOW, WHILE YOU CAN!

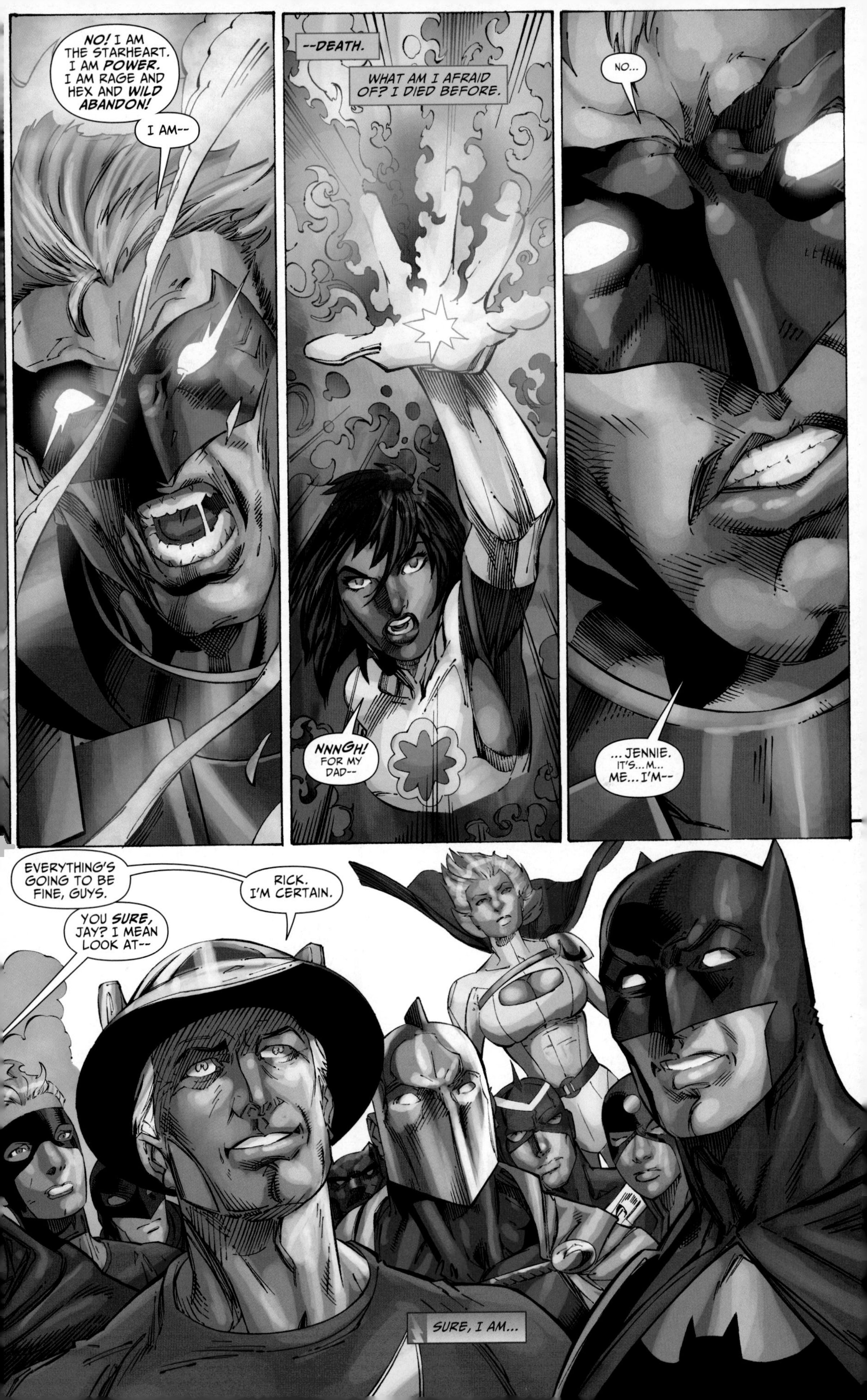

NO! I AM THE STARHEART. I AM POWER. I AM RAGE AND HEX AND WILD ABANDON!
I AM--
--DEATH.
WHAT AM I AFRAID OF? I DIED BEFORE.
NNNGH! FOR MY DAD--
NO...
...JENNIE. IT'S...M... ME...I'M--
EVERYTHING'S GOING TO BE FINE, GUYS.
YOU SURE, JAY? I MEAN LOOK AT--
RICK. I'M CERTAIN.
SURE, I AM...

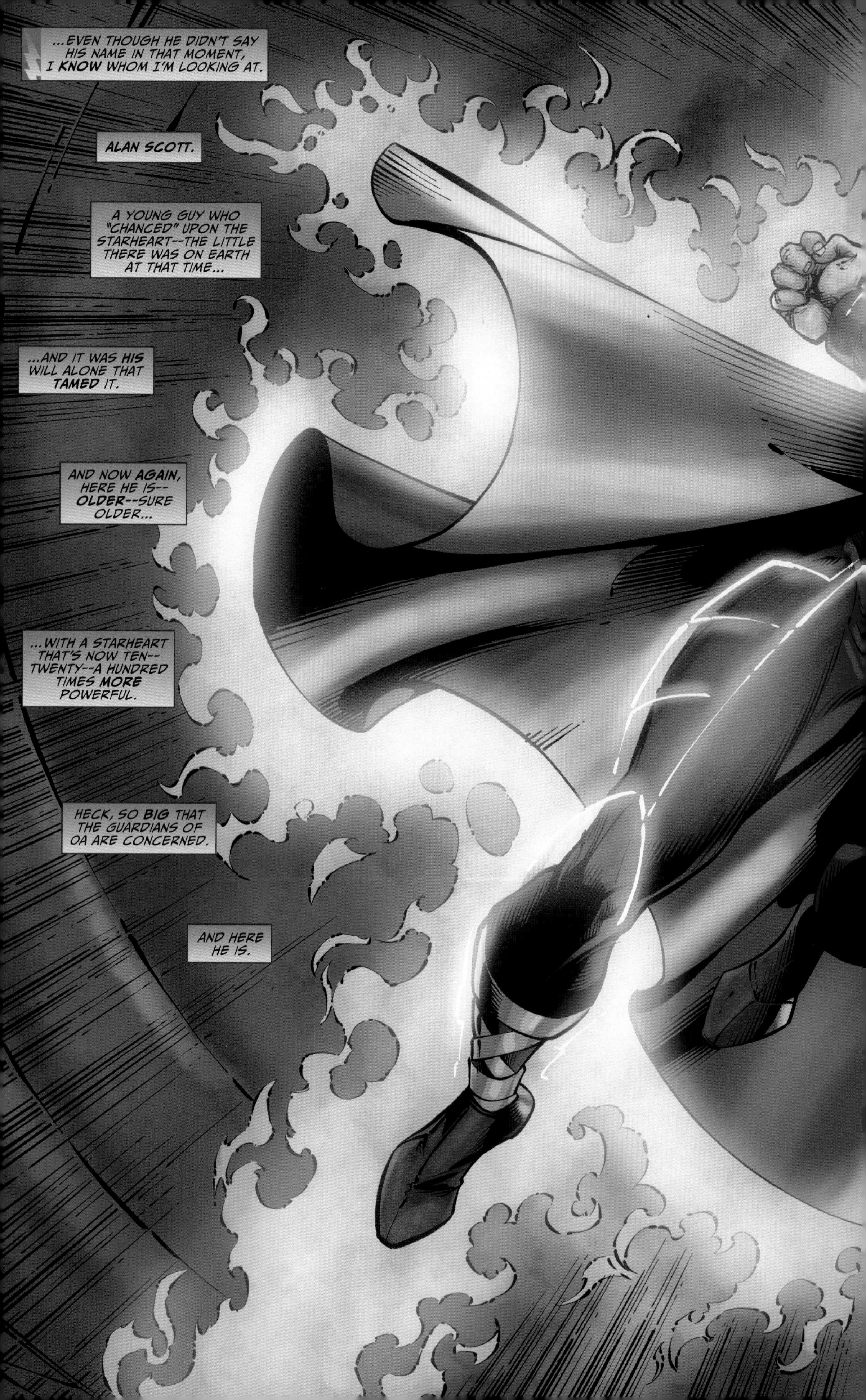
...EVEN THOUGH HE DIDN'T SAY HIS NAME IN THAT MOMENT, I KNOW WHOM I'M LOOKING AT.
ALAN SCOTT.
A YOUNG GUY WHO "CHANCED" UPON THE STARHEART--THE LITTLE THERE WAS ON EARTH AT THAT TIME...
...AND IT WAS HIS WILL ALONE THAT TAMED IT.
AND NOW AGAIN, HERE HE IS--OLDER--SURE OLDER...
...WITH A STARHEART THAT'S NOW TEN--TWENTY--A HUNDRED TIMES MORE POWERFUL.
HECK, SO BIG THAT THE GUARDIANS OF OA ARE CONCERNED.
AND HERE HE IS.

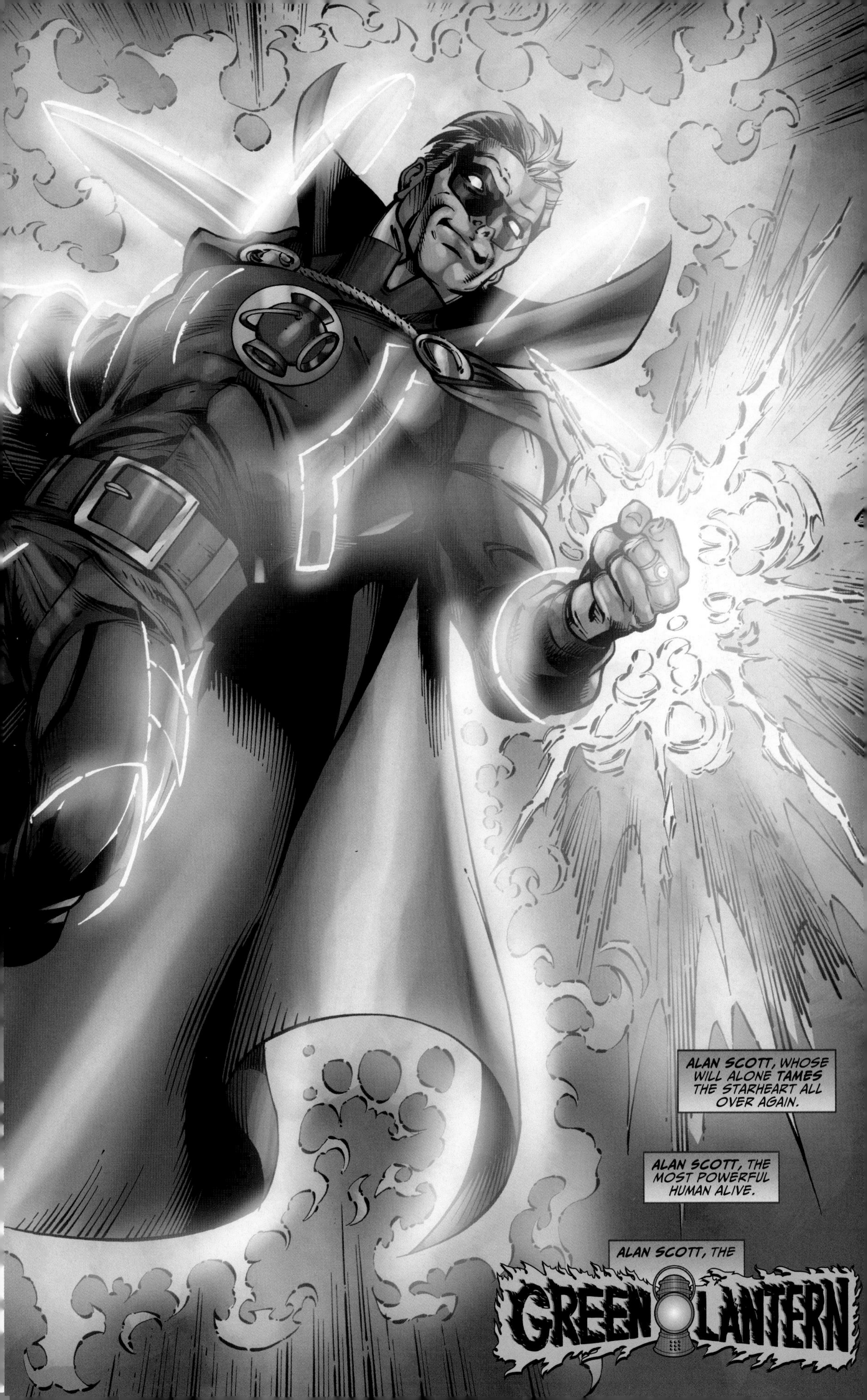
ALAN SCOTT, WHOSE WILL ALONE TAMES THE STARHEART ALL OVER AGAIN.
ALAN SCOTT, THE MOST POWERFUL HUMAN ALIVE.
ALAN SCOTT, THE
GREEN LANTERN

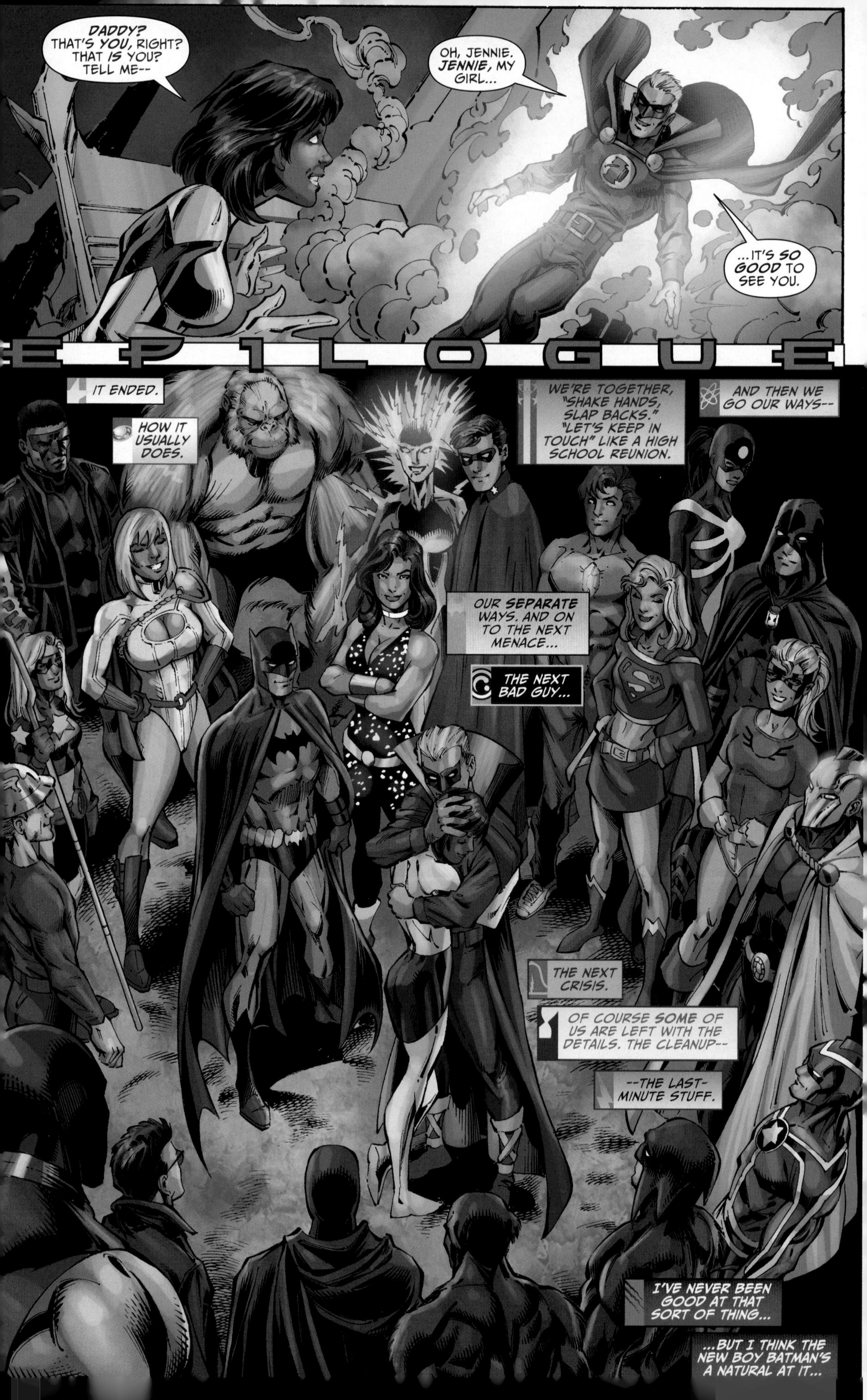
DADDY? THAT'S YOU, RIGHT? THAT IS YOU? TELL ME--
OH, JENNIE. JENNIE, MY GIRL...
...IT'S SO GOOD TO SEE YOU.
EPILOGUE
IT ENDED.
HOW IT USUALLY DOES.
WE'RE TOGETHER, "SHAKE HANDS, SLAP BACKS." "LET'S KEEP IN TOUCH" LIKE A HIGH SCHOOL REUNION.
AND THEN WE GO OUR WAYS--
OUR SEPARATE WAYS. AND ON TO THE NEXT MENACE...
THE NEXT BAD GUY...
THE NEXT CRISIS.
OF COURSE SOME OF US ARE LEFT WITH THE DETAILS. THE CLEANUP--
--THE LAST-MINUTE STUFF.
I'VE NEVER BEEN GOOD AT THAT SORT OF THING...
...BUT I THINK THE NEW BOY BATMAN'S A NATURAL AT IT...

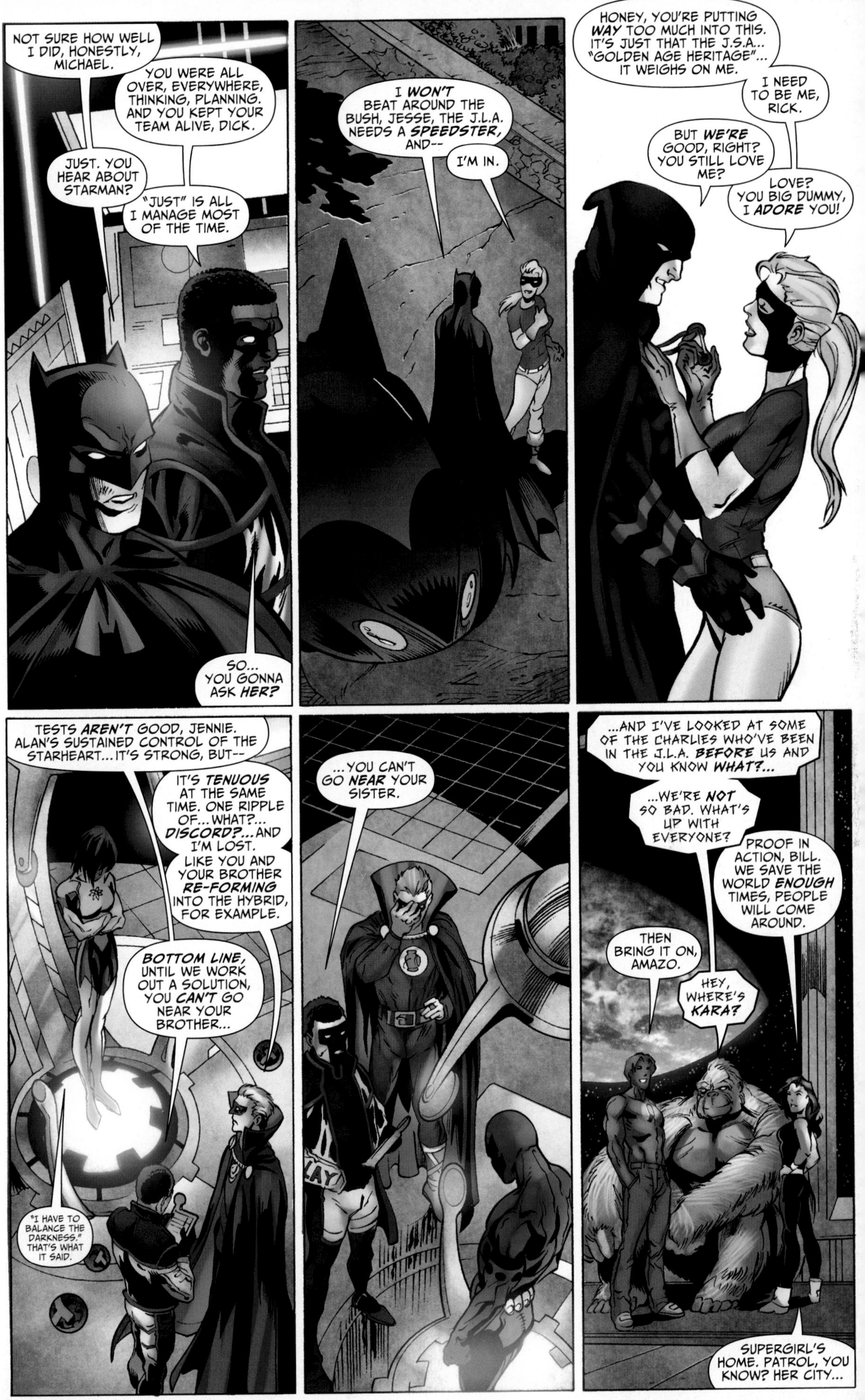
NOT SURE HOW WELL I DID, HONESTLY, MICHAEL.
YOU WERE ALL OVER, EVERYWHERE, THINKING, PLANNING. AND YOU KEPT YOUR TEAM ALIVE, DICK.
JUST. YOU HEAR ABOUT STARMAN?
"JUST" IS ALL I MANAGE MOST OF THE TIME.
SO... YOU GONNA ASK HER?
I WON'T BEAT AROUND THE BUSH, JESSE, THE J.L.A. NEEDS A SPEEDSTER, AND--
I'M IN.
HONEY, YOU'RE PUTTING WAY TOO MUCH INTO THIS. IT'S JUST THAT THE J.S.A... "GOLDEN AGE HERITAGE"... IT WEIGHS ON ME.
I NEED TO BE ME, RICK.
BUT WE'RE GOOD, RIGHT? YOU STILL LOVE ME?
LOVE? YOU BIG DUMMY, I ADORE YOU!
TESTS AREN'T GOOD, JENNIE. ALAN'S SUSTAINED CONTROL OF THE STARHEART... IT'S STRONG, BUT--
IT'S TENUOUS AT THE SAME TIME. ONE RIPPLE OF... WHAT?... DISCORD?... AND I'M LOST. LIKE YOU AND YOUR BROTHER RE-FORMING INTO THE HYBRID, FOR EXAMPLE.
BOTTOM LINE, UNTIL WE WORK OUT A SOLUTION, YOU CAN'T GO NEAR YOUR BROTHER...
"I HAVE TO BALANCE THE DARKNESS." THAT'S WHAT IT SAID.
...YOU CAN'T GO NEAR YOUR SISTER.
...AND I'VE LOOKED AT SOME OF THE CHARLIES WHO'VE BEEN IN THE J.L.A. BEFORE US AND YOU KNOW WHAT?...
...WE'RE NOT SO BAD. WHAT'S UP WITH EVERYONE?
PROOF IN ACTION, BILL. WE SAVE THE WORLD ENOUGH TIMES, PEOPLE WILL COME AROUND.
THEN BRING IT ON, AMAZO.
HEY, WHERE'S KARA?
SUPERGIRL'S HOME. PATROL, YOU KNOW? HER CITY...

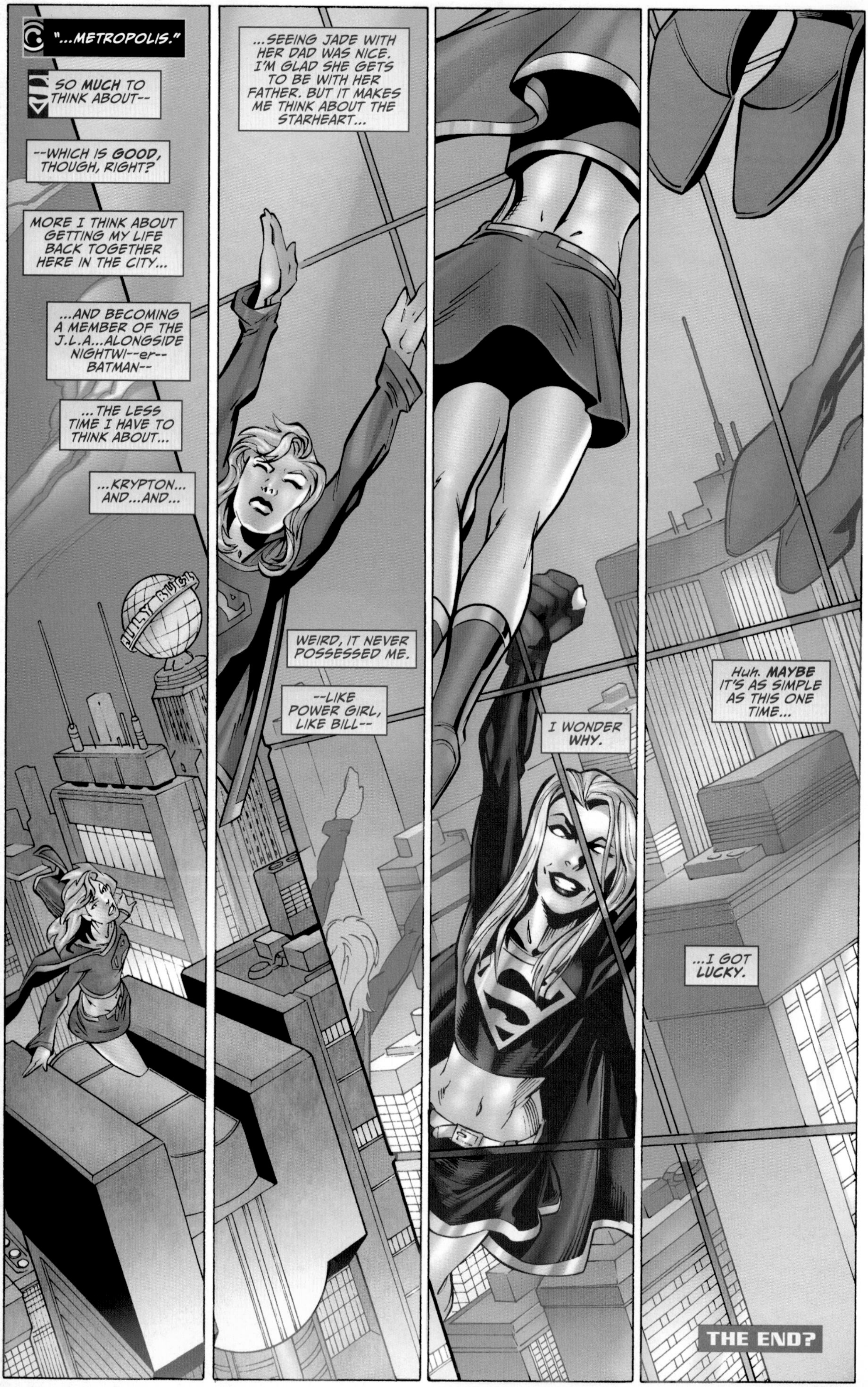
"...METROPOLIS."
SO MUCH TO THINK ABOUT--
--WHICH IS GOOD, THOUGH, RIGHT?
MORE I THINK ABOUT GETTING MY LIFE BACK TOGETHER HERE IN THE CITY...
...AND BECOMING A MEMBER OF THE J.L.A....ALONGSIDE NIGHTWI--er--BATMAN--
...THE LESS TIME I HAVE TO THINK ABOUT...
...KRYPTON... AND...AND...
...SEEING JADE WITH HER DAD WAS NICE. I'M GLAD SHE GETS TO BE WITH HER FATHER. BUT IT MAKES ME THINK ABOUT THE STARHEART...
WEIRD, IT NEVER POSSESSED ME.
--LIKE POWER GIRL, LIKE BILL--
I WONDER WHY.
Huh. MAYBE IT'S AS SIMPLE AS THIS ONE TIME...
...I GOT LUCKY.
THE END?

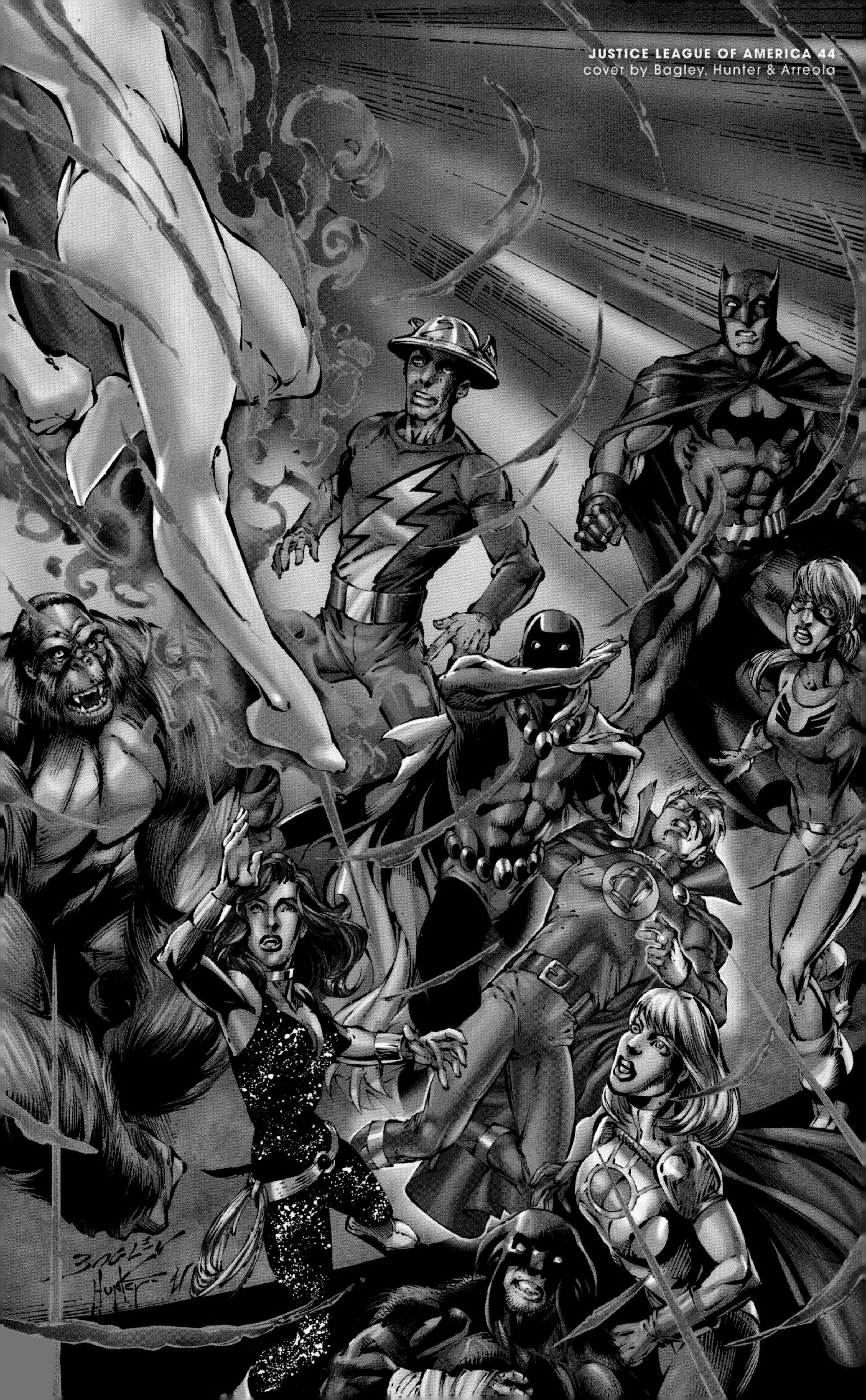

JUSTICE LEAGUE OF AMERICA 44
cover by Bagley, Hunter & Arreola

JUSTICE LEAGUE OF AMERICA 45
cover by Bagley & Hunter

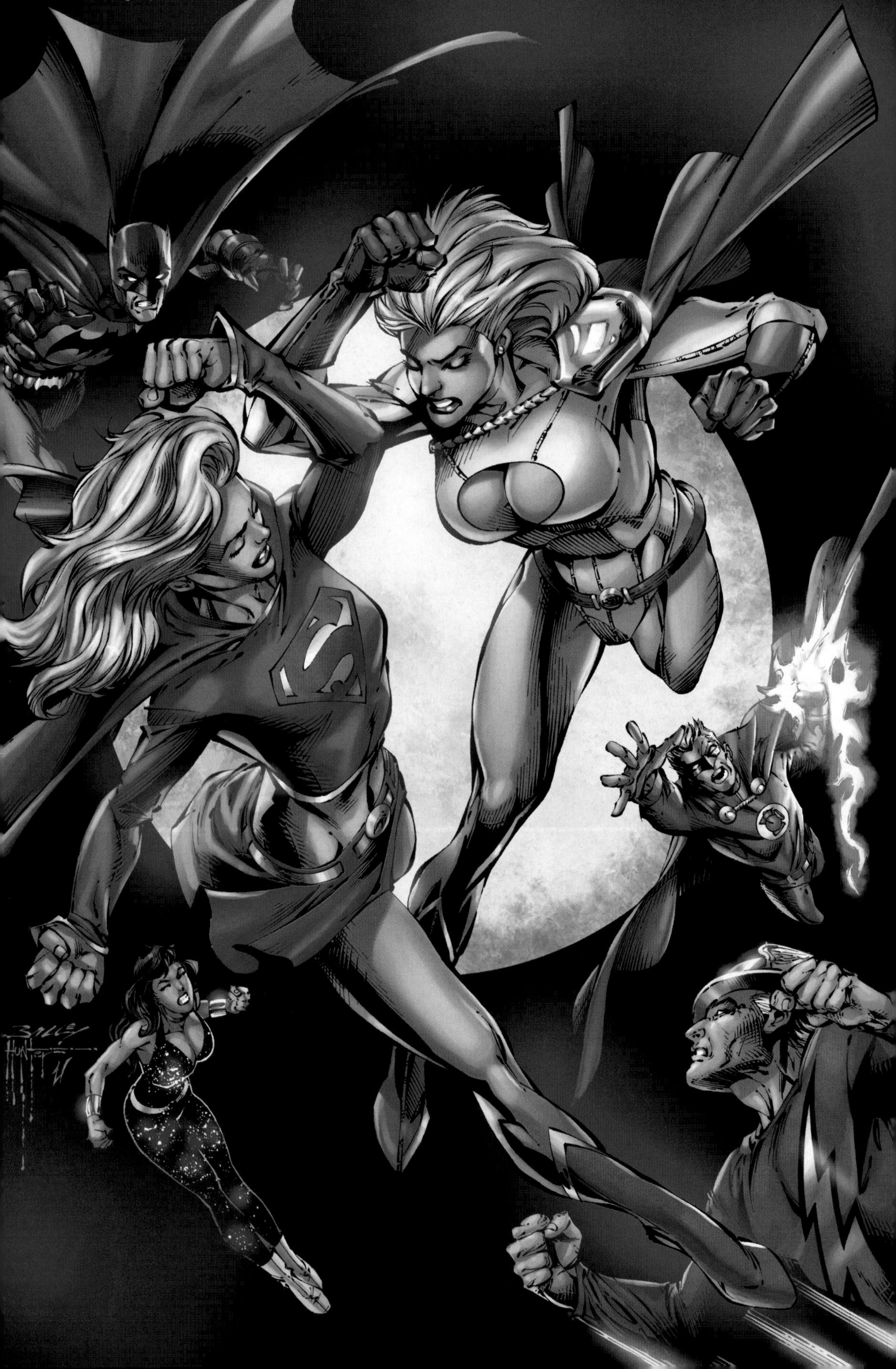

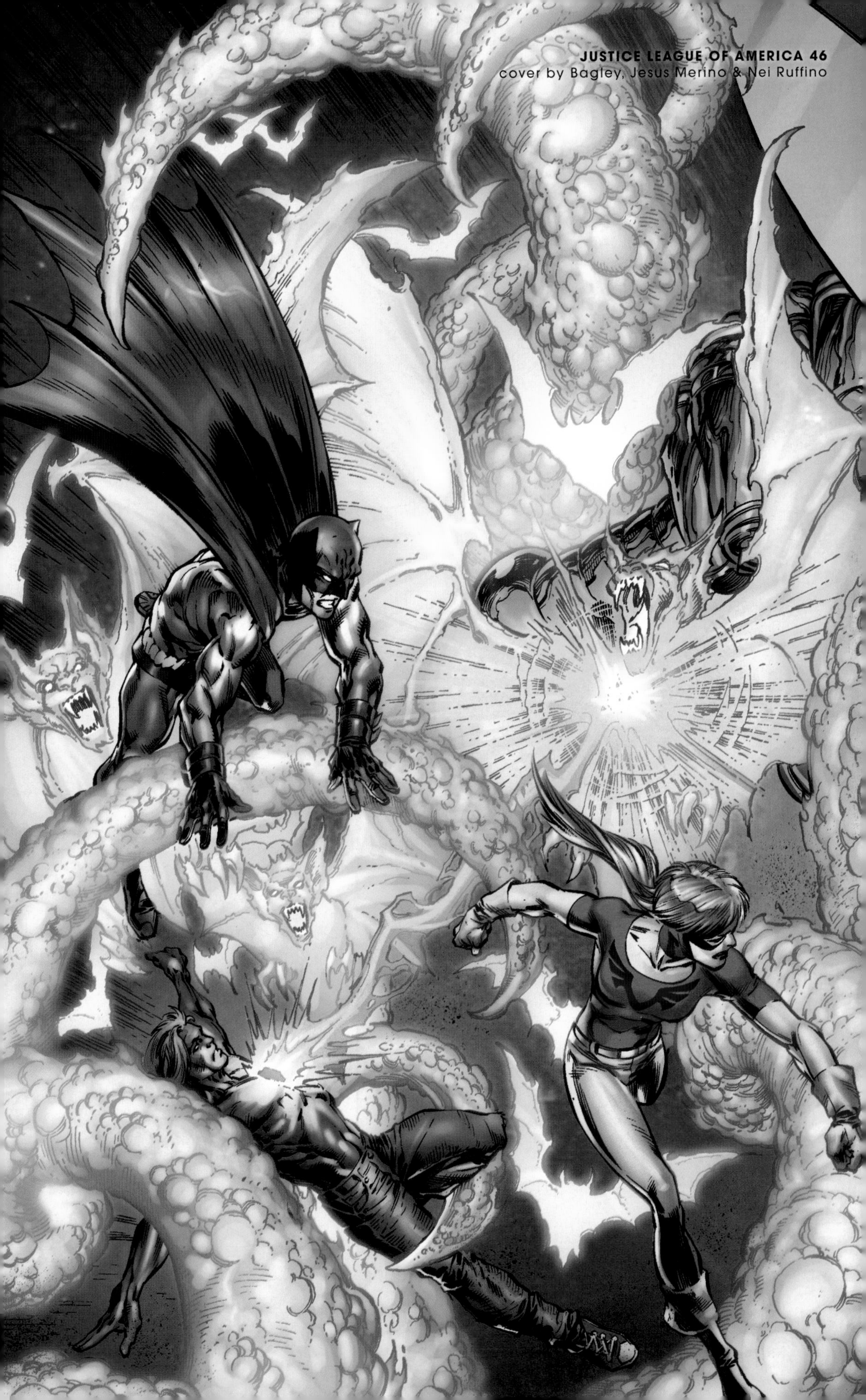

JUSTICE LEAGUE OF AMERICA 46
cover by Bagley, Jesus Merino & Nei Ruffino

JUSTICE SOCIETY OF AMERICA 41
cover by Bagley, Jesus Merino & Nei Ruffino

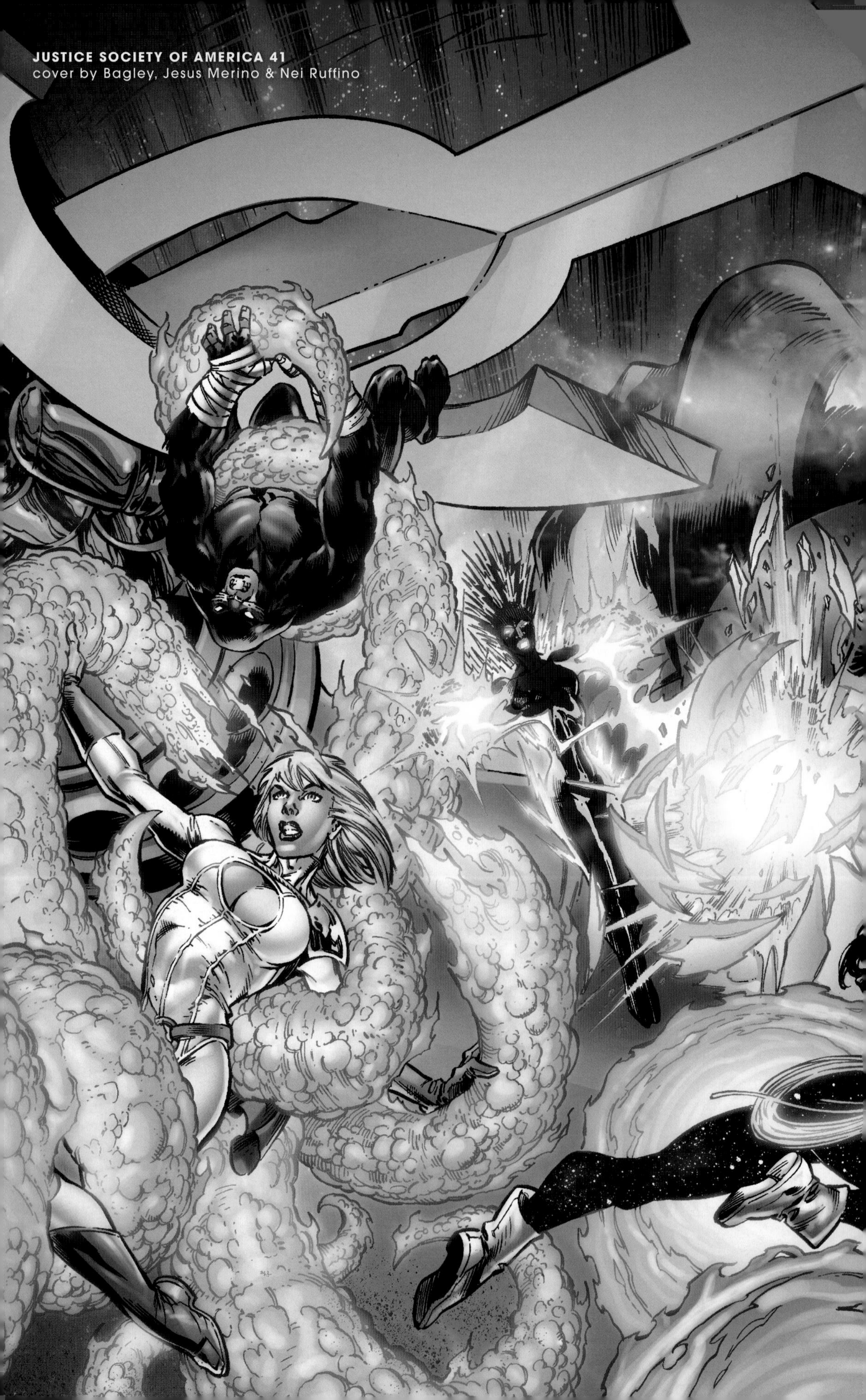

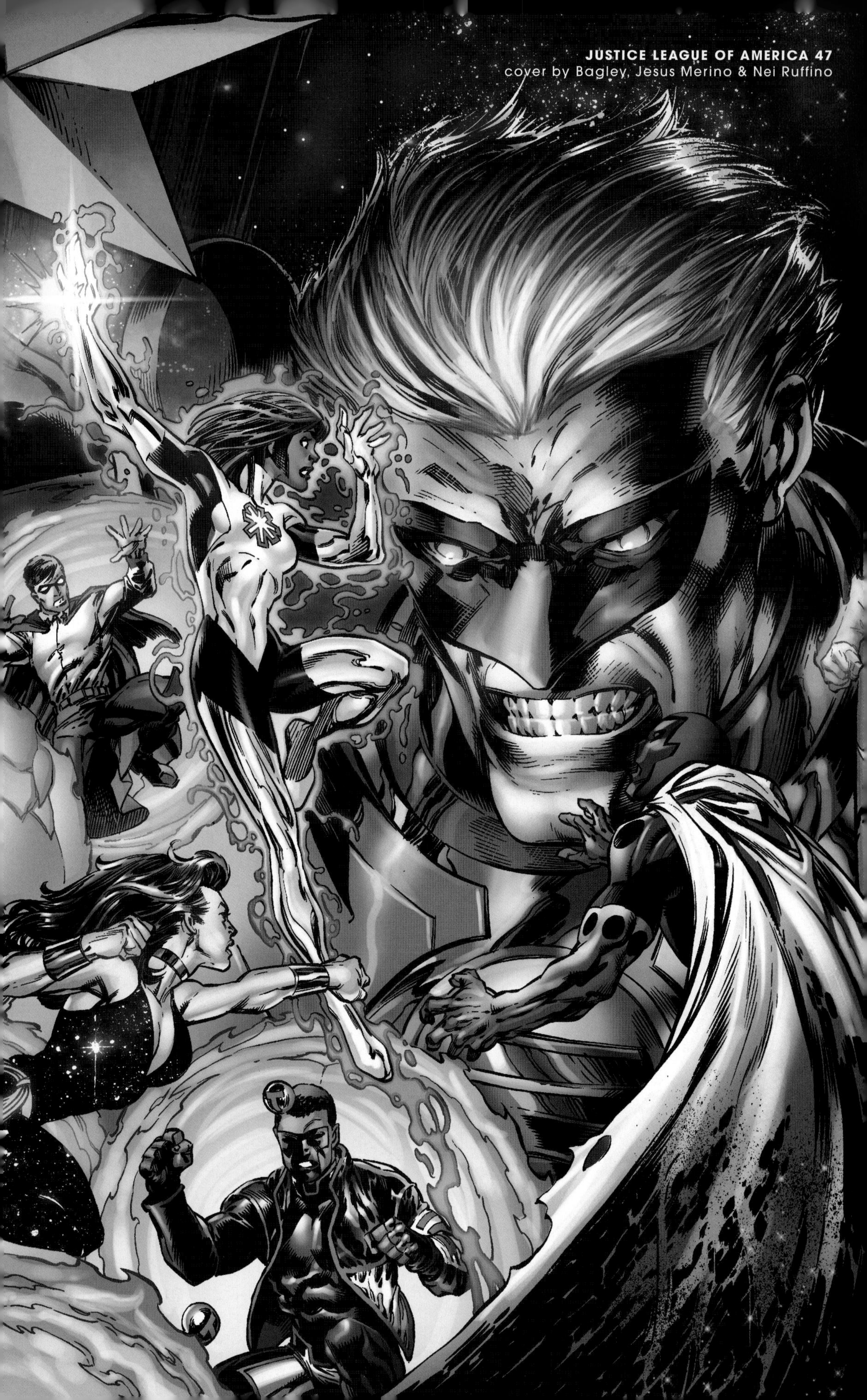

JUSTICE LEAGUE OF AMERICA 47
cover by Bagley, Jesus Merino & Nei Ruffino

JUSTICE SOCIETY OF AMERICA 42
cover by Jesus Merino & Nei Ruffino

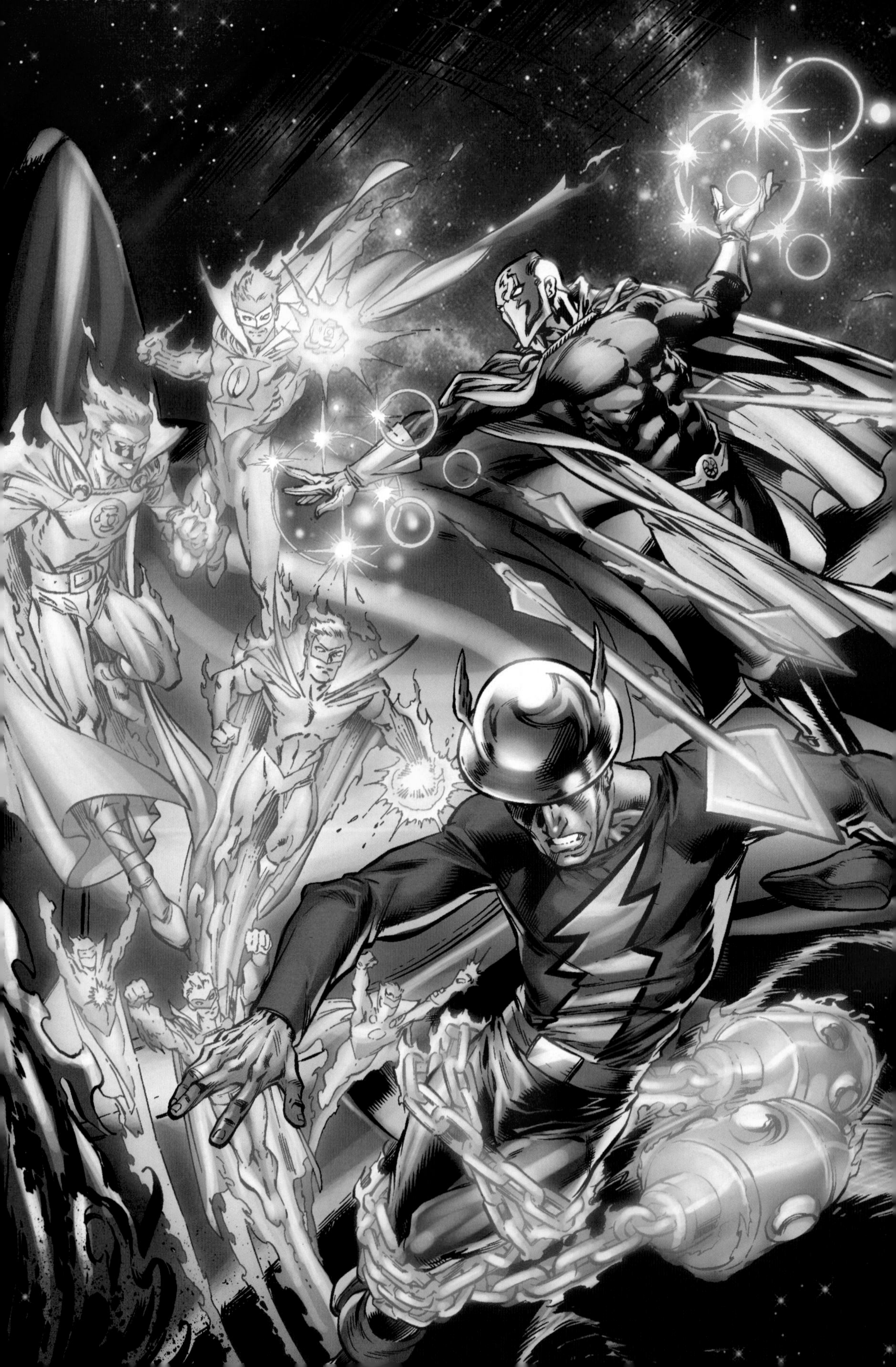

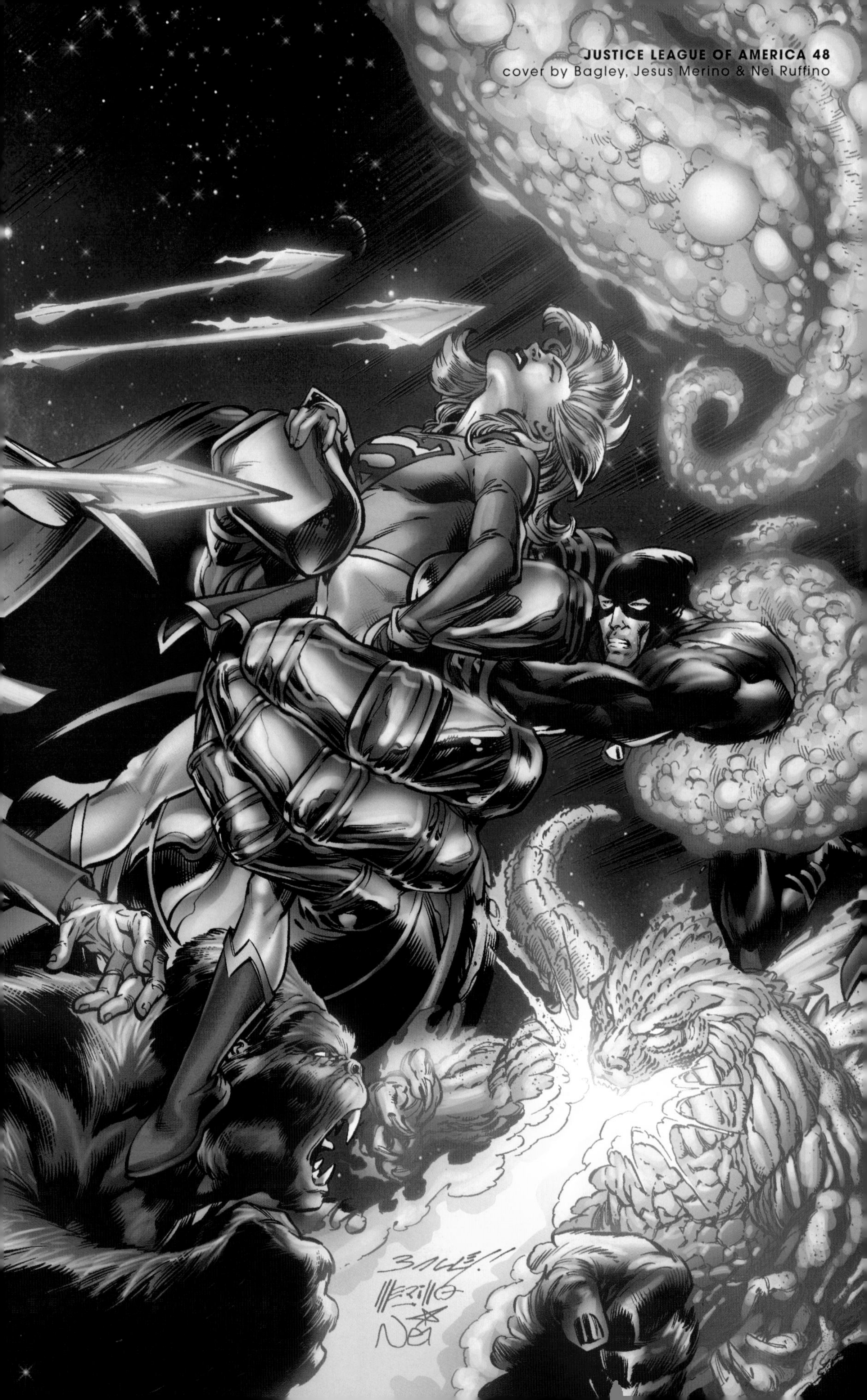

JUSTICE LEAGUE OF AMERICA 48
cover by Bagley, Jesus Merino & Nei Ruffino

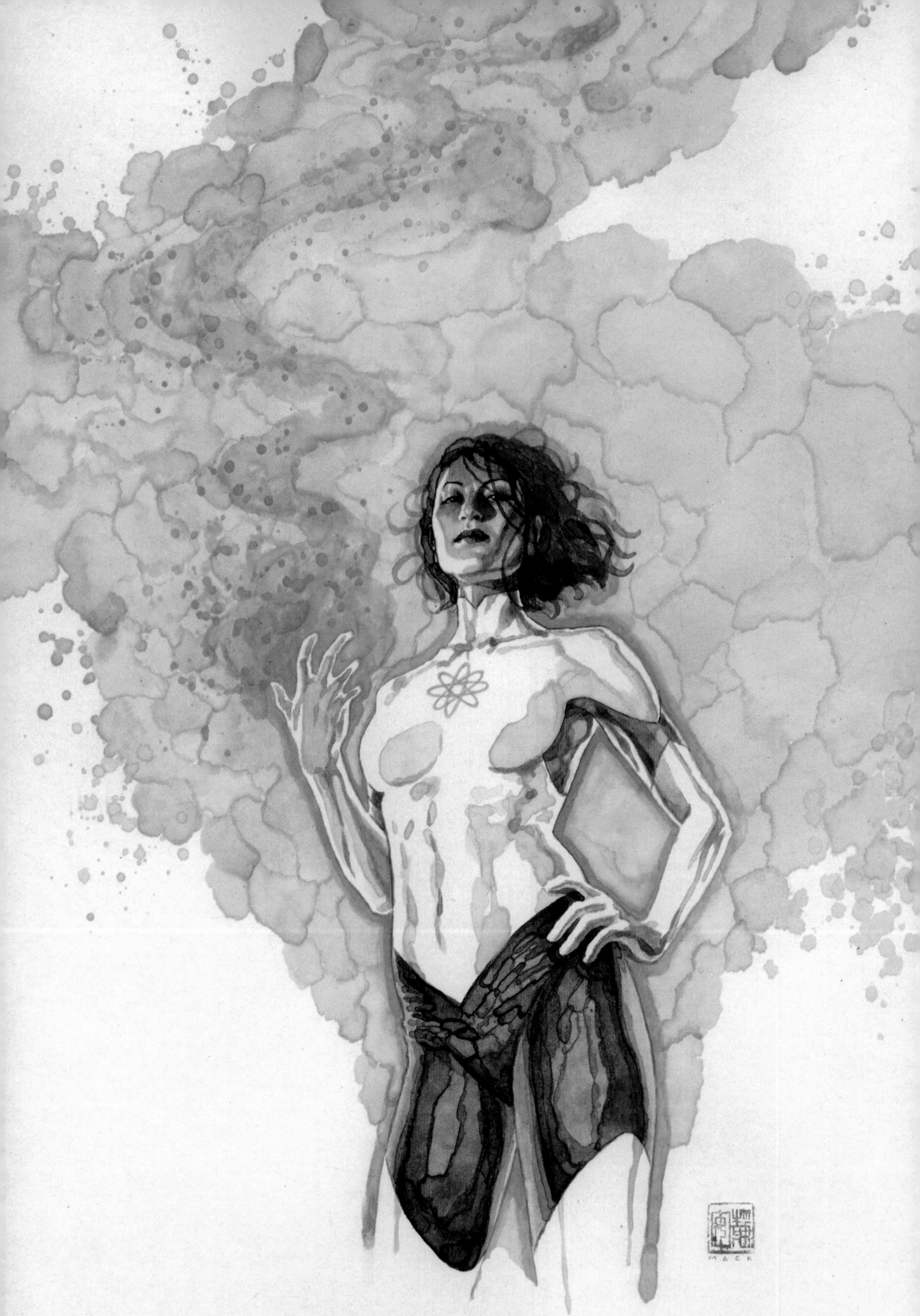
MACK

JUSTICE LEAGUE OF AMERICA 44
variant by David Mack

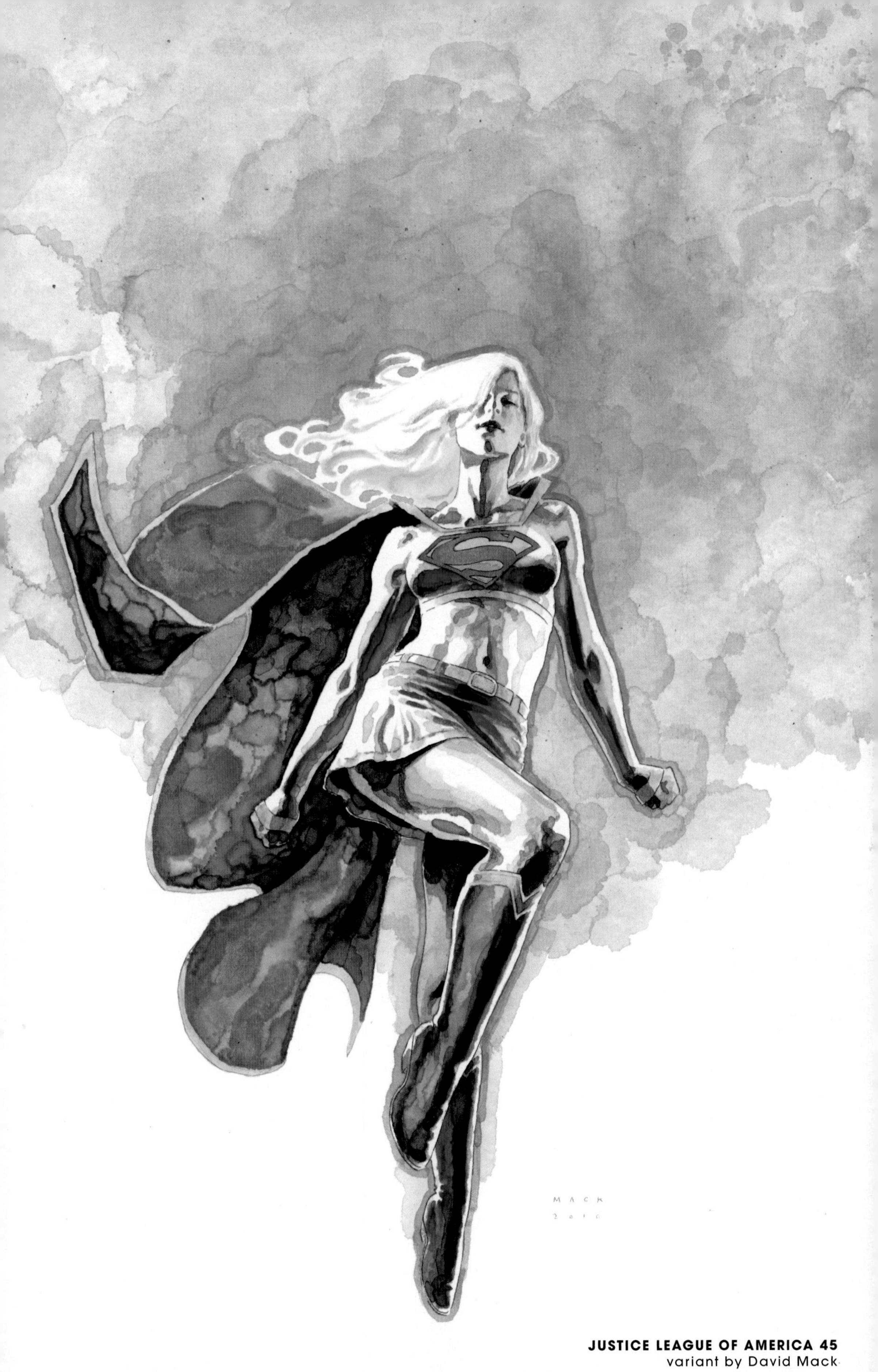
MACK

JUSTICE LEAGUE OF AMERICA 45
variant by David Mack

JUSTICE LEAGUE OF AMERICA 46
variant by Francis Manapul & Brian Buccellato

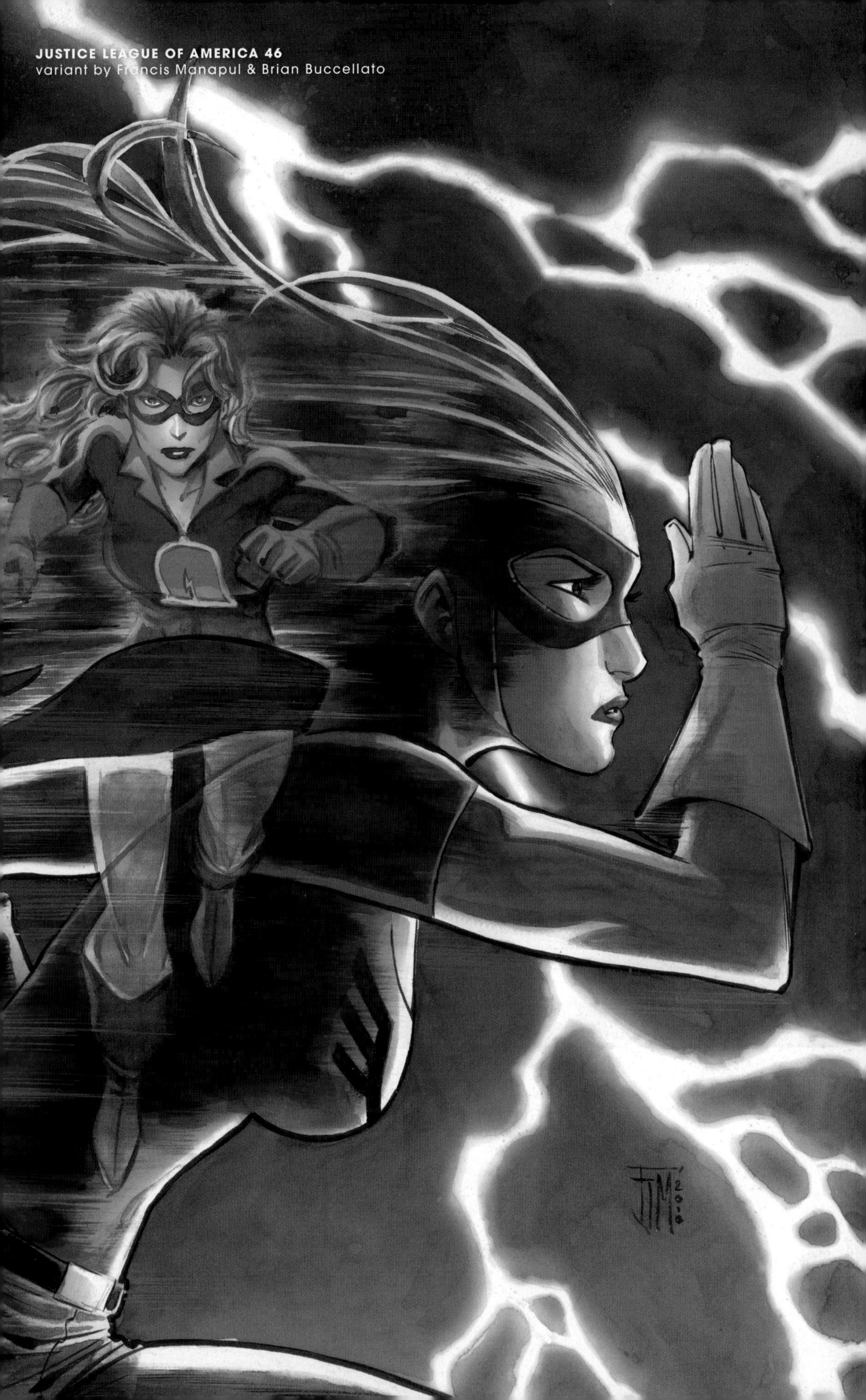

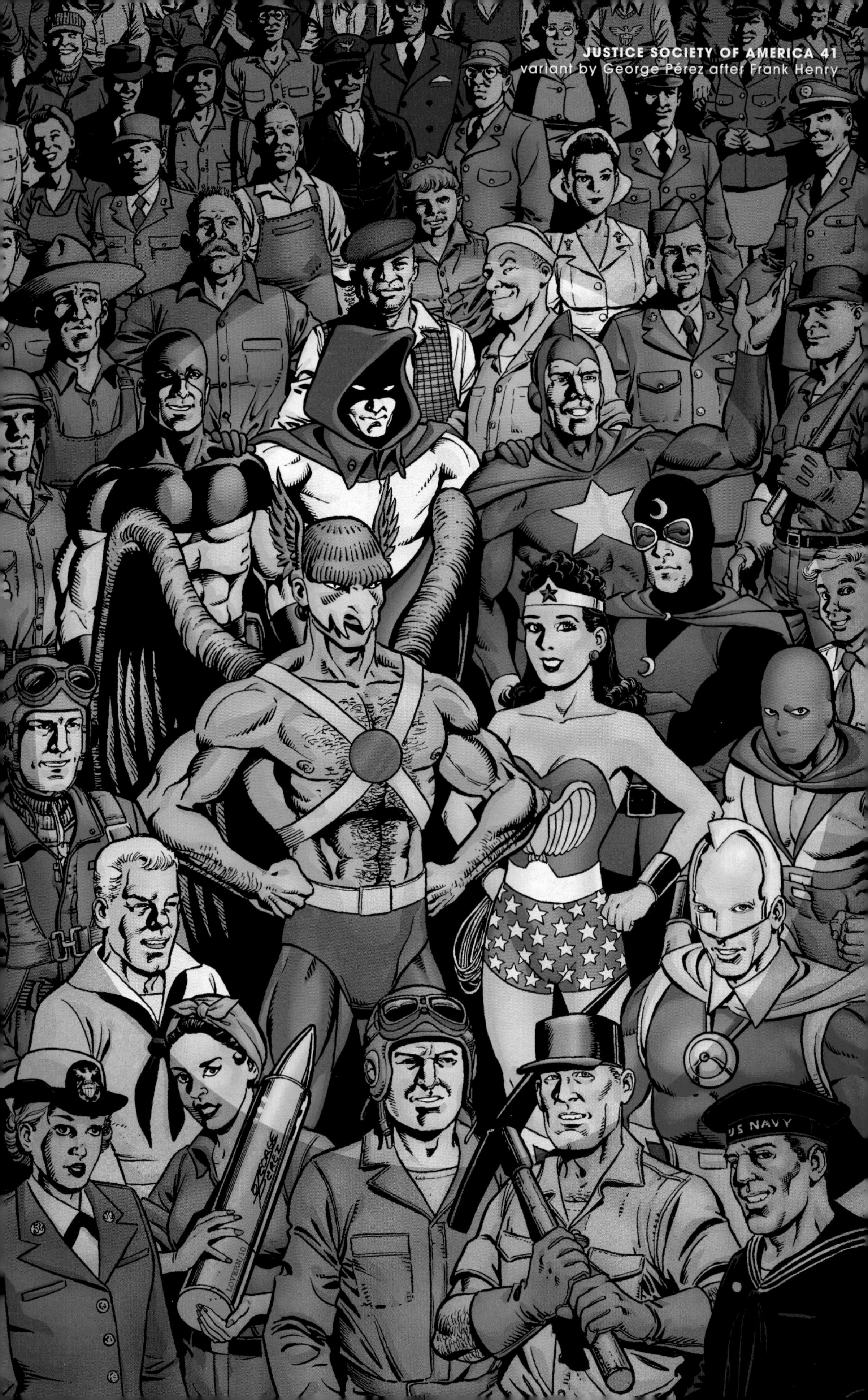
US NAVY

JUSTICE SOCIETY OF AMERICA 41
variant by George Pérez after Frank Henry

JUSTICE LEAGUE OF AMERICA 47
variant by Alex Garner

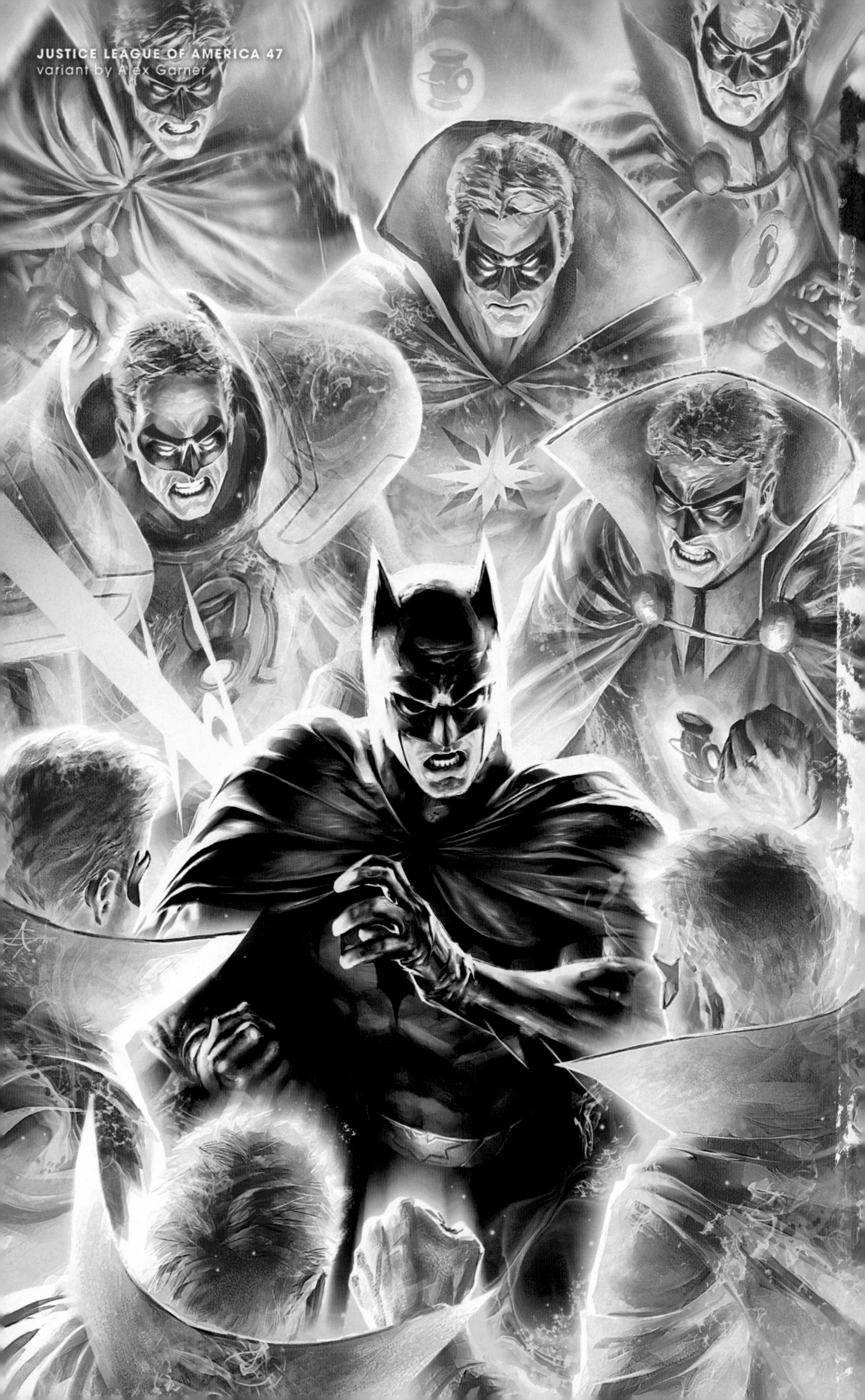

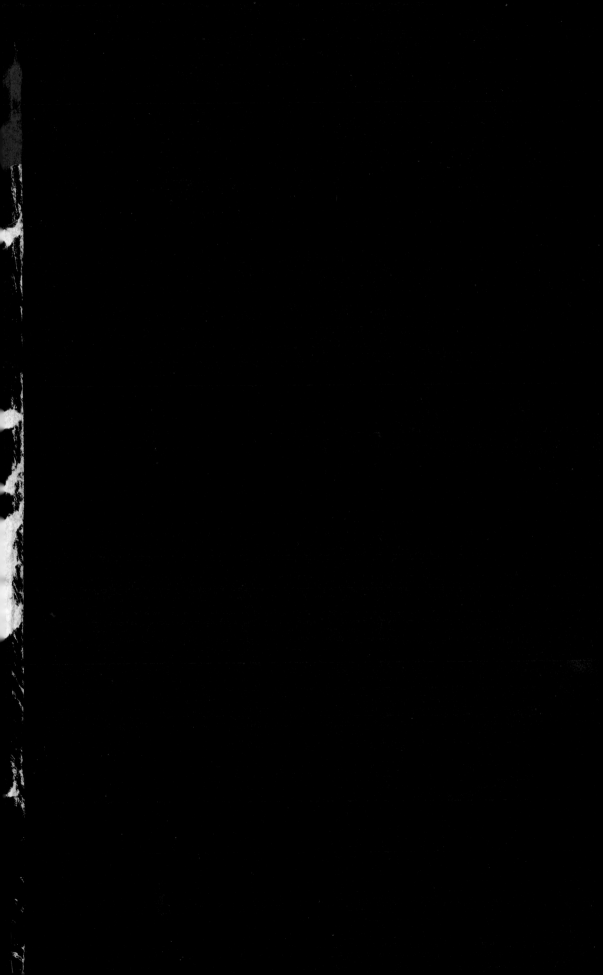